Postmodern Legal Movements

# Postmodern Legal Movements

## Law and Jurisprudence at Century's End

*Gary Minda*

New York University Press
*New York and London*

NEW YORK UNIVERSITY PRESS
New York and London

Library of Congress Cataloging-in-Publication Data
Minda, Gary.
Postmodern legal movements : law and jurisprudence at century's
end / Gary Minda.
p. cm.
Includes bibliographical references and index.
ISBN 0-8147-5510-0 (acid-free paper)—
ISBN 0-8147-5511-9 (acid-free paper)
1. Jurisprudence—United States.  I. Title.
KF380.M56  1995
349.73—dc20
[347.3]  94-24934
            CIP

New York University Press books are printed on acid-free paper,
and their binding materials are chosen for strength and durability.

Manufactured in the United States of America

10   9   8   7   6   5   4   3   2   1

What appears on one level as the latest fad, advertising pitch and hollow spectacle is part of a slowly emerging cultural transformation in Western societies, a change in sensibility for which the term *postmodern* is actually, at least for now, wholly adequate. The nature and depth of that transformation are debatable, but transformation it is.

—Andreas Huyssen, *Mapping the Postmodern,*
33 New German Critique 5, 8 (1984)

# Acknowledgments

This book would not have been possible without the help and insights of many of my life-long teachers, colleagues, friends, and fellow-travelers. I would like especially to thank my editors, Despina Gimbel, Niko Pfund, and David Updike of New York University Press, and Robert Batey, Mark Brown, Neil Duxbury, Stephen Feldman, David Lyons, Richard Posner, Pierre Schlag, and Tony Sebok for commenting on drafts of the manuscript. Sharon Gisclair did terrific work in typing early drafts of the manuscript, and her moral encouragement helped me to stay on course. Laurie Stitzer, Pamela Jacobs, and Carlos Lozano did outstanding work as research assistants. I was extremely lucky to have Sharon, Laurie, Pam, and Carlos to work with on this project. Finally, I am indebted to the faculty and staff at Brooklyn Law School and Stetson University College of Law for their academic support and encouragement.

This book draws from my previously published essays on modern legal movements: Gary Minda, *Jurisprudence at Century's End,* 43 J. LEGAL EDUC. 27 (1993); *The Jurisprudential Movements of the 1980's,* 50 OHIO STATE L.J. 599 (1989); *The Lawyer-Economist at Chicago: Richard A. Posner and the Economic Analysis of Law,* 39 OHIO STATE L.J. 439 (1979). I have also drawn from previously published articles dealing with substantive law topics. *See* Gary Minda, *Title VII at the Crossroads of Employment Discrimination Law and Postmodern Feminist Theory,* 11 ST. LOUIS U. L.J. 89 (1992); *The Dilemmas of Property and Sovereignty in the Postmodern Era,* 62 COLO. L. REV. 599 (1991); *Interest Group Theory and Antitrust,* 41 HASTINGS L.J. 907 (1990).

# Preface

The objective of this book is to present a general overview of the state of law and jurisprudence at twentieth century's end. The idea for this book is based on Karl Llewellyn's THE COMMON LAW TRADITION (1960), and Grant Gilmore's THE AGES OF AMERICAN LAW (1977). In these two books, Llewellyn and Gilmore set out to characterize the dominant styles of judicial decision making that have set the course of modern American jurisprudence since the early 1880s. Llewellyn called his effort the "periodization" of American law, while Gilmore called his the "Ages of American Law." It is hardly necessary to say that these two legal scholars have provided extraordinary insights for understanding the nature of modern jurisprudential studies.

In the following chapters, I offer my modest effort to carry on this tradition in the intellectual history of American law by aiming my sights on the more recent movements and intellectual developments in jurisprudential thought. My study of postmodern legal movements begins with an examination of *modern* modes of traditional jurisprudential thinking in the United States that developed in this century; then it analyzes and describes five movements in legal thought active in the 1980s, and concludes with an examination of the emergence of *postmodern* jurisprudence at century's end. My aim is to explore how the new forms of *scholarly* discourse at the end of this century have ruptured the modern "styles" of jurisprudence as described by Llewellyn and Gilmore, and how those discourses have themselves been reshaped by a new postmodern perspective. In so doing, I hope to offer some thoughts on the future of jurisprudence for the next century.

In order to make my task remotely feasible, I have tried to focus on major themes and general theoretical developments in American jurisprudence, with primary emphasis placed on the development of the modern legal movements arising in the late 1970s and 1980s. My effort here is to try and capture the general jurisprudential climate by reviewing some of the "great" books and law review articles on jurisprudence and legal theory. I attempt to highlight the continuity as well as the disruption in American jurisprudential thought. I make no attempt to comprehensively cover all the significant jurisprudential writings or developments in the period considered, as such an undertaking would not be possible in the context of a single text such as this. The scholarly works I have selected are, I believe, highly relevant for evaluating the complex set of ideas and theories that have shaped the diverse contours of law and jurisprudence at century's end. My hope is that this text will provide the interested reader with a useful interpretation as well as overview of modern and postmodern developments in American jurisprudence. Suffice it to say that this book aims at providing a general introduction to modern and postmodern legal movements and their significance to the contemporary study of jurisprudence.

# Introduction

After several decades of interdisciplinary work in academic legal scholarship, it is impossible for one not to notice how obscure theories of economics, sociology, philosophy, anthropology, literary criticism, and other fields have infected recent academic writing and thinking about law and adjudication, or what is commonly understood as *jurisprudence*.[1] Ever since the New Deal, legal studies have become more sophisticated and more eclectic.[2] This expanding eclecticism has brought about sharp debate in jurisprudence. Diversity and fragmentation of jurisprudence have been stimulated by a profession that has itself become splintered as a result of competition and rivalry between new jurisprudential movements, five of which are the subject of this book: *law and economics, critical legal studies, feminist legal theory, law and literature*, and *critical race theory*.

These movements are jurisprudential because each of them claims a membership of legal and nonlegal academics and practitioners who adhere to a particular understanding about modern law and adjudication. The five movements distinguish themselves by advocating different jurisprudential discourses, conceptions, and practices that challenge the way modern jurisprudential scholars have understood law and adjudication. They are the product of diverse intellectual tendencies, moods, and aesthetic styles, including late-nineteenth- and early-twentieth-century trends in legal theory. However, because the intellectual sources of these movements have involved overlapping intellectual moods or tendencies, the five movements appear at times to share common characteristics. Finally, each movement introduces a new form of jurisprudence that departs from the perspectives and methods of "mainstream" or modern scholarship in the field. One of the more interesting developments in recent American legal thought has been the almost simultaneous emergence and maturation of these five jurisprudential movements during the decade of the 1980s.

More recently, a shift in theoretical perspective came about as contemporary legal scholars associated with these movements turned from interdisciplinary methodologies to more robust and less determinant modes of interpretation. This "interpretive turn" in jurisprudence coincided with a new interest in the possibility of replacing foundational truths, transcendental values, and neutral conceptions of law with a more pluralistic, contextual, and nonessential explanation of law and legal decisionmaking developed for a multicultural society. My central thesis is that the five jurisprudential movements of the 1980s have consequently come to reflect the emergence of a new skeptical aesthetic, mood, or intellectual condition in American jurisprudential studies, which many have identified as *postmodern*. Hence, I shall refer to the five movements as *postmodern* legal movements.

Postmodernism is an elusive term not easily defined or captured by standard dictionaries or interpretive strategies.[3] Postmodernism thus poses an intellectual dilemma for contemporary writers and thinkers. How do we get at the meaning of postmodernism if postmodernism does not allow us to use foundational concepts or a metanarrative to fix its meaning? The predicament of postmodernism is that postmodernism is a condition, an aesthetic, an intellectual style that recognizes and embraces the contradictions and paradoxes it discovers in traditional conditions, aesthetics, and intellectual styles. Postmodernism announces something that resists a stabilized identity; it problematizes the very form, the very discourse used to announce its existence without attempting to offer an alternative theory or discourse. One does not get a better sense of postmodernism by excising this critical reflexivity (and its attendant difficulties). On the contrary, one loses what one was trying to understand (i.e., postmodernism) by any attempt to either cabin postmodernism within the modernist's conceptual framework of understanding or, paradoxically, to insist that the postmodernist present *the* "postmodern" account or history of American jurisprudential thought.

At one time, the term "postmodernism" was used to refer to the rejection of modernist aesthetics in the fields of architecture and art.

Today, the term is used by a variety of contemporary academics to signify a new mood or aesthetic in *intellectual* thought. In law, postmodernism signals the movement away from interpretation premised upon the belief in universal truths, core essences, or foundational theories. In jurisprudence, postmodernism signals the movement away from "Rule of Law" thinking based on the belief in one true "Rule of Law," one fixed "pattern," set of "patterns," or generalized theory of jurisprudence. Postmodernism is an aesthetic practice and condition that is opposed to "Grand Theory," structural patterns, or foundational knowledges. Postmodern legal critics employ local, small-scale problem-solving strategies to raise new questions about the relation of law, politics and culture. They offer a new interpretive aesthetic for reconceptualizing the practice of legal interpretation. However, because postmodernism is an unstable category (and because the condition it announces is unstable), it ends up meaning many things to many people. Postmoderns would in fact resist the effort to reduce the meaning of postmodernism to statements made by a single author or text.

Perhaps the best that can be done is to try and describe very loosely what postmodernists tend to believe and what they do in their intellectual practices. They seem to be united in their resistance to the sort of conceptual theorization and system building routinely practiced by legal academics and analytical philosophers. The postmodern writer is in the position of a philosopher working without theory and rules to investigate how the production of intellectual work serves to establish a certain normative form or "lifeworld." Some postmodernists claim that the intellectual projects of modern legal scholars have unduly emphasized abstract theory at the expense of "open-minded" pragmatic and "no-nonsense" skeptical forms of reason. Other postmodernists claim that the production of intellectual work, in theory and practice, has been concerned more with the perfection of a particular form (pragmatic or theoretical) than with the accomplishment of some social objective.

Some postmodernists tend to believe that modern theory has come to reflect the self-identity of the professional academic who has become obsessed with the ideal of realizing self-perfection, freedom, autonomy, and professional status. These postmodernists claim that the identity of this professional academic is a social, cultural, historical, and linguistic creation of a normative vision of a particular individual subject. They explore the various ways in which the legal and social identity of this subject has influenced the construction of texts, discourses, and institutions. Postmodernists claim that modern jurisprudence has indulged in the dubious fiction that a lone author is in control of the text, that law is a creation of a rational author, and that this author is capable of standing outside the system and is thus capable of objectively evaluating its functions.

Postmodernists do not claim that they can successfully avoid the predicaments and paradoxes they have found in the modernist's conceptual narratives. Indeed, postmodernists recognize and embrace these predicaments and paradoxes in their own narratives. They do this because they believe that texts, discourses, vocabulary, and grammar of the professional field cannot "intentionally" be overcome or avoided by a lone author. Moreover, the existence of predicament and paradox in the texts of postmodernists, as well as those in the texts and discourse of everyone else, are seen by postmodernists as part of the "situation" they call the postmodern condition. In other words, postmodernists do not claim that they stand outside of the system they criticize.

It is important to note, however, that there is probably no one who believes in all of these propositions. Indeed, postmodernists would reject the effort to identify a postmodernist with a series of propositions. To identify postmodernism with a set of propositions, beliefs, or "postmodern narrative" would be too essentialist, too modernist, to be postmodern. Such an effort would too closely resemble the type of academic work now practiced by modern legal academics and analytical philosophers. Postmodernists claim that everyone is influenced and shaped by the rational aesthetic of modernism; the difference between various writers and thinkers is said to be in the extent to which they take critical cognizance of the predicaments and paradoxes of their current intellectual situation. What distinguishes postmodernists from all other legal critics is that they warmly embrace these predicaments and paradoxes.

Postmodernism exhibits different critical manifestations. Some postmodernists have adopted a *neopragmatic* outlook as an antidote to the postmodern condition. These postmodern critics are skeptical of the truth claims of modern theory, but they have not given up on theory. On the contrary, they believe that theory can have utility when used as a tool for the empirical investigation of problems. They understand truth as merely the belief structures of a particular professional community or social milieu. They emphasize the importance of "common-sense" experimentation and instrumental approaches in their work. Other postmodernists are more critical of appeals to "reason," even prygmatic ones that emphasize the virtues of common sense. They embrace the predicaments and paradoxes of the current intellectual condition in order to better understand the world of legal, social, and philosophical thought, and they attempt to bring out the *irony* of the experience of living in a postmodern world. I will refer to these postmodernists as *ironists*.

Before confronting postmodern forms of jurisprudence, we must first explore what came before postmodernism, that is, modernism. Part One will, therefore, begin this study with an examination of the dominant themes of *modern* American jurisprudence in this century. These themes reflect the intellectual background of twentieth-century *legal modernism*. Legal modernism, as distinguished from *artistic modernism*,[4] is a term I use in this book to describe the intellectual position of jurisprudential writers who believed a lone author could discover "right answers" for even the most difficult and controversial problems in the law. Modern legal theorists believe that they can discover the "right answers" or "correct interpretation" by applying a distinctive legal method based on deduction, analogy, precedent, interpretation, social policy, institutional analysis, history, sociology, economics, and scientific method. Legal modernism symbolizes the progressive union of scientific objectivity and instrumental rationality in pursuit of the intellectual project of *twentieth-century Enlightenment*—the century-old quest for universal truth based on faith in the "omnipotence and liberating potential of reason and science . . . to penetrate to the essential truth of physical and social conditions, thus making them amenable to rational control."[5] Legal moderns, influenced by the modernist's tendency to create "movements," express the intellectual and artistic quest for perfection through the process of *uncovering* and *unmasking* the secrets of the world by transcending contexts that limit human understanding.

Much of modern jurisprudential discussion has thus accepted the possibility of developing conceptual and normative arguments to explain how subjective preferences in legal decisions might either be restrained or justified. Conceptual jurisprudence attempts to confine itself to the operational study of legal concepts and reasoning. Normative jurisprudence emphasizes the importance of considering the moral and ethical dimension of law. For many legal thinkers, normative legal thought is believed to be pitted against the technical doctrinalism of conceptualist legal thought. But it turns out that the tension between normative and conceptual legal thought is overstated. While the opposition is real, the two modes of legal thought must be understood as different sides of the same whole. This is because these two forms of modern jurisprudence share a common orientation: both express faith in the Enlightenment search for a universal method to resolve law's many problems. As former solicitor general of the United States and Harvard University law professor Charles Fried expressed the idea, "[T]here is a distinct method which is the legal method . . . that it can be deployed more or less well . . . that it yields a distinct set of answers more or less out of itself."[6]

Legal modernism also characterizes the interpretive practice of modern liberal legal scholars.[7] This practice is based on an understanding of language that assumes that words and conceptual ideas are capable of objectively capturing the meaning of events the law seeks to describe and control. The professional language of law uses abstract categories such as object/subject, law/society, substance/process, core/penumbra, etc., to construct Rules of Law that satisfy jurisprudential requisites of generality and objectivity. Modern liberal scholars assume that these representational dichotomies permit the legal system to produce neutral decisions by constraining the power of judicial interpretation.

New developments in legal theory, however, have brought about a breakdown and fragmentation of this representational practice. A "crisis of representation" occurred as the traditional canons of interpretation in theory and language of modern jurisprudence no longer seemed capable of constraining the power of judicial interpretation. The current mood of jurisprudential studies in the academy suffers under conditions of anxiety created by a loss of confidence in the "Rule of Law" ideal of modern liberal legal thought.

Chapters 1 through 4 examine the key features of mainstream or modern jurisprudence prevailing in the legal academy between 1871 and 1980. Chapter 1 locates the early origins of legal modernism in the jurisprudence of two highly influential nineteenth-century American lawyers and scholars, Christopher Columbus Langdell and Oliver Wendell Holmes. Chapter 2 traces the development of modern jurisprudence from the American legal realist movement to the 1950s theory of adjudication known as *neutral principles*. Chapter 3 examines the modern jurisprudential theories of the 1960s, which established the basic argumentative styles of modern normative jurisprudence. Chapter 4 then examines how the faith in modern jurisprudence was questioned throughout the 1960s, 1970s, and 1980s. The social and cultural changes unfolding during the 1960s provide some clue for understanding why there was a loss of faith in legal modernism. Also of significance was the publication of Charles Reich's THE NEW PROPERTY and Ronald Coase's THE PROBLEM OF SOCIAL COST, both published in the early 1960s.

Part Two surveys the five jurisprudential movements that influenced and transformed modern jurisprudence during the late 1970s and 1980s. Chapters 5 through 9 describe and analyze *Law and Economics, Critical Legal Studies, Feminist Legal Theory, Law and Literature,* and *Critical Race Theory,* respectively. These new movements in American jurisprudence brought to the legal academy a new feeling of excitement as well as unease. As a result of these movements, people debated and argued about basic concepts in jurisprudence and law, and there has been much disagreement and academic dissent over the continuing validity of traditional notions surrounding law and adjudication. What seemed secure in the 1960s and much of the 1970s became hotly contested in the 1980s. New players in the legal academy advanced new ideas about the nature of law and adjudication. For some, modern-day jurisprudence had become like "a stew that is being constantly fed with spices and flavorings and endlessly stirred."[8]

By the end of the 1980s, the jurisprudential "stew" had simmered to a boiling point. The legal academy was embroiled in fundamentally different discourses and perspectives on law and adjudication. Devotees of the law and economics movement argued that law and adjudication would be best understood as a discourse about economics. Critical legal studies devotees claimed that law and adjudication were best understood as an ideological discourse shaped by power relations. Feminist legal theorists believed that law should be analyzed as gender discourse. Meanwhile, critical race theorists advanced a discourse of race to challenge the "race-neutral" stance of mainstream legal discourse. Those in the law and literature movement argued that law and adjudication would be more fruitfully approached from a literary perspective. Jurisprudential discourse mushroomed into a number of different professional *discourses* that advanced different normative and theoretical methodologies for understanding the nature of law and adjudication.

What has not been fully recognized is that the jurisprudential movements of the 1980s set the stage for a new form of legal criticism, which precipitated a much broader debate about the validity of traditional canons for interpreting legal texts, new definitions of law, and different linguistic and cultural practices. This "canon debate," as it is known in the general university,[9] questions the possibility of disinterested scholarship, objective knowledge, and shared intellectual traditions for discovering ultimate truths about American jurisprudence. At stake is the belief that law rests on solid ethical and epistemological foundations. The canon debate revealed that there is no longer a consensus on the possibility of a comprehensive theory for explaining the nature of law. Multiculturalism in legal studies has shaken the once dominant hold of large-scale, homogenizing explanations of law and culture. A new generation of skeptical legal academics has consequently rejected the divine project of developing foundational arguments or "canons" of construction for discovering the ultimate "truths" about law and social phenomena.

Part Three explores the meaning of the canon debate for the future of jurisprudential studies. Chapter 10 explores how the jurisprudential movements of the 1980s set jurisprudence on a transformative course leading unwittingly and unconsciously to a new postmodern form of jurisprudence. Chapter 11 examines the reactions of jurisprudential scholars to postmodern forms of jurisprudence, and speculates on how these reactions are characteristic of a major paradigm shift in academic practice. Chapter 12 explores the nature of this new postmodern jurisprudence by examining how it has come to be reflected in the work of two prolific contemporary postmodern writers and scholars, Richard A. Posner and Pierre Schlag.[10] Posner and Schlag represent two sides of postmodern jurisprudence, just as Langdell and Holmes represented two sides of legal modernism. The Conclusion speculates on the significance of postmodern jurisprudence for the future of law and jurisprudential studies.

My thesis is that the breakdown of comprehensive forms of jurisprudence and the proliferation of multicultural jurisprudential discourses is characteristic of the postmodern aesthetic or temperament in intellectual thought. Postmodernism emerges from the view that the search for new legal theories and metanarratives to solve law's problems has been exhausted.[11] It "announces or implies that a rupture has occurred, an irreparable break with the past, and that nothing can ever be the same again."[12] Some claim this has happened in jurisprudential studies. There has been a loss of faith in a secular and autonomous jurisprudence as the Rule of Law for all rules. My purpose in subsequent chapters will be to explore how the modern legal movements of the 1980s have themselves fostered the emergence of this new postmodern jurisprudential perspective.

*Part One*
# Modern Jurisprudence, 1871–1980

# 1. Origins of Modern Jurisprudence

Modern American jurisprudential studies began when the dean of Harvard University Law School, Christopher Columbus Langdell, published the first modern law school casebook, SELECTION OF CASES ON THE LAW OF CONTRACTS, in 1871. Langdell's casebook ushered in the modern era because it offered a new methodology and pedagogy for law study that was nothing more than an expression of faith in the scientific method. He declared in the preface to his Contracts casebook: "It is indispensable to establish at least two things, first that law is a science; secondly that all the available materials of that science are contained in the printed books."[1] In keeping with the spirit of Enlightenment, Langdell had faith in the powers of science and reason to uncover universal truths.[2] The late Grant Gilmore,[3] a distinguished twentieth-century contracts and commercial scholar, called Langdell a "symbol" of "the Age of Faith."[4] Another way to describe this is to see Langdell as an architect of what Thomas Grey called the "classical orthodox system" of American legal thought.[5]

The refinement of Langdell's classical orthodox system was premised on the view that law is a complete, formal, and conceptually ordered system that satisfies the legal norms of objectivity and consistency. Completeness meant that this system was capable of providing uniquely correct solutions or "right answers" for every case brought for adjudication.[6] Formality meant that the system was capable of dictating logically correct answers through the application of abstract principles derived from cases.[7] The system was conceptually ordered to the extent that its substantive bottom-level rules were coherently derived from a small number of relatively abstract principles and concepts, creating a holistic system.[8] While it is generally thought that Langdell's classical orthodox system was the antithesis of modern legal thought, in actuality it helped establish the argumentative logic of a form of legal modernism known as conceptualism.

Conceptualism ("law as logic") is what Karl Llewellyn called the "Grand Style" in American legal thought—a form of logic that classifies legal phenomena on the basis of a few fundamental abstract principles and concepts developed from the distinct methods of legal reasoning.[9] Legal conceptualists like Langdell used logic to go from legal premises to legal conclusion: basic legal concepts and definitions (premises) were assumed to be self-evident such that a logical correct choice of premises was thought possible. Logic was used to go from the premises to the legal conclusion.[10] Conceptualism was "the project of structuring law into a system of classification made up of relatively abstract principles and categories."[11] Modern conceptual jurisprudence harkens back to the Langdellian idea that law is a value-free science. Conceptual legal thought includes logical positivism, technical doctrinalism, and court-centered theories of adjudication such as legal process theory and neutral principles of adjudication.

Langdellian conceptualism can be discovered in the way Langdell wrote about law. In his writing, the law is a transcendental object or transcendental subject unaffected by social and economic context.[12] When Langdell wrote of law, he wrote like a precocious antihumanist. He wrote in the third person a lot. For example, "A debtor becomes personally bound to his creditor for the payment of debt."[13] The debtor and the creditor are unnamed individuals who are the legal abstractions of Langdell's analysis of commercial law. Langdell, the propounder of the law, never let the reader know that it was he, rather than the "law," who created the discourse and conducted the analysis.[14] Langdell's analysis of the debtor's liability was conceptual because it represented law as an "intrinsic, essential object" independent of context. In contemporary jurisprudence, this way of talking and thinking about law is known as the "formal style" of conceptual legal thought. Conceptualists who are formalists believe that law should be justified on the basis of uncontroversial rules and self-evident doctrinal premises insulated from external moral and ethical concerns.[15]

Legal conceptualists who followed Langdell's orthodoxy assumed either that law was a transcendental object possessing universal properties unaffected by analyzing subjects, or that law was itself a transcendental subject capable of rendering authoritative pronouncements.[16] Conceptualists thus projected a particular interpretive stance developed for a highly abstract and fictitious mode of analysis. The law of contracts, for example, has been treated as a body of fixed objects, of rules, principles, or policies that could be discovered by someone; or, contract law itself has been assumed capable of rendering its own pronouncements without the assistance of any legal actor. A contract for the sale of groceries was like all other contracts, because all contracts worthy of legal enforcement were required to satisfy certain universal rules established by an objective theory of contract law.[17] The law could declare that "A contracts with B" because the universal pronouncements of contract law defined the rules governing the sale of groceries as well as contracts for employment. In this way, Langdellian rhetoric portrayed law as either a transcendental object or transcendental subject, but in either case the role of the analyzing subject was eclipsed.[18]

Modern legal scholars, judges, and lawyers continue to exclude themselves from the process of interpretation in order to preserve their belief in the autonomous object/subject—the Law. Today, modern legal conceptualists believe that law is an "imminently intelligible enterprise" which "elaborates itself from within."[19] Judges who make decisions and attempt to understand the system are assumed to be only *relatively* autonomous in the sense that they control their own thoughts and actions, but their freedom to act is thought to be limited by the legal texts they interpret, and by the reasoning process they apply in the process of interpretation and decision making. The texts and reasoning of the law define the identity of the modern legal thinker as a *relatively autonomous self.*[20] Legal subjects continue to believe, as Langdell did, that they are capable of bringing order and reason to the objective world of law.[21]

The supposed objectivity of law is today justified by boundary definitions that distinguish the rational process of the law from the domains of politics and popular culture of interpreting subjects. The boundary between law and society has become a familiar way for lawyers to maintain their belief that law can be discovered conceptually in the object-forms of rules, principles, and doctrines. Langdellians believed that the object-forms of the law were immune from the ever-changing nature of society. Society might change, but they thought that the universal principles of law would endure forever. Modern-day legal conceptualists reject the idea of an artificially fixed line between law and society, but continue to believe that law and its methods can be objectively administered by disciplinary rules of the legal community.[22] Conceptual jurisprudence thus describes a whole series of jurisprudential theories devised by legal scholars to develop a less political and more objective understanding of law and culture.

If law could be like a science, then legal studies could aspire to be a serious discipline in the university. The reduction of law to concepts systematized by Langdell's case method of instruction rendered legal apprenticeship obsolete as a means for professional law training, since it was no longer necessary to study law as a practice; all that one needed to learn the law was a classroom, casebooks, and a teacher trained in the Socratic method of instruction.[23] The modern American law school, modeled after Langdell's Harvard Law School, could subsequently claim membership in the university community, with equal, if not greater stature and status.[24] Law professors could aspire to join university professors in the common quest for the discovery of truth. These developments permitted law to be studied as a "normal science."

Langdell gave American legal studies a new faith in the powers of law to dispel the darkness of the ancient common law, with its confusing and incoherent terminology and theories. Gilmore said that "if Langdell had not existed, we would have had to invent him."[25] Indeed, modern legal thought would not have been possible without Langdell, or someone like him. Langdell's great idea that "law is a science" was consistent with the modernists' belief that reason and science could and should rationalize and control the dark mysteries of the ancient law. For American lawyers at the dawn of the twentieth century, the spirit of Enlightenment could be found in the Langdellian faith in the omnipotence and liberating potential of reason and science to penetrate the essential truths of legal relations.[26]

The course of modern American jurisprudence was influenced by another great legal modernist, Oliver Wendell Holmes.[27] As Grant Gilmore put it: "If Langdell gave the new jurisprudence its methodology, Holmes, more than anyone else, gave it its content."[28] Indeed, the *modern era* in jurisprudence did not bloom full-flower until Holmes gave a series of lectures at the Lowell Institute in Boston in November and December of 1880. These lectures were the basis for Holmes's great book, THE COMMON LAW, published in 1881,[29] and marked the beginning of the modern era in jurisprudential studies: they set the basic themes of American law in a distinctively pragmatic direction.

In the opening passage of THE COMMON LAW, Holmes enunciated what contemporary legal thinkers have identified as "central, pragmatic tenets" of American law.[30] His view of law was pragmatic because it situated law in the world of "felt necessities" of intuition, prejudice, tradition, and social context. He declared: "The life of law is not logic but experience."[31] In conceiving "law as experience," Holmes expressed the pragmatic version of the philosophy associated with John Dewey, William James, and Charles Sanders Peirce, who rejected the foundationalist tradition in Western philosophy in favor of the thesis that knowledge and human thought are situated within the social and habitual practices or "forms of life" of culture.[32] For Holmes, "law [was] constituted of [human] practices—contextual, situated, rooted in custom and shared expectations."[33]

In evaluating law within situated social practices, Holmes argued in favor of a pragmatic approach to law, which viewed law as a means for achieving desired social ends of people. His view was that "continuity with the past is no duty but only a necessity";[34] for him "adjudication should and must be result-oriented, fundamental [and] legislative."[35] Influenced by American pragmatist philosophers of his day,[36] Holmes renunciated faith in the ability of a rationalist epistemology to distinguish truth from falsehood and instead favored a practical, functional understanding of truth and knowledge. He shared the pragmatists' belief that facts and values were derived from experience, and that knowledge about the world was possible only through experimentation.[37] For Holmes, truth was a function of social power, and law expressed that power.[38] "Thus, while Holmes felt that law ought to be a science, it was a science of experience, facts, and induction."[39] Like Langdell, Holmes believed that law was a "science" of categorization and deduction. But Holmes's jurisprudence, unlike Langdell's, was a science of categorization and deductions based on antiformalistic ideas of pragmatic thought as well as logical reason.

Although Holmes was critical of Langdell's emphasis on formal logic, he was also a conceptualist.[40] Holmes criticized Langdell for giving too much importance to the power of syllogism and logic.[41] He believed that any generalized theory of law would have to take human social conditions into account and respond to them. For Holmes, the conceptual order of the legal system was merely a "practical aid in teaching and understanding law."[42] As Thomas Grey recently explained: "Unlike Langdell, Holmes did not believe doctrinal conceptualization could produce a deductive system that would make legal reasoning formal and scientific."[43]

Holmes revolted against Langdell's idea that law and legal decision making were governed by rules alone. In place of Langdellian formalism, Holmes argued in favor of a pragmatic and instrumental approach, which subordinated logic to the "felt" experience of human history. Holmesian jurisprudence subsequently set the stage for the modern style of jurisprudence known as *normative legal thought*.[44] In modern times, normative legal thought has become associated with "conclusion-oriented" instrumental policy analysis.[45] It establishes the normative structure of legal policy in the law; what Pierre Schlag called "rhetorical levers" used by official authorities to instrumentally summon and coerce individuals and institutions.[46] Normative legal thought describes "the prime cultural ·pieces by which lawyers manipulate the self-image of jurors, clients, judges and other lawyers to get more of what it is lawyers ostensibly want."[47] In other words, normative legal thought describes a type of means-end rationality that subordinates the logic of law (positivistic law) to a broader cultural inquiry of history, economics, politics, or what Holmes called "experience."[48]

Holmes's pragmatic jurisprudence attempted to mediate between "tough-minded" instrumentalism and "tender-minded" moralism.[49] On the one hand, Holmes questioned Langdell's faith in autonomous law by rejecting the essentialism of Langdell's formal logic. Legal logic, in Holmes's jurisprudence, was subsidiary to practical reason and considerations of public policy. Holmes believed that law and its institutions evolved from views of public policy, social context, history, and experience. His pragmatic insight has since enabled contemporary legal scholars to accept the modern idea that "the creation of legal meaning— 'jurisgenesis'—takes place always through an essentially cultural medium."[50] Holmes's hypothesis, Gilmore said, "was that inquiry is a never-ending process whose purpose is to resolve doubts generated when experience does not mesh with preconceived theory."[51] This hypothesis led modern-day critical legal scholars to argue that law must be understood as a contingent political social practice driven by an underlying ideology.[52]

On the other hand, Holmes's pragmatic thesis about judge-made law also helped to support a form of policy instrumentalism in law. His thesis evolved from his *prediction theory*. As Holmes put it: "The prophecies of what the courts will do in fact, and nothing more pretentious, are what I mean by law."[53] By this Holmes meant that law should be studied pragmatically as a profession or business.[54] For example, in advocating a "bad man" perspective for evaluating law, Holmes argued that law was merely the expression of majority will, whether right or wrong. The role of normative judgment in Holmes's jurisprudence was understood from the practitioner's view, who approached law as a means to an end. Holmes's "bad man" perspective focused on the "material consequences" of law practice rather than on utopian possibilities,[55] and reflects the modern-day law and economics view that private law is "primarily a device for distributing risk according to the variable demands of public policy."[56]

Holmes's jurisprudence was *modern* because Holmes, like Langdell, placed faith in the ability of logic and reason to solve legal and social problems. However, unlike Langdell, Holmes believed that the law must be understood to develop from the practices of social life, rather than the abstract rules found in judicial opinions. He admonished law students of his day to seek an explanation for the nature of law in practices and customs of social life, that is, to look outside of law for law's inner rationality.[57] Holmes urged law students to study economics, statistics, and history in their endeavor to discover the mysteries of the common law. Legal thinkers who followed Holmes's instrumentalist jurisprudence took the position that the law should establish the moral rightness of its rules. Benjamin N. Cardozo, following Holmes's pragmatic philosophy, for example, seemed to have taken Holmes's position to the extreme in proclaiming the process of law involved "not discovery, but creation."[58] Apparently for both Holmes and Cardozo, discovery and creation "react upon each other." Holmes's jurisprudence, as consolidated by other great American legal thinkers, subsequently came to symbolize a new form of jurisprudence.

## The Two Sides of Legal Modernism

In the legal academy, there are now two dominant professional representational practices of modern jurisprudence: conceptual and normative.
Modern conceptualists who follow Langdell's type of conceptualism,
place a high priority on abstract principles and concepts logically derived
from a secure and bounded legal system. For conceptualists, the autonomy of law must be preserved in order to prevent external moral and
political concerns from corrupting the universal principles, rules, and
doctrines of law. Conceptualists believe that law's analysts can distinguish between questions of fact and value, the "is" and the "ought," law
and politics. They attempt to identify legal norms within the self-contained logical systems of law and legal reasoning.

Normative legal scholars follow the pragmatic or instrumental side of
Holmes's jurisprudence. They view law as an instrumental or pragmatic
process shaped by factors outside of law—experience, history, economics, and culture. Normative and pragmatic legal thinkers favor open-
ended justificatory arguments that embrace practical and ethical judgment. Normative legal thinkers believe that "law is dependent upon
moral or value choices, that law is not neutral, or otherwise exempt
from the contestable, value-laden character of politics generally." [59] For
these legal moderns, law is an "essentially cultural medium, mediated by
a universal pragmatic subject." [60] They share the Langdellian belief in
autonomous law, but understand law's autonomy to be shaped by an
antonomous culture and honogeneous society. [61]

These two sides of modern jurisprudence are expressed today in
jurisprudential styles, which owe their legacy to Langdell and Holmes.
Gilmore stated that "Langdellian jurisprudence and Holmesian jurisprudence were like the parallel lines which have arrived at infinity and have
met." [62] The lines of legal thought derived from these two American
legal thinkers establish the contours of the dominant styles of legal
modernism in American jurisprudence. Langdell's faith in the scientific
method (formalism) combined with Holmes's belief in the evolutionary
progress of law (pragmatic instrumentalism) worked together to affirm
the conflicting objectives and diverse styles of modern legal studies. The
most extraordinary aspect of modern jurisprudence has been the belief
that Langdellian formalism and Holmesian pragmatism could somehow

be synthesized to establish an autonomous and universal jurisprudence based on the belief in the ideal of one true Rule of Law. The history of modern legal thought has been a story of a series of failed attempts to reconcile and synthesize these two styles of jurisprudence.

The attempt to synthesize the ideas of Langdell and Holmes has never worked, because these two great legal thinkers developed different legal styles or aesthetics that expressed contradictory views about law and culture. Langdellian formalism protected law's autonomy by minimizing the instability arising from the diversity of culture. Holmesian pragmatic instrumentalism, on the other hand, valued and protected law's autonomy by permitting law to adapt and change to societal circumstances. The two styles of legal reasoning known as *formalism* and *instrumentalism* capture the essence of two conflicting sides of normative and conceptual legal thought embedded within the discourse of law. They are the source of the patterns, shifts, and pendulum swings reported in the commentaries of American jurisprudential history.[63]

The relative autonomy of modern law has thus come to be defined in the contradictory space between a style of analysis which "sees the law as an autonomous and closed system whose development can be understood in terms of its 'internal dynamic'" (legal formalism) and an opposing style, which "conceives of law as a reflection, or a tool in the service of dominant groups" (legal instrumentalism).[64] It is in this space that modern legal scholars attempt to develop theories to justify their view of law as a relatively autonomous activity.[65] The Rule of Law ideal of modern jurisprudence, for example, reflects the stability of formalism and the dynamic of instrumentalism under the legal doctrine known as *stare decisis:* like cases should be treated alike, unless circumstances warrant otherwise. *Stare decisis* is the "safety valve and brake" working to internalize normative justifications in conceptualist doctrine.[66] Judges read cases formalistically when they want to preserve the stability of precedent; they read cases instrumentally when they want to depart from precedent. Patterns of legal precedent were disrupted as legal decision makers shifted from one style of analysis to another.

Legal modernism characterizes the intellectual aesthetic that has evolved according to its own relatively autonomous and paradoxical mind-set.[67] This mind-set remains firmly grounded in the belief that legal thinkers can remain outside the realm of culture and politics and in control of the objective world symbolized by law. The mind-set of the legal subject is only *relatively* autonomous, however, because the legal modern's concept of self is also a creature of the legal texts they interpret. The forms of this rationality define the self of the legal thinkers as autonomous.[68] The forms of American jurisprudence, which emerged from Langdell's formalism and Holmes's pragmatic instrumentalism, reflect the paradoxical conviction of legal thinkers who accept the notion that judges must avoid making their own value choices in deciding cases, but who believe that interpretation and decision are matters of free will of an autonomous subject. This mind-set allows legal moderns to believe that law could be analyzed as a holistic system of abstract thought evolved from the logical and pragmatic investigations of relatively autonomous subjects.[69]

The dilemmas of modern legal theory have never been resolved, however, even though lawyers, judges, and legal scholars believed that a synthesis of sorts was possible. Modern legal thought is instead defined by a set of conflicting and paradoxical abstract propositions about the nature of the legal system and the power of legal actors within the system. The classical orthodoxy of modern jurisprudence developed on the assumption that law was a transcendental object or subject unaffected by particular contexts, including the subjective gaze of the observer. The legal analyst, the subject in control of the analysis, was presumed to be a neutral, objective interpreter; but paradoxically, the analyst was also required to faithfully follow the legal meaning embedded in the texts they interpreted. Legal moderns' dominant self-image of a universal individual self was a social construct defined by the fiction of an "autonomous human agent" capable of controlling the objective world through reason and free will.

Modern legal thinkers continue to believe, as Langdell did, that the objective order of the law is discoverable so long as the analyst remains disinterested and detached from the object. The analyst is assumed to be a mere instrument in the process leading to the discovery of the objective order of law. In positing the object, that is, the law, and the subject, that is, the analyst, as relatively autonomous, legal modernists were able to maintain their faith that law could be like science. In Langdell's world, law was a science with a rational order that could be discovered by an autonomous subject who used the correct legal methodology. This "depersonalization and deprivileging of the individual subject" remains a hallmark of both the conceptual and normative styles of legal modernism.[70] In the modern world, however, law is assumed to be only relatively autonomous, because law is assumed to have a social and historic dimension. Normative and conceptual legal discourses are thus used by legal moderns to situate law within the larger culture.

# 2. Modern Conceptual Jurisprudence

During the first part of this century, the study of jurisprudence was like an inductive science: principles of law were pragmatically derived from the raw data of appellate opinions much in the same way that the laws of nature were derived from scientific experiments. Law students were instructed on how to dissect appellate court cases like medical students were instructed to dissect cadavers—both dissected for purposes of discovering the universal truth of their objects. The conceptualism of this era was also associated with the substantive due process tradition of constitutional law—a time when the Supreme Court incorporated common law concepts of free contract into the constitution and froze the meaning of liberty in the Due Process clause of the Fourteenth Amendment. The common law rules of contract were constitutionalized by the Supreme Court, thereby preventing state and federal governments from regulating social and economic affairs. Langdellian formalism thus became the dominant constitutional jurisprudence. But, as Grant Gilmore colorfully stated: "A hurricane howl[ed]; the foundation slip[ped] away; the wisdom of the past could not save." [1]

The "crucible of events" that brought constitutional formalism to its knees was the confrontation between the pre-New Deal Supreme Court and the progressives associated with President Roosevelt's New Deal. [2] Also important was the work of the "Great Dissenters," Holmes and Louis Brandeis, who authored strong dissents in the economic due process decisions of the Supreme Court. Holmes and Brandeis provided scathing critiques of Langdellian formalism that were read and studied by New Deal progressives during the 1920s. [3] Following their example, a new group of legal scholars and teachers emerged offering a response and critique of the Supreme Court's substantive due process decisions. Academic battles waged by the legal realists; a political and constitutional crisis created by the Supreme Court's unwillingness to accept New Deal social welfare legislation, and general discontentment with formalistic reasoning in the law generally, shook the foundations of the Age of Faith until it crumbled. Modern conceptual jurisprudence arose from what Gilmore called the dawning of the *Age of Anxiety*. The anxiety of this particular epoch was heightened with the rise of the *American Legal Realist Movement.*[4]

## The American Legal Realist Movement

Legal realism, dominant during the 1920s and 1930s, transformed and undermined nineteenth-century assumptions of Langdellian conceptualism and set the stage for the emergence of modern jurisprudence. The legal realist movement of the 1920s and 1930s, according to conventional accounts, revolted against both Langdellian and constitutional law formalism. It is true that the legal realists shaped modern legal thought by developing and exploiting the strand of pragmatic instrumentalism that originated with Holmes. The realist movement also provided legal scholars with new interpretive ideas for reconstructing modern jurisprudence along the lines of a contextual and purposive understanding of law. "It was by insisting that one always needed to look to purpose in order to interpret even the plain meaning of words that the realists unfroze rules, shattering their brittle form and dissolving them back to their constituent policy goals."[5] Legal realism was also a radical intellectual movement in American legal thought; it also exemplified a new political attitude of American legal thinkers.

Arising almost exclusively within the world of legal academics, legal realists were represented by the law faculties at Columbia and Yale Law Schools, who were pitted against Langdell's Harvard Law School. The body of work that gave rise to the American legal realist movement consisted of a series of law review articles provoked by a brief essay written by Dean Roscoe Pound of Harvard Law School. Pound sought to identify the characteristics of a new movement in legal thought that he called "Realist Jurisprudence."[6] Pound's essay, which had not identified any realist by name, was viewed by the realists as an unsympathetic attack on their movement. Two of the best-known legal realists, Professor Karl Llewellyn of Columbia University and Judge Jerome Frank of the Federal Court of Appeals, published under Llewellyn's name a response to Pound, called *Some Realism about Realism.*[7] Their article is attributed with formally announcing the legal realist movement.

Llewellyn and Frank rejected Pound's description of legal realism, but failed to offer a more correct alternative definition of the movement. Instead, Llewellyn and Frank emphatically declared: "There is no school of realists. There is no likelihood that there will be such a school."[8] Llewellyn and Frank claimed that legal realists were "related . . . only in their negations, and their skepticism, and in their curiosity."[9] Llewellyn's description of legal realism has been a principal bane of confusion for traditional legal scholars who insist on knowing the foundational definitions of American legal thought.[10] The only foundational belief shared by the realists was their common skepticism about the claims of legal formalists. What united and defined the legal realist movement was the criticism it raised about the formal style of modern jurisprudence.[11] Legal realism has since remained somewhat of a mystery in the history of modern legal thought.

The work of legal realists was comprised of conflicting impulses and alternative strands of oppositional thought developed from Holmes and the *sociological movement* in jurisprudence, associated with Pound and later, Benjamin N. Cardozo.[12] Pound's theory of sociological jurisprudence called for judicial decision making in which judges would explicitly weigh social and economic consequences. Pound's theory was in many ways the first modern step in the development of modern legal thought.[13] Legal realists also took inspiration from Justice Holmes, especially immortal Holmesian phrases in dissenting opinions such as: "General propositions do not decide concrete cases";[14] and "the Constitution does not enact Mr. Herbert Spencer's *Social Statics.*"[15] These Holmesian "nuggets" were popular slogans for the legal realist movement.

Some of the leading legal decisions responsible for generating the American legal realist movement were the Supreme Court's economic due process decisions. The most notorious was *Lochner v. New York.*[16] In *Lochner,* the Supreme Court made a "political decision" in concluding that a state law regulating the hours of work for bakers violated the "liberty of contract" clause of the Fourteenth Amendment. The issue in *Lochner* concerned the constitutionality of a New York statute fixing a ten-hour day for bakers. The bakers claimed the law violated the clause of the Fourteenth Amendment prohibiting a state from depriving "any person of life, liberty, or property without due process of law." The Supreme Court, in the majority opinion authored by Justice Peckham, declared the New York baker law unconstitutional, because it interfered with the liberty of bakers to employ workers beyond the ten-hour restriction. *Lochner* effectively defined a jurisprudential era insofar as it reflected the structural traits of legal consciousness of classical legal thought. The conflict between private law and public constitutional law was "resolved" by a judicial determination that constitutional liberty includes freedom of contract, so that state restrictions on the freedom of contract were found to abridge constitutional freedom.

The legal realists helped explain why *Lochner* represents an example of bad decision making—a mistake that should be avoided. Following Justice Holmes's dissent in *Lochner,* the realists argued that *Lochner* was wrong because it involved judicial partisan decision making: the court decided the case by favoring the ideology of *laissez-faire economics.* The realists contended that the problem with this way of thinking was not just judicial activism, but the way the Court conceptually defined the word "liberty" in the due process clause of the Fourteenth Amendment.[17]

The Supreme Court had assumed that common law concepts of contract and property furnished the definition of the concept of liberty. The realists argued that the Court's conception of liberty was assumed to be self-evident when in fact it was a contested policy choice (laissez-faire economics). *Lochner* was thus said to be traceable to the premises underlying the Court's definition of liberty rather than bias or a mistake in logic. As a result of legal realist critique, modern legal scholars acknowledge that the problem with *Lochner* was that the Court selected the wrong "baseline" for defining the concept of "liberty."[18]

The realist movement was also marked from the beginning by a deep skepticism about the possibility of decision making according to rule. Realist skepticism was based on two closely related ideas.[19] The first idea was that "reality" is too complex and fluid to be capable of being governed by rules. The realists explained how the relationship between law and society is, as Lon Fuller once put it, like "two blades of a pair of scissors."[20] If we keep our eye only on the law blade, as legal formalists were prone to do, we will fail to see how society contributes to the cutting. The relationship between law and society, or as Fuller called it "law and life," thus enabled the realists to argue in favor of "nontechnical" or "extra-legal" considerations in legal decision making.

The other basis for the legal realists' distrust of rules lies with their critique of the conceptualism and abstraction in Langdellian formalism. Justice Peckham's majority opinion in *Lochner v. New York,* for example, relied upon an abstract and highly formalistic understanding of contract to privilege the bakers' liberty of free contract. The formalism of *Lochner* was condemned because the Court failed to address the reality of the disparate bargaining power between workers and employers. The Court's abstract legal analysis simply assumed that background rights defined by the common law were the best expression of the type of freedom and liberty protected by the Constitution. The Court ignored the prevailing inequalities in property and wealth that denied different groups the substantive liberty to contract freely. The realists showed how the abstractions of legal contract doctrine were but shadowy fragments of a political decision disguised by *liberty-of-contract* metaphors.[21] The most vocal advocates of this form of political skepticism were Felix Cohen[22] and Walter Wheeler Cook,[23] though many other realists advanced this view.[24]

One strand of legal realist thought, *radical legal realism,* was reflected in the scholarship of legal realists who emphasized a "political critique" to criticize public law such as constitutional law.[25] Radical realists attempted to expose the illogic and ideological implications of Langdellian formalists who believed that the dangers of exogenous value judgments in legal decision making could be avoided by the logical application of general rules to specific contexts. Felix Cohen, for example, taught that legal scholars should be skeptical of formalistic claims of legal objectivity; that many of the key categories of legal doctrine were incoherent; and, that a paradigm of "applying the law" through the formal logic of legal syllogism relied nonetheless on political judgments about the role of law in society.

According to Felix Cohen, "[T]he question of whether the action of the courts is justifiable calls for an answer in nonlegal terms. . . . To justify or criticize legal rules in purely legal terms is always to argue in a vicious circle."[26] The danger in this was that "the author, as well as the reader, of the opinion or argument, is apt to forget the social forces which mold the law and the social ideals by which the law is to be judged."[27] The early work of Karl Llewellyn[28] and Jerome Frank,[29] based on rule and fact skepticism, also illustrates this strand of legal realist thought. The radical potential of American realists has been largely ignored because the radical perspective lost out to progressive legal realism as World War II broke out and America embraced more traditional and apolitical ideologies.

Radical realists such as Felix Cohen,[30] Walter Wheeler Cook,[31] and Robert Hale[32] were the first to develop an anticonceptual jurisprudence to expose the political context of public and private law. Robert Hale, for example, argued that the law of contract drew its justifications from the coercive power of law rather than the ideal of freedom of contract.[33] By exposing the latent political power of law, Hale and the radical realists wanted lawyers, judges, and practitioners to understand how legal logic maintained and justified legal and economic coercion through rationalizations that accepted the reality of inequality and raw social power. The radical realists wanted to replace the conceptualism of Langdellian formalism with a realistic understanding that analyzed law and legal reasoning within its specific historical and social contexts. In the view of the radical realists, law needed to be transformed in order to deal with the underlying power relations of American society.

The radical realists believed that "[l]aw and legal reasoning [were] a part of the way [people] create [their] form of social life."[34] In analyzing the formalistic nature of the Supreme Court's liberty of contract cases, radical realists thus "emphasize[d] the inevitable ideological character [of the] representational activity [of the judiciary]."[35] The radical realists argued that orthodox jurisprudence had little relevance to the actual process of judicial decision making.[36] Radical legal realism was thus linked with the conceptualism of Langdell in a negative way. The radical strand of realism attempted to expose the political ideology of conceptual legal thought.

The other strand of legal realist thought is known as *progressive legal realism*. It developed out of Holmesian pragmatism, and describes the work of legal realists commonly identified with the pragmatic legal philosophy of Holmes, Pound, and Cardozo. Modern legal scholars have emphasized the significance of this strand of legal realism, and as a result they have ignored the significance of radical realist thought. Grant Gilmore is among many contemporary legal scholars who have equated the legal realist movement with the work of progressive realists. Gilmore's revisionist account of the legal realist movement in THE AGES OF AMERICAN LAW, for example, focused on Llewellyn's social policy orientation to realist criticism.[37] Karl Llewellyn, late in his career became the principal author of the Uniform Commercial Code, and thus served to nurture the reconstructive projects of liberal legal scholars such as Gilmore who wanted to restructure the law of sales under a Uniform Commercial Code. Gilmore thus shared the older Llewellyn's urge to "improvise" in order to shape the law in accordance with "novel business practices" of the modern commercial world.[38]

*Progressive realists* accepted the basic tenets of Langdellian jurisprudence that "law is a science," but for them law was a social science. Progressive legal realists took a more constructive and apolitical approach to their legal criticism. They rejected the conceptualism of legal formalists and turned to social science approaches in developing new objective policy analyses of the law. They did not, however, succeed in escaping the tenacious hold of the essentialism of conceptual legal thought. They made the same false move of legal formalists in believing that the essential concepts and categories of social sciences, such as economics, were natural, universal, and fundamental. The policy instrumentalism of progressive realism was like Langdellian formalism; progressives substituted a nonlegal and apolitical form of conceptualism (social science conceptualism) for legal conceptualism (Langdellian formalism).[39] The progressive strand of legal realist thought thus attempted to perfect the logic of Langdellian formalism by giving it a nonlegal and apolitical source of authority and certainty.

Progressive legal realists were successful in bringing a more pragmatic intellectual stance to legal studies. They argued that law must be studied as "it works in practice by making use of the social sciences" to establish what Karl Llewellyn called a new "Realistic Jurisprudence."[40] Progressive realists associated realism with a "postformalist" method of law study; practiced the empirical scientific method, and viewed the pragmatism of law as "skilled craftsmanship." Karl Llewellyn's legal realism, for instance, focused on human behavior as the basis for understanding what "officials do about disputes."[41] He attempted to free law from its past by articulating a coherent conception of the public interest and by developing legal policies to advance that interest.[42] Llewellyn's proposal for restructuring commercial law by distinguishing between merchants and nonmerchants was an example of the progressive realist notion that law should reflect the "realities" of commercial society.[43]

Progressive legal realists thus devoted their efforts to the goal of reconstructing public and private law so that law might better achieve the interests of society. The reconstructive effort of progressive legal realism served to meld the older legal formalism with a new-policy instrumentalism.[44] Modern social science became the new basis for controlling and limiting the open-ended type of policy narratives found in the law. The objective stance of the social science theorists also became an attractive alternative to the critical stance of the political realists.

But progressive realists were not that different from the traditional legal scholars they criticized. Like the Langdellian theorists who argued that "law is a science," progressive realists advanced the similar idea that "law is a social science." As Grant Gilmore ironically explained, "[These] [l]egal Realists or whatever they should be called no more proposed to abandon the basic tenets of Langdellian jurisprudence than the Protestant reformers of the fifteenth and sixteenth centuries proposed to abandon the basic tenets of Christian theology."[45] The irony of this was that these progressive legal realists became the new Langdellian policy analysts, "fact gatherers" and "improvisors" of the Restatement and Uniform Code projects Gilmore supported. The new Langdellians developed legal paradigms that offered a type of systematization, authenticity, and "puzzle solving" which is the hallmark of normal science.[46] Their efforts culminated in the modern forms of jurisprudential discourse of "reasoned elaboration," "institutional competence," and "neutral principles" of the legal-process school of the 1950s.

These two analytic strands of legal realist thought—one radical and one progressive—provided examples of how the two sides of legal modernism might give rise to new forms of jurisprudence. The radical strand of legal realist thought became known as a negative reaction to Langdellian formalism which championed a political critique of law. This strand of legal realism was largely forgotten as modern legal scholars during the 1950s developed new conceptual theories of law. It wasn't until the late 1970s that radical realist thought resurfaced when it was rediscovered by the critical legal studies movement. The progressive strand of realism, "realism as science," sought to ground legal realism in the modern social sciences. The progressive realists attempted to refine the pragmatist cast to Holmes's jurisprudence by giving it a quasi-scientific authenticity.[47] The progressive strand of legal realism was picked up and refined, first by the legal process theorists of the 1950s and 1960s, and later in the 1970s by law and economics scholars. Progressive realism has become the "official" version of the legal realist movement.

The American legal realist movement nonetheless shaped the future course of contemporary jurisprudence.[48] Langdellian conceptualism "crumbled" during the period between the two world wars, but a form of Langdellian conceptualism remained alive and well in modern jurisprudence.[49] Modern legal thinkers who followed Holmes's pragmatic jurisprudence returned to a more rigorous and sophisticated form of conceptual jurisprudence represented by legal process theory. Progressive realism also became a bridge that enabled legal thinkers to rediscover a new form of Holmesian instrumentalism represented by legal policy science. A new synthesis of Langdellian formalism and Holmesian instrumentalism seemed possible.

Most law teachers today regard themselves as legal realists. This is because most legal academics associate legal realism with the work of the progressive realists, the pragmatic strand of legal realism. The lessons of legal realism are accepted by most law professors in the academy, although many continue to have faith in the possibility of an objective and autonomous law. Contemporary legal scholars claim the realists as inspirational heroes for demonstrating that the missing disciplinary authority of law could be found in a discipline outside of law. Contemporary legal scholars could also celebrate the work of the legal realists for demonstrating how one might apply scientific methods and technocratic craftsmanship to legal study in an effort to render law more objective and determinate.

The possibility of making scientific statements about law continues to be a comforting myth that never really died. The "comforting myth" of legal certainty, however, has never successfully suppressed contradiction, paradox, aporia, and so on, from the law.[50] Williston and the law "codifiers," who formulated uniform statutes and restatements of the law during the 1920s,[51] helped keep the Langdellian faith alive for a time. However, the effort to "restate" the governing rules of the law was controversial; its success depended on the ability of the "restaters" to disguise, deny, and marginalize opposing views, contradiction, and paradox in doctrinal law. Moreover, the pretense of neutral law disintegrated as President Franklin D. Roosevelt's New Dealers developed new political theories to justify an activist welfare state.[52]

Recollections of the misadventures of Justice Peckham and the 1930s substantive due process era of the Supreme Court have remained vivid in the minds of modern legal scholars, but there was a renewed sense of optimism following World War II that encouraged jurisprudential scholars to accept the social-welfare activism of the Roosevelt administration, but reject the rule skepticism of radical realists. This new confidence was encouraged by the turn toward objective methods in the law, and a new faith in the ability of "man" to solve social problems through rational techniques. The era of ideological struggle seemed to be at an end and a new era of "reasoned elaboration" seemed possible. Social, political, and moral issues of the law became legal problems to be solved by modern policy "experts."

This new generation of legal scholars responded to the crisis provoked by legal realism and constructed new theories of law and adjudication. These scholars accepted the possibility of a public interest or social engineering strand of legal realism, while rejecting the radical claims of political realists. Modern conceptual jurisprudence was thus born. The merger of Langdellian formalism and Holmesian instrumentalism seemed possible as a new theory of the legal process gained popularity and influence.

## Legal Process and the "Synthesis" Theories

During the 1940s and 1950s American jurisprudential writers responded to the implications of realism by explaining how judges might engage a more rigorous policy analysis in the law. Harold Lasswell and Myres McDougal, together with a dedicated group of scholars they inspired at Yale,[53] endeavored to demonstrate how the indeterminacy of law enabled judges to be more creative in legal decision making. Their central premise was that judges could develop a policy-oriented analysis by balancing the competing policy interests involved in legal controversies. Legal thinkers of this period attempted to develop a "jurisprudence of interests" by focusing on problems of legal interpretation and interest analysis. Their central jurisprudential project was to tame the radical skepticism of legal realism by explaining how the intellectual criticism of the realists could be answered by a more "prudential" rather than "empirical" understanding of the process of law and adjudication.[54]

Legal scholars at Yale argued that law was essentially a process of social engineering that enabled judges to formulate and classify decision making rules for various types of legal controversies. Consequently, judges were encouraged to resolve legal disputes by "balancing interests." Legally protected interests were placed in three principal categories: (1) public interest; (2) individual interests; and (3) social interests. In balancing these interests, the primary concern was the long-term benefit of society. The ultimate determination was based on social welfare considerations. The goal of such work was to reconstruct legal doctrine on a systematic legal policy foundation by rekindling interest in the role of practical reasoning in the law. The most elaborate attempt to refine such an approach has been the legal process school associated with Harvard Law School professors Henry M. Hart Jr., and Albert M. Sacks.

The development of the legal process school can be traced to the unpublished legal process materials used by Hart and Sacks,[55] who explained how respect for procedure and principled decision making might lead judges to outcomes that conform to institutional and democratic norms. Process theorists at Harvard Law School during the 1950s sought to develop a process explanation of law and adjudication that would achieve social purposes through the institutional settlement of disputes. Process theorists defended the view that right answers in legal decision making could be developed from a conceptual understanding of the institutional functions and competency of different governmental agencies of the legal system. Process theorists believed in the possibility of "right" answers, so they rejected the indeterminacy claims of the realists. Because they asserted the autonomy of the legal process, process theorists rejected the claims of those realists who advocated the development of non-legal criteria for judicial decision making.

Legal process theory was conceptual because it relied upon conceptual models to explain, describe, and evaluate institutional competency. In public law areas, process theorists relied on the political theory of *pluralism* in their analysis of the functions of democratically elected legislatures and they used this analysis to expose the antidemocratic nature of judiciary. They never questioned the democratic character of the legislative process because they were wedded to a model of political pluralist theory[56] that assumed that interest group representation would ensure a democratic process. In private law areas, process theorists urged the "reasoned elaboration" of the principles and policies of the common law. This meant that judges, unlike legislators, had limited discretion; they were supposed to decide like cases alike under the guiding force of case precedent and statutory law. Judges were supposed to "elaborate" rational "reasons" for their decisions.

In confronting the realists' dilemma of law and politics, Hart and Sacks proposed that a distinction be drawn between process and substance. The process-substance distinction was mediated by their "principle of institutional settlement."[57] Recognizing the realist's insight that what judges did was often no more than policy-making, Hart and Sacks offered a sophisticated analysis of institutions and procedures for enabling judges to engage in a form of legal policy-making that was supposed to avoid the evils of subjective value decisions. Legitimate legal decision making would turn on process values, not substantive theory.[58] Procedure provided the objective process through which the law would achieve ethically desirable outcomes.

Legal process theorists in the 1950s understood the relation between law and society in a way that accepted some, but not all, of the legal realists' insights. They accepted the realists' claim that judges engage in policy-making when they decide legal cases, and they agreed that legal abstractions alone cannot explain what judges really do. They "emphatically accepted the social welfare implications of realist work in assuming the range of questions across the substantive field [of law] were rooted in issues of social policy."[59] Process theorists, however, rejected the realists' skeptical conclusion that legal policy-making had to be subjective and unprincipled. They argued that public law disputes (constitutional, antitrust, and administrative law) could be rationally decided by "reasoned elaboration" of the institutional procedures for dispute settlement. They claimed that private law disputes (property, tort, contract, and commercial law) could be conceptualized under a refined legal policy analysis of the "facts" and "procedure" of the dispute. Process theorists attempted to tame legal realist insights about the political nature of judicial activity by showing how judicial discretion might be limited by a rationalistic aesthetic defined by a peculiar understanding of the institution of judging. The rule skepticism of the radical strand of legal realist thought was rejected in favor of a new understanding of the institutions of the legal system.

For example, Hart and Sacks began their study of the *Legal Process* by examining the dispute-resolution procedures used by different governmental institutions. They concluded that "different procedures and personnel of different qualifications, invariably prove to be appropriate for deciding different kinds of questions." [60] Hart and Sacks next argued that a rational theory of the legal process could be devised from the systematic analysis of these procedures that would enable decision makers to match different types of disputes with the appropriate institution of government competent for rendering the correct dispute-resolution solution. Legal process theory was then offered to provide a new framework for synthesizing the jurisprudence of formalism and instrumentalism. Process theorists believed that instrumentalism, as a policy-oriented technique, was more appropriately a matter for the legislative process because legislative process was presumed competent in dealing with questions of value. They believed that the logical consistency was an essential feature of case adjudication because it was appropriately suited for the judicial task. Process theorists believed that disputes could be classified by a conceptual framework of process structured by the spheres of competence of different institutions in the American legal system. [61]

The idea of "institutional competence" has since become a basic regulating principle for synthesizing the two sides of legal modernism. [62] The rhetoric of this principle reflected the belief that legal reasoning and legal method could generate right answers for even the most difficult and controversial legal questions of the day. Legal formalism was to be reformed by a new conceptual understanding of institutional form of rationality about procedure. Shifting the emphasis away from Holmes's idea that the "life of the law" was "experience," the 1950s process theorists argued that judges should place their confidence once again in the powers of "process" and "reason." As Henry Hart, Jr., declared in the 1958 *Foreword* for the HARVARD LAW REVIEW: "[The Supreme Court was] predestined . . . to be the voice of reason [because] reason is the life of the law." [63]

## Neutral Principles of the 1960s: The "Highwater Mark" for Modern Conceptual Jurisprudence [64]

The generation of legal academics attending law schools in the 1950s laid the foundation for a set of widely shared notions about judicial decision making, known in the 1960s as the "Reasoned Elaboration" or the "Neutral Principles" school. This post-World War II generation of jurisprudence scholars attempted to construct a theory of constitutional adjudication that accepted the necessity of judicial discretion, but rejected the radical skepticism of the legal realists. They hoped that judicially conceived notions of self-restraint and the duty to render a "reasoned decision" would establish constraints on the freedom of a judge to decide difficult legal problems based on the judge's particular policy predilections. "Right" answers could be discovered through the development and application of the "right" reasoning for adjudication. The best way to ensure that the "right" reasoning was employed in adjudication was to require judges to deliberate and give reasons for their decisions, which satisfied a consistency test—all similar cases should be treated alike. The problem of "subjectivity" in judicial decision making would thus be avoided by the logical consistency of the "legal reasoning" process.

The values of consistency and reasoned elaboration gave legal process theorists during the late 1950s a basis to criticize Chief Justice Earl Warren's celebrated 1954 school desegregation decision in *Brown v. Board of Education.*[65] The charge was that *Brown* was symptomatic of unprincipled decision making of a result-oriented Court. For legal process scholars, the *Brown* opinion was no better than the Court's turn-of-the-century decision in *Plessy v. Ferguson*[66]—both epitomized an act of "constitutional politics" in which the moral agenda of nine justices was imposed under the guise of constitutional interpretation.[67] In *Plessy,* the Supreme Court made a different "political decision" by upholding the authority of state legislatures to enforce social patterns of discrimination based on color. *Plessy* partially defined an era in American history and helped define the agenda for social struggle over the question of race and the meaning of slavery throughout the next century.[68]

Legal process scholars during the 1950s argued that *Brown* and the Warren Court should be condemned for the same reason *Plessy* and *Lochner* were condemned—all disguised politically driven outcomes as decision making according to rules. Legal process scholars believed that a methodology was needed to engage true decision making according to rules in hard constitutional cases. In the face of what was perceived as an openly interventionalist Supreme Court, process theorists sought to rehabilitate the idea of an autonomous neutral law.

Professor Herbert Wechsler of Columbia University attempted to do this in his 1959 Holmes lecture at Harvard Law School, entitled *Toward Neutral Principles of Constitutional Law*.[69] Wechsler surprised the academic world by launching a broad-scale attack on the Warren Court and some of its leading civil-liberties decisions. He engaged the concept of "reasoned elaboration" to criticize the Warren Court decision in *Brown* as well as decisions in cases involving the white primary[70] and the enforcement of racially restrictive covenants.[71] The lecture charged the Warren Court with choosing outcomes in these cases merely because the justices agreed upon the substantive policies those outcomes affirmed. Wechsler believed that the Warren Court was becoming a dangerous "naked power organ" rather than a court of law.[72] His antidote was a call for reasoned elaboration in constitutional adjudication. For Wechsler, this meant the Court should commit itself to a form of legal reasoning that is "genuinely principled, resting with respect to every step that is involved in reaching judgment on analysis and reasons quite transcending the immediate result that is achieved."[73]

Wechsler believed that Chief Justice Warren's opinion in *Brown* flunked his "neutral principles" test, because Warren failed to identify a reason or principle for his outcome that would transcend the immediate result of the case. He argued that *Brown* relied upon flimsy empirical evidence to establish that racial segregation in public education was a denial of constitutional equality. Wechsler believed the Court failed to provide a principled reason why the right to a desegregated school should trump the segregationist right not to associate. He thought someone should attempt to identify a principle to justify *Brown*, but he was pressed to admit that even he could "not yet [write] the opinion."[74]

Yale University Law School professor Alexander M. Bickel responded to Wechsler's challenge by offering a new category between policy and rationality, which Bickel dubbed "passive virtues" in his influential 1962 book, THE LEAST DANGEROUS BRANCH.[75] Passive virtues referred to the various legal doctrines and procedures judges frequently employed to limit the court's power to review cases. Thus, Bickel's solution to the problem of an unprincipled judiciary was to limit judicial review in cases where it would be possible to rely on a neutral principle. Through the exercise of passive virtues, Bickel thought that the Supreme Court could avoid adjudicating controversial issues, which raised essentially political questions, more appropriately resolved by the legislative and popular vote. Bickel believed that the Court should save its activism for the day when it was really needed, for instance, the day a dictator marches his troops down Massachusetts Avenue in the capital.

The problem with judicial review, Bickel explained, is that it is a "counter-majoritarian force in our system." When the Supreme Court decides to declare a legislative act unconstitutional "it thwarts the will of the representatives of the actual people of the here and now; it exercises control, not in behalf of the prevailing majority, but against it. That, without mystic overtones, is what actually happens."[76] Thus, Bickel's commitment to the idea of reasoned elaboration and neutral principles was nothing more than a version of the philosophy of judicial restraint. Bickel believed the Court should stick to "matters of principles that legislators and executives do not possess."[77]

Wechsler's criticism of *Brown,* and Bickel's criticism of judicial review, inspired the next generation of legal academics to debate the pros and cons of Warren Court activism. Progressive realists rejected the idea of neutral principles and instead argued in favor of a "result oriented, sociological jurisprudence."[78] Others wondered whether Wechsler's demand for "neutral principles" and Bickel's "passive virtues" were themselves an ideology that camouflaged political objections to Warren Court activism. Substantive policy decision making by the judiciary was condemned by Wechsler and Bickel, because they wanted judges to apply principles that satisfy the "neutral values" of generality and consistency. These values, however, favored the status quo values that the Warren Court found repugnant to its conception of the Constitution.

The factual reality of race discrimination under the law became invisible under Wechsler's approach of generality and consistency. Wechsler's manner of looking at the *Brown* decision favored an abstract analysis ("freedom of association"), which prevented the courts from inquiring into the actual effect of segregation. Generality thus favored the position of those who desired to uphold the racial segregation of public facilities in the South.[79] As Yale University law professor Jan G. Deutsch argued in the late 1960s: "Adequate generality in a judicial decision—neutrality, if you will—is generality perceived as adequate by the very society that imposes the requirement of adequate generality to begin with."[80]

For other legal scholars, neutral principles of adjudication was an "impossible" theory because no neutral principle could be found whenever two constitutional principles were in conflict. Wechsler found in *Brown* two competing claims: the claim of racial minorities demanding the right to send their children to racially integrated schools; and the claim of segregationists demanding the right to send their children to racially segregated schools. These claims were in turn supported by two competing constitutional principles: the freedom to associate interracially; and the freedom to associate on a racially segregated basis. The problem with Wechsler's analysis was that there would never be a "neutral" principle found to mediate the conflict. UCLA law professors Addison Mueller and Murray L. Schwartz complained in their 1960 essay, *The Principle of Neutral Principles:* "The difficulty . . . is that there will *always* be a point at which an extension of the logic of my constitutional principle of decision will run into the similarly extended logic of competing principles."[81]

Legal scholars sympathetic to Wechsler's theory attempted to defend the *Brown* decision by rewriting the opinion to support the Court without offending the doctrine of neutral principles. Yale University Law School professor Louis H. Pollock's 1959 essay, *Racial Discrimination and Judicial Integrity: A Reply to Professor Wechsler,*[82] offered as a "neutral principle," the idea that the Equal Protection clause of the Fourteenth Amendment prohibits state governments from using their laws to stigmatize and denigrate a group of citizens because of their race.[83] Yale University Law School's Alexander Bickel, in turn, sought to defend Wechsler by showing how his idea of a neutral principle supports the exercise of judicial restraint. Instead of attempting to vindicate Wechsler's theory through its application to different problems of adjudication, Bickel argued for understanding Wechsler's argument about adjudication as part of the "passive virtues" that permit the Court to refrain from deciding a case when the "right" answer might be too controversial or costly.[84]

Finally, former Yale University law professor and former judge Robert H. Bork argued in his infamous 1971 INDIANA LAW JOURNAL article[85] that "[w]e have not carried the idea of neutrality far enough."[86] According to Bork, neutrality and reasoned elaboration forbid Supreme Court justices from deriving constitutional principles from ambiguity in the Constitution. Bork wrote: "Where constitutional materials do not clearly specify the value to be preferred, there is no principled way to prefer any claimed human value to any other."[87] For Bork, neutral principles require that "judges[s] must stick close to the text and the history, and their fair implications, and not construct new rights."[88] Bork believed that *Brown* could be justified by the text and history of the Equal Protection clause of the Fourteenth Amendment—namely, the recognition of a general principle of equality that forbids state-enforced discrimination.[89]

In Bork's view, judges must adjudicate according to rule or constitutional standards. Neutral principles form a restraining principle forbidding judges from imposing their own views and policies in adjudication. Bork argued that the Warren Court's decision in *Griswold v. Connecticut*,[90] which struck down a Connecticut statute making it a crime, even for married couples, to use contraceptive devices, was "unprincipled" because the Court's discovery of a constitutional right to privacy was not derived from any specific text or history of the Constitution. Justice Douglas's *Griswold* opinion attempted to locate the right in the undefined "penumbras" of various specific guarantees in the Bill of Rights.[91] Bork believed that the *Griswold* decision "failed every test of neutrality" because there was no way to decide between the right to sexual gratification and the right to economic gratification.[92] He believed that Justice Douglas's *Griswold* opinion transformed the Constitution's Equal Protection clause into an "equal gratification clause." For Bork, Wechsler's theory of neutral principles became a reason for requiring judges to decide cases according to rules.

A fundamental source of difficulty posed by the idea of neutral principles and process theory is that the theory assumed that conscious sovereign legal subjects were situated to apply the rules, and thereby limit their own discretion in choosing between competing principles and different interpretations.[93] There was a paradox here. Even if one were to accept the existence of "reasoned elaboration," "neutral principles," or "objective interpretation," judges would still need guidelines to know how to choose between any number of possible competing principles ascertainable from different interpretations of the constitution, legislation and prior court decisions. The necessity of remaining neutral and principled, however, was not a reasonable option for those judges who had to render decisions.

Judges and legal theorists were assumed to be autonomous. However, the legal subject was also a creature of legal texts that sharply limited his or her autonomy, even though these same texts assumed that its subjects were autonomous. The definition of legal subject presumed autonomous free will, but interpretation of legal texts created this definition and limited its expression. "[T]his self [was] a creature whose structure [was] in part constituted by legal texts, but who [was] in part constituted to act and understood itself to be autonomous." [94] The object to be interpreted (the law) required legal thinkers to be autonomous in order to preserve law's objectivity. But the object defined and constituted the autonomy of the subject. Legal thinkers could not demonstrate that they stood outside the system that defined the legal process. Legal process could not be separated from substance because there was no neutral "outside" vantage point for drawing distinctions between substance and procedure.

There was also a real danger presented by neutral process thinking— there was the possibility that process theorists might fail to support morally correct results in particular cases. [95] Process theorists failed to establish that there was a necessary analytical link between their theory of process and the achievement of social justice. The reality of racial inequality and disadvantage, justified and enforced by the judiciary, was hardly the basis for believing in legal process claims of justice through *neutral* modes of decision making.

Modern conceptual jurisprudence was thus both a reaction to the American *realist movement* and a continuation of Langdellian formalism. [96] Legal realism did not die; it evolved into new forms of postrealist jurisprudence. The radical strand of legal realism laid dormant after World War II until it was rediscovered in the late 1970s by critical legal studies scholars. The progressive strand of legal realism remained active in legal studies, but it became largely the theory of the legislative process as legal process scholars of the 1950s and 1960s developed new conceptual theories based on the values of principle and consistency to explain how judicial law making could be consistent in a constitutional democracy that allocated law making authority to the legislature. In public law areas, progressive legal realism marked the turn to neutral principles and judicial restraint. In private law areas, progressive realism sustained forms of conceptual analysis that viewed tort, contract, and commercial law in terms of economic risk distribution and loss minimization. Langdellian formalism remained active in forms of postrealist jurisprudence that nurtured new conceptual methodologies of process rationality and the application of quasi-scientific methods of the social sciences in law.

# 3. Modern Normative Jurisprudence

During the 1960s, modern legal thinkers sought to be more *normative*. They attempted to develop legal theories for instructing judges and lawyers on how to bring values of justice, fairness, social utility, etc., into their legal practices. Normative legal thought during the 1960s and 1970s was based on the conviction that legal theory and legal reason could make law more normative.[1] However, "despite its obvious desire to have worldly effects, worldly consequences, normative legal thought remains seemingly unconcerned that for all practical purposes, its only consumers are legal academics and perhaps a few law students—persons who are virtually never in a position to put any of its wonderful normative advice into effect."[2] American law professors were able to satisfy their desire to be normative without becoming politically engaged. "Normative legal thought" defined the operational rhetoric needed to bring out the normative content of law suppressed by conceptualist jurisprudence.[3]

At the end of the 1960s, two intellectual works were published that indicated a new direction for conceptualist jurisprudential studies. The first was Alexander M. Bickel's 1969 Holmes lecture at Harvard Law School.[4] In this lecture, entitled *The Supreme Court and the Idea of Progress*,[5] Professor Bickel conceded that the idea of neutral principles in constitutional adjudication was often unworkable. He concluded that there were no neutral principles to guide the court in resolving conflicting value choices central to many controversial problems of constitutional interpretation. Bickel, one of the most respected academic authorities of the Legal Process School, seemingly recanted, acknowledging that the Supreme Court could not always be a "voice of reason."

44

Professor Bickel abandoned the attempt to define neutral principles because he began "to doubt in many instances the court's capacity to develop 'durable principles,' and to doubt, therefore, that judicial supremacy can work and is tolerable in broad areas of social policy."[6] Bickel followed Wechsler's neutral principles theory to its logical conclusion and announced that the courts were "a most unsuitable instrument for the foundation of policy."[7] Evidently, by 1969, Wechslerian analysis had led one of the most respected liberal legal scholars to the extreme view that the Supreme Court should stay out of "social policy" adjudication altogether. By the early 1970s, Bickel embraced Burkean conservatism to justify limiting the role of the Court.[8]

Burkean constitutional conservatism was not, however, a philosophy American legal academics, judges, and practicing lawyers were willing to embrace. By the 1970s, many American legal thinkers favored the open-ended value talk of fundamental rights in constitutional adjudication and increasingly distrusted the political processes of legislation. One problem was that the legal process tradition failed to produce a jurisprudence that would permit judges to utilize normative and ethical considerations in legal decision making in controversial cases. Another was that Wechsler's theory of neutral principles appeared to be a defeatist theory in light of Bickel's candid recognition that neutrality was not possible in many constitutional adjudications.

The other intellectual "event" was District of Columbia circuit judge J. Skelly Wright's stunning essay, *Professor Bickel, the Scholarly Tradition, and the Supreme Court*,[9] published in the 1971 issue of the HARVARD LAW REVIEW. Judge Wright argued that the scholarly tradition associated with Professors Wechsler and Bickel had come "full circle." Wright meant that Wechslerian analysis had brought the postwar legal process scholars to accept the logical implication of the "progressive realists" who left the legal academy and joined the New Deal to focus their sights on legislative policy-making, rather than judicial decision making. Ironically, the Wechslerians of the 1950s and early 1960s attempted to refocus attention on the judicial process. But, as Wright explained:

With *The Supreme Court and the Ideas of Progress*, the scholarly tradition fathered by the progressive realists had come full circle. The confinement of constitutional value choices to the political process is again the true faith. . . . [T]he Wechslarians had in practice, if not in theory, strayed not far at all from the fold. Their demands of principle were so rigid that they could rarely be met. So their ultimate prescription of the court's proper role amounted to almost the same thing: decision on those policy issues known as constitutional issues would actually be left to the legislative and executive branches of government.[10]

Wright claimed that Wechslerian criticism of the Warren Court rested upon an essentially "political" idea of process theory: namely, that government by legislation is inherently legitimate. He pointed out that the foundation of this "political" theory was premised upon ideas of democratic pluralism championed by political pluralists such as Robert Dahl.[11] Wright argued that there was now "a rapidly growing body of literature by students of politics" that doubted the optimism of political pluralists, who trusted the ability of the democratic process to represent the views of all groups in society.[12]

Wright concluded his essay with a stinging indictment of Bickel and the World War II Wechslerians. Wright saw within Bickel's and Wechsler's criticisms of the Warren Court a "profound value relativism"[13] that accepted the dark vision that " 'justice' and 'injustice' [were] no more than passing societal value choices of no inherent meaning."[14] Upon finding that Bickel adopted the perspective of a moral relativist, Wright condescendingly stated that the "professor" wanted to "paralyze" the Court with his value-neutrality talk.[15] Although the debate over neutral principles was presented by Bickel as a debate over "fundamental method," Wright argued that the real issue involved the view of the "good life." He explained: "It is useful . . . to pierce the veil of the scholarly tradition and to see its quarrel with the Warren Court for what it really is. It is, I believe, a fundamental dispute over the good society as well as over judicial method."[16]

Wright predicted that the "new generation of lawyers," educated in the 1960s, would reject the scholarly tradition of the New Deal Wechslerians. He claimed that this new generation would see "no theoretical gulf between the law and morality."[17] They would see that "the Supreme Court *was* the Warren Court." Wright felt that the 1960s generation, inspired by the moral leadership of President John F. Kennedy, "was prepared to act on the ideals to which America is theoretically and rhetorically dedicated."[18] Wright stated that this new generation of "young lawyers know that a country which hoards all of its moral capital in the form of windy rhetoric is likely to die rich—and soon."[19] He believed that they would accept the role of an activist judiciary in a constitutional democracy: "They [had] seen that it can be done: The Warren Court did it and the heavens did not fall."[20] History proved Wright's prediction to be correct.[21]

For the new generation of professors, judges, and practitioners, the social issues provoked by the school desegregation litigation leading up to *Brown v. Board of Education* raised fundamental value choices that could not simply be left to the political process of government. Chief Justice Warren's opinion, rejecting the "separate but equal" doctrine of *Plessy* in *Brown,* may have been "unprincipled" and "unsatisfactory" for the legalistically inclined legal process scholars,[22] but for others in the legal academy, *Brown* symbolized a new normative form of legal analysis.

The normative justification for *Brown* made the intellectual position of 1950s legal process scholars untenable. It was difficult to square decisions like *Brown* with the process-oriented perspective, which un-critically accepted that the American legislative process was fair and democratic. After all, the racial segregation issues in *Brown* were the product of a pervasive social system of state-endorsed institutionalized racism. Legal process scholars failed to acknowledge that the law's process contributed to the legal construction of the social reality of Black Americans and other minorities. Decision making according to rules failed to account for "twentieth-century developments since *Plessy*" that "undermined the interpretive premises" and supported the *Plessy* Court's reading of "equal protection."[23] To understand why this was so, it is necessary to review the dispute in American jurisprudence over legal positivism and the separation of law and morality.

## Modern Legal Positivism and the Separation of Law and Morality

Following World War II, English legal positivists advanced a modern theory of legal positivism that precipitated a heated debate and contro-versy in America during the 1960s. Legal positivism, as developed by the English philosopher H. L. A. Hart, grew out of the monumental work of nineteenth-century philosopher John Austin, who defined the essence of law as a distinct branch of morality or justice.[24] Austin and the English positivists believed that the key to understanding law could be found in the simple idea of an order backed by threats.[25] Legal positivists believe that the study of jurisprudence should concern itself, as Austin believed, with the analytical as opposed to ethical meaning of the rules of a sovereign authority. Hart and the modern legal positivists, however, offered a general theory of rules that was more complex and normative than Austin's version of legal positivism.[26]

Hart's monumental book, THE CONCEPT OF LAW,[27] published in 1961, offered a *modern* version of legal positivism. Hart, a moral philosopher, wanted to define a theory of rules to explain why a community might, as a matter of convention, require its citizens to obey the same rules as a matter of obligation. His CONCEPT OF LAW relied on a distinction between "primary" and "secondary" rules. Primary rules granted rights and imposed obligations on individuals (for example, the rules of Contracts or Criminal Law). Secondary rules determined the application, validity, and source of the primary rules (for example, Article II of the U.S. Constitution, which determines the power of Congress to legislate).

Hart sought to avoid the "mistakes" of Austin, who failed to see that the authority of law was located within the internal perspective of legal actors of the legal system. Hart argued that the authority of primary rules did not rest solely on the physical authority of a sovereign. Rather, the binding authority of these rules rested upon two sources: custom and the community's secondary rule of recognition, that is, the ultimate Rule of Law that stipulates the validity of all primary rules. Hart's concept of law thus located the binding authority of law within the internal context in which legal rules operate. The normative background of community custom and a particular Rule of Law gave Hart's concept of law the "call of obligation that the naked commands of Austin's sovereign lacked."[28]

Hart's concept of law posited that every modern society has a fundamental secondary rule that determines how that society's primary rules are to be identified and justified. In identifying a society's rule of recognition, Hart believed that it would be possible to posit theoretically an objective and morally justifiable concept of law for reasoning about legal obligations. Hart's concept portrayed law as a self-regulating system derived from social fact and convention. The rule of recognition and other secondary rules established a "master" set of legal rules as the law of all rules. Hart's concept of law thus laid the seeds for the idea of a normative theory of jurisprudence as the Rule of Law for all modern legal systems.[29]

Modern legal positivists believe that problems of legal indeterminacy (the failure of rules to guide decision-makers to correct answers) were minor difficulties in decision making that could be resolved by institutional choices based on the competency of the decision maker to resolve ambiguity in language. Hart argued that legal terms had a core of settled meaning and a penumbra of debatable meaning.[30] In the core, judges must decide a case by following the settled meaning of legal terms. In the penumbra, judges are allowed to make a policy choice similar to the one typically rendered by legislators.

The core-penumbra distinction was a new normative basis for synthesizing the tension between formalism and instrumentalism. In the core, judges would be formalists. In the penumbra, judges would be policy instrumentalists. Logical consistency characteristic of Langdellian formalists was therefore relegated to the judiciary function. The open-ended nature of Holmesian instrumentalism was justified by the judiciary only when courts were required to perform a legislative-like function. In Hart's famous example involving a hypothetical statute prohibiting vehicles in the park, for example, Hart asked whether such a statute should apply to a bicycle. Hart's answer was that judges must determine if the word "bicycle" fell within the core or penumbra of the dictionary definition for the word "vehicle." Hart assumed that the rule excluded cars and trucks since they were in the rule's "core" of settled meaning and application.[31] Bicycles, however, fell within the penumbra, thus allowing judges to render a policy decision. The indeterminacy to be filled in by legal decision makers was therefore limited to cases following the "penumbra" of debatable meaning.[32]

Legal positivism as practiced in English jurisprudence never really caught on in America for a number of reasons. First, as Gilmore had noted, the "trauma" of the American Revolution and the events that led to the War of 1812 "instilled in many, perhaps in most Americans, a hatred of England and all its ways."[33] Those events turned American lawyers and judges away from English legal materials in the early history of the common law. This Anglophobia in the early history of America contributed to the foundation of a uniquely American jurisprudence.

English legal positivism was also largely unsuited for America because American lawyers needed an interpretive theory of law to explain and justify what America's highest appellate court, the United States Supreme Court, was doing—namely, revising, reinterpreting, and sometimes overruling legislation under vaguely worded phrases of the U.S. Constitution. In England, as a result of Blackstone's influence, judges are far more restrained by case law, precedent, and statutes. In America, judges have greater power under the United States Constitution, which, as a result of the Constitution's supremacy clause, sometimes supersedes acts of the legislature. The higher-order principles of the United States Constitution give American judges greater power to decide controversial issues of human rights, which in England would be a political rather than constitutional issue.[34] This facilitated the move away from the idea of positive law to the notion of *purposive* and *normative* law.

Harvard Law School professor Lon Fuller, for example, challenged Hart's concept of law by questioning Hart's linguistic assumption that a rule can have a settled core of linguistic meaning.[35] Fuller's famous debate with Hart, following World War II, illustrated how American jurisprudential writers sought to provide a more practical and realistic account of how judges decide difficult and controversial constitutional problems. Fuller, one of the greatest American jurisprudential thinkers,[36] criticized the conceptualism of legal positivists who believed that legal meaning could be determined by interpreting legal concepts in the abstract, without considering human purpose or social policy. For Fuller, there was an "internal procedural morality of law"[37] that explained and justified the power of judges to decide controversial issues. American jurisprudential writers since Lon Fuller have attempted to develop a more normative theory of jurisprudence.[38]

The main line of American jurisprudence followed Fuller's call for a more purposive jurisprudence and established a more normative form of jurisprudence. Fuller's notion of *purposive* interpretation has given American judicial jurisprudence its distinctive character and purpose. American lawyers now view judicial decision making as a purposive process that justifies subjecting human conduct to the governance of rules. For American legal scholars, *purpose, context,* and *policy* are integral to legal interpretation and meaning. The fundamental problem with Hart's positivism was that it failed to respond to the flux of American law, which constantly responds to different factual, social, economic, and political contexts of cases. Legislation and the U.S. Constitution frequently invited, if not required, judicial inquiry into purpose. The ever-changing dynamic of American law is an essential feature that Hart's positivism fails to explain.

Another reason for the unpopularity of legal positivism in America is the fear that positivism encourages obedience to immoral law. For example, Lon Fuller was concerned that H. L. A. Hart's "semantic" brand of legal positivism supported judicial attitudes that would lead to amoral law-obedience.[39] Fuller believed that positivist judges might rely upon their commitment to legal objectivity and the rule of law to justify amoral law, much in the same way that obedience to law was used by the Nazis to justify atrocities. While Hart vigorously and convincingly refuted this causal claim,[40] there remained a creeping suspicion among many American legal thinkers that English legal positivism breeds amoral and immoral law-obedience.[41]

Thus, in America, the study of jurisprudence evolved from a blend of progressive realism and the eclectic views of writers who developed pragmatic and normative approaches to problems of judicial decision making. This is not to suggest that legal positivism is dead in America. American lawyers and legal academics have retained positivistic attitudes to the extent that they regard law to be merely what judges and legislators announce to be law, and to the extent that they disown any allegiance to natural law. Hence, while modern legal theorists object to being called positivists, their cognitive habits (what they do, as opposed to what they say they do) serve to reproduce a positivistic approach to law. Most legal thinkers today remain committed to some version of positivist law because they tend to regard law—cases and statutes—as positivist law. Normative jurisprudence remains positivistic, but modern legal thinkers work hard to suppress the visibility of their own positivistic and conceptual moments.

## The Fundamental Rights Movement

In the late 1960s and early 1970s, a new group of legal theorists sought to avoid the substantive pitfalls of process theory by advancing new theories of adjudication that gained legitimacy by appealing to democratic values and constitutional norms. These theorists believed that law is indeterminate, but argued that adjudication can be more or less objective, constrained, and rational by identifying the best moral theory or by using fundamental values. Following the tradition of moral philosophy, rights foundationalists assumed that the main source of law's objectivity and legitimacy lies in moral and justificatory argument, not divine law of the sovereign. Throughout the late 1960s and 1970s, fundamental rights theorists attempted to ground law's objectivity in the cultural and institutional patterns of American constitutionalism.[42]

The *first wave* of fundamental rights scholarship attempted to identify a set of fundamental rights from constitutional principles and policy. The normative values reflected in the language of American constitutional law became the divine source of law's objectivity. It was believed that fundamental rights could be discovered in the text of the Constitution, case law, and the law's cultural heritage.[43] This phase of the movement focused primarily on issues involving constitutional authority and the source of fundamental rights and values.[44] A *second wave* of fundamental rights scholarship, developed in the late 1970s and early 1980s, and focused on the *process of interpretation*.

Constitutional theorists of the first wave attempted to overcome the "counter-majoritarian difficulty" posed by an independent judiciary, but when conventional legal methods failed, the second wave turned to interpretive strategies to solve the problem.[45] One group, known as *interpretivists*, sought to identify an interpretive framework for fundamental rights from grounded sources such as the text of the Constitution, tradition, or social consensus.[46] Another group, known as *noninterpretivists*, turned to general normative theories of interpretation in their quest to discover the moral foundations of law. However, rights foundationalists of *all* persuasions believe that rights trump positive law because only rights can claim transcendent lawmaking authority.

Interpretivists argued that the judiciary should follow the original intent and text of the Constitution. They argued that originalism was the best guide for the discovery of fundamental rights. Noninterpretivist, on the other hand, sought to identify and describe how textual analysis of the constitution requires the aid of an extra-legal theory to identify fundamental rights. As Stephen Feldman explained: "Noninterpretivists . . . argued that the text and the intent of the framers are hopelessly ambiguous and incomplete and must therefore be supplemented by some other source or sources, such as natural law tradition, or societal consensus."[47] However, a major problem for these scholars was defining which rights were to be accorded fundamental, and hence favored, status under different interpretive theories of the Constitution. Thus, political conservatives such as Richard Epstein argued that property rights are fundamental,[48] while liberals such as Ronald Dworkin argued that the "right to equal concern and respect" is essential in the discovery of fundamental rights.[49] Despite their differences, all branches of the fundamental rights school emphasize the necessity of an elite judiciary to discover and defend fundamental questions and rights in constitutional law.[50]

In turning to interpretation, fundamental rights theorists were unable to defend the integrity, coherence, and actual operation of the normative vision of law they espoused. The normative theories advanced seemed to reflect more the subjective view of the author of the theory than some objective, autonomous, coherent, and rational theory of law. Thus, the fundamental rights theories are normally identified by the name of the author, for example, Epstein's theory, Dworkin's theory, etc. The rhetorical form of these theories, however, prevented the recognition of their subjective nature. Fundamental rights theory, as a manifestation of normative legal thought, developed on the assumption that the expounders of theory were relatively autonomous subjects who were "receptive to moral arguments through a medium of language that is itself weightless and neutral."[51] It is in this sense that fundamental rights are assumed to be relatively autonomous and *authoritative*.

While fundamental rights theorists favor open-ended forms of normative discourse, they also remain committed to a technical normative analysis based on an objective and deliberative understanding of law. Fundamental rights theorists view themselves as working against technical doctrinalism in the law, when in reality their normative position is an authoritarian normative conceptualism, not unlike the position of technical doctrinalists who follow Langdellian formalism.[52] This is because "[t]he appeal of normative legal thought is grounded precisely in the fact that it is rational, deliberative, authentic, and non-coercive."[53] Legal normativity presupposes that a body of autonomous normative material is available and discoverable in shared values and shared understandings of what the law is or what it ought to be.[54] It is in invoking this presumption that normative values and understandings are shared. The normative impulse of legal modernism maintains its authoritarian character by invoking the presumption that a consensus exists for identifying shared values.

## Normative Process-Oriented Theories

Process theory has also been used by legal scholars seeking to identify the ethical and moral dimension of law. At Harvard Law School, for example, Lon Fuller attempted to build a "natural law" theory for a jurisprudence of *process*.[55] Fuller identified an internal set of normative criteria postulated from procedural values to guide purposive interpretation by judges. Fuller's normative criteria were built on the belief that process values could be discovered to restrain subjective preferences of legal decision makers. The hope was that judicially conceived notions of process and the bonds between government and citizens would identify a definition of law based on the ideal of decision making according to rule.

Perhaps the most famous moral theorist seeking to develop a process-oriented approach is John Rawls.[56] He attempted to define a moral discourse based on social contract theory to establish the minimum basic rights that would be essential for a "just society." Rawls first defined a legitimate decision making procedure for rendering fair decisions based on the community's values of fairness.[57] He then defined an institutional process for decision making based on what free individuals would consider just, without knowing where they stood in society—what Rawls called the "the veil of ignorance." Rawls called this the "original position," establishing the framework for identifying principles of justice.[58] The original position would be one in which all individuals would agree that principles of justice have a certain neutrality and noncontroversial character. It would establish a universal method for determining how to rationally analyze questions of justice divorced from the subjective positions of legal subjects.

By the early 1980s, however, many legal scholars took what has been called the "interpretive turn," adopting the view that law *is* interpretation.[59] An early example of this is Owen Fiss's 1982 article, *Objectivity and Interpretation*.[60] In declaring that "adjudication is interpretation,"[61] Fiss attempted to define a process that judges could use to understand and express the meaning of a legal text. He argued that judges can rationally make normative choices about sharply contested issues by identifying the "disciplinary rules" established by the "interpretive community" of the legal system.[62] Fiss postulated that judges are restrained by established rules, customs, and conventions of legal culture reflected in the language of the Constitution, case law, and the prevailing cultural heritage of society. These rules and customs are what Fiss called the "disciplinary rules" found in the "interpretive community."[63]

Fiss's notion of an objective interpretive process for normative decision making is representative of attempts by legal scholars to define a normative process for legal interpretation subject to judicial constraint. Thus, Fiss's "disciplinary rules" of the "interpretive community," are what Bickel and Bork call "original intent,"[64] and what Ronald Dworkin more recently called the judge's "interpretive attitude."[65] These "disciplinary rules," "interpretive attitudes," or "original intent" establish the basis for believing in the possibility of an objective interpretation for "filtering" and discovering community values.

Thus, a growing number of modern legal scholars subscribe to Fiss's claim that "[a]djudication is interpretation: Adjudication is the process by which a judge comes to understand and express the meaning of an authoritative legal text and the values embodied in that text."[66] Dworkin advanced a similar claim, arguing that "we can improve our understanding of law by comparing legal interpretation with interpretation in . . . literature."[67] Modern liberal scholars share the belief that objective methods of interpretation can be discovered to give effect to the fundamental values that epitomize the Warren Court era.[68] In this important sense, fundamental rights theory resembles the older jurisprudential theories associated with ideas of natural or divine law dominant during the premodern era. Fundamental rights theorists seek to describe "an objective moral reality" constructed from a set of authoritative legal principles and case precedents.[69]

Process-oriented normative theorists such as John Hart Ely argue that both interpretivism and noninterpretivism fail to ground constitutional adjudication in an objective source.[70] Ely sought to ground law in a moral foundation based on a presumed consensus about fundamental process values. He believes that a proper interpretive concept can be applied to the democratic process.[71] Ely insists that the proper role of the Supreme Court is to ensure that process of democracy is democratic and fully participatory. His argument rests on the belief that there is "one conception of democracy [which] is the right conception—right as a matter of 'objective' political morality—and that the job of the Court is to identify and protect this right conception."[72] Moral theory is relevant, not as an end in itself, but because it helps make sense of the law's commitment to the process of democratic representation for ascertaining moral values.[73]

Modern liberal theorists such as John Rawls, Ronald Dworkin, and Owen Fiss have attempted to construct new interpretive theories of rights and the judicial process by elaborating on community norms, "shared values," and fair procedures to which autonomous individuals would consent. The goal of such scholarship is to create a new theory of rights based on the belief in an autonomous normative legal process. Normative legal scholars presuppose that the process of norm selection and norm justification can be a rational, deliberate, and noncoercive legal exercise divorced from political or rhetorical manipulation.[74]

The goal of *modern rights* discourse: to specify fair decision-making standards for filtering community values, has never been realized. Process-oriented theorists hypothesize how community values would emerge from an objective and authoritatively defined choice situation. The process-oriented approach rejected the idea of fundamental rights, but imagined the existence of a neutral medium for discovering shared values of process. Interpretive rights theorists rely on descriptive and normative arguments to objectively prescribe fundamentally shared values, while process-oriented theorists rely on a process framework to develop their theories for the law. Authoritative legal materials prescribed the relevant process and the range of normative rights for resolving substantive issues for both groups.

Ronald Dworkin, highly critical of modern legal positivists and legal process theorists, forcefully defended the importance of normative and justificatory arguments in judicial decision making.[75] Dworkin argued that judges can justify the *Brown* decision using justifications deduced from interpretive practices not unlike those used in literary criticism.[76] Rather than policy analysis, he favored an explanation of judicial decision making as an interpretive practice of "integrity in adjudication," developed from ethical and political norms reflected within the text and history of the Constitution.

Dworkin emphasizes the importance of the right to equal concern and respect in the law. The focus of his work is to defend the notion that a rights foundation exists to ground law in a determinate and reasonably objective source.[77] Thus, Dworkin's project supports the fundamental rights school of constitutional law fostered by the Warren Court.[78] This school developed as a result of the Warren Court's effort to discover a number of fundamental rights in various clauses of the Constitution. Of particular significance was the Warren Court's construction of the Equal Protection clause to require a "strict" constitutional scrutiny of state regulations affecting a "fundamental interest." [79] Rights foundationalists believe that the primary responsibility of the judiciary is to discover fundamental rights and protect them from state intervention.[80] A still-evolving debate has ensued between process theorists, who tend to view judicial review of legislation as presumptively invalid, and rights foundationalists, who tend to favor a more active judiciary.[81]

## Normative Legal Thought—Post-1960s Themes

While process theorists emphasized the importance of defending the artificial process of the law, fundamental rights theorists focused on moral and justificatory arguments. The conceptualism of process and rights theory encouraged legal analysts to focus on doctrinal manipulation in the law. Rights foundationalists concentrated on the logic of rights and principles, process theorists focused on the logic of consensus. Rights foundationalists argued that rights trump process (provided that the particular legal right is normatively justified), while process theorists believed that process values (e.g., the value of protecting legislative will) may trump the assertion of a legal right. Despite these important differences, each side believed in the possibility of grounding law's objectivity in a Rule of Law defined by either process or rights, or a combination of both.

One important theme of modern jurisprudence thus involves the possibility of objectivity of law. Is law objective? Can judges be expected to render objective decisions on controversial matters of social policy? These questions have provoked considerable debate in modern jurisprudence discourse. Process theorists argue that the main source of law's objectivity resides within a theory of legal process, while rights foundationalists argue that law's objectivity can be defended by normative and justificatory arguments. However, both believed that the answer to any given legal question must be provided by the "law." Thus, while the study of jurisprudence exhibited heated debate on questions of legal objectivity, a central core of jurisprudential thought accepted the possibility that law and adjudication can be grounded in some objective source, whether it be a conceptual theory of legal process or a normative concept of rights.

The most ingenious scholarly explanations of decision making, such as Ronald Dworkin's late 1970s "Herculean" account of how judges decide difficult constitutional cases,[82] or Bruce Ackerman's recent treatment of the "countermajoritarian difficulty" of constitutional adjudication,[83] presume that a shared foundation for decisions can be discovered. Hence, Dworkin's effort is aimed at discovering unexpressed moral principles for deciding "hard cases."[84] Meanwhile, Ackerman sought to persuade us "that our present patterns of constitutional talk and practice have a deeper order than one might suppose."[85] The projects of these modern legal scholars are characteristic of modes of legal thought that sought to describe the logic of a monolithic process of morality for law. The assumption was that "there is some normatively charged context that is both retrievable and universally shared."[86]

Modern normative legal scholars have acted as if the "fund of normativity-charged beliefs and ideals [shared in the community] is normatively efficacious."[87] They generally assumed (as legal conceptualists clearly assumed) that judicial decisions that are required by law enjoy some measure of moral justification. This assumption enabled normative legal thinkers to remain committed to the idea of autonomous law. Norm justification was consequently grounded on a rational, deliberative legal process. For modern normative legal scholars, objectivity in the law, in its strongest sense, required legal decision makers to select the "best or correct form of reasoning that would yield distinctive right answers to legal problems."[88] To say that the law provides answers to legal questions is to acknowledge the existence of the Rule of Law. In this sense, normative jurisprudence is no different than conceptual jurisprudence, in that both involve the search for a method that might define an ultimate Rule of Law for legitimating the rules of the legal system.[89] The normative conceptualism of normative legal thought was, like conceptual forms of legal thought such as process jurisprudence, defended and articulated under the assumption that judicial authority was limited by an external, objective source. While normative legal thought is usually viewed as pitted against conceptual legal thought, the rhetorical nature of these two sides of modern jurisprudence are intimately related. Both seek to locate the logical and moral support of law in the faith of "right answers."

The rhetorical field of conceptualism and normative legal thought thus exhibit the Enlightenment vision of one true Rule of Law as the law of all rules. This ultimate Rule of Law perspective characterizes much of modern jurisprudential thinking in America. For modern jurisprudential scholars, "[t]he most promising avenues for correct answers to legal questions are in terms of answers supported by the best reasons or the answers an ideal judge would reach."[90] As Kent Greenawalt, a legal philosopher at Columbia University School of Law, stated: "The idea is that every legal question having a correct answer has a single answer supported by the best reason."[91]

An alternative paradigm born out of progressive legal realism seemed possible to postwar legal scholars—one that was both more "normative" and "conceptual" than the one Langdell offered. It stems from the view of modern legal scholars who have accepted the skeptical, functional approach of the realists but continue to believe in the formalist idea of decision making according to rules. This alternative paradigm was adopted by progressive legal realists who argued that law must look outward for legal justifications,[92] but rejected the implications of radical realists' assault on law's objectivity. The belief in law's objectivity has paradoxically enabled these same legal theorists to retain traces of Langdellian formalism in their work. The spirit of Chris Langdell can still be found in the modern legal theorists' belief in a legal and moral process capable of yielding correct answers for law's problems.

Today, legal scholars continue to think and talk about law in essentialist terms; that is, law as an autonomous, self-generating activity. They continue to practice Langdellian formalism as the rhetoric of the transcendental object or subject in which the legal subject-interpreter is eclipsed, even while they strive to be normative. Normative legal thinkers believe that a distinct legal method is discoverable by a relatively autonomous subject, and that such a method can unlock the door to the ultimate legal truths. The jurisprudential quest to discover, develop, and refine a normative method for the discovery of legal truth remains an important aspect of their modern legal projects. Proponents of this view proclaim that the application of shared public values can settle public policy issues, either through strong adherence to the "basic values as they are reflected in the law"[93] or by adherence to liberal ideals of universalism, fairness, and impartiality.[94]

Modern forms of normative jurisprudence have emerged from the attempt of American writers to bring "enlightenment" to the study of legal objectivity and neutrality. Modern jurisprudential thinkers are thus optimistic about the possibility of achieving an autonomous, objective Rule of Law for the legal system. The idea that legal questions have objectively correct answers, drawn from the "best reasons" and "correct values" found in authoritative legal materials, is believable, since law is assumed to be relatively autonomous. The possibility of discovering normative answers to law's problems inspires modern jurisprudential writers to ground knowledge and truth about law in objective and universal morality. If one believed in the relative autonomy of law, then one could believe "in objectively correct answers to questions within the system, based on the best reasons within the law, even if one were otherwise skeptical."[95] Accepting the ideas of "best answers" and "an ideal judge," modern legal scholars "urge that answers may be objectively correct in a significant sense even when reasonable lawyers disagree."[96]

For modern jurisprudential writers, the idea of law as a self-contained system captures much of the meaning of modern legal thought and reasoning, "explaining how legal materials are used in legal arguments and also explaining how legal questions may have correct answers when the pure moral or political analogies to those questions are highly controversial."[97] Contemporary jurisprudential writers, however, add an important qualification: "An answer to what existing law provides can be correct only if the crucial 'best reasons' are generally accessible."[98] Hence, while "[r]adical skeptics often point out how the legal system embraces contrary values," modern legal scholars continue to believe that "reasoned analysis of the law often [but not always] suggests circumstances in which one value is to be given primacy."[99]

An important theme of modern jurisprudence has consequently involved the recurrent attempt of legal scholars to explain, justify, and defend the idea of legal decision making according to the ideal of an autonomous Rule of Law. The "ideal judge" perspective of normative jurisprudence was conceived to defend this "ideal." Modern legal scholars sought to defend decision making according to rule by distancing themselves from the various "pejorative connotations of the word 'formalism.'"[100] They have thus "appli[ed] [their] intellectual faculties to the rewriting of the law so as to make it more principled, coherent, and morally appealing."[101] For modern legal scholars, the ideal of the Rule of Law remains at the heart of their normativity, and they have little sympathy for or understanding of the "avant-gardist sensibility" of those who have recently lost faith in law's autonomy. Legal moderns reject the view of skeptics who question law's claim to authority, because they revere legal traditions and are hesitant or unwilling to accept different intellectual perspectives.[102] They find the avant-gardist sensibility of postmodernism unintelligible because their modernistic cognitive orientations and gestalt do not allow them to embrace the critical reflexivity of postmodernism. Ironically, some legal writers and thinkers would deny that they are postmodernists even though their work exhibits an unwittingly postmodern character.[103]

# 4. Decline of Modern Jurisprudential Studies

Legal process and fundamental rights theories dominated much of modern jurisprudential discourse throughout the 1960s and 1970s. The average law teacher's jurisprudence combined interest balancing, fundamental rights analysis, and institutional coordination between courts, agencies, and the legislature.[1] Legal studies at many law schools were regarded as an autonomous discipline because legal reasoning and legal methods were thought to be sufficiently distinct from the methods of other academic disciplines in the general university. The autonomy of legal thought was relatively secure as the 1970s began, but then events, both internal and external to law, caused legal thinkers to question their faith in law's autonomy. The *Age of Faith* had passed; the *Age of Anxiety* had finally arrived.[2]

The Age of Anxiety reflected a common condition prevailing within both the fine arts and the academic disciplines of literary theory, philosophy, social sciences, and the law throughout the 1970s and 1980s. This condition was brought about by what contemporary social critics have called a "crisis of representation" in the traditional representational structures utilized by artistic, philosophical, literary, social, and scientific languages to control, predict, and describe the social and physical worlds. By the early 1970s, the representational structures of modern discourse seemed incapable of maintaining their distinctive knowledge claims of universal truth.

The "crisis of representation" created anxiety over the possibility of sustaining the intellectual projects of modernity. "Postmodernism" became the term to describe this "crisis" in the fine arts and within the intellectual disciplines of literary theory, philosophy, the social sciences, and recently the law. Preservation of tradition and the status quo was no longer a central project inspiring the interest of these intellectual and artistic communities.[3] The search for truth and knowledge became a *performative enterprise*[4]—one in which the goal was to increase the performance and operation of a theoretical model, paradigm, or social action. The objective was no longer truth but performativity.[5] There was a loss of performative significance in this enterprise because the puzzle-solving character of theoretical work had become recognized as a "language game" easily subjected to rhetorical manipulation.[6] The old ways of defining reality were no longer perceived as credible, as language itself became a "language game." In jurisprudence, the first telling sign of boundary dissolution was the breakdown of the distinction between law and society. The breakdown in the law/society boundary, central to the idea of autonomous law, created anxiety and crisis in the modern forms of jurisprudential thought. This crisis of representation can be traced to events that occurred during the early 1960s.

## The External Social and Cultural Forces of the 1960s

As Judge J. Skelly Wright reported in 1971, for most lawyers trained in the 1960s, the "outside reality" of American culture rendered the modernist vision of American law out of touch with social reality. The new generation of professors, judges, and practitioners were concerned that traditional jurisprudence had failed to address the pressing social issues of the day. Worse yet, jurisprudence had little if anything to say to this generation about the burning social issues of the day. As Robert W. Gordon stated: "The appeal to a deep social consensus was hardly a winner in a society apparently splintering every day between blacks and whites, hawks and doves, men and women, hippies and straights, parents and children."[7]

It was also painfully apparent that many crucial policy issues in the law, especially in constitutional law, could not be resolved without judicial resolution of controversial value conflicts. Even legal process scholars, who argued that Chief Justice Warren's opinion in *Brown v. Board of Education* was illegitimate, were unable to offer a "principled" argument to justify *Brown*. The idea that judges should defer from deciding controversial policy issues merely because a value choice was required seemed unrealistic.

De jure forms of racial discrimination, for example, could be eliminated only after the courts decided that freedom to associate interracially prevailed over the freedom not to associate interracially. The "leave it to the legislature" response of Wechslerian process theorists was an unacceptable approach in the school desegregation cases because the legislatures themselves were a reason for judicial intervention. Jim Crow discrimination had been sanctioned by state legislators committed to the cause of white supremacy. The institutional competency analysis of process theory seemed to rest upon what Gary Peller called an "analytic loop"[8]: Wechslerian scholars argued that the judiciary had to defer social policy value judgments to the political branches of government, the legislative or the executive branch, because the judiciary was unelected and therefore incompetent to make social policy value choices. But the democratic character of the legislature, the ground for judicial deference, was never seriously questioned by the courts. The courts never questioned the legitimacy of democratic process, because that question depended on the resolution of issues that were beyond judicial competence. Many lawyers educated in the 1960s could sympathize with Peller's complaint that "it [was] difficult to conceive of the basis for the purportedly 'principled' concern about [legal decisions such as] *Brown* voiced by [Herbert] Wechsler and other fifties legal scholars."[9]

While legal process scholars were aware that legislatures and state bureaucracies were capable of implementing discriminatory policies, those errors were considered "isolated blunders, not the product of systemic failures."[10] Many progressive legal academics committed to the civil rights movement and the cause of racial equality, however, found it difficult to accept the legal process theorists' rationalizations of weaknesses in the legal process.[11] For many legal scholars educated in the 1960s and 1970s, the process-oriented theorists' "concern with the institutional integrity of the Supreme Court seem[ed] hollow and abstract, hard to distinguish from the 'principled' commitment to 'states rights' claimed by the most vociferous and racist southern opponents of the Warren Court reforms."[12] The baby boomer generation believed that a deeper structural failure was to blame.

The problem was that traditional legal analysis had failed to recognize that law contributes to the construction of social reality. Traditional analysis of legal problems adopted a "naive" understanding of the relationship between law and culture. Most legal scholars assumed that the directive force of legal rules had an independent existence, such that law could function autonomously of culture. Many now recognize that the *Brown* decision embraced a new idea, that law contributes to the construction of social reality.[13] Chief Justice Warren's opinion in *Brown* repudiated the "separate but equal doctrine" of *Plessy*, because the Court recognized for the first time that Jim Crow laws influenced the social "choices" that stigmatized persons of color. The Court saw a structural link between law and culture that modern process theorists failed to consider. Mainstream, liberal legal scholars such as Bruce Ackerman now acknowledged that Chief Justice Warren's opinion for the Court "look[ed] better than many of the scholarly 'improvements' offered up over the years," because his opinion "turns on the crucial synthetic point: twentieth-century developments since *Plessy* have undermined the interpretive premises that informed Justice Brown's reading of 'equal' protection [in *Plessy*]."[14]

The baby boomer generation also noticed linkages between the discourse of contemporary American politics in the 1960s and the discourse of traditional legal scholars who criticized the *Brown* decision. Legal process theory became suspect because it failed to come to terms with the social disintegration of the cultural consensus of the fifties generation. American culture was changing, but the legal practice taught in law schools continued to cling to old paradigms of social and cultural legitimacy. The problem was that the Wechslerian generation was trained under a legal mind-set influenced by the cultural images and practices of the fifties. For a time, the attitudes and authority of the fifties generation prevailed, but evidentially the 1950s cultural images gave way to less-ordered and more fragmentary images.

For baby boomers like Gordon and Peller, the legal process appeal to "neutral principles" and "reasoned elaboration" seemed strangely like the appeal of the "best and brightest" who were then directing and rationalizing the war in Vietnam[15] and defending the "institutional integrity of the Supreme Court" voiced by Herbert Wechsler and other liberal legal scholars throughout the 1950s.[16] Gordon felt that "[t]he fluent optimistic jargon of policy science in the middle of such unspeakable slaughter and suffering seemed not only absurdly remote from any real world of experience, but literally insane."[17] Peller believed that "the discourse about the Vietnam War only brought into wider view what was already contained within the process analytic in the 1950s, an unwillingness on the part of mainstream American intellectuals to identify social domination." [18]

Law students of the 1960s and 1970s lived in a vastly different culture than that of the fifties generation. The 1960s generation began to question the purpose of their lives and the meaning of a materialistic mass culture, which had defined the "good life" of the fifties generation. There was also the problem of race. The belief in a color-blind society with equal process was hard to square with the events unfolding on the streets of Selma, Montgomery, and countless other communities in America during the 1960s.

Wherever they turned, the baby boomer generation was bombarded with cultural symbols of dissolution and fragmentation. The dynamics of class, race, age, religion, and sexual orientation made it very difficult for them to accept the idea that an objective, autonomous law was capable of providing "solutions" for contemporary social problems. The romantic belief in the possibility of legal "solutions" for the problems of the day was no longer capable of fostering a consensus, because the authority of the law was seen as part of the problem.

Fundamental rights theories of the 1960s lost performative significance as it became increasingly difficult to explain and justify which rights were "fundamental," and why fundamental rights should trump other rights, democratic choices or, for that matter, politics. Conservatives emphasized the foundational role of property rights; liberals emphasized the right to equal concern and respect, and collectivists focused on the rights of disadvantaged groups. [19] For some, the theory of rights seemed to collapse into what Richard Posner subsequently called a "transparent apology for judicial activism." [20] For others, the problem was that "rights talk" encouraged an abstract way of analysis that confused social roles and people. [21] Many believed that rights talk was blind to the inequities that prevailed in particular social contexts.

The claims of process-oriented theorists were also hard to square with the reality of American culture. The idea of a representation-reinforced process seemed nice in the abstract, but it was far too indeterminate to guide Supreme Court decisions. [22] Ely's idea of a process theory of judicial review was structured to facilitate the representation of minorities, but the theory fell prey to the problem of determining which societal groups constitute minorities. "The categorization of groups as protected minorities require[d] the Court to engage in exactly those unconstrained substantive value choices that representation-reinforcement theory [was] supposed to forbid." [23]

Disillusionment was also brought about by a new technocracy associated with the modern bureaucratic state. With the rise of the modern welfare state erected after the New Deal and strengthened during the Kennedy-Johnson years, government became a major source of power and wealth. The power and wealth was administered by a new professional class of administrative "experts" who sought to manage social problems through government largess. This new technocracy manifested itself in law by fostering a new technocratic form of policy discourse. Cost-benefit analysis, empirical analysis, and general scientific lure was replacing the common law craft tradition. A new technocratic theory of the legal process was needed to deal with new social problems resulting from the bureaucratization and technocratization of American law.

The consensus theories of the 1950s became less believable by the late 1960s as American society entered a new period of political, intellectual, and social transformation. During the 1950s, "[l]ife in America, it appeared, was in all ways going to get better: a new car could replace an old one, and a larger, more modern refrigerator would take the place of one bought three years earlier, just as a new car had replaced an old one." [24] By the end of the 1960s, general feelings of the good life and expanding affluence of consumerism had peaked. The new American car was not as good as it had been in the past; the Japanese and Germans had better alternatives. The values of market consumption were replaced with a new social awareness of scarcity and human poverty. In the midst of the emerging new culture, the optimism of the legal process tradition could no longer hold sway; a new generation had become more skeptical. For those who attended law schools during the 1960s and 1970s, the contrast between the "reality" portrayed by the legal curriculum and the reality of the world outside the law school classroom was like that between night and day.

This is even more true today for the current generation of law students who were born during the Watergate era and came of age during the 1970s. The current generation, full of angst and disillusionment, is even further removed from the Wechslerian generation of the 1950s and 1960s. Its members are entering their professional careers at a time when secure, lucrative jobs (partnership positions in law firms and tenured academic positions) are shrinking. This new generation of law students, the so-called Generation X,[25] has come to the law school as the much larger baby boom generation challenged the authority of the Wechslerian generation and established diverse new intellectual legal movements. The Generation X of future lawyers, judges, and legal academics is coming of age during an extremely contradictory and confusing era in legal education. It is experiencing the breakdown in the theories of law that had defined traditional jurisprudence. The breakdown is a manifestation of the skepticism and criticism of the current intellectual and social condition. This generation, Generation X, belongs to a particular epoch, namely, that of postmodernism.

## The Internal Forces of Change—The Law and Culture Nexus

During the early 1960s, two highly influential law review articles were published that exemplified a new course in American jurisprudential thinking. The two articles were Charles Reich's *The New Property*[26] and Ronald Coase's *The Problem of Social Cost*.[27] These were path-breaking articles in legal theory because they advanced a new jurisprudential attitude about law and culture.[28] Reich's *New Property* attempted to reconstruct a new rights-based jurisprudence, while Coase's *Problem of Social Cost* was aimed at developing a new transaction cost analysis for microeconomic theory.[29] Although lawyers trained in the 1950s and early 1960s were taught to understand law as an ongoing interaction between the court, bureaucracy, and legislature; Reich and Coase argued that traditional notions about legal process and rights had to be revised to accommodate the goals and interests of a legal system operating within the modern bureaucratic state. Their work put contemporary jurisprudence on a trajectory that has since sought, unsuccessfully, to ground jurisprudence in sources outside law. After Reich and Coase, law as an autonomous discipline was no longer a central tenet of modern jurisprudence.

## Charles Reich's New Property

Charles Reich's 1964 article, *The New Property*,[30] attempted to explain how governmental power to regulate wealth created new forms of property that affect individual liberty interests. According to Reich, one of the most important developments in America since the 1950s was the expansion of the modern bureaucratic state. He reported that government grew into a "gigantic syphon" drawing in resources and pouring forth "wealth: money, benefits, services, contracts, franchises, and licenses."[31] A wide range of dependency relationships was created between government and citizens in the growth of "government largess, accompanied by a distinctive system of law."[32] Reich argued that legal entitlements to this wealth were a new form of property that performed the function of traditional property.

Reich believed that the new forms of government-created wealth—welfare benefits, government employment, occupational licenses, franchises, government contracts, subsidies, privately available public resources, and services such as education—were often critical to an individual's survival in the modern bureaucratic state. He wrote that these forms of government largess were "taking the place of traditional forms of wealth—forms which are held as private property."[33] He felt that property conferred power on the individual to maintain his or her independence and survival.

Reich explained: "Property is to the individual as the enumerated powers are to government."[34] In 1964, he surveyed the various ways that government largess created forms of individual wealth—licenses, franchises, government contracts—and discovered that these new forms of individual wealth had helped to create a new society in which the underpinnings of individualism and independence had changed. In the modern bureaucratic state, there was an increased dependency of citizens on their relationships with government. These relationships, encoded by the legal system as legal entitlements, were what Reich called the "New Property."

Reich's New Property basically functioned in the same way that the legal realists' idea of property functioned. Legal realists such as Felix Cohen argued that legal concepts had to be understood as a function of concrete decisions within a particular social context. Thus, for Cohen,

"[The] general idea [of] property [was] to be found in all the examples and consequences of . . . specific [social] situations."[35] Like Cohen, Reich surveyed the social forces creating the sources of wealth that were traditionally defined as property. Like Cohen, Reich viewed the legal concept of property as a social institution that performed many different functions.

Reich's observation was that the "legal" concept of property drew a boundary between public and private power.[36] Within the private boundary the individual was "master, and the state must explain and justify any interference."[37] Outside the private boundary, individuals "must justify or explain [their] actions, and show [their] authority."[38] Reich argued that this legal concept of property was no longer relevant for dealing with the New Property of government largess. He concluded that "there must be a zone of privacy for each individual beyond which neither government nor private power can push—a hiding place from the all-pervasive system of regulation and control."[39]

In calling for a new understanding of the relationship between citizens and government, Reich argued that government's power over wealth defined the liberty interests of individuals, and that the law should grant protection to these interests as a "new property." He seized the historical moment by recognizing that the development of the bureaucratic state and government largess had transformed the legal meaning of property rights, and he believed that the legal system should respond to these changes by moving toward a New Property jurisprudence. Legal entitlements to welfare benefits would be a form of property that would be legally protected as any other form of property right. In the 1970 decision *Goldberg v. Kelly*,[40] the Supreme Court seemed momentarily to embrace Reich's New Property theory in ruling that statutory welfare grants were legal entitlements that could be withheld or terminated only in accordance with due process of law.[41]

## Ronald Coase and the Problem of Social Costs

In 1961, Ronald Coase published his famous article, *The Problem of Social Cost*,[42] which challenged the conventional wisdom of economic theory that had justified governmental regulation of externalities[43] in private production. This conventional understanding, which Coase ascribed to the English economist A. C. Pigou, assumed that when private production produces an undesirable externality such as smoke pollution, the law should respond by compelling the responsible party to internalize the cost of the externality. In other words, social costs of undesirable externalities would be internalized, either through liability rules enforced by judges or alternatively by tax codes or other statutory regulation enacted by the legislature.

Coase revealed logical flaws in the "internalize the externality" approach of Pigouvian economists.[44] He argued that the traditional analysis of externalities would fail to bring about economically efficient outcomes in cases where the transaction costs (the cost of private bargaining) were zero.[45] Coase's argument (subsequently characterized by George Stigler as "the Coase Theorem") focused on how the legal system's regulation of private activity can create transaction costs that adversely affect the private production and allocation of goods.[46]

Coase's so-called theorem was really not a theorem at all, but a logical proposition about the potential of market transactions to rearrange the effect of legal rights. If private bargaining and the pricing system work without costs—if there are zero transaction costs—Coase predicted that the allocation of rights by law will not affect the maximization of the value of production and the allocation of costs. On the other hand, as Coase argued, legal enforcement of rights may adversely affect the value of production to the extent legal enforcement results in greater transaction costs.

Coase's "theorem" was based on the simple but brilliant insight that individuals can always bargain their way around legal rights when transaction costs are minimal or zero. In cases where transaction costs were zero, the initial allocation of rights would thus not affect the allocation. Coase's overall point was twofold: first, transaction costs are generally positive and will often preclude a reallocation of goods among parties; second, the various ways in which legal entitlements are defined and enforced affects the magnitude of transaction costs. Coase's argument was critically aimed at economists who had failed to recognize the affects of transaction costs within their models.

While Charles Reich's *New Property* focused on how individual liberty was affected by the modern bureaucratic state, Coase's article focused on the economic consequences of bureaucratic regulation of private markets. Coase's *The Problem of Social Cost* is one of two major works credited with launching the law and economics movement of the late 1970s,[47] and for establishing a theoretical justification for limiting the growth of the modern regulatory state. As Coase himself declared: "It is my belief that economist[s] and policy-makers generally, have tended to over-estimate the advantages which come from government regulation."[48]

Coase's work has also been interpreted by other law and economic scholars as laying the foundation for a new instrumental form of normative jurisprudence—a jurisprudence of wealth maximization. While Coase has never associated himself with this jurisprudence, his theorem has been associated by others as laying the ground for deregulation of the welfare state. Law and economic scholars believe that the legal system should focus its attention on minimizing transaction costs and reduce, if not eliminate, the legal system's intervention in private affairs. For Coase, however, facilitation of market efficiency was an important justification for state intervention in private markets. He believed that legal intervention was necessary in a world with positive transaction costs. One goal of Coase's approach was to enable judges to identify rules, procedures, and legal outcomes that would maximize society's wealth by maximizing private production and minimizing costs. In theory, the law would facilitate wealth-maximizing transactions by recognizing the centrality of transaction costs in market transactions.

## The Reciprocal Nature of Law and Society

While Ronald Coase's focus and concern were different from those of Charles Reich (e.g., Coase was concerned with transaction costs and common-law regulation, while Reich was concerned with constitutional liberties and government largess), a common jurisprudential perspective can be found in these two path-breaking articles. Both articles exhibited similar critical responses to the role and function of law in society. Coase's *The Problem of Social Costs* was designed to recognize the reciprocal character of harmful interactions of an externality in the economy; Reich's theory of *The New Property* was designed to recognize the reciprocal character of governmental entitlement and the nature of property. For Reich, law could not be divorced from considerations of political power: individual survival was dependent on governmental largess. For Coase, law could not be divorced from the logic of markets; legal entitlements meant nothing if private bargaining was costless.

Both authors implicitly rejected traditional faith in the efficaciousness of the legal process and the autonomy of fundamental rights. Charles Reich argued that a new concept of rights was needed, functionally shaped by social forces, including government power, to protect new forms of wealth. He believed that the idea of "new property" was necessary, because the old property failed to consider the dynamic changes caused by the bureaucratic state. Ronald Coase provided the intellectual case for the view that lawyers' preoccupation with legal rights failed to take the reality of market exchange into account.[49] In Coase's view, legal rights made sense only in terms of transaction costs.[50]

Reich and Coase thus developed surprisingly similar ideas about law from insight about the reciprocal nature of law and culture. For Reich, individual liberty stands in a reciprocal relation to governmental largess. He argued that the "growth of governmental largess" was having "profound consequences" for individuals and their rights under law: "[Government largess] affects the underpinnings of individualism and independence. It influences the workings of the Bill of Rights. It has an impact on the power of private interests, in their relation to each other and to government. It is helping to create a new society."[51]

For Coase, transaction costs stood in a reciprocal relation to market exchanges and conflicting resource uses. In cases of conflicting resource use, Coase argued that the conflict must be viewed from the merger of both activities. He claimed that the relevant question in such cases was: Which outcome would minimize the total costs arising from the conflict? In Coase's view, the solution to problems involving competing uses of scarce resources depended on whether significant transaction costs are present and, if so, which legal arrangement will minimize those costs.

Coase and Reich believed that new solutions were needed to respond to the reciprocal relationship between legal rules and the cultural context to be regulated or affected. They argued that traditional solutions to problems of individual liberty or economic welfare were unhelpful, if not noxious, because the traditional solutions failed to consider the link between law and society. With respect to problems of individual liberty, Reich believed that new concepts of property were needed to deal with the new forms of wealth created by governmental largess. With respect to problems of economic welfare,[52] Coase claimed that the traditional liberal approach to regulation, which favored state intervention in the economy to eliminate the costs of externalities, was "at once impossible and unhelpful," because the real economic issue in such cases depended on identifying "[w]hich legal regime minimizes the total costs arising from unfortunate encounters."[53]

Reich and Coase reformulated the relevant questions of legal analysis. Reich demonstrated that the legal definition of individual liberty was linked to governmental power, or what he called "government largess." Coase demonstrated that private law problems involving harmful effects are reciprocal in nature: "To avoid the harm to B would inflict harm on A. The real question that has to be decided is: Should A be allowed to harm B or should B be allowed to harm A?"[54] Reich and Coase raised new questions and encouraged lawyers and judges to better understand the role of law and legal decision making in society.

The reciprocal nature of the problem to be regulated by law, however, imposed new difficulties and challenges for modern legal scholars. If effective legal solutions to society's problems required a context-specific legal response, then decision making could not be said to depend on general rules. The problem exposed by Reich and Coase is that law could not be analyzed as an autonomous object separate from culture.[55] Reich and Coase also cast doubt on the view of those who believed in the autonomy of "basic theory" whether it be law or economics. For them, theory could not be divorced from social and economic context.

The Supreme Court's decision in *Brown* (decided before Coase and Reich wrote their articles) reflected a somewhat similar idea about law and legal theory. In *Brown,* the Supreme Court rejected the theory of "separate but equal" because legal analysis had failed to take into account inequality arising from cultural context, and because the theory itself failed to take account of the role law played in reinforcing the cultural values of race discrimination. The Court concluded that separate but equal had "no place" in public education because legally sanctioned segregation in the schools perpetuated culturally based forms of discrimination. In *Brown,* the Supreme Court thus implicitly recognized that the law cannot ignore the social reality of the norms and practices of culture. As Bruce Ackerman has recently argued, Chief Justice Warren's opinion in *Brown* "looks a lot better" today when compared to various scholarly "improvements offered up over the years."[56] Warren's interpretation of "equal protection" in *Brown* looks a lot better today because the decision embraces the idea that culture helps define the social and the legal meaning of *equal protection*.

In *Brown*, Warren saw the system of public education established by Jim Crow laws as a factor contributing to the process by which groups made their "choices" in American society.[57] Compulsory public schooling affected individual "choices" about the social reality of racial segregation. Warren declared that "education is perhaps the most important function of state and local governments."[58] Recognizing this, the Court rejected the logical premises of the "separate but equal" doctrine of *Plessy v. Ferguson*.[59] As Ackerman explained: "Whatever Justice Brown in *Plessy* might have thought, it [was] now absurd to dismiss the 'badge of inferiority' imposed by state officials as they shunt black children to segregated schools as if it was 'solely' the product of a 'choice' by the 'colored race . . . to put [a degrading] construction upon it."[60] The crux of Chief Justice Warren's *Brown* opinion was the recognition of the need for decision makers to take into account the reciprocal nature between law and culture.

## Disintegration of Modern Jurisprudence

Modern jurisprudence teachers assumed that a distinctively legal method or theory was capable of yielding correct answers to law's problems, and that legal analysis could provide a representational method for defining, analyzing, and evaluating legal problems in a credible and principled manner. Yet the scholarly achievements of Charles Reich, Ronald Coase, and the leading constitutional decision of the modern era—*Brown*—demonstrated that the old modes of representation were no longer credible. A new representational mode for understanding the relation between law and society was needed—one constructed from the social and economic context in which the legal system operates. Reich's and Coase's articles, and Chief Justice Warren's opinion in *Brown*, laid the foundation for a form of jurisprudence based on a new understanding of the dialectic relation between law and society.

The new jurisprudence proved highly influential because its approach to social problems attempted to account for the reciprocal nature of law and social phenomena. The appeal of Reich's and Coase's articles was that they offered new strategies for dealing with the technocratic and social changes of the modern bureaucratic state. In *Brown*, the Court set the stage for this when it considered social changes brought about by the growth of compulsory public education since the time *Plessy* was decided. After *Brown*, it was no longer possible to ignore law's contribution to the construction of social reality. However plausible the claim of autonomous law had been, *Brown* made that claim untenable, ushering in a new era in jurisprudence.

A new era in jurisprudence was needed to deal with the complexities of the modern activist state following the New Deal of the 1930s. The New Deal was significant because government was viewed as an active contributor in the process where various groups in society made their choices and exercised their free will.[61] Liberty-of-contract and laissez-faire policies were replaced by a new regime of welfare legislation, because individual freedom to choose appeared to depend on the prevailing legal and economic baseline. Freedom to choose meant nothing in the absence of legal and economic resources. Governmental intervention was seen as necessary to give citizens the freedom of choice. With the rise of diverse new technocracy and new forms of bureaucracies, new legal solutions were required. Judges and lawyers needed new solutions to the new forms of wealth and power of the bureaucratic state.

To say that legal problems had a reciprocal nature meant there were no easy solutions or easy fixes for law's problems, an unacceptable view for jurisprudential thinkers who remained committed to the idea of law as an autonomous, objective activity. Correct answers to legal questions required judges to access the underlying value choices—competing claims of welfare and wealth. Judges desire to remain relatively autonomous and neutral at the same time. Analysis of the underlying value choices in the·law meant that judges had to decide essentially political and moral questions. Even the belief that there is *always* a correct or best answer rested on the dubious assumption that broader sources for decision might yield the best answers.[62] One source was the discovery of a shared consensus for selecting normative justification for legal decision making. Another was the development of a basic theory for making normative decisions in law. By the late 1960s, however, there was a rising skepticism about the possibility of maintaining the political or theoretical consensus necessary to sustain the thesis that there is *always* a correct answer in the law. This skepticism reflected the disintegrated nature of the once solid foundation of autonomous law.

By the late 1960s it was apparent that the political and legal consensus of the World War II generation of jurisprudence teachers and writers no longer reflected the mood and temperament of those who personally experienced the conflict and divisions of Vietnam, the race relations crisis, and the cultural, sexual, and gender revolutions. American society was becoming ethnically, racially, and economically divided. Those divisions were reflected in contemporary legal controversies. There was no consensus to which law could appeal, because there was no consensus "out there." The contradictory mood and temperament of the 1960s made it difficult for anyone to argue the possibility of reaching a consensus through law.[63]

Throughout the 1970s, a new generation of legal academics, versed in the work of Reich and Coase, began to write a new genre of legal scholarship that openly challenged modern notions of jurisprudence. This new genre rejected the notion that law was distinct from political and moral philosophy; it also rejected the idea that law could be rendered coherent by a comprehensive legal theory. Examples of 1970s scholarship of this genre included Abram Chayes's ground-breaking article, *The Role of the Judge in Public Law Litigation*,[64] which claimed that the traditional view of adjudication, as a process for resolving disputes between private parties, failed to account for public law implications of litigation. Another example is Duncan Kennedy's 1976 article, *Form and Substance in Private Law Adjudication*,[65] which argued that private law opinions, articles, and treatises were structured by two opposing rhetorical modes of argumentation called "individualism" and "altruism." There were also the stunning examples set forth in Richard A. Posner's 1972 book, ECONOMIC ANALYSIS OF LAW,[66] which boldly proclaimed that lawyers and judges should turn to the study of economics to resolve law's problems. Robert M. Cover's 1975 book, JUSTICE ACCUSED,[67] took the opposite stance in arguing that legal positivism employed by legal scholars had stripped law of its moral and philosophical resonance.

This new genre of legal scholarship served as a springboard for a new type of "law and . . ." jurisprudence that attempted, throughout the 1970s, to combine law with different social science disciplines. This new body of scholarship deepened the insights of the Reich and Coase articles by employing interdisciplinary approaches to legal analysis to show how the legal regime was linked to social, economic, political, and cultural contexts. Law was no longer studied as a purely self-contained, autonomous system. Coase's and Posner's articles thus helped foster the *law and economics* movement, while Abe Chayes's, Robert Cover's, and Duncan Kennedy's articles set the stage for a more political approach to legal studies. It was during this period that others predicted the "coming renaissance in law and literature."[68] The "law and" genre of legal scholarship subsequently flowered, developing new theoretical approaches and comprehensive changes in legal theory that culminated in new jurisprudential approaches for understanding law and adjudication.

Doctrinal legal scholars correctly saw these new "law and" movements as challenging the central core of beliefs of autonomous, objective law. For many, the "law and" movements were radical departures from conventional legal thought. As the late Arthur Leff of Yale University Law School complained in 1974: "The critical questions were henceforth no longer to be those of systematic consistency, but of existential operations. You could no longer criticize law in terms of logical operations, but only in terms of operational logic."[69] For Leff, these changes in legal scholarship were "terrifying" because they seemed to compel legal theorists not only to become "empirists" of "social facts," but also experts on good and evil. Leff believed that the difficulty with these developments was that there was "no way of 'proving' that napalming babies is bad except by asserting it (in a louder and louder voice) or by defining it as so, early in one's game, and then later shipping it through, in a whisper, as a conclusion."[70]

The "law and" movements, nonetheless, became part of the established jurisprudential landscape throughout the 1970s and 1980s. By the early 1980s, law and society scholarship had attempted to transcend the categories of "law" and "society" by developing an interpretive sociology of law, which set a new empirical agenda for the study of law's institutions and institutional processes.[71] New jurisprudential discourses of law and economics, critical legal studies, feminist legal studies, law and literature, and critical race theory developed and seriously questioned the once dominant hold of modern jurisprudence. Yet, while the "law and" movements of the late 1970s and early 1980s subverted the disciplinary authority of legal formalism and the autonomy of law, these movements also served in their own way to reproduce a type of interdisciplinary formalism similar to Langdellian formalism.

The "law and" scholarship reproduced a form of interdisciplinary formalism by bestowing upon law a foreign discipline that was given the status of privileged authority.[72] Arthur Leff was mistaken about the new "law and" movements, as they were not really radical departures from traditional modes of legal thought at all. Rather, they were novel applications of the same "good old fashioned lawyer-academics" that characterized much of modern legal scholarship. The "law and" movements simply shifted the frame of analysis away from "applying the law to the facts" (the traditional frame) to "applying the theory to the law."[73] The same legalistic rhetoric, however, was used in the age-old search for the disciplinary authority of the law. As Pierre Schlag amusingly put it: "The interdisciplinary travels of traditional legal thought are like a bad European vacation: the substance is Europe, but the form is McDonald's, Holiday Inn, American Express."[74]

## Crossing the Modernist Divide

It is only now becoming clear that the new legal discourses of the "law and" movements of the late 1970s and 1980s have themselves become transformed by a general disenchanted condition that has affected contemporary legal scholarship—*postmodernism*. By the mid-1980s, new scholarly trends in the legal academy consumed and modified the structuralist and deterministic modes of legal scholarship of the early 1970s and 1980s. Early "law and" scholarship, wedded to a foundational and structural explanation of law, adopted an antifoundational and more skeptical explanation of law.

The inability of rights or process foundationalists to ground their particular rights in a stable meta-ethics, moral epistemology, or interpretive practice made it increasingly difficult for legal scholars to accept the idea of objective and autonomous law. Fundamental rights theory encouraged lawyers to look outside the law for the profound reflection available in Western literature.[75] The turn to "Great Books" of the Western tradition, however, "only emphasizes the elitism involved in removing fundamental questions from the democratic process."[76] By the mid-1980s, constitutional scholars "began to argue that the initial distinction between interpretivism and non-interpretivism may have been misleading; even supposed non-interpretivists always claimed to be interpreting the Constitution. . . . Jurisprudence thus began its interpretive turn."[77]

The "interpretive turn" in jurisprudence reflected developments in the social sciences and humanities that rejected the scientism and positivism of the social sciences and the conventional understanding of language and literary criticism.[78] By the early 1970s, Thomas Kuhn[79] and Paul Feyerabend[80] questioned the belief that scientific theory developed on the basis of objective description and instead demonstrated that "scientific models were themselves partial interpretations, dependent upon the perspectives and disciplinary conventions of scientific observers."[81] The intellectual reactions against empiricism in the social sciences were similar to reactions in literature and literary criticism. Stanley Fish, a literature and law professor at Duke University, drew from his reader-response theory of literary criticism to show how the interpretive process of law defines meaning in reference to the constitutive power of the interpretive community.[82]

Legal scholars turned to the nonlegal work of literary critics such as Stanley Fish[83] and the continental philosophy of Hans-Georg Gadamer[84] or Jacques Derrida.[85] Contemporary legal academics looked for novel and sophisticated theories of interpretation to apply in their analyses of law. As legal scholars contemplated the interpretive turn in its fullest sense, they found themselves confronted with a dilemma. They turned to new critical interpretive practices to stabilize the objective foundation of law, but they discovered that those interpretive practices undermined the very possibility of an objective foundational theory for law.[86]

By the late 1980s, the direction of the new scholarly movements seemed to have shifted away from the goal of achieving a particular social vision through interdisciplinary approaches to law, to the view that law is contingent upon the perspective of the analyst. The rhetoric of transcendental subjects and objects was losing to a new form of legal criticism aimed at bringing the missing subject, and the context of the objects they analyze, back into the analysis. This did not mean that legal modernism had failed or was dead. The normative and conceptual strands of modern legal thought remained pervasive. The problem for contemporary legal thinkers was that the normative and conceptual vocabulary was the only acceptable vocabulary. To deepen the insights of the new scholarly movements in law, a new discourse and vocabulary was thought necessary. To appreciate these developments in contemporary legal theory, we must examine how the new scholarly movements of the 1980s developed and matured.

*Part Two*

# Jurisprudential Movements
# of the 1980s

# 5. Law and Economics

The sources responsible for the expansion and transformation of the law and economics movement of the 1970s and 1980s have never been adequately explained. One fact remains clear: this movement coincided with the rise of interdisciplinary legal studies and the growing disenchantment with the legal process and fundamental rights schools. In the midst of the disintegration of and disillusionment with mainstream jurisprudence, legal scholars looked outside law to economics for law's missing authority and the autonomy of legal discourse. Of all the social sciences, economics was the most promising candidate offering "right answers" for law's problems.

While the use of economic analysis in some legal subjects, such as antitrust law, has been rich and long-standing, much of what is included in the law and economics movement developed within the last two decades.[1] The new law and economics involves the application of economic analysis to common law subjects such as Tort, Contract, and Property, where the relevance of economics is less apparent. The birth of the *new* law and economics occurred in the early 1960s when Ronald Coase published his seminal article on nuisance law[2] and Guido Calabresi published his economic analysis of tort law.[3] Law and economics as an academic movement did not "coalesce," however, until Calabresi published his widely acclaimed book on accident law in 1970,[4] followed by Richard A. Posner's textbook, ECONOMIC ANALYSIS OF LAW, in 1973.[5]

This movement has since evolved for more than two decades, creating two generations of law and economics scholarship united by quite different theoretical jurisprudential orientations. The first generation responsible for forming the movement were united by their faith in the merger of law and the quasi-scientific method of economics. The second generation has taken a more pragmatic and no-nonsense stance toward economic analysis of law: economics is found to be useful for verifying empirical observations about legal behavior. The jurisprudential source supporting the lawyer's faith in the economic analysis of law, however, remains a subject for debate.[6]

The economic analysis of law, as presented by one of the most famous practitioners—judge and legal theorist Richard Posner—epitomizes the ambiguity and confusion surrounding the jurisprudence of this movement. Posner's ECONOMIC ANALYSIS OF LAW, descriptive of first-generation analysis, for example, was initially viewed by many, including myself, as a refined, modern version of the Langdellian idea that law consists of a universal system of scientifically discoverable principles. Posner staunchly maintained in his early writing the basic tenet of Langdellian faith, claiming that "it may be possible to deduce the basic formal characteristics of law itself from economic theory."[7] However, unlike Langdell, who searched for enduring principles in appellate court decisions, Posner's ECONOMIC ANALYSIS OF LAW was single-minded in its effort to reconstruct legal doctrine out of a limited number of basic economic concepts. Economic analysis of law seemed to offer a modern version of the type of instrumental analysis associated with progressive legal realism: it attempted to offer lawyers a new instrumental logic developed from the social science of economics to "solve" the problems of traditional jurisprudence.

The paradox of law and economics is that it attempts to bring together two inconsistent forms of jurisprudence: Langdellian formalism and progressive legal realism. This paradox helps to explain the confusion concerning the jurisprudence of the movement. Encouraged by the new interest in interdisciplinary legal studies and an overall desire to improve and refine mainstream jurisprudence, the first generation was correctly understood as claiming to have advocated a type of Langdellian formalism. On the other hand, these same legal scholars later renounced faith in law's autonomy and turned instead to a new instrumental analysis to critique the intellectual position of their process-oriented and fundamental-rights-oriented mentors and teachers. These two jurisprudential themes played themselves out differently with different generations of law and economics scholarship.

First-generation scholars were the "young Turks" who renounced the modernist's commitment to an autonomous or fundamental law, but did not totally reject the possibility of universal legal truth. They sought to reinforce modern jurisprudence by claiming that the authority and autonomy of law could be discovered in the "hardest" of the social sciences. Economic analysis, as applied to law, committed these scholars to a form of economic formalism not unlike Langdellian formalism. First-generation scholars believed that "economics could be the master discipline, itself autonomous, but which might explain results in other non-autonomous disciplines like law."[8]

Indeed, while much was made of the differences between traditional legal and law and economic scholars, those differences were minor when compared to what they shared in common. Mark Kelman, a critical legal theorist and professor at Stanford Law School, noted that the law and economics movement (in its early stages of development) was "the best worked-out, most consummated liberal legal ideology" that characterized the modern jurisprudence of traditional legal scholars.[9] Belief in the omnipotence and liberating potential imminent in the application of economic analysis to law revealed the lingering influence of both Langdell and Holmes on the first generation. It was the influence and hold of legal modernism that brought jurisprudential ambiguity to the work of the first generation. It served to align the first generation with the unresolved ambiguities of modern jurisprudence.

In the mid-1980s, the influence of the first generation peaked and a new generation of law and economics scholars emerged. This *second generation* rejected the strong scientific-like claims and the economic formalism of their intellectual fathers and seem to have adopted a more pragmatic jurisprudential outlook. They have embraced the idea that the authority and autonomy of economic analysis was limited; and that truth, knowledge, and legal understanding no longer be explained from an objective economic perspective. Second generation scholars, emphasizing the pragmatic-instrumentalism of Holmes, accepted that law must be understood as fundamentally indeterminate. The second generation thus attempted to distance itself from the "new Langdellians" of the first generation, who embraced Langdell's "great idea" that law might be a science. The second generation now associates itself with a post-Chicago form of economic analyses of law.

One way to examine the relationship between first- and second-generation law and economics scholars is to consider how one leading law and economics scholar has, at different moments, positioned the law and economics movement in relation to Holmes and the legal realist movement of the 1920s and 1930s. In 1981, for example, Posner traced the origins of the law and economics movement to Holmes's THE COMMON LAW and the *Legal Realists*. Posner argued that in THE COMMON LAW, Holmes applied the *modern method* of social science in his attempt to discover the true meaning of a legal doctrine from the study of its historical evolution. Posner claimed that Holmes's method was later picked up by legal realism, a movement Posner said had "fizzled for want of a theoretical framework to guide research." [10] Posner concluded: "The scholarly movement that is today's counterpart to Legal Realism as the foremost alternative to doctrinal analysis is economic analysis of law, or, as it is sometimes called, '*Law and Economics.*' " [11]

By 1990, Posner published a somewhat different historical account of the movement. [12] This time, Holmes's THE COMMON LAW was compared to Nietzsche's great work, THE GENEALOGY OF MORALS, which Posner found to "employ an effective method of skeptical analysis: the genealogical." [13] Apparently Posner rediscovered a new Holmes who was no longer the pioneer of the social science method, but rather the founder of the legal *pragmatic* method, a method that Posner now views as "Nietzsche-like." [14] Posner now espouses a Nietzsche-like outlook, which he says is "progressive (in the sense of foreword-looking), secular, and experimental, and that is commonsensical without making a fetish of common sense." [15] Posner's contemporary outlook is said to have been shaped by Holmes's pragmatism, not his realistic jurisprudence (law as experience, rather than logic) which helped shape the legal realist movement.

Posner's pragmatism, unlike that of Holmes, emphasizes the importance of language rather than experience, reason, or economics. His pragmatism is suspicious of the very idea of a "scientific theory." He now insists that law and economics projects be judged "by their conformity to social or other human needs rather than to 'objective,' 'impersonal' criteria." [16] Posner also rejects the idea that there is an affinity between law and economics and legal realism. He believes that the relationship between law and economics and the American legal realism movement is "equivocal";[17] that the law and economics movement is "closer to the father of legal realism, Holmes, than to the legal realists themselves with their emphasis on liberal meliorism."[18] Picking up "the thread of philosophical pragmatism" from Holmes and Cardozo, Posner seems to have made a change in intellectual direction to the postmodern strategy of neopragmatism.[19]

The neopragmatist is more concerned with developing instrumental and practical approaches to problems than discovering the way things "really" are. When applied to the economic analysis of law, the neopragmatic attitude is less concerned with maintaining legal objectivity and consistency than bringing about results that "work." The neopragmatic attitude is also skeptical of the claims of basic economic theory and is instead drawn to the *experimental* and *predictive* uses of economic theory.[20] Neopragmatic economic analysts are "can do" types; they are interested in empirical methods and the proprieties of factual phenomena only to the extent that such knowledge serves an instrumental function in resolving some problem or getting the "job done well." Neopragmatists are antidogmatic and skeptical of foundational claims about the nature of "truth." They disassociate themselves from economic formalists, who believe in basic economic theory, and progressive legal realists, who claimed that the answers to law's problems can be discovered in another discipline such as economics.

Posner's revisionary history of the law and economics movement provides clues for understanding second-generation law and economics scholarship. The first generation tended to view its work as a continuation of progressive realism, and it advanced a strong thesis that law is, and ought to be like a social science—that is, economics. First-generation law and economics scholarship was thus steeped in the jurisprudence of legal formalism, especially Langdell's idea that law is like a science. The second generation has since broken free from the "law as science" idea, and instead advocated a new institutional economics that is decidedly skeptical about the scientific-like and formalistic claims of the first generation. Drawing inspiration from Coase and neopragmatic philosophers, the second generation of law and economics scholars tend to favor the study of institutions and economic behavior of bureaucratic organizations rather than economic models and "theory."[21] The shift from abstract theory to concrete institutional analysis has been nurtured by a new understanding of economic theory—an understanding that views "theory" merely as a tool for investigating what may "work" as a solution to some problem. While the first generation of law and economics scholars approached economics as a *theoretical* science, the second generation views economics as an *applied* science. By 1990, the foundations of "science" were "kicked away" such that Posner could proclaim: "Today we are all skeptics." [22] The second generation has thus become postmodern in its aspirations, attitudes, and aesthetics.

## First-Generation Law and Economics Scholarship

The initial impetus for the law and economics movement came from the work of economics scholars—Ronald Coase, Gary Becker, Aarron Director—at the University of Chicago who devoted their efforts to the economics of nonmarket behavior. [23] In deepening what many regard as the "Chicago School" perspective of economics, these scholars employed a "rational-actor" model of human behavior in their analysis of nonmarket subjects such as discrimination, family, and the law. This model "assumes that an actor will choose the course of action that will maximize his personal expected utility, which may, of course, reflect a concern for the welfare of others." [24] Self-interested profit-maximization behavior was assumed to be a reliable predictor of the principal motivating factors of human endeavor, including human behavior in the law. [25] While the work of these so-called Chicago School economists focused on *applied* economics, their work came to be associated with *theoretical* economics as legal academics adopted the "theory" of the Chicago School and applied it to their analysis of law. As initially propounded, economic analysis of law developed conceptually as a new "basic theory" of the law. The "theoretical" economic analysis of law drew essential insights about the law from a limited number of fundamental economic concepts. This phase of the movement resembled the jurisprudence of conceptualism in law.

A cardinal principle of economics, from which early law and economics work emerged, was based on the assumption that "man [sic] is a rational maximizer of his ends in life." [26] From this assumption, law and economics practitioners erected the rational-actor model of human behavior: "It is implicit in the definition of man as a rational maximizer of his self-interest that people respond to incentives—that if a person's surroundings change in such a way that he could increase his satisfaction by altering his behavior, he will do so." [27] It was assumed that behavior is rational whenever it conforms to the rational-actor model, even when the actor is unaware of his or her rationality and even though many individuals may act irrationally. Most individuals are assumed to act rationally, and those who do not are assumed to represent random exceptions unlikely to alter the predictive ability of the rational-actor model. It is also accepted that selfishness is not the same as self-interest— "happiness (or for that matter the misery) of other people may be a part of one's satisfactions." [28]

From the rational-actor model, law and economics practitioners derived three fundamental concepts for the economic analysis of law.[29] First is the "inverse relation between price charged and quantity demanded (the Law of Demand)." [30] According to early practitioners of law and economics, the law of demand has many applications for the law:

The convicted criminal who has served his sentence is said to have "paid his debt to society," and an economist would find the metaphor apt. Punishment is, at least from the criminal's standpoint . . . the price that society charges for a criminal offense. The economist is led to predict that an increase in either the severity of the punishment or the likelihood of its imposition will raise the price of crime and therefore reduce its incidence. The criminal will be encouraged to substitute other activity.[31]

The second fundamental concept is the economic definition of cost. Cost to the lawyer-economist means "opportunity cost"—the benefit forgone by employing a resource in a way that denies its use to someone else. Law and economics practitioners claimed that the opportunity cost concept was useful in legal analysis. For example:

Among the many applications of the concept of opportunity cost to law, consider the problem of computing damages for the loss of a child's life. If the child has no earning power, his death will not have imposed a pecuniary cost on the parents. However, we can compute the opportunity costs of the resources invested by the parents in rearing the child by determining the alternative price of the parents' time and other inputs (food, clothing, education, etc.) into its rearing. The sum of these prices is a minimum estimate of parental loss.[32]

The third basic concept is "the tendency of resources to gravitate toward their most valuable uses if voluntary exchange—a market—is permitted." [33] Law and economics theorists believe that through a process of voluntary exchange, scarce resources will be shifted to those uses that are the most valued by people, as measured by their willingness to pay.[34] When resources are put to their most valuable uses, economists say that they are being employed "efficiently." It is the "efficiency criterion" that establishes the basic normative standard for economic analysis of law.

The last concept, the economist's notion of efficiency, is the most important concept of the three for understanding the methodological theme of early law and economics scholarship. For the lawyer-economist, "efficiency means exploiting economic resources in such a way that 'value'—human satisfaction *as measured by aggregate consumer willingness to pay* for goods and services—is maximized."[35] Early law and economics scholarship sought to show that common law judges should, and do, decide cases so as to maximize wealth. First-generation practitioners argued that judges can "approximate" the efficient outcome in decisions by assigning the right to the party who values the right the most, measured by the willingness to pay standard.[36] As an alternative to the "approximation principle," law and economics practitioners argued that the efficient outcome could be attained through the law by minimizing the cost of bargaining.[37]

Much of the theoretical support for first-generation scholarship can be traced to Ronald Coase's *The Problem of Social Cost*,[38] and what later came to be known as the *Coase Theorem*. As we have seen, the Coase Theorem arose out of Coase's effort to show how economists had neglected the importance of transaction cost in their theoretical models of markets. Richard Posner argues that in bringing attention to the centrality of transaction cost, Coase declared "war" on those economists who focused on economic theory at the expense of practical investigation of market behavior.[39] One would think that Coase's influence in law and economics would have led to a less formal and more realistic economic analysis of law. But this is not what occurred, at least in the early stages of this movement.

This is because Coase was read formalistically by lawyers. Legal academics, advocating the new economic analysis of law, read Coase's work as a "theory" about market transactions to be applied to the "facts" of legal problems. The first generation of law and economics practitioners consequently embraced a version of economic formalism not unlike legal formalism. Coase's theorem was seen by legal academics as supplying the missing theory of authority lacking in traditional forms of doctrinal legal analysis. For many legal academics, Coase's work established the theoretical case for the deregulation movement in American law.

As it turned out, Coase's "theorem" had undermined the confidence in the "interventionist" programs of welfare economics of the 1960s, and thereby strengthened the influence of laissez-faire market conservatives at the University of Chicago and elsewhere.[40] Coase's preoccupation with private property rights committed the first generation of law and economics scholars to an underlying conservative political perspective which favored laissez-faire markets, and a theory of jurisprudence which championed the view that law should facilitate free choice and private contract.[41]

Ironically, while Coase advocated the advantages of private market ordering, he also recognized that in real markets, transaction costs would be positive. Coase thus acknowledged that governmental intervention would be needed to make markets work efficiently. The type of intervention Coase seemed to advocate, however, was seen by others as calling for a "market-like" solution: The law should try to make the market work and, if that fails, the law should mimic the market. The type of legal intervention envisioned by Coase was interpreted to be like the type of private "regulation" to be expected by markets.

The success of Coase's theorem was largely due to his insightful analysis of the problem of externalities in the economic system. The existence of externalities troubled economists because they are viewed as a source of inefficiency in the private market activities of individuals and firms. Because spillover effects of an externality are normally not reflected in market prices or costs, it was thought that private wealth-maximizing behavior failed to account for the total "social" cost of economic activities. Economists feared that either too much or too little would be produced, resulting in the inefficient allocation of resources.

In treating externalities as an example of "market failure," economists who followed the analysis of the English welfare economist A. C. Pigou concluded that the way to prevent inefficiency in resource allocation would be to use the legal system to make those responsible for harmful interfering activity bear the cost of spillover consequences.[42] Pigouvian economists thus advocated that the law should be structured to ensure that all undesirable externalities are "internalized" by those responsible for such costs. In THE PROBLEM OF SOCIAL COST, Coase uncovered an apparent oversight in the logic of traditional Pigouvian analysis—the costs of market transactions.[43] Coase claimed that if the costs of market transactions (transaction costs) are minimal, legal intervention would have no significant consequences on resource allocation. He demonstrated that if transaction costs are low, individuals would bargain their way to an efficient allocation of resources, regardless of the assignment rights and liabilities. Private bargaining would achieve efficient outcomes regardless of the judicially dictated outcome.

For example, if transaction costs are zero and a factory owner is initially assigned a right to emit smoke at will and the smoke adversely affects neighboring property owners, the property owners will have an interest in offering the factory owner a bribe to refrain from exercising the right to emit smoke or, alternatively, to adopt smoke avoidance measures. On the other hand, if the property owners have a right to be free from the adverse effects of smoke pollution, the factory owner will have an interest in offering compensation for the resulting smoke damage in order to maintain factory operations. In either case, the bargain that is ultimately struck will be based on who values the right the most— the factory owner or the property owners. If the factory owner values the right the most, then no matter where the law places the right, the factory owner will end up with the right.

While the logic of the Coase Theorem suggests that liability rules have no effect on efficiency, in the real world where transaction costs exist the rule of liability does matter. As Coase recognized, there are simply too many imperfections in the marketplace to permit parties to bargain efficiently. When the assumptions of the Coase Theorem are not satisfied, which is typically the case, the rule of liability will determine whether liability rules are helpful in bringing about efficient outcomes. This will occur when the cost of bargaining is prohibitively high, when the requisite information is imperfect or expensive to obtain, when there are too many parties to make bargaining feasible, or when it is not possible to exclude nonpaying users or "free riders" from the benefits of a bargain.

The significance of the Coase Theorem was that it provided academic lawyers with a new theoretical basis for analyzing common law rules of Contract, Property, and Tort. In bringing attention to the importance of transaction costs, the theorem called for a complete change in the standard legal analysis of problems involving interfering harmful activities such as pollution. The regulatory approach attributed to Pigou—internalizing the externality—was rejected in favor of deregulation and the minimization of transaction costs. For the first generation of law and economics practitioners following Coase, the ultimate issue was what the market would do if private bargaining were feasible, and whether the logic of Coase's Theorem was applicable. These practitioners embraced a type of economic formalism not unlike the legal formalism of Langdell.

Adopting Coase's market perspective, law and economics scholars initially aimed their sights at demonstrating that the governmental regulation of the economy was unnecessary, and some cases were detrimental. Hence, the standard nuisance question: "Who caused what harm?" was restated by Coasian analysts as: "Which legal regime minimizes the total costs arising from the unfortunate encounters?"[44] And the answer most frequently given was: "The legal regime of nonregulation."

These early versions of law and economics scholarship were vulnerable to forms of criticism made against the legal formalists. Thus, first-generation law and economics scholars were initially called the "New Langdells" or "New Conceptionalists" of the legal academy.[45] The work of the law and economics scholar was criticized for failing to take into account the "realities" of real markets. Economic theory was said to be based on unrealistic assumptions which should be distrusted because the assumptions would devalue and "relativize" the values of law.

Early law and economics scholars followed two basic defensive strategies in response to their critics. First, in response to those who claimed that law and economics would lead to immoral law,[46] they argued that a distinction must be made between *positive* and *normative* economic analysis. Law and economics scholars claimed that the purely descriptive or "positive" forms of analysis helped clarify the cost of various alternatives that might be selected by the *normative* decision maker. Law and economics scholars offered no opinion on the ultimate normative question to be decided, other than saying that moral questions are best left to the elected branches of government.

In response to those who argued that law and economics assumptions fail to conform to the "real world,"[47] law and economics scholars argued that economic theory must be evaluated on its ability to make accurate predictions, not on the "realism of its assumptions." Law and economics scholars believe that the lack of realism in a theory's assumptions is a merit, not a demerit. As Posner explained in the second edition of his ECONOMIC ANALYSIS OF LAW: "A scientific theory must select from the welter of experience that it is trying to explain, and is therefore necessarily 'unrealistic' when compared to actual conditions. Newton's law of falling bodies, for example, is unrealistic in its basic assumption that bodies fall in a vacuum, but it is still a useful theory because it predicts with sufficient though not complete accuracy the behavior of a wide variety of falling bodies in the real world." [48]

The orthodox defense of law and economics was developed by Posner and a cadre of law and economics scholars working at the University of Chicago. It was the "hardliners" of the Chicago School (the founding fathers) who, throughout the 1970s and early 1980s, advocated strong claims based on the *law and efficiency* hypothesis. This hypothesis, normally associated with Posner's initially staunch efficiency perspective, asserted that the common law is, or at least should be, a primary vehicle for promoting efficiency—what Posner later called the principle of *wealth maximization.*[49]

The first generation soon devoted its effort to the goal of redefining common law concepts of Contract, Property, Tort, and Criminal Law to fit what Posner called the "capitalist conception of justice." [50] According to the capitalist conception, the ethical basis for determining whether a particular state of affairs is "just" is determined by the criterion of whether that state of affairs promotes the maximization of wealth. Because the economic value of wealth is determined by willingness to pay, "The only kind of preference that counts . . . is . . . one that is backed up by money—in other words, that is registered in a market." [51]

While the first generation initially avoided making normative claims about the law, it was not long before they began making such claims. Early law and economics scholarship held strong ideological claims about the common law and the function of the legal system in the market economy. Law and economics scholars argued that judge-made law should maximize the value of legal entitlements as measured in dollar equivalents. They argued that the common law is, and ought to be, efficient. First-generation law and economics scholars soon claimed that law and adjudication could be best understood as profit-maximization activity. Market efficiency was their normative standard for evaluating legitimate law and effective legal decision making. They believed that law was economics, and economics was a neutral, apolitical science of "reason." A popular first-generation law and economics slogan was that "law should be efficient."

The law and economics movement was also, in the early stages of its development, a conservative reaction to the judicial activism of the Warren Court era. The Warren Court's fundamental rights discourse in constitutional law was rejected by these scholars as too simplistic and underdeveloped to deal with theoretical and institutional aspects of the modern bureaucratic state. By focusing on the dynamics of market mechanisms, law and economics analysts placed less attention on the legal conception of rights as a normative or descriptive framework, and focused instead on behavioral consequences of different rule systems. For these scholars, legal rights became mere tropes for the economic analysis of law.

## Second-Generation Law and Economics Scholarship

By the mid-1980s, however, the influence of the Chicago School peaked. A new generation of law and economics scholars emerged and distanced themselves from the orthodoxy of the Chicago School and developed alternative approaches to the economic analysis of law. Distance was necessary for those law and economics scholars who rejected the Chicago School's conservative agenda and desired a more liberal one. Although most law and economics scholars now agree that efficiency analysis is a beneficial tool for understanding behavior under law, most practitioners now reject the notion that efficiency should be regarded as the only legal norm in common law adjudication.[52]

Moreover, there is now a new breed of law and economics scholars who favor a genuinely reformist law and economics philosophy to address the problems of the modern welfare, regulatory state.[53] These scholars no longer believe that legal rules should be affirmed or rejected solely on the basis of efficiency. Instead, they have shifted their attention away from the common law to an examination of public law and the normative justifications for the activist state. This second wave of law and economics scholarship helped establish a *liberal* school of law and economics, known as the *New Haven* or *Reformist School* of law and economics.[54]

This second generation is now quite diverse. One group attempts to construct a more sophisticated understanding of the Chicago School approach by developing nonmarket theories to explain bureaucratic and institutional behavior.[55] Law and economics scholars associated with the University of Virginia adopted the Chicago School's conservative perspective in advancing theories of strategic behavior to explain long-term bargaining relations.[56]

Another strand of second-generation law and economics scholarship embraces the Chicago School's perspective in developing a theory of *public choice* for analyzing legislative behavior.[57] This theory developed from Kenneth Arrow's book, SOCIAL CHOICE AND INDUSTRIAL VALUES, published in 1951, which is known in law and economics literature for establishing *Arrow's Impossibility Theorem*.[58] This theorem demonstrates that under certain conditions, groups attempting to choose among three or more alternatives by majority vote may be unable to reach a consistent decision. It questioned the optimism of political pluralists who in the 1960s assumed that interest-group representation would lead the legislative process to socially preferred legislation.[59] Arrow's Theorem also suggested that majority voting in appellate courts may prevent judges from reaching consistent and "principled" decisions.[60] Public choice theory became a vehicle for criticizing liberal pluralistic premises of democratic and judicial theory of the post–New Deal era.

Post-New Deal intellectuals attempted to construct a new democratic theory known as *interest group pluralism*.[61] This theory provided a conception of democracy that optimistically accepted the legitimacy of interest group influence in the political process. Pluralists viewed the political process as a legitimate battle between competing interest groups, whose interaction ensured that the democratic process was representative of all interests in society. They believed that interest group competition in the political process would operate much like the mythical "invisible hand" of the market (i.e., that the group pursuit of self-interest would lead to the aggregate social welfare of society).

Pluralists favored a process-oriented perspective that supported the views of the legal process school.[62] Because pluralists viewed interest group competition as essential for a well-ordered, modern democratic process, pluralism became a central concept for establishing the legitimacy and authority of lawmaking process. For this reason, process-oriented legal pluralists believed that political lawmaking (i.e., legislation) was the ultimate authority of lawmaking of all other institutions, particularly the courts.[63] The legal process school accepted the pluralist concept of politics and advanced a new methodology of legal analysis— a methodology that promised an objective *process* for resolving subjective questions of *public policy*. Through belief in the possibility of consensus and agreement, interest group competition was believed capable of resolving substantive disagreements about political values. During the 1950s and 1960s, legal theorists believed that the ethical relativism of legal realism could be tamed by a democratic process structured by interest group compromises and political action.

Public choice theorists rejected the optimistic vision of the political process on various grounds. Raising the dilemma presented by Arrow's Impossibility Theorem, these theorists argued that majority rule may be unable to resolve the choices among competing political alternatives. Drawing from Mancur Olson's work on collective choice,[64] public choice theorists argued that *"free rider"* problems (the tendency of one person to freely take the benefit created by the efforts of others) prevent interest groups from representing large and diverse groups. Public choice theorists thus predicted that political activity is likely to be dominated by small interest groups seeking to advance their own special interests, frequently at the expense of the public good.

Public choice theory raised serious questions about the efficacy of the "proceduralism" of legal process scholars who, following the process tradition of Hart and Sacks, uncritically assume that judges should exercise judicial restraint and leave "political issues" and substantive questions of value to the legislature for resolution. At the same time, public choice theorists questioned the efficacy of first-generation scholars who assumed, as their process-oriented intellectual fathers had, that the theory of adjudication could be objective and autonomous, "free" from political distortions. Second-generation law and economics public choice theorists thus distanced themselves from the first generation.

Although second-generation scholarship accepted the methodological approaches of the founding members of the Chicago School, tension erupted between the first and second generations. This tension was exhibited by differences in tone as well as anxieties about the distinct conservative agenda of the Chicago School of economics reflected in the work of conservative economists such as Milton Friedman, Gary Becker, and George Stigler. The second generation is more modest in its claims about the role of economics in law, and less accepting of the Chicago School's conservative orientation toward property-rights analysis. Only a small number of methodological issues appeared to be settled between the two generations, such as the ideas that microeconomic theory is a basis for analyzing law, demand curves are downward sloping, and that cost-benefit analysis and the economic definition of cost (opportunity cost) are essential for intelligent policymaking. Second-generation scholars retreated from the orthodoxy of "efficient" analysis for nearly every legal question. Instead, they admit that "[m]ost law and economics questions are still open and likely to remain so for a long time."[65]

Second-generation law and economics scholarship is also more eclectic than the early law and economics scholarship.[66] The second generation has developed a new institutional economics that promises a more realistic, yet inchoate, understanding of the bureaucratic, institutional, and relational contexts of modern transactions, legal relations, law, and adjudication. One recent avenue of inquiry involves an attempt to construct a new version of economic analysis that goes beyond individual self-interest and supports cooperation.[67] New theories of relational contract and strategic behavior were offered to modify or replace the static models and assumptions of neoclassical microeconomic theory used by Chicago School practitioners.

Public choice theorists offer an interest group theory for understanding the economics of statutes and the behavior of legislators.[68] Public choice theorists attempt to explain how political and bureaucratic organizations make collective choices under models which assume that political actors, like economic actors, are self-interested maximizers.[69] Other law and economics scholars seek to resuscitate a liberal, reformist vision of law by using economic analysis to defend various liberal conceptions of law and adjudication.[70] Law and economics has grown to encompass a host of divergent theoretical perspectives and normative conceptions about law and adjudication.

Even though the law and economics movement is diverse in theory and perspective, there are some common premises that all law and economics scholars accept. Lewis Kornhauser, a second-generation law and economics scholar, recently identified four premises that he claims describe the corpus of law and economics scholarship: (1) a *behavioral claim,* which asserts that economics can provide a useful theory for predicting behavior under rules of law; (2) a *normative claim,* which asserts that the law ought to be efficient; (3) a factual or *positive* claim, which argues that the common law is in fact efficient; and (4) a *genetic* claim, which asserts that the common law selects efficient rules, even though not every rule may be efficient.[71] According to Kornhauser, "Every article in law and economics adheres, explicitly or implicitly, to one or more of [these] logically distinct [claims]."[72]

Only the scholarship of the Chicago School founding fathers, who adopted the *law and efficiency* hypothesis, embraced all four claims of law and economics that Kornhauser identified. These law and economics practitioners accepted the behavioral claim that individuals respond rationally to incentives and that legal rules affect behavior. Because they assert that the *normative* claim identifies efficient behavior and is, therefore, the criterion for choosing among rules, they use the *behavioral* claim of economics to identify legal rules that induce efficient behavior. These scholars view judging as an exercise in cost-benefit analysis, transaction cost reduction, risk assessment, and wealth maximization. Such an economic perspective places the judge in the role of "social engineer," with the single-minded purpose of shaping rights and liabilities in the name of efficient resource allocation.

The *positive* and *genetic* claims identified by Kornhauser describe the position of Chicago School practitioners who view the common law as a system of rules having a factual or natural (genetic) tendency to induce efficient behavior under the law. Their underlying legal perspective is the product of a worldview that pursues truth about law within a paradigm that evaluates legal rules under the single universal standard of wealth maximization. For these practitioners, the law and efficiency hypothesis became a comprehensive organizational principle for understanding the nature of legal relations.

Second-generation law and economics scholars either reject the normative and genetic efficiency claims identified by Kornhauser or remain *agnostic* about whether these claims are persuasive. While recent law and economics scholars adopt a positive claim regarding economic analysis of law, it is different from the one identified by Kornhauser. Second-generation law and economics scholars merely claim that "a given rule can be fruitfully examined using microeconomic theory,"[73] or emphasize that the tools of microeconomic theory provide "explanations of the law and predictions of the consequences of legal rules."[74] The positive claim of law and economics scholars is now more modest. It simply assumes that law can be understood as a rational system of behavior based on economic interest. In rejecting the idea that *efficiency* is the foundation of law, these scholars embraced a more "common-sense" working hypothesis, which claims only that economic efficiency is the "best approach for the American legal system to follow."[75]

Thus, the only claim identified by Kornhauser that characterizes the dominant methodology of the movement today is the behavioral claim. This claim commits *all* law and economics scholars to the view that rational, self-interested calculation of individual cost and benefit is the best key for understanding and evaluating the nature of legal relations and various rule systems. Practitioners of the movement believe that rules of law are like prices, and that legal actors are like perfectly rational consumers.

While the second generation distanced itself from the conservative influence of the Chicago School, the vocabulary and methodology of their practice ensured that these scholars remained committed to the conservative agenda bequeathed by Coase. If there is an ideological tilt to the law and economics movement, it is no longer the result of the conservative perspective of the law and efficiency hypothesis. Rather, the ideology of this movement is best explained today in terms of a particular worldview, which assumes that the rationality and economic self-interests of legal subjects are the best tools for understanding law and adjudication. The behavioral and positive claims of second-generation scholars hold that law and the larger social world can be viewed as a system of rational behavior, sometimes influenced by impulses toward efficiency, other times not, but always a product of the "pragmatic" reason of the analyzing subject. The phrase "law is pragmatic" characterizes the worldview of second-generation scholars who accept the possibility of developing a pragmatic subjectivity for "muddling through" the hard problems in the law.

Second-generation law and economics practitioners maintain a pragmatic perspective about the world that accepts the utility of *abstraction, universalism,* and *scientific rationality.* Their pragmatic and economic approach assumes, however, that legal analysis must proceed in the way that *applied* science proceeds—the examination of complex phenomena must be explained on the basis of hypothesis testing. This quasi-scientific perspective presumes that lawyers can discover a relatively stable basis for justifying legal results by universalizing legal propositions abstracted from hypothetical examples structured by behavioral assumptions about economic motivations of homogeneous individuals. Second-generation law scholars nevertheless remain "open-minded, forward-looking, respectful of fact, willing to experiment, disrespectful of sacred cows, antimetaphysical." [76]

## Post-Chicago Law and Economics

By the 1990s, the second generation shifted away from the deterministic efficiency analysis of the first generation to a more indeterminate, pragmatic intellectual stance. The second generation moved away from strong "scientific" claims of economic formalism. Instead, they embraced the pragmatic view that law and economics must be approached from a more common-sense, instrumental perspective focusing on human goals and aspirations. [77] Hence, while law and economics analysts continued to believe that efficiency is the test for evaluating good and bad law, they understood legal efficiency as a practical concept that is instrumental, adoptive, and functional.

Today, law and economics scholars have moved beyond the "rational-actor" model and the efficiency analysis of early law and economics analysis. They develop less ambitious but more complicated approaches to the economic analysis of law. Some contemporary law and economics scholars argue that the economic approach must be supplemented with insights from "modern psychology and sociology," [78] while others seek to qualify economic analysis of the law by highlighting the limitations of its analysis. [79] New institutional analyses developed from game theory [80] have been created to explain bureaucratic behavior. Attempts have been made to make economic analysis of law more realistic by explicitly incorporating a more realistic understanding of the interrelation between substance and procedure, and the study of institutions has caused economically oriented legal scholars to reject the economic formalism of the first generation. [81] The fact that so many practitioners have "moved beyond" the original analysis of the Chicago School is evidence of an emerging second-generation "*Post-Chicago* law and economics." [82]

Advocates of the post-Chicago economic approach to legal studies recognize that economic analysis is one of many different modes of analysis relevant to the task of developing a realistic concept of law in jurisprudence. This socio-economic view seems to be catching on. Even the founding father of the law and economics movement, Richard Posner, has softened his economic views about law and adjudication and adopted a more philosophical perspective. Posner's recent defense of law and economics in his book, THE PROBLEMS OF JURISPRUDENCE, for example, represents the post-Chicago shift from the jurisprudential view found in his earlier work, ECONOMIC ANALYSIS OF LAW.[83] Posner, who once argued that law is best understood through the objective lens of efficiency analysis, now argues for a form of legal pragmatism that accepts the idea that "large changes in law often come about as a result of a non-rational process."[84]

In ECONOMIC ANALYSIS OF LAW, Posner was confident about the possibility that judges could discern economically correct answers for legal problems by consulting a handful of simple economic concepts. In PROBLEMS OF JURISPRUDENCE, Posner is less confident and more skeptical about the possibility of right answers in law. PROBLEMS OF JURISPRUDENCE is thus offered as a "Pragmatist Manifesto" encouraging judges to rely on their intuition and common sense in deciding legal problems. Posner acknowledges that there "is no such thing as 'legal reasoning,' " distinct from "the use of simple logic and the various methods of practical reasoning that everyday thinkers use."[85] He concluded that the "methods of practical reason are inarticulate," because such reason relies on "prejudgment that cannot be empirically established."[86] Posner thus argues for a flexible jurisprudence—one that favors the rational outlook of scientific inquiry but rejects the metaphysical search for unity and order.[87]

According to the new pragmatic Posner, legal objectivity merely demands that legal decision makers exercise "reasonableness" in the resolution of particular cases.[88] Change in the law is seen "as a result of a non-rational process akin to conversion," and that "law is an activity rather than a concept or a group of concepts."[89] Economic analysis is still relevant to Posner's jurisprudence, but only as a tool for problem solving. In Posner's current pragmatic stance, "The essence of interpretative decision making is considering the consequences of alternative decisions. There are no 'logically' correct interpretations; interpretation is not a logical process."[90]

Posner thus rejects the idea of autonomous law. He asserts that our legal system is the product of different enterprises,[91] and that the primary goal of law is the functional goal of reaching sound effects.[92] He believes that the true test of every legal analysis is whether it "works" instrumentally to maximize human goals and aspirations.[93] The incursions of economics in law are justified on a practical level: economics wins over other approaches because it "gets the job done" better than any other method.[94] Without a doubt, Posner's PROBLEMS OF JURISPRUDENCE is more eclectic theoretically and far more accepting of the contingent nature of law and adjudication than his earlier work, THE ECONOMIC ANALYSIS OF LAW.

The shift in tone and temperament in Posner's current jurisprudence may be the result of a conscious strategy developed to insulate *his* movement and *his* place in history from the criticism of the academic Left and Right during much of the 1980s.[95] Perhaps Posner's ultimate objective is to offer pragmatism as a middle ground between the Right, which he feels exaggerates the formalist nature of American law, and the Left, which he feels exaggerates its indeterminacy. On the other hand, Posner is also the consummate intellectual who is willing to change his position after reflection. It is more likely that his thinking has been affected by broader intellectual shifts in the academy, which are currently precipitating a crisis of faith over legal modernism. Perhaps for Posner, neopragmatism is the best postmodern alternative for dealing with the "incredulity" of the scientific-like claims of early law and economics scholarship.

Posner has emphasized that his jurisprudence rejects the possibility of developing a new metanarrative or grounding foundation for jurisprudence.[96] He also rejects the idea that law is an autonomous, self-generating activity and instead accepts the socially constructed nature of legal knowledge. And yet this is ironic, because Posner's jurisprudence is now detached from its economic foundations. His jurisprudence is best explained today in terms of a particular worldview that regards economic analysis as a form of practical reason, which is peculiarly suited to a jurisprudence without foundations.

Contemporary law and economics practitioners, like Posner, seem to be moving away from strong "scientific" claims of legal determinacy. Instead they accept the pragmatic view that law is too indeterminate to be ruled by the determinate, scientific-like analysis of economics. It is true that contemporary law and economics analysts continue to believe that economics is relevant for legal analysis, but they now approach economic analysis of law from a more practical, functional perspective.

Indeed, by the late 1980s the law and economics movement shifted away from deterministic analysis to a more indeterminate, pragmatic approach defined in part by postmodern trends in the academy.[97]

Unlike Chicago School law and economics scholars who focused their research under the efficiency thesis, post-Chicago scholars look beyond efficiency norms in developing economic predictions based on what they expect rational, self-interested legal actors to do when confronted with cooperative-choice situations.[98] Traditional economic analysis, focusing on efficient outcomes, is said to "blind [law and economics analysts] to the ways in which the distributive and productive dimensions of legal and political constraints are united in rational cooperation."[99] Post-Chicago law and economics scholars incorporate into their economic analysis of the law "a normative component that has traditionally been associated with social contract theory and which is championed today by philosophers."[100] The new power talk of economics thus encourages lawyers and judges to make a shift in their analytical perspective to a new normative perspective of rationality that recharacterizes legally relevant factors such as costs and benefits, and frames normative issues previously missed by the narrow context of microeconomic theory. This shift in analytical perspective allows post-Chicago theorists to restructure the economic analysis of law in fundamental new ways.

First, post-Chicago theorists attempt to correct the "efficiency" implications of Chicago School law and economics by refocusing economic analysis of law on distributive consequences.[101] Thus, post-Chicago analysis acknowledges that while "[i]t may have appeared useful at one time to distinguish the efficiency of legal rules from their distributive dimension," it "was never analytically possible, nor is it now normatively defensible to do so."[102] Post-Chicago theorists also acknowledge that private negotiations frequently involve nontrivial transaction costs that lead to market failure. These practitioners now accept the notion that "market failure . . . calls for legal intervention which is intended to replicate the outcome of a hypothetical costless market."[103] In giving more emphasis to the problem of market failure, post-Chicago practitioners argue that a "more sophisticated understanding" of transaction costs is needed.[104] Hence, Jules L. Coleman argued that "transaction costs are a black box that needs to be filled in."[105] To better understand the nature of transaction costs, Coleman argued that decision makers should follow a new law and economics perspective. Post-Chicago analysts consequently argue in favor of a more sophisticated and complex understanding of transaction costs.[106]

Post-Chicago law and economics also offers a new approach to legal scholarship. Its followers believe that legal scholarship should give greater consideration to formulating and testing more realistic and complicated theories about social life. The underlying approach is that law can be studied and understood *pragmatically*. Law and economics scholars agree that traditional legal scholarship is flawed by ambiguity in purpose and method, but nonetheless argue that the current doctrinal justifications of the law can be *grounded* by economic insights. While only the Chicago School advocates that the principle of wealth maximization can ground legal analysis, all law and economics scholars believe that judges can pragmatically implement economic analyses to improve law and society.

The economic analysis of law encourages the legal profession to look beyond the law to discover a new medium for resolving contested policy views, which in turn necessitates a new understanding of law's legitimacy. For economics to become the new source of law's authority and autonomy, it was necessary that economics master every area in which law operates—including legal reasoning. The second generation of law and economics scholars realized that economic analysis cannot deliver on this promise. As Posner now concedes, economics is not the "reason behind the reason of the law."

Hence, law and economics scholars continue to believe that economic analysis is instrumental, adaptive, and functional. The jurisprudence of law and economics now associates itself with a version of legal pragmatism that clings to the belief in a flexible, intuitive understanding of law. However, it remains committed to the belief that practical reason can do what economic analysis has not been capable of doing—that is, locate the authority and autonomy of law. The law and economics movement has thus shifted away from deterministic scientific-like analysis to a more indeterminate, ambivalent stance defined in part by postmodern trends in the academy.

# 6. Critical Legal Studies

While law and economics attracted the attention of legal scholars, a distinct movement in legal studies established itself as a major critic of both traditional and law and economics scholarship. This new academic movement—critical legal studies (CLS)—surfaced in 1976 when a group of legal scholars met at the University of Wisconsin Law School and formed a social and professional network called *The Conference on Critical Legal Studies*.[1] The diverse intellectual projects of these writers established the thematic character of this movement. The intellectual component of this movement known as CLS continues to grow and expand, despite the fact that there has been considerable opposition to CLS ideas in the legal academy. From the outset, CLS has aspired to be a social and political movement that links its various intellectual projects with the political and social aspirations of its membership.[2] It is the overtly political message of this movement that has caused some contemporary legal scholars to vehemently reject the intellectual insights of CLS scholars.

CLS seeks "to explore the manner in which legal doctrine and legal education and the practices of legal institutions work to buttress and support a pervasive system of oppressive, inegalitarian relations."[3] While CLS scholarship evinces a richly diverse set of opinions and perspectives, CLS scholars (Crits) rediscovered the political critique of radical legal realism, and have gone beyond it to show how the dominant tradition in legal scholarship (as well as the interdisciplinary tradition of progressive legal realism) helped to justify an abstract legal discourse that ignored the politics of power. CLS "spoke to lawyers and academics in a way that connected theoretical speculation to their daily experience [of] the law, rather than merely their abstract curiosity."[4] In this sense, CLS "offered not merely a theory of law," but a hopeful self-conception of a "politically active, socially responsible [vision] of a noble calling."[5] Crits thus sought to move the political criticism of legal realism to a new intellectual and political level.

Commentators have suggested that the intellectual component of CLS is difficult to characterize because Crits share only antipathy toward traditional views of law and do not advocate a common method or approach to legal scholarship. It had been said that "while law and economics scholars seem 'divided by a common methodology' critical legal scholars seem united only in a shared antagonism."[6] Critical legal studies is characterized as a "negative" or "destructive" movement, one that criticizes without offering either a constructive program or specific standard of reference for judging.[7] One legal educator suggested that scholars who share the CLS ideology of "nihilism" have an ethical obligation to leave the law schools and seek work elsewhere in the academy.[8]

There are also differences of opinion about whether CLS is an authentic intellectual movement in law. Mark Tushnet, a well-known Crit at Georgetown University Law Center, suggested that "critical legal studies is less an intellectual movement in law (though it is that too) than it is a political location."[9] Tushnet doubts whether it makes sense to talk about CLS as a "movement" or "school."[10] He concludes that "the project of critical legal studies does not have any essential intellectual component, which is why [he] cannot readily identify a great deal that is common in the intellectual production going under the heading of critical legal studies."[11] He asserts that "[t]here should be nothing surprising about this conclusion, [since] . . . most CLS authors [believe] that law is politics."[12]

Tushnet doubts that CLS is a "movement" because he finds that people, both inside and outside CLS, cannot agree on what CLS is about, other than propounding the "law is politics" claim. Tushnet characterizes CLS by identifying the various interest groups within CLS: "At present one might describe the political location of critical legal studies as occupied by certain feminists ('fem-crits'), certain theorists concerned with the role of rule in law (critical race theorists), a group influenced by recent developments in literary theory (postmodernists), a group of cultural radicals (multiculturalists), and a group that stresses the role of the economic structure in setting the conditions for legal decisions (political economists)." [13]

Martha Minow, however, a legal feminist and CLS fellow-traveler at Harvard Law School, believes that CLS is more than a political location. She argues that the CLS "school is recognizable in its commitment to explain both that legal principles and doctrines are open-textured and capable of yielding contradictory results, and that legal decisions express an internal dynamic of legal culture contingent on historical preferences for selected assumptions and values." [14] Minow identified four "activities" in which CLS scholars were known to engage in the early 1980s: (1) "The critical scholar seeks to demonstrate the indeterminacy of legal doctrine: any given set of legal principles can be used to yield competing or contradictory results"; [15] (2) "[t]he critical scholar engages in historical, socioeconomic analysis to identify how particular interest groups, social classes, or entrenched economic institutions benefit from legal decisions despite the indeterminacy of the legal doctrines"; [16] (3) "the critical scholar tries to expose how legal analysis and legal culture mystifies outsiders and legitimates its results"; [17] and (4) "the critical school may elucidate new or previously disfavored social visions and argue for their realization in legal or political practice in part by making them part of legal discourse." [18]

The "four activities" depicted by Minow contain implications drawn from the different projects of various critical legal scholars and establish the eclectic intellectual projects of CLS. CLS scholars following Duncan Kennedy's notion of a "fundamental contradiction" [19] seek to demonstrate the "indeterminacy" of legal doctrine by describing in minute detail how various legal doctrines rotate around contradictory values or opposing polarities such as objective/subjective and public/private. Other critical legal scholars moved beyond legal doctrine to critique the liberal theory of the state, upon which modern legal theory is said to rest. Roberto M. Unger's 1975 book KNOWLEDGE AND POLITICS [20] demonstrated how liberal theory masked subjective and political choices by portraying knowledge and truth as separate essences distinct from politics, passion, and subjective desire. In describing how legal rights favor particular interest groups or "mystify" their results, other critical legal scholars developed critiques based on psychoanalytic and ideological concepts to explain legal legitimation and hegemony. [21] Still others sought to develop a new historiography to describe how American legal history can be understood as a "winner's story," where a long-term political tradition (liberalism) displaced other traditions (civic republicanism),[22] and how law developed to serve the needs of American corporate enterprise and industrialization.[23]

On the other hand, because critical legal studies is such an unstable and diverse movement (and because the criticism of law advanced by its members is socially, politically, and intellectually unstable), CLS ends up meaning different things to many people. In attempting to define the intellectual core of CLS thought, authors are thus faced with the same predicament peculiar to postmodernism. They both seem to be moving targets that are difficult to hit. Part of the problem in explaining CLS is that Crits practice a form of legal criticism that resists a stabilized identity or definition. Indeed, Crits practice a "chameleon-like" form of criticism that exhibits different manifestations which frequently conflict in practice. Thus, while Duncan Kennedy announces that law is hopelessly embroiled in a fundamental contradiction, he has resisted arguments that establish the fundamental contradictions as the next new category for legal criticism. Like postmodernists, Crits problematize the very form, the very discourse they use in advancing their own announcements about law. They recognize and embrace the predicaments and paradoxes of their texts and discourse.

Tushnet is therefore correct in concluding that there is no single method or epistemology that describes critical legal studies. But this does not mean that CLS is not a "movement" or "school" of jurisprudential thought. As an intellectual movement, distinguished from the political location described·by Tushnet, CLS represents a rich, albeit diverse, set of views and theoretical approaches for understanding the nature of law and adjudication in the modern era. Critical legal studies offers a distinctive and progressive form of jurisprudence developed from eclectic intellectual sources. The writing of this movement is "critical" because it is consciously associated with the counterculture and new-left politics of the 1960s. The critical legal studies movement has advanced its intellectual projects by rediscovering the political potential of a political critique of law presented by the radical strand of legal realism, which remained dormant after the 1930s. CLS is distinctive in that it purports to link radical realism to left-wing legal radicalism. The contours of CLS jurisprudence developed in stages, involving different generations of CLS scholarship—an early modernistic generation and a late postmodern generation.

## Early Critical Legal Studies Scholarship

CLS scholarship from the mid 1970s to the early 1980s focused on demonstrating the indeterminacy of legal doctrine. The CLS indeterminacy critique was premised on the legal realist insight that various substantive categories of law consisted of principles and counterprinciples, rules and exceptions, policies and counterpolicies that were resistant to attempts to reach determinate resolution. Following the radical strand of legal realist thought, Crits argued that there are no foundations for grounding otherwise indeterminate law because law and its doctrines were philosophically committed to contradictory norms and policies. For Crits, the argumentative structures of law established the link between the legal consciousness of lawyers, judges, and scholars and their liberal ideology and practices.

In the late 1970s and early 1980s, CLS scholars developed and "pushed to the limit" the strand of legal realist thought that pursued a deconstructive type of legal criticism. This approach rejected the idea that law consists of a coherent body of principles and policies that inform and rationalize fundamentally shared values. CLS scholars enriched the deconstructive analytic of the legal realists by drawing from the critiques of continental philosphers and new-left thinkers who were then revolting against modernist dogma. The goal of CLS scholars was to reveal how law justified domination and privilege through an abstract professional discourse, which claimed neutrality in process and outcome.

Initially, CLS scholars asserted that law is "rational" or "objective" only because it appears to conform to a particular liberal political ideology. They claim that this ideology sought to justify and explain race, class, and gender disadvantage and privilege as the logical consequences of rational private choice. CLS scholars viewed legal doctrine as a series of ideological constructs that supported existing social arrangements by convincing legal actors and ordinary citizens that the legal and social systems were inevitable and basically fair. Critical legal analysts argued that there is no politically neutral, coherent way to talk about law because law's internal logic depends on fundamentally contradictory concepts and principles. Moreover, Crits claim that the worldview of modern legal thinkers either ignores or diminishes the reality of race, class, and gender differences. In other words, CLS practitioners analyzed law as a political ideology that has operated to re-create and legitimate American society in accordance with the political philosophy of liberalism.

The CLS indeterminacy thesis opened the way for a form of oppositional scholarship known as *trashing*.[24] The idea was to demonstrate the indeterminacy and incoherence of liberal legal thought by "trashing" the doctrinal categories lawyers, judges, and legal scholars relied on in their work. Early CLS work developed various explanations of the indeterminacy embedded within mainstream conceptions of law. The goal was to "unpack" legal doctrine to expose its internal inconsistencies and reveal the paradoxical worldviews imbedded within the doctrine. After exposing the indeterminacy of legal doctrine, CLS scholars would examine the political choices justified by the doctrine.

Duncan Kennedy's early scholarship on private law portrayed the doctrinal categories of the common law as a set of tensions and oppositions structured by a *fundamental contradiction* posed by the pervasive conflict between the individual and the group, the self and the other.[25] Unger's KNOWLEDGE AND POLITICS attempted to show how liberal theory was plagued by an ideology that denied the *contradiction* inherent in liberalism's emphasis on individual autonomy and its fear of community. Unger argued, with considerable force, that the contradictory values of autonomy and community were basic human values necessary for the coherence of liberal legal thought. Both Kennedy and Unger demonstrated that the coherence of liberal legal thought rested on the questionable belief that there are essential meanings to words such as "neutral," "objective," or "free will."[26] Peter Gabel's work on reification in legal reasoning demonstrated how this form of essentialism became like a religion held together by clusters of belief reproduced in doctrinal formula.[27] He described how the structure of legal authority influences the smallest, most routine, and ordinary interactions of social life.

CLS criticism attempted to push traditional legal scholarship from the "dry world" of doctrine and abstract theory to an examination of popular culture and the experiences of daily life. Social behavior became a relevant source for examining the politics of law. Liberal legal scholars attempted to defend liberal legal thought by offering new forms of interpretive theory that located law's objectivity in interpretive practices based on culturally shared values and meanings.[28] Crits responded to these efforts by showing how the "indeterminacy critique" applied to culture as well as language, that the fundamental contradiction existed everywhere—in art, literature, music, language, culture, and virtually every field of law.

The intellectual projects of CLS were also based on the view that practice informed theory. Progressive legal theory was said to emerge from progressive political practice. CLS thus focused on the "doing" rather than just the "theorizing." Crits became politically active at the law schools, advancing proposals for curriculum reform supporting clinical modes of instruction, and arguing for more diversity in hiring, promotion, and tenure.[29] The CLS critique of liberal legal education was popularized by Duncan Kennedy's "little red book," LEGAL EDUCATION AND THE REPRODUCTION OF HIERARCHY: A POLEMIC AGAINST THE SYSTEM,[30] an underground CLS publication intended to be the activist's guide for resisting structures of illegitimate hierarchy at law schools. The rapidly expanding CLS movement gained considerable momentum during the 1980s because many scholars were already disillusioned with Langdellian pedagogy and the banality of traditional legal studies. Intellectual outrage at the rigidity of conventional legal thought was as much a driving force as CLS politics.

Another example of CLS practice involved counterhegemonic legal conferences and annual summer camps for law professors and students. Crits made their presence known at the annual conventions of the Association of American Law Schools (AALS), the professional and quasi-political organization representing law schools and law professors. At the 1993 AALS convention, for example, CLS members organized a picket line of law professors in support of hotel and service employees who were on strike at one of the convention hotels.[31] At the conclusion of a plenary session of the conference, approximately one hundred law professors joined a smaller ad hoc group of CLS organizers to march on the picket line in solidarity with striking hotel employees. At the same time, CLS organizers asked the governing body of the AALS to adopt a policy to support worker rights and the policies of federal labor law.[32] For Crits, intellectual debates about the legal profession could not be divorced from the actual social practice occurring outside the convention hall doors. A central political goal of CLS is thus aimed at stimulating a more active social consciousness within the legal profession generally.

CLS scholars' descriptions of the legal system attempted to demonstrate how the forms of professional law practice reflect and "create a political culture that can persuade people to accept both the legitimacy and the inevitability of the existing hierarchical arrangement." [33] Peter Gabel and Paul Harris argued, for example, that the judicial function is "heavily laden with ritual and authoritarian symbolism" that "signifies to people that those in power deserve to be there by virtue of their majesty and vast learning." [34] They maintained that when "[t]aken as a whole, this display of legal symbolism lays the deep psychological foundation for a political culture that substitutes identification with authority for real democratic participation and that substitutes fantasies of patriotic community for an actual community founded upon love and mutual respect." [35] The "conservative power of legal thought is not to be found in legal outcomes which resolve conflicts in favor of dominant groups, but in the reification of the very categories through which the nature of social conflict is defined." [36]

Early CLS scholarship was initially devoted to showing how traditional modes of legal analysis reflected the phenomenological experience of living within a society that values autonomy, but yearns for community; glorifies reason, but longs for passion. Hence, while traditional legal scholars offered a new technocratic discourse to legitimate the universal perspective of mainstream legal thought, CLS scholars interjected a new phenomenological discourse of political critique. *Liberal legalism,* the label CLS attaches to mainstream law and legal scholarship, denied the values of community and human connection by a universal perspective that emphasized the importance of only certain values—the values of autonomy and individual self-interest.

The early CLS view of law assumed that the preferences of legal actors were shaped by the ruling orthodoxy. CLS scholars asserted that "[l]ike religion in previous historical periods, the law becomes an object of belief which shapes popular consciousness toward a passive acquiescence or obedience to the status quo." [37] CLS scholars purported to show how the dominant discourse in law obstructed the realization of democratic ideals. CLS scholars sought to reveal how a commitment to the ideals of law would require more, not less, discussion about how people can learn to actually realize the ideals of a participatory democratic society. Hence, a popular CLS slogan during the early 1980s was "law is politics."

Critical legal thinkers advanced constructive proposals for legal education. They argued that lawyers must be trained to deemphasize their role as technical experts by understanding the moral and political consequences of the work they perform. William Simon, for example, argued that lawyers must represent clients to advance the clients' interests and values, instead of the lawyer's interests.[38] Simon's goal was to reconceptualize the attorney's facilitating role in the creation of nonhierarchical communities of interests. Instead of asserting their expertise as a function of hierarchical power, lawyers would empower those who are disempowered by the cultural and intellectual hierarchies of the legal system.

CLS perspectives on judging reflected the way critical scholars viewed the law. In his essay on the critical phenomenology of judging,[39] Duncan Kennedy described the experience of a judge struggling to reach a specific outcome in the context of choosing between competing conceptions of law. He argued that the "experience" of judging "is a kind of work with a purpose, and here the purpose is to make the case come out the way [the judge thinks] justice tells [him] it ought to [come out], in spite of what seems at first as the *resistance* or *opposition* of the 'law.' "[40] Kennedy offered a phenomenological description of the reasoning process judges use in creating legal justifications for decisions they make based on precedent, policy, and social and historical arguments. From the perspective of his hypothetical judge, Kennedy imagined how judges are constrained by the "felt objectivity" of "applying the relevant rules," and yet are pulled by the contingent experience of arbitrariness in the process of selecting outcomes.[41] This critical view of jurisprudence sees adjudication as a process for objectifying and rationalizing the felt-experience of rule indeterminacy.

During the early 1980s, the intellectual projects of CLS scholars advanced a structuralist methodology for analyzing law and legal doctrine. The structuralist approach depicted law as resting upon an underlying structure of meaning, which is neither objective nor fixed but rather dependent on the relationship law shares with the dominant cultural and social patterns of society. CLS scholars set aside questions concerning law's origin, consequence, and meaning, and focused instead on the recurring rhetorical structures of legal texts and legal arguments. The goal was to connect the theoretical explanations of law found in legal texts with the daily experiences in order to show how law failed to deal with social problems. CLS structural analysis of law attempted to show how legal doctrine created a system of "signs" that signified the meaning of law. This work led to the development of *legal semiotics.*[42]

Duncan Kennedy's article *The Structure of Blackstone's Commentaries,*[43] for example, employed the method of structural anthropology found in the work of the French anthropologist Claude Lévi-Strauss. Kennedy demonstrated how common-law doctrinal categories (such as Contract, Property, and Tort) attempted, unsuccessfully, to mediate a fundamental contradiction between self and others. By studying the "twists and turns" of various arguments used by judges and lawyers at early common law to mediate this *fundamental contradiction,* Kennedy offered an explanation of how legal doctrine actually works in practice to legitimate existing social practices. He claimed that the more sophisticated a person became in the law, the more likely he or she would understand that all issues within any particular doctrinal field are reduced to a single dilemma or fundamental contradiction between the self and others, the individual and the collective. Kennedy argued that this fundamental contradiction between "self" and "other" permeated a wide range of legal materials.

Early 1980s CLS scholarship typically claimed that a given legal doctrine was hopelessly trapped between two opposed values such as individuality/community, subjective/objective, public/private. The goal of such work was to illustrate how legal doctrine, as a manifestation of the ideology of liberalism, contributed to an unjust, hierarchical social structure. CLS scholars also attempted to demonstrate that legal doctrine was not inevitable, but contingent. In this sense, early CLS scholarship was linked to but not completely aligned with the Frankfurt School of Critical Theory,[44] which emphasized the roles of ideology, legitimation, and mystification in justifying the power of the state. The Frankfurt School attempted to explain how law was an "ideology" that operated to the overall advantage of those classes in society that make up the ruling elite. The purpose of such work was to reveal what was "under the doctrine" of the law; a picture of the underlying ideology that law reflects. CLS scholars employed ideas and concepts associated with the

Frankfurt School of Critical Theory, but rejected the Frankfurt School's attempt to construct an empirically informed theory of moral and political truth.

And, yet the commitment to a structuralist and ideological account of law created a dilemma for CLS scholars. In their early work, as critical legal scholars seemed to say, there was a "true" and "essential deep structure" to the law.[45] As James Boyle explained: "[T]he structuralist method put critical legal theorists oddly close to classical doctrinalists such as Samuel Williston. . . . In both the high formalism of Williston and the high radicalism of critical legal thought, connections are made between very abstract political concepts and very concrete fragments of legal doctrine."[46] Classical doctrinal scholars found the "true, essential" structure of the law in the natural, objective categories of the common law. Crits in the early 1980s found the "true, essential" structure of legal doctrine in the fundamental contradiction between self and others. This rendered CLS work subject to the critique of false essences.[47] Thus, Boyle, a second-generation CLS scholar, noted how "the high formalism of the 1880s and [the CLS] structuralist analysis from the 1980s [had uncomfortable] similarities. Both present a privileged abstraction from a large amount of information. Both say, in other words, 'this is the *true,* the essential deep structure.' "[48]

## Second-Generation Critical Legal Studies Scholarship

By the mid-1980s, a number of important CLS articles applied postmodern critiques of deconstruction to legal doctrines and cases.[49] Their goal was to demonstrate how every legal interpretation of legal texts "privileged" one meaning over other possible meanings. Instead of arguing, as Duncan Kennedy did in *The Structure of Blackstone's Commentaries,* that "all issues within a doctrinal field reduce to a single dilemma (or fundamental contradiction),"[50] CLS deconstructionists asserted that fundamental contradictions are essential impossibilities because they take for granted that a heirarchy of meanings exists to support stable interpretations of legal doctrine. Deconstructionists argue that all hierarchies in legal thought, even those proclaiming the existence of a fundamental contradiction, can be undermined and reversed by a deconstructive reading.

CLS deconstructionalists revealed how the privileging process of legal hierarchies can be reversed by inverting the hierarchy of legal doctrine or case law. Deconstructive practices in CLS legal criticism have consequently sought to liberate the reader from the author's text. Advancing a political deconstruction thesis, Crits attempted to show how legal meaning about the world comes from interpreting subject which is itself constituted by an external social and cultural environment. The deconstruction of legal concepts is said to help inform the underlying social vision legal doctrine supports and justifies in the law's analysis of concrete problems. As Jack Balkin explained: "[T]he deconstructor deconstructs *ideologies,* which are manifested in particular legal doctrines. By challenging what is 'given,' deconstruction affirms the infinite possibilities of human existence. By contesting 'necessity,' deconstruction dissolves the ideological encrustations of our thought." [51]

Deconstruction, as applied to law, is an *interpretive practice* of translation that seeks to bring out the complexity and imprecision of legal texts.[52] Deconstruction is a *poststructuralist* technique of analysis because it is used by practitioners to defeat the belief in foundational structures or concepts. Deconstructionalists claim that interpretation, or what they call "translation," can never fully capture the meaning of the original. In its simplest form, the deconstructive practice involves the identification of a hierarchy of opposing values and an attempt to reverse the hierarchy. Jacques Derrida's favorite example is the Western bias favoring speech over writing.[53] Derrida argued that speech is a special type of writing, and that the hierarchy of speech could be reversed by a translation that viewed speech as a form of writing. Derrida's translation of Plato's arguments in favor of speech, for example, revealed how speech was a form of writing inscribed within the mind or soul of the listener or reader. Derrida argued that because speech or oral discourse is a special type of writing, the Western bias in favor of speech rests upon an essential impossibility. Derrida calls his project a *grammatology* for investigating the biases of Western thought.[54]

Derrida explained that Western philosophy was structured by a system of similar hierarchies that prevent the reader from realizing the existence of alternative conceptions and interpretations. Derrida argued that this privileging process of conceptual hierarchies was not an accident, but was reflective of a more general tendency of Western thought to ground or foundationalize preferred conceptions and interpretations of phenomena. Derrida called this inherent bias the *logocentric* bias of Western thought.[55] Logocentric bias refers to the way hierarchies in analytical conceptual thought favor or privilege one idea over another. Derrida's strategy was to expose this bias through his form of translation of "texts." His *reverse-the-hierarchy* translation of the text is what is known as *deconstruction*. The goal of Derrida's analysis was not to establish a new conceptual hierarchy, but rather to investigate what happens when the "common sense" understanding is reversed. Deconstruction is thus a form of criticism that attempts to defeat foundational claims of conceptual knowledge.

Derrida described this critique the "logic of the supplement" or the "dangerous supplement."[56] Common sense suggests that the "presence" of some preferred or privileged concept is parasitic or dependent on its opposite. Binary oppositions such as speech/writing, objective/subjective, public/private, reason/passion are based on the logic of this "dangerous supplement" because one concept of the binary relation relates to the other, even while it also is in opposition to the other. One goal of deconstruction is to show how the privileging of one concept over another—what Derrida called "logocentrism"[57] (a word that signified to Derrida the privileging of speech over writing, for example)—can be reversed. The overall purpose of such work is to show how every "text" (a metaphor for reality) can be translated as a form of writing supplemented by a language of signs. "The World as we know it is only a world of representations, and representations of representations, *ad infinitum*."[58] Deconstruction thus reveals that "there is nothing outside the text."[59] Derrida wants to show how the hierarchies of the "text," which are frequently taken for granted, are essentially impossible to use for justifying foundational claims of knowledge.

Gerald E. Frug's 1984 article, *The Ideology of Bureaucracy in American Law*,[60] relied on Derrida's notion of a "dangerous supplement" to explain how legal doctrines relevant to corporate and administrative law have relied upon a set of conceptual hierarchies to "assuage the long-standing fear that bureaucracy is a form of human domination."[61] According to Frug, administrative and corporate law can be viewed as stories designed to tell listeners that the dangers of bureaucratic power can be managed and controlled through law. These legal stories embedded within legal doctrine are said to "share a common structure, they attempt to define, distinguish, and render mutually compatible the subjective and objective aspects of life."[62] Bureaucratic power is thought to be "constrained by some kind of objectivity—'neutrality' and 'pursuit of a common purpose' are examples."[63] On the other hand, the concerns of personal freedom and self-expression have led to the development of bureaucratic doctrines that attempt "to make bureaucracy consistent with subjectivity—with the values of individuality associated with the unique desires that distinguish each person from others in the world."[64]

For Frug, legal doctrines regulating bureaucratic power in administrative and corporate law attempt to distinguish and render compatible the subjective and objective aspects of organizational life. He views this goal as impossible, because "no line between subjectivity and objectivity can ever be drawn."[65] The reason is that relationships between objective and subjective realms of doctrine are defined by a "dangerous supplement." Neither the object without subject, nor subject without the object seems possible, because the use of one term always seems to imply the existence of the other.[66] Frug thus concluded that "every attempt to separate objectivity and subjectivity in bureaucratic thought has instead resulted in a relentless intermixing of them. This intermixing—this insertion of subjectivity and objectivity into their antithesis as dangerous supplements—has actually been brought about by the very people who sought to prevent it."[67]

Frug's deconstruction of corporate and administrative law doctrine is not designed to propose a new improved method for combining subjective and objective categories, nor does he suggest that one category should be favored over the other.[68] Instead, he argues that lawyers and judges should simply "abandon the attempt to understand the world in terms of the subjective/objective dichotomy; [they] should [instead] deal with the problems of human association in other ways."[69] Frug's point is that the subjective/objective dichotomy, "like so many categories through which we experience the world, is a human creation and not a reflection of what the world 'is really like.' "[70] Legal doctrines reflect and regulate social life, but the doctrines themselves are not real or objective representations of the world.

Frug's deconstruction of legal doctrine sought to reveal how important human values and possibilities were overlooked or forgotten in the privileging of particular legal ideas about objectivity and subjectivity. Viewed this way, deconstruction in CLS scholarship was neither nihilistic nor self-defeating. As Jack M. Balkin explained: "[B]y recalling the elements of human life relegated to the margin in a given social theory, deconstructive readings challenge us to remake the dominant conceptions of our society."[71] Thus, Frug employs a deconstruction strategy to encourage alternative ways to control the power of bureaucratic organizations. He claims that the "alternative to 'foundations' is not 'chaos' but the joint reconstruction of social life. . . . Acting together, we could begin to disassemble the structure of bureaucratic organizations—not all at once, but piece by piece. In their place we could substitute forms of human relationship that better reflect our aspirations for human development and equality."[72]

Frug's analysis of administrative and corporate law differs from the forms of analyses typically advanced by the first generation of Crits, because he rejects the false essence of a fundamental contradiction. Instead, he revealed how both determinate and indeterminate claims about law were possible in the various doctrinal fields he investigated. Frug's deconstruction practice in *The Ideology of Bureaucracy in American Law* presents a postmodern strategy that works to undermine deterministic and indeterministic knowledge claims in the law. Structuralism is a modern rather than postmodern strategy because all structuralist accounts of theory assert the existence of a true, real structure. Structuralists claim that the underlying structures of knowledge (the symbolic categories, theories, and myths) are the real, objective source of meaning and reality. As a postmodern strategy, deconstruction rejects the essentialism of the structuralist's accounts of law by reversing the hierarchies embedded within structural analysis.

Second-generation CLS scholars also employed a social construction thesis in their work to destabilize modern legal scholars' claims of neutrality and objectivity. The social construction thesis posits that law both affects and is constituted by values, norms, practices, and fads of the larger culture it attempts to regulate. Law is thus said to be a social construction. For example, Gary Peller uses deconstructive strategies in his article, *The Metaphysics of American Law*.[73] Peller showed how nineteenth-century *liberty of contract* doctrines of constitutional law depended on legal constructions of a realm of knowledge separate from superstition or a faculty of reason separate from passion. Peller explained how the Supreme Court's due process analysis viewed government intervention as necessarily peripheral to the preserving of the "private" choices of individuals.[74] The privileging of subjective and private choices was essential to the "historical myth" of the original social contract, where the government or public sphere was assumed to be created by a group of atomized, free, and autonomous wills.[75] Peller argued that this historical myth provided the grounding of liberty of contract doctrine during the nineteenth century.

Peller argued that the jurisprudence of the *liberty of contract* era, underlying Supreme Court opinions such as *Lochner v. New York*,[76] was dependent on the public/private dichotomy as a primary representational construct.[77] The public/private dichotomy divided the legal doctrine into two mutually exclusive spheres, with the government confined to regulating that which fell within the public, as opposed to the private sphere.[78] The private and public spheres were defined against each other in terms of the presence or absence of free will.[79] Because the private sphere was comprised of autonomous individual subjects freely entering into relationships with one another, the government was not authorized to intercede on behalf of private parties in the absence of evidence of coercion or duress.[80]

Peller demonstrated how the public/private dichotomy in the Supreme Court's liberty of contract doctrine was socially constructed. The public/ private dichotomy and its attendant manifestations of private rights were assumed to be self-evident, when in fact they were actually judicial or "public" creations. Peller argues that there is no objective reference point autonomous from culture and politics to enable modern legal scholars to distinguish truth from ideology, fact from opinion, or representation from interpretation. For Peller, however, social construction helps to remind us that our rational vision of law functions like a text; legal meaning is not based on human nature as it really is, but rather on an interpretation of human nature, a metaphor, a privileging.

Deconstruction and social construction practice motivated CLS scholars to reject essentialist-like claims based on the idea of a fundamental contradiction because the very idea of a fundamental contradiction can itself be deconstructed. What seems fundamental may be peculiar to a particular social construction of legal doctrine. Social phenomena are too complex and confusing to be explained by a fundamental contradiction. Hence, while early CLS scholarship attempted to produce elegant maps of the fault lines along which the fundamental contradictions of American law were organized, CLS deconstructionalists argued that modern legal theory is merely part of a larger belief system that is too complex and flexible to permit any conclusions based on a privileged structuralist's account of legal doctrine.

Another interesting example highlighting the shift in the scholarly practice of CLS is Peter Gabel and Duncan Kennedy's article, *Roll Over Beethoven*,[81] which appeared in a widely read symposium on CLS published by the STANFORD LAW REVIEW in 1984. It was in this article that Duncan Kennedy recanted his own theory of "fundamental contradiction." What is significant about *Roll Over Beethoven*, however, is the style and manner in which the piece was presented.[82] *Roll Over Beethoven* is not really an article, but rather a self-conscious dialogue between "Peter" and "Duncan" on the role of theory in the CLS movement. The conversational tone of the article reads like actual dialogue between two people intimately engaged in intellectual discourse. The authors explore how their own subjective understanding about the law has been constituted and shaped by critical legal theory. The authors argue with each other about the meaningfulness of their theoretical practices, and they reveal to the reader their fears and vulnerabilities in attempting to advance progressive ideas about law. In *Roll Over Beethoven*, the law is understood to be a social construction of legal subjects; the authors do not hide behind the veil of a relatively autonomous subject (author). In this sense, the piece represents a critical counterpoint to the type of scholarly dialogue engaged by the Wechslerian generation.

The political significance of *Roll Over Beethoven* can be judged by the effect it had on its audience. It has been reported that one "well-known professor was so upset when Kennedy presented *Roll Over Beethoven* at the Columbia Legal Theory Workshop, that he totaled his car on the way home."[83] Another law professor, David Luban of the University of Maryland School of Law, admitted that his "initial reaction" to the piece was that it was a "pile of crap."[84] These reactions illustrate how the second generation of CLS scholarship is now perceived as even more radical and dangerous than the first. As Luban acknowledged, *Roll Over Beethoven* begins to change the whole way we think of a scholarly article. The piece "keeps working on you after you have set it aside."[85]

## Late-1980s Critical Legal Studies

By the late 1980s, CLS provoked heated debate and controversy in the legal academy. The phenomenon of CLS trashing was seen by traditional legal scholars as an irresponsible tendency to critique for critique's sake.[86] Both liberals and conservatives found CLS politically unappealing because it offered criticism but no vision for replacing what was rejected.[87] For some, CLS was merely a form of legal nihilism.[88] For others, CLS's "central failing" was the "banal" and "irrelevant" insight that the law is but "a mass of contradiction."[89]

CLS deconstructionists were tagged as *legal nihilists* because they were understood by modern legal scholars as rejecting the belief in shared standards of rationality or shared values.[90] Crits are said to be nihilists because they accuse liberal scholars of believing in false essences and fail to offer anything positive or constructive in the process of criticizing modern legal thought.[91] Legal moderns assert that Crits should first develop a normative vision of the law before they trash the normative vision of liberal legalism. The word "nihilist" has thus been used to refer to different arguments raised in objection to the deconstructionalists or irrationalists. Legal nihilism has become a red flag for labeling the negative sensibilities of postmodern practice of second-generation CLS scholars.

For Crits, the fears of legal nihilism are more like a smoke screen to cut off debate than a plea for cogency in legal analysis.[92] If anything, CLS deconstructive practice was highly cogent in its effort to show how modern legal doctrine itself failed to support cogent analysis in the law. Crits debate among themselves about modern and postmodern strategies generally, and they were highly sensitive to the perceived weaknesses of deconstruction practice.[93] Nihilism-fear (the fear of the abyss resulting after radical deconstruction) may well be a manifestation of legal modernists' "Cartesian anxiety."[94] *Nihilism-fear* is an anxiety arising whenever legal criticism fails to support the belief in a fixed foundation for legal analysis. It is generated by the legal modernist's general reaction to nonliberal, that is, nontraditional, forms of legal criticism. Crits argue that nihilism-fear is a "linguistic marker for a sort of free-floating and diffuse orthodox fear of difference, a fear of otherness."[95] CLS criticism is said to be nihilistic because it leads them to resist and ultimately reject the normative visions of law and conceptual approaches of liberal legal scholars. What is amazing is that of all the different legal perspectives currently in the law, CLS is by far one of the most politically committed and optimistic perspectives available. The "nihilism" label attributed to CLS scholarship is thus totally inappropriate; Crits exhibited an extraordinary degree of belief and political passion in their work. The anarchist tendencies of some CLS work do not mean that it was nihilistic; anarchism is very different from nihilism. And there were very few anarchist tendencies within the CLS movement.

The criticism that CLS insights are "banal" or "irrelevant" fails to engage the theoretical insights of CLS criticism. The driving force behind the intellectual critiques of CLS developed from an argument that the political viewpoints in the law, from liberal to conservative, represent an ideology that was characteristic of modern Western thought. CLS political deconstruction practice attempted to unpack the structures of this ideology to show how those structures reproduced and reinforced a general ideological system based on the belief in false essences. Crits argued that the presence of contradiction in legal thought is "banal" only if it is assumed that contradiction is natural, organic, or predetermined. The reproduction of particular argumentative oppositions within doctrinal structures of the law, what Crits call "nesting," are said to give the logic of the system the appearance of coherence and closure.[96] CLS scholars argue that the unpacking of doctrinal nesting in the structures of legal argument is the first step toward social transformation. Their overall goal is to open up space to think and act in order to foster political energy for engaging in a more robust opposition at the academy—hardly a banal endeavor.

It is difficult to find anyone in CLS who believes that all law is indeterminate; even Duncan Kennedy has renounced the idea of fundamental contradiction.[97] One problem was that the fundamental contradiction thesis was leading the movement down the wrong road. Legal theorists, opposed to the CLS political agenda, might invoke CLS scholarship as an excuse for gradualism and restraint. Why should we do anything about law's problems if every reform program is founded upon a theory of contradictory and indeterminate rights? The main problem with the idea of fundamental contradiction was that it promoted the type of "philosophical" abstraction in law that CLS was trying to avoid.[98] CLS was becoming like a "normal science" and Crits resisted the normalization and institutionalization of their movement. Like the law and efficiency thesis of law and economics scholars, CLS practitioners viewed the fundamental contradiction thesis as merely a beginning for progressive legal analysis.[99]

The move from the structuralist approaches of the early 1980s to the poststructuralism of the late 1980s marked a shift in the politics of the social movement known as the *Conference on Critical Legal Studies*. By the mid-1980s, conference activities became diffused and fragmented. As the movement expanded, subgroups within CLS emerged, the most important being the Fem-Crits and the critical race scholars.[100] Symposia were organized around feminism and race theories, and the Conference expanded its membership to include other marginalized groups within the legal academy seeking progressive alternatives to the traditional modes of legal thought. However, the phenomena of "groupism" provoked internal challenges and degrees of diversity within the movement.[101] The splintering of meetings into different groups made it difficult for the movement to advance a common position necessary for successful progressive strategies. Moreover, fragmentation gave way to the formation of new critical intersectional interests between groups, resulting in the formation of new subgroups. CLS conferences were organized around themes that focused on the importance of promoting group identity and group diversity in law and legal education, but fragmentation and diversity made it difficult for CLS to effectively organize.[102]

By the late 1980s, CLS scholars deemphasized the indeterminacy thesis in their work and instead focused on how identity issues, such as race, gender, and sexuality, help to construct legal values and practices. Second-generation CLS scholars advanced a social construction thesis that attempted to reveal how various legal categories were constructed by judges and legislatures from their understanding of a universal subject as white, male, and middle-class.[103] This thesis was advanced to undermine claims that categories such as law/culture are natural or essential, and to explain how legal meaning reflects and reproduces the *ideology of the subject*.

CLS scholars now argue that the various left, liberal, and right-wing positions on the supposed determinacy or indeterminacy of the law are the products of highly contested interpretations based on the belief in an autonomous legal subject. A new type of postmodern identity politics has surfaced within CLS scholarship, exhibiting a postmodern perspective that focuses attention on the role and responsibility of interpreting legal subjects in the reproduction and maintenance of the legitimating rhetorical structures of *American Legal Thought*.[104] *Postmodern critical legal studies* scholars resist all tendencies to locate progressive legal criticism in some authoritarian practice, theory, or interpretation. Instead, they argue for a more self-conscious and reflective attitude in accepting the limitations and pitfalls of theoretical perspectives. These postmodern critics claim that modern legal analysts are prisoners to the perspective they bring to law, and that there is no place "outside" that perspective from which they can gain an unbiased vantage point for political or intellectual analysis.

The liberating energies of early CLS politics seemed to have dissipated by the end of the decade. Several explanations for the recent dispersion of CLS energies can be identified. CLS always lacked a central organization, because it has been a type of syndicalist movement that depended on individual initiative rather than a top-down governing structure. Syndicalism may not be the most efficient structure for sustaining progressive movements. An exchange between two well-known Crits, Mark Tushnet and Gary Peller, in a recent GEORGETOWN LAW JOURNAL,[105] illustrates that CLS is also enmeshed in generational conflict between the first and second generations of CLS scholars. The mid-1980s shift in CLS methodology to deconstruction and poststructuralist approaches alienated a number of older progressive legal thinkers.[106] The dominance of deconstruction left little room for progressives to argue for grand theories of legal reform. Because deconstruction does not postulate a political agenda, some fear that the values of postmodern politics will fail to sustain new social movements like CLS.[107]

However, despite heated opposition, controversy, and well-publicized denials of tenure to a handful of well-known legal academics associated with CLS,[108] CLS enjoyed considerable visibility and popularity throughout the 1980s. There are now a number of legal academics of national reputation who publicly identify themselves as Crits. The number of Crits and "fellow travelers" (people who have participated in CLS events but who would not regard themselves as Crits) has grown, albeit at a steadily declining rate in recent years. The fact that the literature on critical legal studies shaped the intellectual agenda for legal theory throughout the 1980s is evidence of the continuing appeal of CLS.[109] Many legal scholars regard CLS as offering valuable insights about the nature of law and adjudication. The continuing influence of CLS, however, is mainly felt in the world of legal scholarship. Much of the CLS critique remains, to this day, unanswered. It rests in the pages of the law reviews, like the works of the legal realists; a critical project ready to be taken up by the next generation.

# 7. Feminist Legal Theory

In the late 1970s, a powerful new theory of jurisprudence also emerged offering a distinctively feminist perspective on law and adjudication. Feminist jurisprudence grew out of the feminist liberation movement of the 1960s, as feminists critiqued law and society from a woman's perspective. There are a number of stereotypes and misconceptions about what it means to be a *feminist*. As Leslie Bender explained: "Feminists are portrayed as bra-burners, man-haters, sexists, and castrators. . . . We are characterized as bitchy, demanding, aggressive, confrontational, and uncooperative, as well as overly sensitive and humorless. No wonder many women, particularly many career women, struggle to distance themselves from the opprobrium appended to the label."[1]

Certainly more than misinformed stereotypes and offhand generalizations are needed to assess the ideas of the feminist movement. There are many types of feminists, but all feminists adhere to two basic positions: first, that society is shaped and dominated by men and is therefore *patriarchal*; and second, that society *subordinates* women to men.[2] Using these two basic ideas, feminists have examined American law and concluded that it too is patriarchal and gender-prioritized in favor of men. Feminists have taken these two positions into their feminist scholarship in developing a feminist-based critique of American law.

American judges have historically relied on assumptions about gender that reflected and reinforced patriarchal values in legal decision making, which feminists claim have justified legal forms of gender inequality.[3] Assumptions about women's roles, in particular the primary responsibility of women for bearing and rearing children, have historically justified legal exclusion of women from the public sphere of society.[4] These assumptions denied women many important political and economic opportunities. At early common law, married women were denied the right to own or convey property, to retain their own wages, enter contracts, or initiate legal claims.[5] By challenging such restrictions, and the legal assumptions that reinforced gender inequality, advocates of women's rights laid the foundation for the legal feminist movement. Legal feminists argue that law and culture, not nature, have put women in a "private sphere" of domesticity, making women economically dependent on men.

During the 1960s and 1970s, demands for gender equality were fueled by women's increased need for economic independence and equal opportunity.[6] The development of oral contraceptives and the astronomical increase in the divorce rate meant that a substantial percentage of American women were choosing professional careers and independent living arrangements.[7] The sexual revolution of the 1960s also transformed rigid sexual stereotypes that previously restricted the personal freedom of many women.[8] A growing number of women expressed their frustrations in consciousness-raising groups and feminist publications. What Betty Friedan called "the problem [that] has no name" was gaining recognition and claiming a name—the feminist movement.[9]

In response to these social forces, feminists working in the law developed legal strategies designed to protect women from gender inequality reinforced through the law. The early focus of such work was to give greater recognition to the cause of women's rights: to expand reproductive freedom, to eliminate sex-based discrimination in employment, education, family, and other contexts, and to deter sexual abuse generally. In doing so, women's rights advocates developed feminist legal theories to "challenge unequal opportunities and the ideology that had legitimated them."[10] The feminist legal theory movement emerged from the development of a women-based theory of law.

The first published use of the phrase "feminist jurisprudence" occurred in 1978 when Professor Ann Scales published an article called *Toward a Feminist Jurisprudence.*[11] Feminist legal theory is diverse, and anything but monolithic. Many feminists believe that it is difficult to generalize about feminist jurisprudence.[12] It is, however, possible to understand feminist legal theory as a reaction to the jurisprudence of modern legal scholars (primarily male scholars) who tend to see law as a process for interpreting and perpetuating a universal, gender-neutral public morality.[13] Feminist legal scholars, despite their differences, appear united in claiming that "masculine" jurisprudence of "all stripes" fails to acknowledge, let alone respond to, the interests, values, fears, and harms experienced by women.[14] The jurisprudence of this movement is unique to the law—it challenges traditional attitudes and beliefs about gender, which are said to be basic to professional legal discourse. Yet feminists are deeply divided by sharp differences in method, approach, and perspective.

During much of the 1970s and 1980s, for example, feminists argued about whether women should be legally treated the same as men or different from men. Considerable intellectual energy and ink were devoted to this "sameness/difference" or "equal treatment/special treatment" debate. Employing phrases like "the equality trap," some legal feminists argued that the inequality of women in the law was the result of the romantic paternalism of men who accorded women different legal treatment. Feminists thus argued that women should seek formal equality with men by eliminating gender-based rules that treat women differently. Others argued that because women *are* different from men, women should sometimes be accorded "more than equal treatment." [15]

The "sameness/difference" debate placed legal feminists within a "double bind" created by "the old dream of symmetry" [16] which historically required women to prove that they were like men. The double bind was that women could claim legal protection only by comparing their experiences to the universal experiences of men. Since neither "equal" nor "special" treatment effectively erodes male-oriented gender hierarchy, the sameness/difference debate functioned to encourage women to meet the male norms, without questioning why the masculine norms set the benchmark for equality analysis.[17]

In response to the dilemma of the sameness/difference debate, feminists sought to develop a distinctive feminist jurisprudence "built upon feminist insights into women's true nature, rather than upon masculine insights into 'human nature.' " [18] Some believe, however, that a feminist jurisprudence is a "political impossibility" as long as it fails to incorporate the feminist method of taking women's humanity seriously.[19] If there is a "feminist method" to be described, it is the "method of consciousness raising—personal reporting of experience in [a] communal setting to explore what has not been said."[20] The methodology of consciousness-raising has caused feminists to rely on experiential discourse in their legal criticism to validate the experiences of women. Feminists claim that the "evidence" in support of their theory is based on proof that is "experientially felt and material based."[21] As feminist legal theorist Ann Scales explained, "Feminist method proceeds through consciousness raising."[22] The idea of consciousness raising establishes the epistemological framework feminists use to express and validate the experiences of women, and to expose how the content of those experiences has been invalidated in the law.

As part of their consciousness critique, some feminists have developed a *hedonic* jurisprudence that speaks directly to the "oppressed, dominated and devalued" experiences of women.[23] These feminist theorists use experientially based narratives and stories of personal experiences, from rape to spousal battery, to advance substantive messages about hedonic values of women in order to explain how women experience gender inequality and sexual abuse.[24] Hedonic feminists do more than just describe and imagine what it is like to be oppressed—they report actual experiences. They emphasize that their method is aimed at explaining "attributes historically linked to women."[25] The objective of such work is to explain how the law subordinates women. The experiential point of view is used to discover women's authentic sexuality and the reality of their condition. Following Michel Foucault's critical insight that "power comes from everywhere,"[26] legal feminists argue that the power of patriarchy is "everywhere."

Feminist legal discourse challenges the various ways in which modern legal discourse favors masculine ways of knowing.[27] Feminists contend that modern modes of jurisprudence are masculine in character, and that the way to challenge the dominance of masculine jurisprudence is to develop an alternative hedonic jurisprudence based on women's experience. Feminist legal theorists use narratives based on personal experiences to present alternative ways for understanding why women's interests and ways of knowing are ignored by modern discourse, and why they "should occupy a respected, or in some cases a privileged position, in [legal] analysis and argumentation."[28] As Kathryn Abrams explained: "Most feminist narrative scholars start from a few shared premises: a preference for particularity of description, a belief that describing events or activities 'from the inside'—that is, from the perspective of a person going through them—convey[s] a unique vividness of detail that can be instructive to [legal] decisionmakers."[29] By acting on their feminist premises, feminists seek to provoke a jurisprudential debate about the gender of law.[30] The goal is to challenge dominant legal categories and theories, to capture and report on the complexity of gender oppression, and offer new substantive proposals for law reform.[31]

In offering an alternative feminist jurisprudence, feminists have debated questions about "method, knowledge, and critique."[32] These questions challenged a number of core assumptions dealing with the nature of truth, justification, knowledge, and normativity that define the various projects of seemingly modern jurisprudence. By challenging the modernist stance on these topics, feminist legal theory positioned itself as an oppositional movement that questioned the modes, manners, and methods of modern jurisprudence. From the feminist perspective, the legal tradition of modern jurisprudence had an inevitable historical record of unearned gender privilege.[33]

The feminist legal movement can be viewed as a reaction to legal modernism. Feminists view the twin goals of legal modernity—scientific objectivity and instrumental rationality[34]—as the legitimating props of male dominance. Feminists claim to have discerned a "sense of the historical connection between *rationalist ideals* and the belief in a *hierarchical opposition of 'mind' and 'nature'* which has equated human freedom with an objective and universal male perspective."[35] They struggle against the legal modernists' ideas of rationality, objectivity, and the universal concept of self. Contextuality, subjectivism, and difference have become feminist methods used to challenge modernist assumptions about knowledge, language, and the nature of criticism.

Feminist legal thinkers question legal moderns' belief in foundational legal methods for discovering knowledge about law. Feminists emphasize the importance of telling different stories in the law to create new legal understandings about women. As Robin West, a feminist legal scholar at Georgetown Law Center, put it: "We need to flood the market with our own stories until we get one simple point across: men's narrative story and phenomenological description of law is not women's story and phenomenology of law."[36]

In rejecting the legal modernist's belief that the language of law expresses a universal discourse for men and women, feminists assert that a discourse must be developed within law to prevent the alleged masculine discourse of jurisprudence from suppressing the interests and experiences of women. Feminists consequently attempt to decode the "language of domesticity," embedded within law's distinctively modern discourse, to enable women to speak with their own voice.[37] Feminists claim to have discovered a new epistemology of law based on knowledge acquired from the "different voice" and "different ways of knowing" developed from the feminist discourse.

The feminist legal movement appears to be developing a form of jurisprudence that rivals the conceptual and normative forms of modern jurisprudence, as well as all critical forms that fail to take account of gender. In marked contrast to the legal modernist's faith in objective theory, or the critical theorist's emphasis on "ideology," feminists claim that there exists a "nonlingual" and "nonrational" way of understanding women's humanity. As Robin West explained, an "intersubjective sensitivity to the needs of others" is what distinguishes legal feminist theory from Enlightenment modernism and post-Enlightenment critical social theory.[38] The female "experience of nurturance," based on biological materialism, is said to give feminist legal theory its unique character. Feminists assert that "women" know that there is a nonlingual domestic world of human needs that compel fulfillment—"a world of bodies, of babies, of babies sucking milk, of babies' shit, of babies' sleeplessness, of children, of children's needs, of children's appetite—lurking beneath"[39] the objective world of men.

In some respects, however, early legal feminist thought was a typically *modern* movement.[40] Feminists advanced the project of modernity in their attempt to construct a feminist jurisprudence untainted by the patriarchal tradition of jurisprudence. Feminists seemingly embraced the project of modernity in their effort to make law more pure by purging its discourse of the biases and oppression of illegitimate gender hierarchies.[41] This effort committed feminist scholars to the Enlightenment project of modernity. Feminist legal scholars sought to develop a new unitary theory of law based on the "essential" experience of women theorists. Feminist legal scholarship developing within the early 1980s consequently illustrates how the stylistic forms of legal modernism influenced and problematized the development of the early "schools" or "theories" of feminist jurisprudence.

## Early 1980s Legal Feminist Scholarship

In the early 1980s, feminist legal theorists presented three different "schools" of *modern* feminist jurisprudence: *liberal feminism, cultural feminism,* and *radical feminism.*[42] These three schools of feminist legal thought worked together to establish a modern feminist jurisprudence aimed at uncovering the position of women in a patriarchal legal system. Although the three feminist "schools" presented fundamentally different feminist methodologies for analyzing law, they were united in their common effort to expose the various ways that law perpetuates gender hierarchy.

The *liberal strand* of feminist legal thought is associated with the work of liberal legal scholars who focus on women's legal rights. Liberal feminists are united by their commitment to formal equality as symbolized by the Equal Rights Amendment and the civil rights movement. One group of liberal feminists is called "symmetrical feminists" because they argue that men and women should be treated alike and should be permitted to compete on equal terms in the public world.[43] These liberal feminists seek to narrow the different treatment accorded to men and women under various gender-based distinctions recognized in the law. They advocate an equal treatment approach that challenges "the assumptions of female inferiority—the belief that women fall too short of the unstated male norm to enjoy male privileges or benefits inappropriate for them."[44] Professor Wendy Williams of Georgetown Law Center captured the essence of the credo of these liberal feminists with her slogan: "[W]e can't have it both ways, [so] we need to think carefully about which way we want to have it."[45] Liberal feminists who choose the equal treatment approach demand equal symmetry under the law; they "fight for the equal rights and respect that sameness demands."[46]

Other liberal feminists focus on gender differences to expose male dominance and to establish a new legal paradigm that promotes women's rights. These liberal feminist legal scholars argue that the current application of "equal treatment" theory prevents the pursuit of equality under the law and hinders the attainment of meaningful freedom for women, because it treats gender differences in ways that sustain gender hierarchy between the sexes.[47] They thus defend "difference" as a basis for advocating *special treatment,* arguing that women deserve special benefits because they are different from men.[48]

Martha Minow provided a version of the *difference* approach, focusing on the value of difference and arguing for the creation of a new comprehensive discourse committed to the feminist goal of thoughtfully considering all minority perspectives.[49] Taking minority perspectives seriously calls "for a process of dialogue in which the listener actually tries to reach beyond the assumptions of one reality, one version of the truth."[50] A debate exists within the liberal camp of feminists, however, as to whether women should be treated the same or different than men. This is known as the "sameness-difference" debate.

The *cultural feminist,* or "different voice" strand of feminist legal thought, is associated with the path-breaking scholarship of feminist Carol Gilligan, a psychologist at Harvard University specializing in child development.[51] Gilligan's "different voice" perspective asserts that "there is a distinctively feminine way of approaching moral and legal dilemmas [that has] been ignored or downplayed in legal doctrine and scholarship."[52] The goal of her project was to expose the gender biases in the work of child psychologists who relied mainly on masculine values to explain the psychological development of children.[53]

Gilligan's research has been called a "status report"[54] on feminist ideology because feminists view her analysis as demonstrating the psychological dynamic of gender hierarchy.[55] One of Gilligan's major findings is that "femininity" reflects an "ideology of domesticity," which views "motherhood as the central and defining female role, the mother as nutrient and empathic."[56] Feminists who advocate Gilligan's "different voice" perspective are thus called "cultural feminists," because they tend to equate women's liberation with the development and maintenance of a female-centered counterculture. Cultural feminists differ from liberal feminists in emphasizing women's fundamental differences from men—women raise children and men do not.[57] Cultural feminists claim that "women are more nurturing, caring, loving, and responsible to others than are men."[58]

One way to understand this strand of feminist legal thought is to consider the images of "hierarchy" and "the web" in Gilligan's classic study of the responses of two eleven-year-old children who participated in a moral development problem, that is, the "Heinz dilemma" devised by psychologist Lawrence Kohlberg. Two children, Jake and Amy, were presented with the following dilemma: "[A] man named Heinz considers whether or not to steal a drug which he cannot afford to buy in order to save the life of his wife."[59] The children were told that Heinz does not have the money for the drug and the druggist refuses to give him the drug without payment. The question posed was "should Heinz steal the drug?"[60] Jake responded that Heinz should steal the drug because "human life is worth more than money."[61] Gilligan reported that Jake approached the problem as "sort of like a math problem with humans."[62] He treated the problem as an algebraic equation and proceeded to work out the solution. Jake's reasoning process was based on rational deduction, or what Gilligan called "a hierarchical ordering" of values.[63]

Amy, on the other hand, responded differently, using a different reasoning process. Gilligan reported that Amy felt that Heinz "shouldn't steal the drug" *and* that "his wife shouldn't die either."[64] Instead of searching for a correct answer based upon a hierarchy of values, Amy saw the dilemma "not as a math problem with humans but as a narrative of relationships that extended over time."[65] Thus, Amy suggested that there might be other ways besides stealing: "Heinz could talk to the druggist to explain his wife's situation and perhaps borrow the money or make a loan or something" to get the drug.[66] In an attempt to resolve the dilemma in a way that emphasizes the relationship involved, Amy rejected the idea that Heinz should steal the drug, because "[i]f he stole the drug, he might save his wife then, but if he did, he might have to go to jail, and then his wife might get sicker again, and he couldn't get more of the drug, and it might not be good."[67] Ultimately, Amy concluded that "they [Heinz, the druggist, and the wife] should really just talk it out and find some other way to make the money."[68]

Gilligan demonstrated that Amy's approach to the moral dilemma was based on a very different way of looking at the world—a way that conformed to women's experiences and images of relationships. Gilligan called this experience the image of the web. "[S]eeing a world comprised of relationships rather than of people standing alone, a world that coheres through human connection rather than through systems of rules, [Amy] finds the puzzle in the dilemma to lie in the failure of the druggist to respond to the wife."[69] According to Gilligan, "Both children thus recognize the need for agreement but see it as mediated in different ways—[Jake] impersonally through systems of logic and law, [Amy] personally through communication in relationships."[70] Gilligan used the image of a hierarchy to describe the perspective of Jake (the experience of males), and the connection of the web to describe the perspective of Amy (the experience of females). These images were used to criticize the view of traditional psychologists who assumed that Jake's response to the problem reflected a "higher stage" of moral development.[71]

Cultural feminists, who follow the *different voice* strand of feminist legal theory, use these images to show how Jake's image of hierarchy is the dominant image embedded within liberal theories of the law, and how Amy's image of the web is a strong counterideology that has been marginalized or excluded. Cultural feminists argue that the "woman's voice," missing in the traditional discourse of law, must be reconstructed in order for law to explicitly take into account feminine values of relationships and connections, or what Gilligan calls the "ethic of care."[72] This theoretical orientation motivates cultural feminists to support liberal reform measures, such as mandatory child-raising leaves and pregnancy protection laws, aligning them with liberal feminists on many legal issues.

Recently, Gilligan's work was the subject of empirical controversy causing some to doubt the empirical basis of her claims.[73] Gilligan herself has rejected essentialist claims about the differences between men and women that others drew from her early work.[74] Some recently claimed that there is a great overlap in the way males and females reason on moral issues.[75] Detractors who claim lack of empirical support for Gilligan's original findings, however, have assumed that feminist scholarship should be judged by traditional objective standards. Gilligan's book is viewed by cultural feminists as embracing an experiential or material explanation of women's difference. These "[m]aterial explanations require a willingness to engage in a form of speculative inquiry which is contrary to now dominant academic modes of proof."[76] For many legal feminists, the moral difference between men and women reflected in Gilligan's work "feels" right.

The third strand of feminist legal thought is *radical* feminism. This strand is frequently associated with the "dominance" approach of Catharine MacKinnon, a well-known feminist at the University of Michigan Law School. MacKinnon claims that gender inequality in law is not the result of irrational discrimination, but rather the result of the systematic social subordination of women.[77] She argues that gender hierarchy and sexual domination between men and women are taken as unobjectionable, natural, and even "intrinsic" to traditional gender roles.[78] MacKinnon seeks to develop the idea that sexuality was socially constructed by men to establish *gender* hierarchy. She considers heterosexuality to be the product of a culture controlled by men to protect male domination. MacKinnon argues that "[b]ecause the inequality of the sexes is socially defined as the enjoyment of sexuality itself, gender inequality appears consensual."[79] Thus, MacKinnon claims that women who find pleasure within heterosexuality find pleasure in their own subordination. This critique of heterosexuality became fashionable throughout the 1980s.

MacKinnon believes that "[g]ender neutrality is thus simply the male standard, and the special protection rule is simply the female standard, but do not be deceived: masculinity, or maleness, is the reference for both."[80] She views gender as a power issue, "specifically of male supremacy and female subordination," and sexual abuse is the "product of women's subordination in society."[81] In defining the dominance approach, MacKinnon asserts:

The goal of this dissident approach is not to make legal categories trace and trap the way things are. It is not to make rules that fit reality. It is critical of reality. Its task is not to formulate abstract standards that will produce determinant outcomes in particular cases. Its project is more substantive, more jurisprudential than formulas, which is why it is difficult for the mainstream discourse to dignify it as an approach to doctrine or to imagine it as a rule of law at all. It proposes to expose that which women have had little choice but to be confined to, in order to change it.[82]

Like cultural and some liberal feminists, radical feminists emphasize the differences between women and men. The most important difference is that women are "those from whom sex is taken," just as "workers, definitionally, are those from whom labor is taken."[83] A more explicit description by radical feminists is that "women get fucked and men fuck." The radical feminist categories of "sex-class" are vulnerable to the type of criticism raised to criticize the cultural feminist category of "woman's experience"—both are steeped in feminist essentialism about the true difference between men and women.[84] The radical feminists' critique of heterosexuality, however, has not been widely accepted because it seems false to many women who find pleasure and connection within fulfilling, heterosexual relationships.[85]

Throughout the 1980s, these three schools of feminist thought developed new insights for understanding how prevailing jurisprudential notions of American law deny women the opportunity to compete on equal terms with men. Feminist legal scholars sought to reveal how law has adopted a conception of human nature that uses "male as the reference point and treat[s] women as 'other,' 'different,' 'deviant,' 'exceptional,' or 'baffling.' "[86] Liberal and cultural feminists argue that the prevailing legal concept of law is based on a male perspective that fails to recognize the "female voice"—the way women approach moral and legal issues. Radical feminists argue that mainstream conceptions of law reflect social practices and structures that subordinate women; for example, that sexual harassment and pornography are forms of sex discrimination, which reflect socially constructed practices that are highly destructive to women.[87]

The three schools of legal feminist thought initially stood in a paradoxical position to legal modernism. On the one hand, all three schools seemed to use the conceptual framework of legal modernism in asserting a universal feminist perspective for discovering the essential truth of feminism.[88] The work of early feminists seemed to assert essentialist claims about the nature of women or the universal oppression women experience at the hands of men. This opened feminists to the criticism that they had failed to escape the influence of modern jurisprudence which feminists associated with masculine forms of legal discourse. The assertion of an authentic "woman's voice" or "different voice" or "lesbian voice" or "blackwoman's voice" was not unlike the assertion of one "true rule of law" of modern masculine liberal discourse. Thus, early legal feminist scholarship could be seen as furthering the spirit of Enlightenment—the perfection of yet another universal moral and intellectual understanding of "human reason."

On the other hand, all three schools of early feminist jurisprudence resisted modern forms of jurisprudence by emphasizing the importance of telling the woman's story—what it feels like to be a woman living in a legal and social world defined and manipulated by male attitudes and experiences. Feminists were united from the outset by their resistance to the way legal moderns tended to universalize the legal conception of the individual in legal analysis. The concept of the individual "self" used in modern legal theory was presumed to be "any" individual. Men and women were treated alike because legal moderns assumed that any individual was as competent as any other to control his/her fate and exercise free will.

Feminist jurisprudence reacted against modern jurisprudence by showing how the individual voice of modern legal theory was really a male voice that spoke the language of patriarchy. Feminist legal theorists consequently offered alternative stories to reveal the gender bias of law, and to expose how legal rhetoric of free choice and autonomy ignored other experiences and other knowledges. In providing a feminist view of rights, feminists focus on the values of love, equality, fairness, and intimacy. Their objective is to "reveal how traditional jurisprudence and the legal hierarchy protect and define men, not women."

Feminist legal practitioners have, however, taken a paradoxical stance in relation to modern jurisprudence. This paradox is illustrated by the conflicting position that legal feminists have taken about whether or not women should seek protection through "legal rights." Some feminists argue that feminist jurisprudence requires the recognition of a feminist concept of rights—a concept that can provide effective remedies for the specific harms experienced by women. This perspective remains wedded to the modernists' belief in true essences. Other feminist thinkers, however, believe that the type of feminist practice necessary to protect women's interests requires a "rich, contextual thinking" denied by a nontraditional notion of legal rights. These feminists argue that it would be even better if "liberal-talk" about rights protected women as well as men against the dangers that characterize their lives.[89] By remaining steadfast in their desire to establish a feminist discourse of law, these feminists positioned themselves in the role of a critic seeking to expose the gender implications of law's discourse. This role has enabled the feminist movement in its early stages of development to maintain its autonomy from modern jurisprudence. On the other hand, by focusing exclusively on the experience of gender, feminist legal thinkers have failed to totally escape the modernist rhetoric of objectivity, truth, and knowledge. And therein lies a paradox for the feminist legal movement.

By the mid-1980s, the feminist movement had established itself within the critical legal studies movement. These feminists, known as *Fem-Crits*, organized and encouraged the creation of a "feminist" perspective within the critical legal studies movement, to advance a political critique of modern liberal forms of jurisprudence based on feminist theory.[90] The affinity between CLS and the legal feminist movement developed from the fact that both movements share an "outsider's status" vis-à-vis modern jurisprudence. The Fem-Crits' feminist perspective diverges from the political power perspective of the first generation of CLS. Fem-

Crits claim that patriarchy is the source of law's ideology; whereas Crits argued that it is hierarchical structures of power that determine law's politics.[91] The crucial difference is that the Fem-Crits emphasized the subjective perspective of women to analyze social structures, gender hierarchy, and sexual objectification missing in the early work of CLS scholars. The CLS critique is said to be a "male-constructed" form of leftist criticism "in which domination and oppression can be described and imagined but not fully experienced."[92] Hence, while CLS critics argued that "law is politics," the Fem-Crits asserted that "law is *sexual* politics."

Fem-Crit criticism has now established a strong feminist presence within CLS. Fem-Crits have focused on a variety of legal problems. They analyzed laws relevant to rape, sexual assault, battery, and self-defense; antidiscrimination legislation applicable to the workplace, education, or housing; reproductive-freedom issues; military combat exclusion policies; family issues involving divorce, custody, and property divisions; and constitutional issues like equality, pornography, and hate speech.[93] Fem-Crits have advanced theories about inclusion, difference, and community, and relate how feminist theories apply to contemporary legal thought.

Instead of merely seeking to describe reality or to disagree with the way other legal scholars see reality, feminist scholarship, attempted to change reality by transforming the way legal academics understand reality. In developing a feminist perspective of law and jurisprudence, however, feminist scholars used the framework of legal modernism to question the dominant practices and methods used by traditional scholars for reading and understanding law. Feminists argued that meaning and interpretation should be examined against a background of interpretative assumptions that employ the "feminist" perspective as the reference point. These scholars claimed to have discovered a new universal norm and evidentiary criteria for evaluating the gender bias of law.

## Late 1980s Legal Feminist Scholarship

A late-emerging stage of legal feminism, *postmodern feminism*, appears to have broken free of legal modernism by challenging notions of objectivity and claims of universality and essentialism in modern feminist scholarship.[94] Postmodern feminists emphasize the importance of understanding how legal language constructs the law's understanding of gender and sexual equality based on contestable assumptions about gender and sexuality. As the late Mary Joe Frug[95] explained: "The postmodern position locating human experience as inescapably within language suggests that feminists should not overlook the constructive function of legal language as a critical frontier for feminist reforms. To put this 'principle' more bluntly, legal discourse should be recognized as a site of political struggle over sex differences."[96] This feminist perspective of modern feminists attempts to avoid the mistakes of the essentialism and universalism of early feminists' work. The late-1980s strategy seemed to be aimed at bringing feminism and postmodernism together to create a "postmodernist feminism."[97]

Postmodern feminism uses critical interpretive strategies to break down the credibility of essentialist claims and the universal categories on which these claims rest. Postmodern feminists use deconstructive strategies in their work to show how modern forms of jurisprudence celebrate masculine interests and values at the expense of those associated with the "difference voice" of women. Joan Williams, a feminist at American University, used Jacques Derrida's notion of the "dangerous supplement" to reveal how the "ideology of conventional femininity (what historians term the ideology of domesticity)" supplements "the strain of mainstream liberalism that enshrines the importance of self-interest."[98] Williams illustrated how these two ideologies are complementary and mutually exclusive: domesticity contrasts women's selflessness with men's pursuit of self-interest, and women's focus on humane values is pitted against men's ambition.

Drawing from Derrida's deconstruction practice, Williams argues that masculine values associated with mainstream liberalism "set the standard"[99] by which the feminine values of domesticity are measured. Williams explains that "Derrida's formulation [of the dangerous supplement] reminds us that subservient "feminine values have the potential to well up and destabilize the group of the dominant liberal ones."[100] She uses deconstructive strategies to show how Gilligan's book, IN A DIFFERENT VOICE, can be read from a postmodern perspective:[101]

Gilligan's book, and recent work in women's history, suggests that domesticity acts as the "dangerous supplement" of mainstream liberal ideology. . . . Gilligan's work demonstrates the neatly matched binary opposites integral to the covert gendering of the liberal pursuit of autonomy. One key dichotomy is between personal affiliation and achievement. While these attributes are not *necessarily* mutually exclusive (how many people advance without interpersonal skills?), the domesticity/liberalism force field formulates affiliation and achievement as opposites. Understanding this formula reveals a central aspect of the cultural arrangement that domesticity/liberalism encodes.[102]

Williams's and Frug's feminist narrative is characteristic of postmodern trends in other disciplines, including history, philosophy, and science, where postmodernism has been used to challenge the modernist conception of reason. Feminist narratives have bolstered postmodern attitudes in the academy by questioning assumptions that form modern scholarly investigation. These narratives question "the possibility that there [is] any objective 'truth' or 'hard facts of the matter' that could be discovered through investigation."[103] Kathryn Abrams claimed that feminist legal narratives "questioned the assumption that objectivist methods for deriving or assessing knowledge—such as abstract logic or empiricism—represented universal standards or exhausted the criteria that would properly be applied to evaluate scholarly claims."[104] These feminist critics implicitly allied their cause with the type of radical questioning characteristic of postmodernism.

Postmodern feminists seek to strengthen the feminist critique of legal modernism by demonstrating how the binary oppositions of legal modernism define a conception of individuality that lacks feminine interests and values. Postmodern feminist critique challenges the modern concept of self as the subject in control of discourse and analysis, by exposing how the identity of the subject is "artifact produced by discourse"[105] of gender. The postmodern position is that "one is not born [a woman], rather one becomes a woman."[106] Gender is, in other words, viewed as a socially constructed artifact. Postmoderns urge feminist discourse to consider the identity politics of gender discourse reflected in the roles and sex depicted in the language of law. "[T]he Postmodern project of feminism [is] nothing less than the subversion, at every turn, of modernist projections of 'woman'."[107]

The perspective of postmodern feminists is that no essential commonality exists among women. They reject the essentialism of "cultural" and "radical" legal feminists, who tend to focus on a single understanding of women's experience. Instead, postmodern legal feminists argue that feminist theory should bring out the multicultural differences in women's life experiences by deconstructing the unitary quality and character of gender identity in the law. They believe that the deconstruction of gender identity can lead to a pluralist conception of equality in the law, which respects gender differences without forcing women to analogize their experience to either the male experience or to some hypothetical experience of a particular woman. As postmodern feminist Zillah Eisenstein explained, "Women's subjectivity will always be open to the plurality of meaning and possibility contained within this plurality will have different political implications."[108] Rejecting the sameness/difference analysis of traditional equality law, postmodern feminists like Eisenstein have stated that the law must allow for "multiple viewpoints available to any one individual."[109] The feminist inquiry is thus redirected by postmoderns to a consideration of the relation between gender and the power of different gender discourses.

In law, feminists have advanced new conceptions about law and adjudication that emphasize the importance of feminist reasoning.[110] Postmodern feminists go further, accepting the notion that law is indeterminate, but rejecting the idea that there is a hedonic "right answer" for deciding hard cases. Postmodern feminists offer different strategies for ending gender-based oppression. For them, theory is merely a tool that can be utilized for strategic purposes. Gender oppression is regarded as a fact—a reality—that can only be understood from the many different perspectives of different women. Building on women's experiences, postmodern feminists argue that there is more than one right answer to law's problem of gender inequality.

Not all feminists believe that postmodernism is appropriate for feminist legal analysis. Nancy Fraser and Linda Nicholson, for example, worry that the localized narratives of postmodernism are too "anemic" to do anything about the structural problems posed by gender hierarchy.[111] They believe that in order to bring about true transformative changes in the law and in society, feminists must focus on "[l]arge narratives about changes in social organization and ideology, empirical and social-theoretical analysis of macrostructures and institutions, interactionist analyses of the micro-politics of everyday life, critical-hermeneutical and institutional analyses of cultural production, historically and culturally specific sociologies of gender."[112] In other words, as English feminist Sabina Lovibond asked, "How can anyone ask me to say goodbye to 'emancipatory metanarratives' when my own emancipation is still such a patchy, hit-and-miss affair?" [113]

Feminists remain ambivalent about postmodernism because they fear that postmodern strategies will fail to counter the social and political conditions responsible for gender discrimination. Lovibond feared that the feminist critique will be lost if it is treated by postmoderns as just another interesting feature in the "postmodern social landscape." [114] West argued that the postmodern strategies used by critical legal studies scholars reproduce the same masculine values and interests of modern jurisprudence. [115] Feminists thus questioned whether feminism will survive postmodern criticism. Postmoderns, on the other hand, have argued that "postmodernism poses no threat to feminism because, properly understood, postmodernism only threatens a conception of reason (the modernist conception) which may have reached the end of its useful life." [116]

Postmodern feminists have attempted to develop a form of postmodern gender analysis for the law that is more responsive to the needs of all women. Instead of advancing a universal concept of gender identity or an "objective" description of gender reality, they argue that the emancipation of women (and men) can be achieved by undoing the power of sex stereotypes embedded within all objectivist representations of reality. Drucilla Cornell, for example, has thus argued that antidiscrimination law must "allow difference to be recognized without women having to show that they are like men for legal purposes or having to make sacrifices because of the specificity of our 'sex' which makes us like men." [117] Joan Williams argued that sex discrimination law must allow for "multiple view points available to any one individual." [118]

Feminist legal scholar Margaret Radin, for example, has embraced a postmodern feminist perspective by offering new pragmatic strategies for challenging the dominant understanding of truth and reality embodied in the legal categories of antidiscrimination law. [119] Radin argues for a feminist perspective that is contextual and nonessentialist in aspiration, a new "mediating way of thinking" that rejects the "P/or not P" approach. Radin's middle or "mediating" way recommends two basic strategies for legal feminists:

(1) We should recognize that sometimes one of the opposing modes of thought is appropriate, and sometimes the other, and no theory—only situated judgement—will tell us which one to adopt and when;

(2)We should recognize that the traditional conceptions of the modes of thought
. . . are inadequate insofar as they are part of a universal world view that denies
the modes on the other list.[120]

Postmodern pragmatists argue that the alternative to the sameness/
difference dilemma of feminist theory lies in the recognition of feminine
differences in those circumstances where women are different, as in the
case of pregnancy, while, at the same time, not reinforcing the very
stereotypes through which patriarchy has limited women's power. This
perspective is reflected within the *pragmatic feminism* of Professor Mary
Becker of the University of Chicago Law School, who argues that feminists should become more pragmatic: "[R]ather than looking to one
approach to solve all problems in all circumstances, we should regard
the variety of approaches available today as a set of tools to be used
when appropriate."[121] The postmodern insight is that the achievement
of gender equality must begin with a reformulation of the sameness/
difference analysis of feminist theory by taking into account the multiple
consciousness and experience of women. As the late Mary Joe Frug
argued, the goal of gender equality should embrace a new form of
feminist identity politics, which redefines and subverts the reigning notions of gender identity to allow for the multiple identities that define
the inner selves of women.

It may be true, as Dennis Patterson claims, that aspects of recent
feminist legal scholarship, such as that of West and Williams, continue
to reflect the modernist framework of a universal method for developing
feminist jurisprudence.[122] Patterson argued that one can detect within
the contemporary discourses of feminist criticism a view that posits an
appeal to some totalizing structure (hedonic values, feminist narratives,
feminist culture, etc.) which purports to offer the promise of some
universal feminist answers to transcend the many feminist discourses.[123]
Patterson claims that this modernist framework, embedded within forms
of feminist criticism, renders feminism vulnerable to the critique of
modernism.[124]

Feminists, however, use the methods of modern jurisprudence to
destabilize modernism. They criticize the objective claims of law in order
to glimpse what law would look like if structured by feminist values.
The relation between legal feminism and legal modernism may be more
like the relation between radical legal realism and Langdellian formalism. Feminists use the logic and conceptual modes of legal modernism to

challenge the political vision embedded within the doctrines of modern legal thought itself. In doing so, postmodern feminists have advanced jurisprudential arguments for considering the diversity of the many voices and perspectives of a multicultural society.

The feminist criticisms of West and Williams, for example, can be seen as furthering the diversity movement by highlighting the multiple perspectives of different women. Their criticism questions the modernist belief in universal or essential gender identities. West and Williams can be seen as writing within an emerging postmodern feminist tradition that seeks to bring out the diversity within the feminist movement. Black feminist writers now claim, for example, that the construction of gender categories of "different voice," "ethic of care," or "dominance" fails to capture the dynamics of racism and sexism in defining the position of black women. The new interest in "intersectionality" analysis of interests has cast the feminist movement squarely within the diversity movement now shaping the postmodern currents in the university.[125]

The intersectionality of interest between Fem-Crits and CLS scholars has, in fact, pushed CLS toward feminist legal theory and worked to "feminize" the CLS movement. Storytelling in feminist legal scholarship has linked feminist legal theory with the pedagogy of narrative jurisprudence used in the *law and literature* movement. The intersectionality between racism and sexism bonded feminist legal theory with minority scholars who advance a new form of critical race theory. Feminist legal theory may, therefore, establish a bridge of intersectional interests for the new scholarly trends of the 1990s. This intersectionality, however, has challenged the identity politics of feminists who have made essentialist-like claims about the experiences of women. Feminist and critical race scholars argue that color blindness and gender blindness of conventional analysis serve to the disadvantage of women and people of color.

*Black feminist criticism*,[126] a recent development in jurisprudence, reacts against the tendency of feminist legal scholars to treat race and gender as mutually exclusive categories of experience and analysis. Kimberle Crenshaw, a black feminist legal scholar at UCLA, has forcefully argued that "a persistent dilemma that confronts black women within prevailing constructions of identity politics: dominant conceptions of racism and sexism render it virtually impossible to represent our situation in ways that fully articulate our subject position as black women." [127] Crenshaw claimed that the problem is that women of color are "overlooked" and sometimes "excluded" by white feminists who claim to speak for all women.[128]

Black feminist criticism attempts to decenter the subject position of feminists who make essentialist claims about race and gender criticism in the law. Theories and strategies claiming to advance the interest of people of color are criticized to the extent that they fail to include an analysis of sexism and patriarchy. Feminist legal theory is similarly faulted for failing to consider the experience and aspirations of non-white women. As Crenshaw declared, "Neither black liberation politics nor feminist theory can ignore the intersectional experiences of those whom the movements claim as their respective constituents."[129] Black feminist criticism has pushed feminist legal criticism to rethink its identity and reconsider the subject position of women in its critical analysis of law.

Black feminism illustrates how feminist legal theory has come to represent the challenge of postmodernism. Postmodernism challenges the primacy of modern theory, seeking to *decenter* the identity of a universal concept of self in contemporary legal criticism.[130] Postmodern feminists question the ability of modern legal theorists to understand and take into account the experiences, interests, and harms of women.[131] In challenging the complacency of the law's dominant conception of a universal gender, contemporary feminist criticism is committed to a *politics of identity,* which seeks to destabilize the modernist's universal concept of self and thereby open up intellectual discourse in law to the diverse cultural politics of postmodernism.

# 8. Law and Literature

The *law and literature* movement can be traced to the 1973 publication of James Boyd White's THE LEGAL IMAGINATION,[1] a book that advanced the idea that the study of literature should be part of legal education, because literary studies have something distinctive to say about law and adjudication. Law and literature was previously a marginal subject consisting mainly of the study of stories about law found in the great works of classical literature.[2] Law and literature practitioners, following the example of Dean Wigmore,[3] explored the way law was used in the great literary classics of Dickens, Kafka, and Melville, and examined the "legal content" of those and other literary works in law. This older, "Great Books approach" to the study of law and literature was based on the belief that the study of literature was necessary to give lawyers a literary sensibility.

## Early 1980s Law and Literature Scholarship

James Boyd White, professor of law and English at the University of Michigan, established the groundwork for the modern movement of law and literature by showing how the study of literature is very similar to the type of interpretive activity involved in the law. Since White's work, the law and literature movement has become increasingly "serious" as a distinct form of jurisprudence.[4] One of the basic jurisprudential claims of this movement is that the study of literature is useful for studying the ethical nature of law; that literary thought and practice offer insight about the human subjects in law. Another claim is that law and literature are intimately related because each depends on language and a way of reading, writing, and speaking that involves similar interpretive practices. A related claim is that law and literature studies represent the development of legal *hermeneutics*,[5] a school of legal scholarship said to be needed to improve our understanding of law as interpretation. These jurisprudential claims have distinguished this movement from the older forms of jurisprudence and schools of legal theory associated with Langdell and Holmes.

The development of the "law as interpretation" or legal hermeneutics was largely responsible for the "interpretive turn" in traditional legal scholarship of the early 1980s.[6] For White and his followers, the relevant law and literature inquiry is: "What happens if we look at the literature of the law as if it really were literature, as though it defined speakers and a world, a set of possibilities for expression and community?"[7] A central point of the law and literature movement is that law *and* literature are united by a view of language as a community of discourse of particular cultural worlds. The world of literature is said to "bind the lawyer to the larger community of which she is a part."[8]

There are now two basic strands of thought in this movement: *law-in-literature* and *law-as-literature*.[9] The *law-in-literature* perspective developed from the Great Books approach in *literary jurisprudence*, which evolved from the study of legal subjects and legal issues in the classics of Western literature. Advocates of literary jurisprudence claim that the great books of literature are useful for understanding standard legal themes, such as revenge or guilt. They are thought to be useful for learning about the hermeneutical possibilities developed from literary insight about legal concepts, such as intentionalism, formalism, and objectivity.[10] The law-in-literature perspective views literary classics such as Kafka's THE TRIAL or Melville's BILLY BUDD, SAILOR, as offering lawyers and judges important lessons about the law. Professor Richard Weisberg of Cardozo Law School is the chief contemporary exponent of this approach to law and literature. His book, THE FAILURE OF THE WORD,[11] for example, is one of the basic texts for the law-in-literature approach.

The *law-as-literature* approach uses a broader range of methods and theoretical practices of literary criticism as a medium for analyzing legal texts and exploring the nature of legal style and rhetoric.[12] This strand of the movement developed from the idea that storytelling is relevant for legal studies because, as the late Yale University professor of law Robert Cover claimed,[13] law is but another story to be interpreted.[14] One version of law-as-literature relies on the technique of storytelling and narrative to offer a new form of legal scholarship that questions the traditional canons of interpretation in the law.[15] Feminists and critical race theorists have recently used storytelling to develop new critical approaches to law based on personal and imaginative experiences. These legal scholars use storytelling in their work to identify a "different voice," which they claim is missing in traditional stories told in the law. Storytelling is said to be capable of describing the personal experience of discrimination, and revealing how legal discourse is blind to the victim's story.

Another important strand of law-as-literature uses literary methods of criticism to construct interpretive strategies for applying and discovering the textual meaning of the law. This hermeneutic approach to legal interpretation "is not so much concerned with literature itself as with the broader issue of hermeneutics, an interest that easily crosses all disciplinary boundaries to include law, philosophy, and the social sciences."[16] This approach employs the investigations used by hermeneutic critics for examining law as a process of interpretation.[17] Legal scholars such as Stanley Fish,[18] Owen Fiss,[19] and Sanford Levinson[20] have used this approach to law-as-literature in developing a form of *interpretive jurisprudence*. This approach is quite popular in contemporary constitutional-law scholarship.

It may be, as Weisberg suggested, that the "Law in / Law as Literature dichotomy no longer needs to hold sway."[21] For Weisberg, the law-in-literature enterprise is sufficiently rich to advance the pedagogical agenda of those who follow the law-as-literature perspective. Thus, the Great Books of nineteenth- and twentieth-century fiction offer what Weisberg calls a "hermeneutic tradition . . . fully responsive to our postmodern concerns" of current legal interpretation.[22] Others reject the "law and literature" dichotomy altogether in finding that legal and literary criticism are deeply unified in method and temperament. Jurisprudential writers as diverse as Ronald Dworkin, Stanley Fish, and Owen Fiss have advanced widely different conceptions about law and adjudication by developing new insights from literary approaches to legal interpretation and meaning.

Although law and literature scholars disagree about important uses of literary criticism in analyzing jurisprudential issues (e.g., can the legal interpreter go beyond the original author's intent?), they share a common perspective that legal interpretation is but a special genre of literary interpretation. James Boyd White captures the literary mood of these scholars best in stating that "the life of the law [today] is thus a life of art, the art of making meaning in language with others."[23] Viewing law in this manner suggests that a study of literature and language is crucial for understanding the humanity of law, and how the law influences the development of humanity. According to White, law and literature must be understood as a creative art; it "expands one's sympathy, it complicates one's sense of oneself and the world, it humiliates the instrumentally calculating forms of reason so dominant in our culture (by demonstrating their dependence on other forms of thought and expression), and the like."[24] Weisberg, on the other hand, takes a stronger view in arguing that the stories about law in the great classics of literature provide narratives that are as valuable to lawyers as any technique of literary criticism.[25] However, despite their differences, all practitioners of this movement seem to argue that "law is a story" to be interpreted as any other literary story. In this way, diverse legal critics such as Ronald Dworkin and Stanley Fish have become proponents of the law and literature movement.[26]

There has also been disagreement about the need to distinguish between the literary use of metaphor in law and the literary use of narrative in literature.[27] Richard Posner argues that while metaphor has a legitimate use in judicial opinions, the narrative form of literature has no legal significance.[28] Literary critic Paul Ricoeur, however, rejects this distinction altogether in claiming that metaphor and narrative are merely different ways of "storytelling."[29] Ricoeur believes that law is itself a specialized form of storytelling, and hence metaphor and narrative are relevant to the task of engaging intelligent analysis of legal storytelling. Law and literature scholars have published a diverse body of critical articles and books in the last few years employing the literary technique of narrative in legal analysis.[30] James B. Elkins and Thomas Shaffer, for example, took the lead in highlighting the concerns of this new form of "narrative jurisprudence" for legal education and practice.[31] Stanley Fish argues that "[l]egal texts might be written in verse or take the form of narrative or parables."[32] Law and literature practitioners thus reject Posner's view that literary narrative is an inappropriate or suspect medium for law.

The basic forms of jurisprudence of this movement—*literary, interpretive,* and *narrative*—advance different agendas for the law and literature enterprise. Richard Weisberg, a leading spokesperson for literary jurisprudence, argues that by studying how law has been used in classical works in literature we can gain insight about legal norms and the nature of jurisprudence itself.[33] He believes that the authors of classical literary works offer the best ethical descriptions of the type of human values that should be created by legal culture.[34] Weisberg believes that literary sources can also teach us important lessons about official forms of tyranny.[35] Weisberg has shown, for example, how a critical reading of Melville's BILLY BUDD, SAILOR, can be fruitful for understanding ideas about writing and speaking, as well as exploring issues of moral responsibility.[36]

In his 1982 article, *How Judges Speak: Some Lessons on Adjudication in Billy Budd, Sailor, with an Application to Justice Rehnquist,*[37] Weisberg examined the "plot" of Melville's BILLY BUDD, SAILOR, to provide the reader with important lessons about literary narrative. Weisberg shows how narrative form can establish authoritative force even when the analytical logic of the narrative is flawed. The "centerpiece" of Melville's story is the trial scene. Billy Budd, the story's title hero, is a twenty-one-year-old sailor in the British fleet during the summer of 1797.[38] Melville reminds the reader that this was shortly after "The Great Mutiny" at the Nore, which had threatened the stability and authority of the British fleet. Billy's fictional Captain Vere is presented as a basically good but pedantic man who was noted for his severe discipline. John Claggart is the fictional master-at-arms of the ship. Claggart is known to "finesse" language in order to achieve ends through indirection.[39] Claggart was obsessed with Billy's apparent inability to accomplish his tasks with directness and ease.

After a "soup-spilling" episode, in which Billy accidentally spills "greasy liquid" in Claggart's path, Claggart falsely accuses Billy of conspiracy to mutiny.[40] Using his customary indirectness, Claggart subsequently forces Billy to defend himself in public. Billy, a stutterer, cannot advance a coherent defense. Claggart yells at Billy: "Speak man!"[41] But Billy cannot. After being pressed to speak repeatedly, Billy strikes out and hits Claggart, who falls to the cabin floor, dead.

A court-martial panel consisting of three senior officers was instituted to consider the charges brought against Billy, who was charged with a capital offense of striking a senior officer at time of war.[42] At the court-martial trial, Captain Vere, addressing the court-martial panel, used his rhetorical skills to explain why Billy must be hanged, and his rhetorical skills influence the court-martial panel. In examining Melville's story of the trial, Weisberg discovered how Melville used what Weisberg called "considerate communication."[43] Thus, Captain Vere, recognizing the audience's need to understand the results of the trial, recounted the events of the Great Mutiny to explain why, if Billy were not hanged, the ship would be in chaos. Vere's audience, along with the reader, is thus persuaded to accept the wisdom of Billy's fate despite his lack of legal culpability for the crime charged. Weisberg shows how Vere's articulated reasons for the hanging of Billy seem plausible even when they fail to stand the test of legal analysis.[44]

According to Weisberg, Melville's use of "considerate communication" was a good illustration of how legal rhetoric can justify results by sparing its readers and audience any discomfort by omitting or even distorting facts in the narration of past events.[45] Weisberg argues that deviations from the truth are permitted when the communication is "considerate" of the reader's right to know "the essence of the underlying reality [of what] he is discussing . . . despite . . . omissions or mild representations of detail."[46] Thus, Melville's fictional Captain Vere, "ever considerate of his audience's needs," recounts the mutinous events in other cases where a sailor disobeyed orders, while omitting that Billy has a stutter, and that his disloyal and murderous conduct was an irrational act.[47]

Weisberg uses the idea of considerate communication to illustrate how authoritative "law speakers" sharply limit their communications of factual events in a way that "is *considerate* both to their own interests and to those of their audience."[48] He also explains how considerate communication exposes Supreme Court Justice Rehnquist's reliance on rhetorical ploys to "dispel critical probing into his logic and use of precedent."[49] According to Weisberg, Rehnquist is not considerate of his readers because his communication and language "subtly deneutralize" the court's reasoning process by omitting or distorting facts and precedent essential to the reader's understanding of the law.[50] Considerate communication illustrates a mode of literary criticism that Weisberg claims lawyers must understand to avoid the undesirable literary exegesis in legal reasoning.[51] More recently, Weisberg examined how this form of rhetoric was used in Vichy France during World War II to facilitate crimes against Jews on French soil.[52]

Literary jurisprudence thus uses the Great Books of literature as a medium for discovering insight about meaning, use of rhetoric, and the values of the law. Weisberg believes that the study of literary jurisprudence provides for the "poethics" of justice, that is, the way language and rhetoric are used in law to translate the legal meaning of justice.[53] He views the language and rhetorical phrases of judicial opinions as more important than the legal outcome, for they determine the perceived rightness or wrongness of the conclusion reached. In order to understand legal justice, Weisberg argued that we must examine the "inner world" of the subjective realm of law found within its language and rhetoric. Weisberg's strategy is to compare and contrast the two worlds of law and literature to see how each involves different visions of the ideal of justice. Narrative jurisprudence, on the other hand, relies on the analyst to develop the text of a story for appraising the narrative content of the official stories told in the law.

For those legal scholars who practice narrative jurisprudence, law is but one story to be read in conjunction with others. By telling alternative stories, based on actual personal experiences or fictional accounts, narrative jurisprudence attempts to expose the universal "mind-set" of modern jurisprudence. Richard Delgado, for example, claims that "[s]tories, parables, chronicles, and narrative are powerful means for destroying mindset—the bundle of presuppositions, received wisdom, and shared understandings about a background on which legal and political discourse takes place."[54] Narrative jurisprudence used in this way is a critical medium for criticizing the formal interpretive style of legal modernism by attacking its claims of objectivity. It is also a medium for interjecting, within the discourse of the law, the perspective of groups of people who are not accounted for in the official stories told in the law.

Throughout the 1980s, narrative jurisprudence as used in legal scholarship, sought to expose the fact that law is made by human beings who are influenced by their own particular experiences and pathologies. Narrative jurisprudence highlights stories that are told in the law and it compares those stories to other narratives about different social or psychological phenomena. It can also take the form of actual accounts of the author's experiences, or imaginative storytelling offering imagined or "made-up" stories that are fictional or "novel-like" accounts of social or psychological phenomena.[55]

Imaginative forms of narrative jurisprudence use storytelling to depict a common experience with which readers are likely to identify, or to evoke a deeply ambivalent experience in the reader.[56] Derrick Bell's book AND WE ARE NOT SAVED: THE ELUSIVE QUEST FOR RACIAL JUSTICE,[57] is based on an imaginary character, Geneva Crenshaw, who describes for Bell a series of stories about social events and law. The book describes a discussion between Bell, Crenshaw, and other imagined characters on whether certain imagined race-restricting laws would be constitutional under contemporary Supreme Court case law.[58] Bell uses this imaginative narrative much in the way novels are used in literary studies to evoke awareness about the human condition. As Linda R. Hirshman explained: "Literature trains people in the reflection, consciousness, choice, and responsibility that make up the ability to engage in moral decisionmaking. It does so by presenting artificial, but concrete, universes in which premises may be worked out in conditions conducive to empathy but ambiguous enough to allow for the formation of moral judgment."[59]

Narrative jurisprudence also offers "anecdotal evidence" of an event or experience, and captures the essence of a social problem such as race discrimination.[60] Thus, Stephen Carter, in his book REFLECTIONS OF AN AFFIRMATIVE ACTION BABY,[61] discusses his own experiences of how affirmative action programs create dilemmas for talented black Americans.[62] Patricia Williams, in her book THE ALCHEMY OF RACE AND RIGHTS,[63] reports on her own experiences and anxieties as an African American woman in American society. Williams describes a shopping visit to Au Coton, a retail establishment near her home in New York City. In the store, three young salespeople are overheard "joking about Jews." Williams examines her silence about their obvious anti-Semitic comments. She concludes that she was unable to say anything because she had been "privileged" to hear what these people thought. "I realized that breaking the bond of my silence was like breaking the bond of *our* silence."[64] The story is then used to discuss how racism is perpetuated by a "bond of silence."[65]

*Interpretive jurisprudence* has developed from a broad range of hermeneutic interpretive strategies used by legal critics to question the official interpretations of legal texts. One strategy is to encourage the reader to discover new meanings and interpretations by questioning the authority of legal texts. Stanley Fish's idea of "reader response" criticism, for example, claims that the meaning of a text is created by the community of interpreters who share social and aesthetic practices.[66] The community of readers becomes, in Fish's view, the source of the text's authority. What is "in" the text is a function of the traditions, practices, and customs of an interpretive community. The official interpretations of the law are viewed by Fish as "fixed" within the context of legal discourse.

The idea of a fixed cultural context for grounding legal interpretations is viewed by others as a cover for the exercise of political power. An early and provocative proponent of this view is Sanford Levinson, a professor of law at the University of Texas. In a 1982 essay, *Law as Literature*,[67] he argued that there will always be as many plausible readings and competing interpretations of law as there are poetry. According to Levinson, "the principle social reality of law" is the political force of official interpretations that require the community to accept the interpretation law requires.[68] Levinson's law-as-literature perspective leads him to contemplate the political dimension of law in its fullest sense.

Interpretive jurisprudence has consequently stimulated a lively academic debate about the proper "interpretive practice" to be applied in judicial interpretations of the Constitution. Constitutional liberals like Owen Fiss reject Levinson's interpretive conclusions and argue that legal interpretation can be grounded in the objective source of the disciplinary rules of the interpretive community.[69] Constitutional conservatives who follow Judge Robert Bork's example use traditional literary notions about the "author's intent" in defending an interpretive canon that the Constitution means only what the drafters who originally wrote it intended it to mean.[70] Supreme Court Justices Antonin Scalia and Clarence Thomas have relied on original intention to defend their conservative view of the Constitution. Some believe that an objective source of legal meaning is embedded within the text of the law or its institutions and culture, while others argue that texts and culture are sufficiently ambiguous to permit readers to invent whatever meaning serves their partisan views.[71]

Hence, while it might appear to some that the law and literature movement does not have a strong ideological program like the law and economics, critical legal studies, or feminist legal theory movements, it has stimulated normative and political perspectives about law. David Papke noted that "political alignments in the movement dance from one end of the spectrum to the other."[72] James Boyd White helps capture the politics of the movement by emphasizing that interpretative activity as a creative art form enables us to better grasp our human capabilities for self-definition.[73] Alternatively, as Richard Weisberg argues, law and literature offers insight about the human condition often missing in legal analysis.[74] On the other hand, other law and literature practitioners like Robin West illustrate how the stories in classics of literature might lead legal analysts to misunderstand the plight of women.[75] Even Richard Posner, the founding father of the law and economics movement, acknowledges that "literature . . . speaks to . . . the eternal problems of the human condition."[76] The politics of this movement seems to be aimed at bringing out the human element missing in law.

The literary perspective has been used by traditional legal scholars seeking to defend modern foundations of law and prevailing jurisprudential conceptions of law. Ronald Dworkin relies on literary forms of interpretation of law to defend and justify liberal legal thought.[77] Owen Fiss uses literary concepts of interpretation to defend the possibility of legal objectivity.[78] Even James Boyd White is a defender of conventionalism: He argues legal interpreters can discover an "ideal" understanding about law and adjudication by adopting an "ideal reader" perspective.[79] Thus, White's view that "[t]he lawyer's work thus contributes to a process of collective or cultural education that is in structure analogous to that experienced by the single reader of the literary text"[80] establishes an interpretive foundation for the enduring belief in law's autonomy similar to the one offered by Ronald Dworkin. Law and literature has therefore not always been opposed to the projects of legal modernism.

What aligns this movement with legal modernism is the distinctive humanistic aspirations of literary jurisprudence. Practitioners of the movement believe that the basic human dimension of modern law can be discovered from the study of the great works of literature, literary criticism, and narrative interpretation. In either case, narrative and literary studies have become powerful tools for capturing the human element missing in legal studies. One might say that the law and literature movement advances the modern project of Enlightenment by offering a unique and humanistic foundation for law, one that takes the humanity underlying law and adjudication seriously. In this important way, law and literature practitioners seek to render law more pure in its aspirations. The law and literature perspective attempts to interject humanistic values in law so as to perfect traditional jurisprudential studies.

## Late 1980s Law and Literature Scholarship— Proliferating Literary Discourses

By the late 1980s, the influence of law and literature could be found in the work of scholars such as White and Weisberg, who claimed that the law and literature perspective would transform the way legal academics talk and think about law and adjudication. The movement questioned the basic universal assumptions shaping the discursive culture of law by "pointing towards a more overt and ethical use of institutional language." [81] A major shift in theoretical practice occurred as other law and literature practitioners discovered new interpretive strategies within the transformative ideas of critical social theorists such as Michel Foucault, Jacques Derrida, Jean-François Lyotard, and Edward Said. The new interpretive strategies of critical social theory (deconstruction, poststructuralism, postmodernism, neopragmatism) have energized the law and literature movement and broadened its theoretical base. By the late 1980s, law and literature scholars took the "interpretive turn" and began arguing that literature and literary criticism were highly relevant sources for understanding the politics of interpretation." [82] Their interpretive arguments developed from a cultural form of literary criticism that sought to bring out the diverse, multiple discourses that had been silent in legal analysis. [83] They claimed that legal interpretation has constrained the "hermeneutic possibilities" in order to maintain and rationalize legal institutions and the social and economic conditions they support. [84]

One interesting manifestation of this involves new imaginative readings of classical literature. Robin West's imaginative interpretation of Kafka's THE TRIAL in a widely discussed HARVARD LAW REVIEW article, for example, was used by West to expose the limitations in the mindset of Richard Posner's ECONOMIC ANALYSIS OF LAW. [85] According to West, Kafka's story reveals the ethical failings of the scientific-like analysis used by Posner in his economic analysis of law. West argued that Posner's vision of the legal world betrays the contradictory impulses of masochistic authority and submission found in Kafka's story. West argued that Kafka's story illustrates how people sometimes exercise freedom to choose in inherently coercive ways. Freedom of choice can be motivated by dark impulses to submit to authority. Posner's theory of individual autonomy as the neutral calculation of *good* and *bad* was shown by West to have potentially immoral consequences.

West thus used Kafka's text to support the validity of the normative argument she constructed in response to Posner's economic analysis of law. Kafka's story was used as a political and rhetorical device for formulating West's normative argument. West makes no attempt to read Kafka's text as a story about real cultural events of a particular historical moment. Nor was there any attempt to remain faithful to Kafka's text or intent. In her "nuanced readings" of Kafka, West sought to persuade readers "that Kafka's characters depict fundamental, timeless truths about human nature that are not confined by the author's own profound personal despair, mental illness, or the extraordinarily bleak social world his novels depict." [86]

West's interpretive reading of Kafka relies upon a reader-response strategy to expose how economic interpretations of law are based on culturally arbitrary" understandings of human behavior. By encouraging her readers to imagine different cultural understandings of human behavior suggested by Kafka's text, West encouraged them to develop their own awareness of the multiple motivations of human behavior. She used Kafka's text as a rhetorical device to bring out the multiple consciousness of "consent" and "authority" in order to challenge Posner's view that human behavior is exclusively motivated by self-interested behavior. [87] Patricia Williams's *Alchemical Notes* [88] follows a similar strategy in using her own personal narrative to provoke questions about the cultural attitudes and perspectives of race that have influenced the traditional legal understanding of race discrimination problems. By the mid-1980s, this form of reader-response storytelling was a popular tool used by legal scholars. This form of narrative jurisprudence seeks to move beyond the historically determined narratives of classical or modern literary studies.

The pedagogy of legal storytelling or "voice scholarship," the genre of law and literature scholarship popular in the late 1980s, had become a powerful tool used by feminists and critical race scholars to show how the narrative perspectives of minority groups were excluded or marginalized in mainstream legal discourse.[89] In 1989, a legal symposium on legal storytelling was held in a major law review,[90] attracting the attention of academic lawyers.[91] By 1992, the prominence of narrative jurisprudence and legal storytelling was featured in the *New York Times*.[92] The objective of the "outsider storytelling" by minorities was to bring out the voices of all people (African Americans, gays and lesbians, other non-white, non-Western people) left out of the discourse of law.[93] This genre of narrative jurisprudence has become a critical methodology for unmasking the universal concept of self in the law-and-literature movement itself.

Another important and highly influential strand of late 1980s legal scholarship that developed from the law and literature movement involves the work of antifoundational literary critics and philosophers such as Stanley Fish and Richard Rorty. These scholars used literary strategies to attack foundational interpretations of literature and law.[94] Fish believes that "literary criticism" is a tool for debunking the foundational claims of theory in law or literature. He sees little point in appealing to "principles" of one's discipline because professional judgments always come down to a matter of consensus or belief. He views professional expertise as merely a matter of literary style or taste; it cannot provide anything more in the way of a legitimating ground.

Debates between legal foundationalists and antifoundationalists reflect pervasive disagreement about the possibility of maintaining a legal or philosophical consensus about the possibility of discovering "right answers" to every legal problem, or reaching a consensus on the values and goals of the legal system.[95] Legal foundationalists believe that right answers can be found within the shared consensus in social values and goals of society. Antifoundationalists reject the ideas of shared intellectual foundations and therefore do not accept the right-answer thesis or view consensus as a possibility. The debate between foundationalists and antifoundationalists is reflected within diverse new movements of literature and philosophy that question traditional philosophers who believe in the possibility of objectivity, rationality, and universal knowledge.[96]

Rorty, a leading antifoundational philosopher, utilized literary criticism and classical literature to develop his particular antifoundational

philosophy of neopragmatism.[97] In CONTINGENCY, IRONY AND SOLI-
DARITY, he found inspiration in the literature of Vladimir Nabokov and
George Orwell, which exposed the temptations of modern liberals to be
cruel and illustrated the "irony" and "contingency" of modern liberal
thought.[98] Rorty thus stretches the term "literary criticism" to involve
something more than the "literary qualities" in a book in order to
explore how canons of interpretation can be broadened to facilitate
moral and political reflection.[99] According to Rorty, the modern critic
"is not in the business of supplying himself and his fellow [critics] with
a method, a platform, or a rationale. He is just doing the same thing
which all [critics] do—attempting autonomy. He is trying to get out
from under inherited contingencies and make his own contingencies, get
out from under an old final vocabulary and fashion one which will be
all his own. The generic trait of [critics] is that they do not hope to have
their doubts about their final vocabularies settled by something larger
than themselves."[100]

In CONSEQUENCES OF PRAGMATISM, Rorty contrasted two stylistic
paradigms used in law *and* literature that were applicable to the styles of
legal argument made in law.[101] He asserts that lawyers are trained to
use a scientific-legal style of analysis that emphasizes the importance of
cogency and formality in legal argument at the expense of discovering
new modes of argument.[102] This paradigm values "[t]he ability to construct a good brief, or conduct a devastating cross-examination, or find
relevant precedent [and the overall ability to] see at a glance the inferen-
tial relationships between all the members of a bewilderingly large set of
propositions."[103] The literary stylistic paradigm, on the other hand, may
involve "argumentation, but that is not essential; what is essential is
telling a new story, suggesting a new language-game, in the hope of a
new form of intellectual life."[104]

While the scientific-legal paradigm "asks that premises be explicitly
spelled out rather than guessed at, that terms be introduced by definition
rather than by allusion," the literary paradigm asks that new stories and
new language games be told in the law so that decision makers and
policy planners might discover new insights for dealing with legal problems.[105] The fact that different stylistic paradigms frequently involve
different normative modes of legal argument is helpful for understanding
the politics of legal form.[106] Thus, the stylistic modes of legal modernism

project different normative visions of legal argument than those of post-modernism.

Rorty's style of literary criticism has paved the way for the revival of pragmatic philosophy in legal studies as well for the use of literary criticism to refute essentialist interpretations of law and legal decision making.[107] The revival and reinterpretation of American legal pragmatism derived from Holmes is known today as *neopragmatism*.[108] Neo-pragmatists exhibit "a profound skepticism about the possibility of consensus in social values and goals."[109] Rorty has been the leading promoter of the neopragmatic philosophy. The primary purpose behind his neopragmatism is to offer a philosophical alternative to the Kantian conception of philosophy as foundational. Rorty believes that the notion of objective knowledge in philosophy rests upon interpretation of a particular literary practice. He thus stretches the word "literature" to cover whatever the literary critics criticize, including the foundational assumptions of philosophy.[110] Rorty uses a form of literary criticism to show how foundational assumptions of philosophy can be refuted.

Contemporary legal critics believe that Rorty's literary criticism and neopragmatism challenge foundationalism in modern jurisprudence. Thus, Joseph Singer relied on Rorty to question the possibility of legal objectivity: "All objectivity means is agreement among people";[111] and Martha Minow and Elizabeth Spelman found within Rorty's writing a valuable insight about language on human cultures: "It [is] better to speak within particular communities about contingent practices."[112] Legal scholars have also used Rorty's pragmatic philosophy to construct antifoundational approaches to legal analysis, some of which rely upon what is known as "practical reason."[113] Practical reason calls for a contextual approach to legal interpretation, one that would provide the "best answers" for the problem at hand based on experience, context, and common sense. Pragmatic legal theorists assert their belief in practical reason to question the philosophical foundations of modern legal theory.[114] Rorty's literary strategies are used by contemporary legal critics to reveal how legal perspective is influenced and shaped by different class-based cultures.

Stanley Fish has also been influential in showing legal scholars how traditional theories of interpretation repeat the mistakes of foundationalism. According to Fish, judgments in law, as in literary criticism, always involve a matter of belief and cannot be based on a legitimating foundation. By claiming that truth is contingent on a particular "interpretive community,"[115] Fish provided legal critics with a powerful interpretive stance for attacking the foundations of modern jurisprudence. Fish views autonomous law as a set of shared assumptions about legal meaning, context, and authorial intent. He encourages legal critics to abandon their search for the one true rule of law. Fish seemingly offers comfort to antifoundational legal theorists who think that law must be understood as a special form of conversation—what some have called "a deliberative practice."[116] On the other hand, Fish is critical of antifoundational theorists who believe that antifoundational theory can avoid the dilemmas and predicaments of modern theory.

Because law and literature scholars disagree about basic literary strategies and goals, it remains questionable whether law and literature will lead to transformative changes in law. Some reject the reliance on traditional literary canons of criticism, while others argue that traditional canons of classical literature are needed to teach the necessary ethical lessons of law and literature.[117] Still others believe that the narrative strategy of this movement offers a promising strategy for engaging a form of leftist politics to expose the racial and gender bias of traditional jurisprudence.[118] The methodological eclecticism of the movement, however, means that law and literature has failed to advance a strong theoretical stance generally.

While it is true, as Richard Posner argued, that "there is no central theory of literature that can be taken and applied to a body of law,"[119] this does not mean that law and literature is a theoretically weak movement when compared to law and economics. James Boyd White believes that law and literature is now primarily an art form.[120] David Papke claimed that the activities within law and economics and law and literature are fundamentally different:

Economics facilitates deductive reasoning regarding the law. Literature, by contrast, is different in its application. Literature consists of poems, plays, stories, novels, and various other primary cultural forms. One does not deduce new propositions from literature, but literature does contribute to our humanity and ability to understand the law. . . . When literature both as a primary art and as a humanistic undertaking is combined with law, the combination is indeed less systematic and predictable than is the combination of economics and law.[121]

Law and literature thus offers a different form of knowledge about law than that offered by modern legal thinkers. A dominant perspective of the current generation of law and literature scholars is aimed at deflating foundational truths and values that legal modernism projected in its stories about law and society.

Law and literature practitioners have expanded and diversified jurisprudential studies through the use of literary criticism in legal analysis. By offering contrasting humanistic views about law and legal decision making, these scholars encouraged lawyers and judges to be more aware of the human and cultural aspects of law. The law and literature movement stimulated new interest in understanding the way law intertwines with the "cultural artifacts" of literature. Encouraged by such developments, other legal academics have argued that the movement should be diversified even more by expanding the varieties of cultural artifacts to include "the interrelationships of law and popular culture."[122] As Rosemary Coombe, a law professor at University of Toronto, recently argued: "Modern (or, more precisely, postmodern) anthropology has made significant contributions to our understanding of cultural context by stressing that cultural context is not a singular structure of constraint that, so to speak, 'descends from above,' but a dynamic of multiple discourses which exist only in their reproduction and transformation of everyday practices."[123]

Finally, the traditional canon of the Great Books approach defended by Weisberg's style of literary jurisprudence has been criticized for failing to include stories about women, people of color, and non-Western people. One critic has stated that "when Richard Weisberg constructs a model reading list for course in Law and Literature, he includes nine weeks of white male authors (Shakespeare, John Barth, Melville, Dickens, and Faulkner) and only one black woman (Toni Morrison)."[124] This causes some to wonder whether the Great Books tradition of law and literature commits the movement to storytelling by white men or other nondiverse perspectives.[125] This may be a misreading of Weisberg's pedagogical purpose, however, since he uses the classics only to explore "literary sensibility in law" from the reader's perspective.[126] Weisberg's postmodern view is that "plain meanings can only be discovered by audiences receptive to them."[127]

Postmoderns have nonetheless moved away from the Great Books idea and started experimenting with the narrative and literary mode to justify a multicultural law and literature movement that has developed into a rather diverse multicultural movement. The readings and teachings of law and literature are held out as "powerful counterunderstandings"[128] about legal decision making. Postmodern trends within the academy have diversified the law and literature movement by fragmenting its members within different theoretical camps.

Postmodernism has thus impacted the law-and-literature movement by questioning the notion of an "ideal" reader or law and literature perspective. Although it is true that the law-in/law-as-literature dichotomy is now passé, so too is the law and literature dichotomy. Law and literature is another field in which postmodern strategies of interpretation have destabilized the autonomy of yet another foreign discipline pressed into the service of multicultural legal analysis. The method and medium of law and literature has become one of many different modes of expressing our understanding of law and jurisprudence. Thus, the law and literature movement merely offers a different vantage point from which to view a different possibility for jurisprudence in legal studies— one that rejects the vision of law as disciplined rhetoric and neutral rationality divorced from context. Reading literary texts and engaging in literary criticism encourages lawyers and judges to approach law from a multicultural and postmodern perspective.

# 9. Critical Race Theory

As the 1980s came to a close, a new movement in legal thought emerged offering a new epistemological source for law derived from the "actual experience, history, culture, and intellectual tradition of people of color."[1] This movement developed as racial-minority scholars within critical legal studies and other progressive networks established "an African American movement"[2] in legal studies to approach problems of race from the unique perspective of African Americans. Critical race theorists asserted that it was time for "different and blacker voices [to] speak new words and remake old legal doctrines."[3] The critical race theory movement emerged as minority scholars developed a *race consciousness* form of legal criticism. "Race consciousness" characterizes the jurisprudential perspective of minority scholars who emphasize the need for fundamental changes in the way the law constructs knowledge about race.[4]

Critical race theorists focus on racial consciousness to address the question of "color" in American law. The traditional view of the law of race discrimination has been structured by a silent category that distinguishes between people of different color. The color "white" has, for example, served as an implicit legal benchmark for determining whether the goal of legal equality has been achieved—equality requires that people of color enjoy the same formal rights and process as the dominant group. Critical race theorists argue that this way of thinking has the ideological consequence of convincing minorities that racial discrimination can only be eradicated through the implementation of color-blind meritocratic standards, which accord whites and blacks the same formal rights and process.[5]

Critical race theorists claim that when color is used in this way, it can reinforce racist attitudes prevailing in society that seek to justify the oppression of racial minorities.[6] They contend that by generalizing the category of race, the law reinforces the stereotypes of minority groups that have historically subordinated all people of color.[7] It is said that the law's generalization of the category of race suppresses knowledge about the different cultural experiences and attitudes of racial groups.[8] Race consciousness is thus the critical method these scholars advance in their struggle to achieve racial equality in the law. Color of skin pigmentation is viewed by critical race scholars as a symbol of cultural and personal identity constructed by white society.[9]

Race consciousness established a unique critique developed by minority legal scholars who advanced a racially distinctive body of civil rights scholarship—scholarship *by* minority academics who asserted *their* racial distinctiveness in their scholarship.[10] The idea of a critical race theory arose as minority legal scholars challenged the foundational assumptions of civil rights scholarship. Richard Delgado's 1984 article, *Imperial Scholar: Reflections on a Review of Civil Rights Literature*,[11] for example, charged that civil rights scholarship was held captive by a group of elite white "imperial scholars" who created a "scholarly tradition" that systematically excluded or minimized the participation of minority scholars.[12] A similar charge was raised by minority scholars who claimed that the *critical legal studies* movement lacked sufficient race consciousness.[13] Critical race theory also developed as minority scholars developed race-conscious critiques in reaction to civil rights law.[14] Critical race theory thus developed as a series of reactions against the typical modes of analysis used by white legal scholars, practitioners, and judges in their legal analysis of the race problem. The jurisprudence of this movement was shaped by something missing in traditional and non-traditional jurisprudence—race consciousness.

Because racial critiques of law are "rooted in the history of American race relations," the intellectual origins of critical race theory are quite old, going back to the early history of slavery in America.[15] The idea of "critical" race theory, however, can be traced to recent developments in the civil rights movement. The movement became visible after a number of important conferences were held at the University of Wisconsin to consider minority perspectives and approaches for responding to the "crisis of confidence" in the civil rights movement and antidiscrimination law in America. By the late 1980s, advocates and critics alike seemed to agree that the civil rights movement in America had run out of steam. Professor Derrick Bell, the most widely known African American civil rights scholar in legal education today, forcefully argued that the civil rights movement and its promise of supposed benefits of legal reforms has been largely a failure.[16] On the other side is the highly regarded conservative African American commentator Thomas Sowell, who believes that the struggle for racial equality under the law has been completed and that continued affirmative action is no longer necessary.[17]

## Color-blind Law

Much of the intellectual debate about civil rights reform in American law is based on the ideal of a "color-blind" society.[18] Traditional legal scholars, influenced by the liberal values of universalism and formal equality, saw the goal of ending race discrimination intertwined with the law's aspiration of objectivity and neutrality. The traditional view posited that the legal system would eliminate race discrimination by ensuring that every citizen, regardless of race, received the same treatment under law. The liberal version of a color-blind society required "color-blindness" in the law of race discrimination. However, once the law performed its proper function of assuring formal equality, color-blindness meant that furthering the rights of one group at the expense of another would amount to race discrimination. Thus, antidiscrimination remedies such as affirmative action would promote race discrimination in a color-blind society. Differences between groups would not be the result of race discrimination in such a society, but the expected consequences of groups competing for societal rewards on the basis of merit. The debate over civil rights hinged on whether or not American antidiscrimination law achieved formal equality between the races.

Conservative race scholars such as Thomas Sowell argued that the ideals of formal equality had been achieved in America. According to Sowell, "The battle for civil rights was fought and won—at great cost—many years ago."[19] Because conservative scholars like Sowell believe that the battle for formal equality was won, they argued that the continued demand for affirmative action and equality in outcomes made civil rights advocates mere lobbyists for special-interest politics.[20] The civil rights movement, with the help of federal judges, was held responsible for the politicization of antidiscrimination law. This conservative criticism of civil rights reform in America was similar to Herbert Wechsler's criticism of the *Brown* decision:[21] both said that judges should not participate in a process that reduces "the law to a question of who has the power and whose ox is gored."[22]

Derrick Bell, on the other hand, argued that the stylistic paradigm of civil rights law had established an argumentative basis for the belief that the races enjoyed formal legal rights, when in fact the reality of race discrimination continued to subordinate African Americans to an inferior position in society.[23] Bell argued that it was the rhetoric of neutral rights which prevented the legal system from doing anything efficacious about the substantive inequality between the races. Bell viewed the Warren Court decisions on civil rights as establishing a false rhetoric of racial equality. As Bell observed: "The modern civil rights movement and its ringing imperative, 'We Shall Overcome,' must be seen as part of the American racial fantasy."[24] He has argued that the Supreme Court's decision in *Brown v. Board of Education*[25] was decided the way it was because the decision coincided with the interests of middle- and upper-class whites.[26]

The different perceptions of these two well-known intellectuals helped shape and focus the political positions of scholars on the question of color-blind antidiscrimination law. The conservative and liberal position is that antidiscrimination law should be color-blind, while the left argues on behalf of race consciousness. Conservatives like Sowell have aligned themselves with the color-blind meritocratic position of modern legal scholars who follow the liberal Wechslerian view that questions of race must be judged under racially neutral standards. Under the color-blind meritocratic position, individuals should be judged on the basis of merit and ability regardless of race. Critical race scholars of the left attempt to develop ideological critiques of civil rights law that deepen the original insights of Derrick Bell's *interest-convergence thesis.*[27] They reject the color-blind, meritocratic position of conservative and liberal legal scholars because they believe that meritocracy and color-blindness are cultural standards that favor the interest of the white majority and fail to respect the reality of racial hierarchy structuring American society. For critical race scholars, color-blind meritocracy is part of racist ideology that prevents the law from affirming the cultural diversity of individuals belonging to the minority community. Critical race scholars thus argue that meritocratic judgments must be made on the basis of race-conscious standards.

## Racial Critiques of Civil Rights Scholarship

Instead of "color-blindness," critical race scholars argue the importance of *race consciousness*—the view that the question of color is more than just an issue of skin pigmentation. To be *race conscious* is to be aware that race is linked to identifiable communities in American society that are "*different* from the community of Anglos in America." [28] Seen from the perspective of race consciousness, the "belief in color-blindness and equal process . . . would make no sense at all in a society in which identifiable groups had actually been treated differently historically and in which the effects of this difference in treatment continued into the present." [29] Critical race scholars thus challenged the epistemological category of color-blind law—a legal category of racial justice that modern liberal legal theorists have used to structure race discrimination law for the past fifty years.

A central aim of the movement focused on the effort to develop a racially distinctive body of race consciousness scholarship. Civil rights scholarship reflects the perspective of white scholars who examine racial problems from the perspective of white culture. Critical race scholars claim that the existing body of scholarship in civil rights fails to adequately address the perceptions and consciousness of racial minorities who experience firsthand the oppression of racial discrimination. [30] They challenge the traditional legal scholar's faith in external, universally accepted meritocratic standards for judging the merits of scholarship. They argue that color-blindness has infected civil rights scholarship thus preventing legal scholars from understanding the meaning of discrimination from the victim's perspective.

Richard Delgado criticized the "scholarly tradition" in civil rights law for its failure to encourage the participation of minority scholars in the development of central areas of civil rights law. [31] Because minority scholars have been excluded from the scholarly tradition, their work is rarely cited by the courts because they are not members of the "inner circle of about a dozen white, male writers who comment on, take polite issue with, extol, criticize, and expand on each other's ideas."[32]

Professor Mari Matsuda, agreeing with Delgado, complained that racial hierarchy in legal academia has favored whites over blacks, creating what she has called "segregated scholarship."[33] Matsuda argued that victims of racial oppression can speak with special authority on problems of race: "The victims of racial oppression have distinct normative insights."[34] She claimed that "[t]hose who are oppressed in the present world can speak most eloquently of a better one."[35] Delgado and Matsuda thus advanced an "exclusion thesis," which asserted that "the intellectual contributions of scholars of color are wrongfully ignored or undervalued."[36]

Critical race scholars also argued a "racial distinctiveness thesis."[37] They asserted that minority scholars share an awareness of racial oppression that permits them to discuss problems of race from a personal vantage point that gives their narrative the authority of "racial distinctiveness." Delgado argued that white scholars see civil rights problems from a fundamentally different perspective than minority scholars. Consequently, they tend to focus on different issues, arguments, and substantive topics.[38] Matsuda argued that the legal elite of academia have established an illegitimate racial hierarchy that has subordinated the academic status of minority scholars.[39] She argued that minority scholars are the ones the law should listen to since "[t]hose who have experienced discrimination speak with a special voice."[40]

The emphasis on race consciousness in critical race scholarship has stimulated a call for stories from and about the experience of people of color. As a result of the new pedagogy of storytelling, a new form of narrative jurisprudence emerged within critical race scholarship. Like the narrative jurisprudence associated with the feminist and law and literature movements, which seeks to reveal the human potential missing in law, race-conscious narratives are offered to reveal the missing race consciousness of legal and social thought. Critical race scholars such as Derrick Bell, Richard Delgado, and Patricia Williams have used rich allegories, metaphors, chronicles, and parables to describe the experience of race discrimination from an African American perspective. Race narratives are another illustration of how "narrative jurisprudence" illuminates a particular experience left out of modern legal discourse.[41]

The "voice of color" is relevant because it gives importance to the perspective of minority groups.[42] The rationale for race narratives in legal scholarship is similar to the argument for feminist narratives in legal scholarship—both seek to bring out the social reality of the victim's story.[43] Critical race scholars, like feminist legal scholars, attempt to provide a perspective for understanding the gender implications of traditional jurisprudence—perspectives that are not easily understood by white men. Race and gender are said to be prerequisites for speaking and writing on the subject of race or gender discrimination. Stories are vehicles for ascertaining knowledge about different cultural worlds.

## Minority Critiques of the Critical Legal Studies Movement

Critical race scholars also developed a "critique of the critique" of CLS scholars and their political criticisms of law in general, as well as race-relations law in particular.[44] Kimberle Williams Crenshaw, for example, focused her race-conscious criticism on the ideological projects of CLS as they related to the left-critique of American law generally. In her path-breaking article, *Race, Reform and Retrenchment: Transformation and Legitimation in Antidiscrimination Law,*[45] published in the HAR-VARD LAW REVIEW in 1988, Crenshaw identified what she called a serious "unintended consequence" of the CLS critique of American legal thought, namely the failure to address the reality of racial oppression.[46] As she explained: "While Critical scholars claim that their project is concerned with domination, few have made more than a token effort to address racial domination specifically, and their work does not seem grounded in the reality of the racially oppressed."[47] Crenshaw also claimed that CLS may have disempowered racial minorities by denying them the transformative potential of liberalism's aspiration and by failing to address the problem of racism in America directly.

Crenshaw asserted that the CLS attack on rights discourse was incompatible with minority efforts to achieve transformative social change through the law. In her view, CLS strategy may have led minorities down a dead-end road. Crenshaw, like other critical race theorists, argued that the CLS critique of rights failed to recognize that rights discourse offered racial minorities "some aspirations that are central to Black demands, and may also perform an important function in combating the experience of being excluded and oppressed."[48] Crenshaw also rejected the standard CLS view of legal ideology as "induced consent," because the CLS view failed to appreciate that racism, not liberal ideology, was the true source of racial domination.[49] Critical race scholars thus argued that the "principal error" of the CLS critique of liberal ideology is that CLS assumes that ideologically induced consent is the source of all forms of domination and oppression.

The CLS position on race discrimination law was shaped by Alan Freeman's 1978 article, *Legitimizing Racial Discrimination through Antidiscrimination Law*,[50] which advanced the distinction between the "victim" and the "perpetrator" perspectives.[51] Freeman, a well-known critical legal studies scholar at the University of Buffalo, argued that civil rights law had internalized the perpetrator perspective, which was concerned with rooting out the behavior of bad actors who engaged in discriminatory practices. The central concern of the law was eliminating discriminatory intent or *fault*. The perspective of the victim, however, was rooted in the experience of racial discrimination and oppression. The central concern of law from the victim's perspective is measured by the success of *results*. The official perpetrator perspective of law was, according to Freeman, unable to account for the experience of inequality from the "victim's" perspective. Central to the victim's perspective is the historical experience of racial oppression embedded within the customs and practice of culture. Racial discrimination involves racist practices of culture which transcend the principle of individual fault. When coupled with the ideology of "induced consent," the perpetrator perspective of antidiscrimination law had the effect of "blaming the victim" for the disparate results of the victim's position in society.

Freeman's analysis placed a premium on understanding the law of antidiscrimination from the victim's perspective. Crenshaw argued that "Freeman's discussion of antidiscrimination law suffers from a failure to ground [the] critique in the historical and ideological conditions that brought about antidiscrimination law."[52] Specifically, Freeman was criticized for failing to analyze how race consciousness in the law affected *his* understanding of the categories "victim" and "perpetrator." Crenshaw claimed that Freeman's categories also failed to explain the racial backlash and retrenchment resulting from the implementation of race-specific affirmative action remedies in the law.[53] As Crenshaw explained: "Without such an analysis of racism's role in maintaining hegemony, [Freeman's] explanation simply does not convincingly capture the political realities of racism and the inevitability of white backlash against any serious attempts to dismantle the machinery of white supremacy."[54]

## The Racial Critiques Debate

Racial critiques of civil rights and CLS scholarship have since provoked a heated debate within the academic community. Randall L. Kennedy, an African American professor at Harvard Law School, published *Racial Critiques of Legal Academia*,[55] an essay that rejected the race-based standing assertions of critical race theorists such as Bell, Delgado, and Matsuda. Kennedy's article provoked what is now known as the racial critiques debate. This debate has, despite its polarizing rhetoric, helped to refocus the arguments about the validity and effectiveness of race-conscious legal scholarship. This debate was a defining moment in the critical race theory movement.

The racial critiques debate was precipitated by Kennedy's claim that the race-consciousness critiques of critical race scholars Bell, Delgado, and Matsuda, were "bad for minority scholars" and "bad for all scholars."[56] According to Kennedy, race-conscious critiques "would be bad for all scholars because race-based criteria for intellectual standing are anti-intellectual in that they subordinate ideas and craft to racial status."[57] In his view, race-conscious criticism reduces to the unthinkable view that the merit of one's ideas depends on *"who* one is."[58]

Kennedy thus claimed that race-based scholarship was dangerous because it set the stage for racist categories in judging the validity or merit of ideas about the law. "If the tables were turned," Kennedy wrote, "if a commentator were to read articles by twenty-eight scholars of color, describe deficiencies found in some of them, acknowledge that some black scholars produced work that avoided these pitfalls, but nonetheless conclude that manifestations of these flaws were attributable to the *race* of the twenty-eight authors—there would erupt, I suspect (or at least hope), a flood of criticism."[59]

Kennedy claimed that race-conscious critiques may have had the undesirable consequence of silencing the important contributions of white race scholars, thus hindering the transformative effort of all individuals interested in eliminating illegitimate racial hierarchies in the law.[60] In Kennedy's view, the problem with "voice of color" scholarship

is that it derogates the individual's ability to have an impact in the
world. The idea of "race-based standing" would prevent white scholars
from working in the field. On the other hand, race scholars such as
Thomas Sowell would be presumed to have standing even though their
scholarly orientation is aligned with the very position critical race scholars seek to change.[61] Kennedy also argued that such a strategy could be
misused for illicit racial purposes and would lead to the diminished
reputation of minority scholars, since the field would be regarded by
other academics as "soft."[62]

Kennedy's article precipitated fierce criticism in legal academia, and
in the popular press. Kennedy was accused of being "insincere"[63] in his
arguments, and he was charged in an editorial in the New York Times
as "willing to speak for whites."[64] In a special Colloquy published in
the HARVARD LAW REVIEW, a number of well-respected legal academics
rejected Kennedy's argument and came to the defense of critical race
scholars.[65] Scott Brewer suggested that the debate provoked by Kennedy's article involved a "more deeply flowing discussion" about a
vital moral question of whether minority scholars should emphasize the
"sameness or difference" between the races.[66] Milner S. Ball, on the
other hand, argued that the debate involved two different worldviews or
ideologies: "What is to be hoped for, then, is not a surrender of standards but translation, the art of 'making it possible for people inhabiting
different worlds to have a genuine, and reciprocal, impact upon one
another.' "[67] Robin D. Barnes complained that the role of critical race
scholarship must be understood in terms of the need for cultural diversity: "In a post-modern world in which we have come to realize that
*truth* is somewhere, if anywhere, in the symphony of experience, the
development of solid legal principles that vindicate the rights of all
Americans requires a platform for marginalized voices."[68]

The racial critiques debate has thus raised issues involving the continuing validity of the conventional analytical framework used by traditional legal scholars for analyzing questions of race in the law. These
issues serve to link the critical race theory movement to intellectual
debates over modernism and postmodernism. The question of whether
race-neutral meritocratic norms should be used in the academy for judging the merits of race-based scholarship and, in particular, whether the
racial distinctiveness of meritocratic norms excludes minorities and their
racially distinctive narratives, is characteristic of the type of critical

inquiry postmoderns make in connection with their criticism of legal modernism.

Postmodernists resist what Duncan Kennedy has called "colorblind meritocratic fundamentalism" because they want academic communities to respect the practices, customs, and knowledge of different cultures.[69] Postmodernists argue that because "[t]he natural, racial and ethnic intelligentsias are internally divided along ideological lines" on a wide range of ideological and cultural issues, consensus needed for developing fundamental standards of merit is not possible.[70] What is needed are academic standards that reflect the intellectual diversity of different cultural communities. Postmodernists thus argue that legal academics need to learn "to talk about political and cultural relations of the various groups that compose our society without falling into racialism, essentialism, or a concept of the 'nation' tied to the idea of sovereignty."[71]

The racial critiques debate links up with larger intellectual debates concerning the possibility of neutral law.[72] Like law and literature scholars, critical race scholars question the relationship between interpretive practices and normative perspective. The racial critiques debate relates to the sameness/difference debate in the feminist legal theory movement.[73] Legal feminists disagree on whether to treat gender as a gender-based standing concept for analyzing gender hierarchy or whether gender should be no more relevant than eye color.[74] Alex M. Johnson Jr., for example, recently argued that the race-consciousness critique of critical race theory parallels Catharine MacKinnon's feminist method of dominance: critical race theorists implicitly create a "dominance strand of Critical Race Theory that may ultimately require the rejection of what has been characterized as the integrationist model of racial equality."[75] Johnson argued that the racial critiques debate suggests that the critical race theory movement is "diversifying along lines similar to those in Critical Feminist Theory."[76]

From a broader vantage point, the debate in critical race theory can be viewed as a debate between the two worldviews of legal modernism and postmodernism. The color-blind meritocratic view of Randall Kennedy seems to be representative of legal modernism's embrace of universal and majoritarian meritocratic standards of judgment, and the racial critique of those standards seems to represent the postmodern stance favoring local, contextualized, and culturally diverse standards. The racial critiques debate spawned within the critical race theory movement is arguably another manifestation of the tension and conflict resulting from the diversification of theoretical movements within law and the diverse intellectual discourse those movements have established. The racial critiques debate reflects the consequences of a larger dialectic transformation of the argumentative modes of legal modernism as law and jurisprudence move to the multicultural discourses of postmodernism.

## Race Consciousness as Identity Politics

Indeed, a key distinguishing feature of critical race theory discourse can be discerned from the prefatory commentary that critical race authors frequently make about the labels they use to describe the identity of their subject. Critical race theorists use labels like "African American" and "black" to refer to the identity of specific minority groups in society. Kimberle Crenshaw uses an upper-case "B" in using the word "black" to denote her view that "Blacks, like Asians, Latinos, and other 'minorities,' constitute a specific cultural group and, as such, require denotation as a proper noun."[77] Patricia Williams prefers the term "black in order to accentuate the unshaded monolithism of color itself as a social force."[78] What these examples illustrate is the idea that racial identity should not be regarded "as merely a color of skin pigmentation, but as a heritage, an experience, a cultural and personal identity, the meaning of which becomes specifically stigmatic and/or ordinary under specific social conditions."[79] The more general categories of "black" and "white," as used in traditional legal discourse, are rejected by critical race theorists because those categories are found insufficient for capturing the richness of ethnic and political diversity provoked by critical race scholarship.

Critical race scholars analyze modern modes of jurisprudence as an ideology structured by racial attitudes and norms that ignore the racial and political diversity of American culture. The focus on race consciousness in critical race discourse can be viewed as a form of *identity politics*. The focus on racial "discourse" in critical race theory attempts to understand how discourse produces particular images and racial identities. The effort to particularize the cultural perspective of specific groups and to break down unitary concepts of race seeks to uncover the ideology within the racial view of the law. Critical race theorists claim that different racial identities are excluded by the current racial categories used in the law and that this exclusion denies racial equality.

Identity-based scholarship attempts to challenge modern jurisprudential notions of objectivity, neutrality, and universality. Mari Matsuda called for a new jurisprudence that looks "to the bottom" of the social structure of race relations to understand the experience of racism.[80] Richard Delgado, in turn, emphasized storytelling and racial narratives as means for understanding the experience of victims of racism in American legal thought.[81] These critical race theorists believe that the identity of race, rather than the color of skin pigmentation, invokes the cultural heritage and personal identity of specific groups in society. Identity-based scholarship is aimed at uncovering the ideological structure of racism in American intellectual practices and discourses. Critical race theory is aimed at exposing the dynamics of this racist ideology.

Race narratives are only one method used for these purposes. Another method involves the critical interpretive practice of deconstruction. For example, Crenshaw used the deconstructive practice of Jacques Derrida to demonstrate how the traditional understanding of race issues in the law is influenced by hierarchical categories structured by whites and blacks. She claims that racist ideology reproduces Derridian dichotomies or polarities to establish what Derrida called a "metaphysics of presence."[82] According to Crenshaw, racist ideology is based on oppositional dualities such as industrious/lazy, intelligent/unintelligent, moral/immoral, and knowledgeable/ignorant, that associate the color white with a privileged or superior image (intelligent, moral, knowledgeable) and the color black with an inferior image (unintelligent, immoral, ignorant).[83] The dynamics of these traits were said to be created and maintained through an "elaborate and systematic process" in which the categories "filled with meaning—Blacks were characterized one way, Whites another. Whites became associated with normatively positive characteristics; Blacks became associated with the subordinate, even aberrational characteristics."[84]

The point of Crenshaw's deconstruction was, first, to show how racist ideology was structured by a hierarchical opposition of ideas and, second, to demonstrate that the opposition could be reversed by inverting the difference defined by the images associated with the colors white and black. Crenshaw saw the exposure of race consciousness within color-blind ideology to be the central task for eliminating the hegemonic consequence of racist ideology. Challenging racial hierarchy was linked to the goal of showing how racial identity is socially constructed by the difference of the "other." Race consciousness defines the notion of identity. Self-identity seems so basic, so "present"; but identity depends on the notion of difference. "Difference is a derivative concept based upon identity: Two things are different if they are not identical." [85] Racial identity is thus comprehensible only in terms of difference with the "other." Racial identity is not itself foundational to problems of discrimination; discrimination stems from the way racial identity is defined in terms of the privileged relation to the difference of others. Crenshaw stated: "The establishment of an 'other' creates a bond, a burgeoning common identity of all non-stigmatized parties—whose identity and interests are defined in opposition to the other." [86] A color-blind society in which racial identity defined and subordinated one's position could not be a just society.

To challenge the legitimacy of racial inequality, critical race scholars like Crenshaw argued that traditional notions of formal equality had to be deconstructed. A color-blind society operating under a race-conscious ideology might give the appearance of formal equality (under law, blacks and whites are equal), when in fact the reality is that legal categories are defined by a racist ideology that subordinates blacks as inferior to whites. Crenshaw believes that civil rights advocates needed new legal strategies to undermine the way racist ideology defined black Americans as the "other." She saw rights discourse as an important means for developing such a strategy, because the rhetoric of rights could be defined to protect the interests of blacks. [87] On the other hand, rights discourse might also co-opt the challenge, as CLS scholars have argued. For critical race scholars, however, "Liberal ideology embraces communal and liberating visions along with the legitimating hegemonic visions." [88] They believed that rights rhetoric could be used for transformative purposes, creating a crisis in the prevailing social order. "The use of rights rhetoric during the civil rights movement created such a crisis by presenting and manipulating the dominant ideology in a new and transformative way." [89]

Critical race scholars have consequently developed their understanding of race ideology from social theorists who studied how ideology is hidden within the meritocratic standards of Western thought. The Italian neo-Marxist, Antonio Gramsci, for example, developed a critical approach for understanding how domination and oppression operate in Western cultures.[90] Gramsci invented the concept of *hegemony* to explain how physical coercion and ideological control are managed by a system of thought that persuades the dominated class to accept its domination as an inevitable state of affairs. Critical race scholars have used Gramsci's notion of hegemony to explain the ideological role of racial classifications in antidiscrimination law much in the same way that CLS scholars have used the same concept in critiquing liberal legalism.[91]

Critical race scholars used Gramsci's ideas of ideology to go beyond the CLS critique of liberal legal thought. These scholars first argued that the CLS "account of the hegemonic nature of legal thought overlook[ed] a crucial dimension of American life—the ideological role of racism itself."[92] To remedy this perceived deficiency in CLS thought, critical race scholars argue that the "hegemonic glue" of racist ideology in America can be discovered by considering what "is believed *about* Black Americans, not what Black Americans believe."[93] They tell stories from their racial perspective in order to develop the actual experience, history, culture, and intellectual position of people of color. Narrative and storytelling represent a new epistemological source for getting at forms of knowledge missing in the standard stories told in the law about race.

Critical race scholars use race consciousness to develop new strategies to confront and transform beliefs held about racial minorities in the dominant consciousness of white society. The goal of the race consciousness critique is to challenge the race consciousness of white society directly.[94] Race discrimination is understood by critical race scholars as an ideology that legitimates the privileged status of white society. Racial stereotypes in white culture attempt to rationalize the oppression of Blacks "by perpetuating a mythology about both Blacks *and* Whites [which] reinforc[es] an illusion of a white community that cuts across ethnic, gender, and class lines."[95] Critical race scholars argue that racist ideology creates the illusion of unity of interests between white and all non-white communities. Crenshaw, for example, argued that the everyday institutional practices of society implement this ideology by embodying "white norms" as neutral, fair, and meritocratic.[96] In this sense, critical race scholars claim that "race consciousness makes it difficult—at least for whites—to imagine the world differently."[97]

## Postmodern Nationalism

Critical race theory reflects the broader intellectual developments that evolved at the end of the 1980s known as "multiculturalism," the "diversity movement," or "postmodernism." Critical race scholars attempted to establish multicultural perspectives of empowered, culturally vibrant racial communities within the legal academy in order to preserve an intellectual foothold for the cultural and personal identity of different racial groups in society.[98] The emergence of the critical race theory movement "is intertwined with parallel and analogous developments in other academic fields, as well as with recent transformations of the American cultural arena, developments often labelled as 'multiculturalism' or the 'diversity' movement."[99] Multiculturalism and the critical race theory movement share a common rejection of the legal moderns' faith in a single meritocratic color-blind standard for resolving questions of race.

Critical race theory is another current in the legal academy that rejects the vision of law as "one right answer" derived from a culturally neutral standard or method. Critical race scholars rejected the notion that law can be studied in a way that is culturally neutral.[100] "From the perspective of race consciousness, being African American means being part of an historically situated community that is *different* from the community of Anglos in America."[101] Critical race theory thus encourages minority legal scholars to develop a scholarship of racial nationality, or what Gary Peller has called *postmodern nationalism.*[102]

To Peller, postmodern nationalism is an attempt to define the cultural identities of different people by reference to the definitions established in cultural practice, rather than "some distant or fantasized past, or to some fantasized future of separation and purity in the way that some black nationalist groups have done."[103] Peller's idea of a postmodern nationalism recognized the historical construction of racial identity, but it does not freeze that understanding forever. He believed in the possibility that racial identity can be transformed in the future. Postmodern nationalism calls for multicultural movements in legal studies to reclaim their cultural heritage and experiences as different racial groups, including African Americans, Asians, Latinos, Native Americans, and other "minorities."

Asian Americans have drawn from the race-consciousness critique of critical race theory and asserted the existence of an "Asian American movement" in legal studies.[104] This "[m]ovement is marked by the increasing presence of Asian Americans in the legal academy who are beginning to raise their voices to 'speak new words and remake old legal doctrines.' "[105] Race consciousness critiques of the critical race theory movement are considered inadequate for addressing the race problems of Asian Americans because "Asian Americans suffer as Asian Americans, and not just generically as persons of color."[106] Because Asians are stereotyped as being "foreign," anti-Asian sentiment is a particular type of racism unique to Asian Americans.[107] The Asian American community has also found itself in conflict with the African American community, as the Los Angeles riots following the Rodney King trial illustrate.[108] Asian American legal scholars thus claim that "[to] focus on the black-white racial paradigm is to misunderstand the complicated racial situation in the United States."[109] Asian American legal academics created their own narratives of discrimination to justify the need for a distinct Asian American legal scholarship.

The most important insight to be drawn from the developing race-consciousness scholarship is that there is no essential concept of race, culture or group identity. The move toward a postmodern nationalism is a strategy aimed at exposing and highlighting the multicultural nature of America. Critical race scholarship is a means of identifying the roots of the diverse voices that make up American culture. Postmodern nationalism exposes how the diversity of race consciousness enhances and diversifies the intellectual currents of American law.

It is still too early to tell where these currents will take the jurisprudence of race relations. Some have argued for the development of new laws to protect the values of cultural diversity. Neil Gotanda, for example, argued in his essay, *A Critique of Our Constitution Is Colorblind*,[110] that a new constitutional right of cultural diversity should be developed by making an analogy to the religious freedom protected under the First Amendment.[111] Alex Johnson, on the other hand, has argued that the debate over the voice of color has been concluded and that it is time to contemplate a new communitarian theory of law—a theory that places "emphasis on community, the individual's situatedness within that community, and the dialogic in the community as a methodology for achieving 'right' actions leading to good consequences."[112]

One thing is clear. Critical race scholars have contributed significantly to jurisprudence by exposing how traditional legal theorists have ignored the importance and significance of race consciousness in their under-standing of law. In rejecting the racial essentialism of color-blind law, critical race scholars have reconceptualized race in a postmodern way, recognizing the importance of the racial context of a multiracial society in which group existence is partial, unstable, and in flux. Critical race scholars argue that race-conscious law is needed to enable different racial groups to live together in a multicultural and racially diverse society. Postmodern race scholars thus state that "[i]t is not a sign of a pathology within the community to have people who are different and say that they are different. It is a sign of a cosmopolitan postmodern nationalism." [113]

*Postmodern race "theory"* attempts to decenter the universalism of modern discrimination discourse by questioning the way modern theo-rists have uncritically relied upon a universal concept of a racial subject in their legal analysis. Legal moderns approach the problem of race discrimination by positing the existence of an autonomous subject who is "color-blind." The goal of racial equality under law is viewed by legal moderns as a goal that requires "color-blind" standards enforced by a "color-blind" judiciary. *Postmodern race theorists* attempt to subvert this formation of subject identity by revealing how it fails to take into account the multiple identities and subjective experiences of people of color. The postmodern strategy aims at *decentering* the legal conception of race by revealing the different experiences of racial groups.

The strategy of decentering the legal conception of race, for example, can be seen in the effort of black feminists who have focused on the intersectionality of race and gender.[114] Black feminists report that they find it difficult to entirely accept the narratives of white feminists or black race scholars. The intersectionality of their identity has required black feminist legal scholars to develop their own narratives of the complicated nature posed by the interrelated forces of racism and sexism in their lives. The multiple consciousness of black feminists helps explain the dilemma Anita Hill faced during the Clarence Thomas nomination hearings that culminated in Thomas's confirmation as a United States Supreme Court justice.[115]

Hill charged Thomas with sexual harassment, but she was unable to represent her position as a black woman. Thomas successfully defended himself by invoking the image of a "high-tech lynching" to associate his position with the plight of black men who suffered brutal forms of discrimination, including lynching, for asserting their manhood. "While Thomas was able to invoke narratives that linked his situation to the sexual oppression of black men and thus have his story understood as relevant to the entire black community, Hill remained unable to represent even herself, much less other similarly situated black women."[116] Anita Hill had a rhetorical disadvantage because her racial identity was itself suppressed by Thomas's assertion of the race issue. To make her case, Hill had the difficult position of establishing the legitimacy of her own intersectional identity as a black woman subordinated within black culture. Responding to Hill's difficulty, Kimberle Crenshaw argued that more attention must be placed on the way race identity is defined and manipulated for rhetorical purposes in the law. Black feminist criticism has unwittingly, by virtue of the postmodern condition, brought postmodernism to critical race theory. Race is multivocal and must be understood within the intersections of power relations of a multicultural and racially diverse culture.

*Part Three*

# Postmodern Jurisprudence, 1990s and Beyond

# 10. Jurisprudence in Transition

The jurisprudential movements of the 1980s deepened and advanced a process of crisis and transition in modern jurisprudence. The most striking facet of this transformation has been the success of new forms of jurisprudential discourse or "law talk" in penetrating, subverting, and decentering the conventional forms of legal discourse. The proliferation of different jurisprudential discourses has erased the lines between description and advocacy, making it much more difficult for traditionalists to maintain their belief in neutral and objective law. A new understanding of language and interpretation has fired the imagination of legal scholars as they reexamined and critiqued the polar categories that had separated the domains of law and society. Different types of theoretical tools have been used for reexamining law as an essentially cultural medium of a multicultural community. The rediscovery of the relation of law and society has led contemporary legal thinkers to the view that the problems of law cannot be "solved" by some "theory" abstracted from context.

By 1990, legal studies in America could no longer claim to be confined to an autonomous narrative or discourse of law. Law talk had developed new dialectical discourses defined by economic analysis, critical legal studies, feminism, literature, and race consciousness. These proliferating discourses have created the critical space in jurisprudence for other discourses to develop within legal studies. The resulting proliferation of discourses has transformed the way legal scholars talk and think about problems of jurisprudence. Many of the basic issues of jurisprudence have been shown to have a cultural dimension that encouraged legal scholars to consider the modes of thought and discourse of diverse cultures in society.

These recent developments in jurisprudence represent a new form of postmodern jurisprudence. Legal scholars only recently began to explore and identify the premises of postmodernism in legal thought. Peter C. Schanck has attempted to capture the meaning of postmodernism by associating postmodernism with four "interrelated concepts." These four concepts react against a particular version of legal modernism. The four concepts are:

(1) The self is not, and cannot be, an autonomous, self-generating entity; it is purely a social, cultural, historical, and linguistic creation. (2) There are no foundational principles from which other assertions can be derived; hence, certainty as the result of either empirical verification or deductive reasoning is not possible. (3) There can be no such thing as knowledge of reality; what we think is knowledge is always belief and can apply only to the context within which it is asserted. (4) Because language is socially and culturally constituted it is inherently incapable of representing or corresponding to reality; hence all propositions and all interpretations, even texts, are themselves social constructions.[1]

Schanck's dissection of postmodernism into basic concepts is contrary to postmodernism, in that any attempt to locate the core concepts or essences of postmodernism falls prey to modernism.[2] Schanck's taxonomy is thus a thoroughly conventional and predictable modern narrative. The desire to categorize the strands of postmodern legal thought into a taxonomy of concepts gives the impression that Schanck is following the modernist's conceptual framework of understanding. A better way to approach postmodernism is to examine how Schanck's interrelated concepts have been used by postmodernists to recover contradiction, paradox, ambiguity, and so on, in the traditional modes of jurisprudence. One must examine how postmodernists use concepts of modernism to shake the hold of modernism. To understand the nature of postmodernism we must also look to contemporary legal criticism and its effect on the current intellectual situation.

The present contours of postmodern jurisprudence have been shaped by legal scholars who have recovered and exposed contradiction, paradox, and ambiguity within the fragmentary features of American jurisprudential theory. Disagreement and debate about the nature of theory, language, knowledge and the primacy of individual subjects have intensified the experience of contradiction and paradox. Instability has been further heightened by proliferating new discourses and intellectual practices for the study of jurisprudence. Diversity and disagreement caused a fundamental transition in jurisprudence. The existence of multiple discourses and methodologies has led to major paradigm shifts in the thinking of many prominent jurisprudence thinkers.

The legal movements of the 1970s and 1980s have come to represent the intellectual themes of *postmodernism—antifoundationalism, antiessentialism, social construction,* and *deconstruction.* These themes can be discovered within the intellectual practices of the new scholarly movements of the late 1980s. These movements depart from legal modernism in that they define themselves against the traditionalists' aspiration to uncover essential and universal concepts of law to govern the temporal conditions of society. Postmodern legal scholars reveal how the language and theories of contemporary legal theory reflect the fragmentary and chaotic nature of politics and culture in the 1980s and 1990s.

## Proliferating Intellectual Practices

Postmodernists currently seek to intensify the different intellectual agendas of different cultural groups, and the intellectual orientation of those espousing them, in order to provoke a debate about the nature of the relation between law, economics, literature, politics, gender, and race. This effort was not so much a matter of style as it was a question of politics and culture.

For example, law and economics scholars had argued that the dominant methodologies of modern legal thought are inadequate because they lack scientific rigor and a persuasive theory for developing a consistent theory of decisions. These scholars believe that "[h]opes for a better society do not justify unreflective treatment of the tradeoffs we must make in a world of scarcity."[3] Some law and economics scholars took issue with liberal scholars who argued that objective decision making standards can be inferred from an interpretive community or from some enduring theory of legal rights. They claimed that judicial decision making has and will become increasingly consistent as the judiciary adopts the law and economics perspective. In place of process values of "harmony," "stability," and "shared-values," law and economics scholars argue that in the "real world," what counts are the "facts of life" —

"scarcity," "choice," and "self-interested conduct."[4] Others accept the liberal vision of shared values, but offered a less determinant methodology for realizing the liberal vision.

Critical legal studies scholars, in turn, advanced a different theoretical agenda. They claimed that modern legal scholars stood in the way of political emancipation. What was needed was a new critical theory of law that had a more realistic understanding of the problems of class, race, and gender in American society. CLS thus attempted to develop a *critical guide* for understanding how the ideology of liberalism embedded within the argumentative structures of modern legal thought prevented the law from achieving its highest ideals.[5] Crits argued that new critical tools were needed for exposing the true politics of liberal legal thought. Crits claimed that legal interpreters were free to choose from a variety of possible techniques, methods, and approaches in dealing with law's problems. Instead of the process virtues of stability and shared values, or the liberal ideals of universalism and impartiality, Crits argued that law and adjudication were the products of "conflict," "struggle," and "politics," and they worked hard to bring out a more contentious and political mood in legal studies.

Feminist legal scholars deepened the ideological work of CLS by exposing how modern legal scholars, and those within critical legal studies, justify a masculine perspective of law shared by men, but not by women. They argued that contemporary legal scholars can claim consistency and fairness only by relying upon a conception of law and adjudication that excludes the perspectives of those who are in the margins of power. Feminist scholars advanced the perspective of women's experiences and feminine values. In place of the process values of "universality" and "objectivity," feminist legal scholars believe that law must explicitly take gender into account, particularly the feminist contextual values of love, commitment, and care.

Law and literature scholars raise yet different theoretical questions about law. They look at the language of law and see a form of life with a real force of its own. These legal critics argue that language and interpretation "do[ . . . ] much to shape both who we are—our very selves—and the ways in which we observe and construe the world."[6] They approach legal studies by offering specific and highly detailed explanations of the dominant cultural and political force of law. It is said that "[l]iterature provides a lively and accessible medium for learning about law in an ethical way."[7] The representational practice of law is critiqued to provide a new vantage point for comparing how literature "understands law." The understanding offered by literature provides a "poetic method of law and a poethics (poetic ethics) of reading."[8] The approach of literary criticism seeks to reveal what is missing in the traditional accounts of reality depicted in the cases found in published legal opinions. The approach of "narrative jurisprudence" offers new stories for learning about what is missing in the standard stories told in law.

Critical race scholars have in turn exposed how the conventional discourse of law rests upon assertions of a color-blind meritocratic view of objectivity and neutrality that is said to perpetuate societal disadvantages based on race.[9] Critical race scholars seek to show how "color-blindness" of affirmative action law covers a particular ideology that mirrors and justifies the dominance of white culture.[10] In telling different stories and narratives about race, critical race scholars have developed an "outsider narrative jurisprudence" that challenges conventional distinctions between law and politics, and reason and race found in traditional jurisprudential notions about law.[11]

The cumulative effect of the jurisprudential movements of the 1980s shattered the consensus underlying modern legal thought. By 1990, new theoretical criticism deepened the attack on legal modernism by challenging a number of core assumptions central to the work of modern legal scholars. Modern notions about legal impartiality, fairness, objectivity, and neutrality were questioned, as postmodern scholars uncovered new connections between law, culture, knowledge, politics, and human identity. In viewing law as an essentially cultural medium, postmodern scholars became skeptical about the possibility of legal values such as objectivity, neutrality, and rationality which were deeply reflexive of the faith in law's autonomy. Thus, law and economics scholars argued that modern liberal scholars had internalized an outworn view of "law as an autonomous discipline"—a view that assumes that law is "a subject properly entrusted to persons trained in law and in nothing else."[12] They asserted that the modern modes of legal thinking are "old-fashioned, passé, tired";[13] that traditional legal scholars ignored the insights of other disciplines (namely economics) and assumed a political consensus can be reached for deciding on an official method for legal decision making.[14] Law and economics scholars believe that it is "wrong" to assume that legal problems can be resolved by one set of premises and one method of argument. They look beyond law to develop new determinate theories for establishing law's legitimacy.

CLS scholars challenged the notion that legal texts contain neutral meanings that can be "correctly" discovered by apolitical "authoritative" legal methods. They argue that "it just isn't possible to do legal scholarship without making [ideological] choices" about how to explore particular issues and paths of theoretical inquiry.[15] Crits argue that "ideology is commitment" whether it is consciously or unconsciously acknowledged. In drawing from Foucault's insight that "power comes from everywhere," Crits have developed a *postrealist* political analysis of the relation between power and knowledge to show how legal institutions and legal analysis itself creates and perpetuates social power. Crits teach that knowledge is a form of power and politics. CLS scholars argue that judges and legal academics who interpret the law are too elitist, too privileged to be trusted as representatives and guardians of the values and interests of all those within the larger society.

Feminist scholars rejected the notion that law can be studied as an autonomous system abstracted from the reality of gender differences. These scholars use the experiences of women to show how allegedly neutral abstractions in the mainstream legal analysis are in reality constructed from the masculine perspective. Feminist scholars argue that claims of objective and universal law mask discriminatory content and application under male-constructed norms of jurisprudence. Feminist critics look beyond law to ascertain how the traditional understanding of adjudication reflects a cultural perspective that fails to respect the realities of women. Like law and economics scholars, feminist legal scholars seek a view of law that evaluates the effectiveness of legal rules by judging their instrumental capacity in promoting the well-being of individuals.[16] Like CLS scholars, feminist legal scholars argue that law must be approached from a multidisciplinary perspective, focusing on gender differences and the social basis of gender power.

Law and literature scholars argued that contemporary legal methods taught in legal education are representative of "a craft that has been dead in the water since the late fifties."[17] They advance insights from literary studies and application of new forms of literary criticism in an effort to "jump-start legal education's engine."[18] Narrative and interpretive jurisprudence of the law and literature movement provide an important literary medium for stimulating a more aggressive and humane understanding about how law might serve human goals in a more just world.

Critical race theory offers its own narratives and critical methodologies of race to underscore how traditional theories about law fail to account for the experiences and perspectives of African Americans and people of color. Critical race theory seeks to expose the "ways in which those in power have socially constructed the very concept of race over time, that is, the extent to which White power has transformed certain differences in color, culture, behavior and outlook into hierarchies of privilege and subordination."[19] The "essentialism of universal sameness [between White and Black] is rejected" in order to acknowledge "differences between Blacks and Whites that are 'sufficiently' real, namely, differences in experience, outlook, and response."[20] Race consciousness is heightened by these scholars who take color-blindness seriously to show how allegedly neutral analysis of race problems in mainstream legal materials fails to account for the experience and reality of race discrimination and racial hierarchy.

The emergence of different theoretical practices in legal studies has weakened the once dominant hold of large-scale, foundational explanations of law. The established foundations of law have been shown to rest upon contested translations of legal text constructed from cultural practices of legal subjects. Members of different cultural and intellectual communities have represented their perspective, establishing an intellectual culture in the legal academy that calls for different theoretical and normative perspectives for jurisprudential studies. Multiculturalism,[21] a word that signifies diversity and culture, has challenged the status and prestige of universal concepts and ideas of modern jurisprudence.

## Proliferating Discourses

Modern legal thought developed on the assumption that the intellectual faculties of interpreting subjects could develop a form of legal discourse that would enable the law to be more principled, coherent, and morally appealing. The projects of legal modernism thus presumed that a universal form of discourse was possible in legal studies. The most significant consequence of recent movements within jurisprudence has been the shattering of this idea of a dominant language or discourse for law.

Indeed, a staggering proliferation of different jurisprudential discourses now exists: economic, political, literary, gender, racial, and so forth. The law is now viewed as a language of different practices, beliefs, thoughts, perceptions, and preferences of different individuals and groups in society. A form of multicultural analysis and criticism has emerged as legal scholars considered different modes of discourse and communal conversation in society. Legal scholars examined how legal discourse established an authoritative conversation for law and critically examined how that official conversation excluded, marginalized, and ignored other discourses in the communal conversation. This culturally based inquiry has led to the discovery of competing communal languages for developing new legal languages in law.

For example, by the late 1980s, openly bisexual, lesbian, and gay legal scholars developed gay and lesbian legal studies, a new form of critical discourse that has sought to correct the biases and inaccurate views of sexual orientation in Western legal culture.[22] William N. Eskridge, Jr., for example, argued that a "Gaylegal Agenda" for jurisprudence must be discovered within the discourse of the counterculture of the gay and lesbian communities.[23] One important goal of gaylegal discourse is "to provide more reliable information and rigorous legal arguments for discussions of issues important to the bisexual, gay, and lesbian communities; and to criticize laws and legal interpretations that penalize or stigmatize [bisexuals, gays, and lesbians]."[24]

The liberal discourse of rights in American legal institutions is said to have denied the interests and perspectives of gays and lesbians because that discourse is found to be "rooted in the moral culture of 1950's" liberalism which marginalized people who differed from the heterosexual white stereotype of the 1950s nuclear family.[25] Gay and lesbian legal scholars of the post-Stonewall generation[26] have proclaimed their desire to change the worldview of modern jurisprudence (the "fifties-liberal culture of pluralism and the melting pot, of law as process and neutral principles, of the Nelsons and Cleavers as the happy nuclear family")[27] by developing a gaylaw jurisprudence. The core principles of this jurisprudence are based on "the morality of [gay and lesbian] intimacy, the need to disrupt rather than merely reform the interconnected social and political obstacles to such intimacy, and an insistence upon equal citizenship for bisexuals, gay men, and lesbians."[28]

Similarly, Native American legal scholars have argued that Western jurisprudence has developed an assimilationist discourse that has been used as a sword against Native American culture to prevent the diversity of their cultures from becoming part of the official American culture.[29] Native Americans have thus struggled to preserve and protect indigenous discourses of law and justice by resisting the assimilationist tide of American law. Like the gaylaw agenda, Native American law is aimed at preserving Native Indian traditions by recognizing the need for protecting tribal legal organizations and their unique discourse from the interference of Western law.[30] Native American law has thus struggled to develop its own unique cultural legal discourse.

Asian legal scholars have also recently joined the legal academy in increasing numbers proclaiming the existence of an Asian American movement that offers a new critical race-conscious discourse to reverse the problem of discrimination against Asian Americans.[31] These scholars offer a narrative account of exclusion and marginalization from the perspective of Asian Americans. Exclusion of race discrimination is thus shown to have many faces; its harms are not the same for all minorities. Asian American legal scholars are now attempting to develop their own cultural discourse for analyzing legal issues relevant to their communities.

Another offspring from critical race theory discourse has been black feminism, which offers its own legal narratives to capture the unique experience and voice of black women.[32] Black feminist discourse arises out of the intersectionality of interests of black women who experience discrimination both as women and as blacks. The intersection between racism and sexism has enabled black feminists to discover a unique discourse of racial and gender discrimination unique to black women. The black feminist critique of antidiscrimination law has addressed how the interplay of race and gender has constructed sexuality and race consciousness in ways that ignore the experience of black women. Embracing the intersection between race and gender, black feminists have started to develop a black feminist critique of law that speaks the language of those women who reside in the intersection.

The proliferation of law talk has refocused the concern of jurisprudence on the importance of culture and how culture shapes and structures the values, beliefs, and thoughts of legal subjects. The study of jurisprudence is consequently becoming the study of diverse legal subjects who inhabit the law. Jurisprudence is becoming a multicultural discipline of rich and diverse theoretical discourses. A renewed interest in forms of legal discourse has started a transformative process in jurisprudence that has broken down the barriers separating law from culture, and between jurisprudence and its interpreting subjects.

The culturally specific character of the gay-lesbian, Native American, Asian and black feminist communities and their distinct communal conversations offer new discourses for engaging jurisprudential studies from the perspective and interests of different people and groups. Gaylaw, Native American, Asian law, and black feminist discourse are examples that affirm the importance of being aware of group affiliation, or group identity, in talking and thinking about law. They celebrate the identity politics of multicultural perspectives and criticism of law.

Communal conversation, or multicultural law talk, encourages the law to be more sensitive to the differences between groups and individuals in society. Subcategorization in legal analysis "might solve the problem of apparent essentialism, by moving us closer to what people are like 'as individuals.' " [33] On the other hand, subcategorization may also "take us further from the particular truth of a consciousness rather than nearer to it, not because the truth is situated at the level of the universal, but because the seductive specificity of 'straight, white, upper-middle-class male' hides as much as it reveals." [34]

The postmodern strategy of legal scholars fosters the proliferation of different cultural discourses of identity in order to render law more "realistic" in its understanding of culture. Thus, black feminist criticism has emerged within the critical race and legal feminist movements challenging the prevailing constructions of identity politics of African American men and white women. The dominant discourses of racism and sexism are critiqued in order to reveal how those discourses render it impossible for black women to fully articulate their interests. [35] The strategy of intersectionality analysis of identity politics seeks to empower groups and individuals who are not sufficiently identified in the grid of subcategories currently used in the law for evaluating social problems. Multicultural law talk developed through consciousness of identity bringing intellectual diversity to the legal academy, and with that diversity an increasing realization of a nonuniversalist law.

## Ironic Shifts and Oscillations

Resistance and reaction against the modern modes of jurisprudence have not consisted of a complete or total rejection of modern legal thought. The 1980s movements in jurisprudence exhibit considerable degrees of antipathy and ambivalence toward modern liberal thought. This too is a tell-tale sign of postmodernism: postmodernism recognizes and embraces the antipathy and ambivalence of the current times. Indeed, postmodernists are quite likely to bring attention to the ironic shifts and oscillations in legal theory. It is just not traditional legal thought that is shifting, but the legal movements of the 1980s as well.

The ambivalence pervading contemporary legal discourse is illustrated by the "legal rights" debate. *Chicago School* law and economics scholars, for example, claim that the assignment of legal rights is theoretically irrelevant in cases without bargaining or transaction costs. Where transaction costs block bargaining, these scholars treat rights as if they were mere "price signals" for allocating scarce resources to their most efficient users. *Post-Chicago* school law and economics scholars have adopted more complex behavioral assumptions that analyze legal rules under market and nonmarket conditions that accept the notion that individuals sometimes act strategically. These scholars, unlike the founders of the Chicago School, no longer give primary significance to the economic value of efficiency in reformulating legal rights in accordance with economic analysis.

The analytical move of law and economics has allowed law and economics scholars to make a shift from rights jurisprudence to an overt instrumental jurisprudence. *Post-Chicago* scholars can now agree with their founding fathers that economics equips lawyers and judges with a new understanding of how to make legal policy analysis more rigorous, scientific, and pragmatic. Rather than deducing meanings from abstract economic concepts for understanding the nature of contract and property, post-Chicago scholars approach economic analysis of law by drawing new pragmatic lessons that depart from the rational-economic actor model of economics. Their goal is to transcend legal rights by unifying law with the empirical methods of the social sciences, thereby erecting a new pragmatic structure for instrumentally approaching law. It is said that "[i]n the economic approach to law, legal rights are designed, in part, to overcome the conditions under which markets fail."[36] To reach this result, some contemporary law and economics scholars attempt to "overcome" the problems of jurisprudence by turning their back on legal modernism altogether.

CLS scholars reject the conception of rights advanced by mainstream legal thinkers for different reasons. Some Crits reject the modern rights theorists' belief in a rational basis for making normative judgments. Such a belief is seen as founded upon unrealistic expectations and controversial criteria that fail to support judgments that progressive legal thinkers would accept. Most CLS scholars point to the existence of doctrinal indeterminacy as a prime example of the controversial nature of the normative judgments made by traditional scholars.[37] A minority faction within CLS seems to have believed that the liberal conception of rights can be socially constructed and reestablished by redefining rights to correspond to the needs of disadvantaged social groups. While substantial disagreement exists, most critical thinkers claim that the trouble with rights thinking is that it reinforces a profoundly self-destructive and alienated form of human consciousness.[38] The rights debate has nonetheless moved CLS toward the position of liberal legal scholars who rely on the modernist's conception of rights to argue for particular normative outcomes.

Feminist legal theorists challenge the rights theories of traditional legal scholars by demonstrating how those theories fail to respond to the social, economic, and political harms of women. A central point of the feminist critique of rights is that abstract formulations of rights actually conceal gender-biased assumptions that foster a coercive legal system. Some feminists claim that the rights discourse of modern scholars "has an unofficial, underground, subterranean potentiality, only occasionally recognized, but nevertheless always there."[39] According to this view, rights discourse must be used carefully to advance feminist interests or to remedy their harms.[40] Other feminist thinkers argue that the concept of rights must be transformed to take into account the differences of women. While feminist legal scholars advance different views on how to "feminize" rights, as a group they believe that prevailing "masculine" theories of rights must be resisted and changed.

In focusing on the human character of law, law and literature scholars reject traditional legal concepts of rights as abstractions distinct from real people and human values. Law and literature scholarship is said to offer "a hope of redemption from a technocratic future" depicted in the rights discourse of modern legal theory.[41] Legalisms and abstract "rights" are seen by law and literature practitioners as obstacles that prevent the achievement of social justice in the law.[42] For those who understand law as an interpretive activity, the idea of legal rights is discounted, and instead more emphasis is placed on the modes of interpretation used to justify, interpret, and discover the existence of rights.[43]

Critical race scholars are more tentative on the question of rights. They want to preserve the transformative potential that the liberal conception of legal rights offers people of color, while sharing the skepticism of CLS and feminist critiques that see rights discourse as an ideology that mystifies and marginalizes different perspectives and ideas critical to black culture. Critical race theorists worry that the trashing of rights consciousness exhibited by CLS scholars may have the "unintended consequence of disempowering the racially oppressed while leaving White supremacy basically untouched."[44] While supporting a race-conscious concept of rights, critical race theorists seem to be arguing that a new race-conscious theory of rights needs to be developed—one that takes the reality of racial domination and oppression seriously. The basic strategy seems to be one of using the logic of rights discourse against itself by highlighting the "contradiction between the dominant ideology (represented by traditional rights discourse) and [the] reality [of powerless people]."[45]

To some, the new scholarly movements may seem to be moving in the direction of legal modernism in advancing legal agendas that seek to reform the law by rendering legal theory more pure and more capable of achieving the Enlightenment aspiration of human freedom by defining legal rights. One might argue, as David Luban argued, that the postmodern developments in legal scholarship of the late 1980s express a *neo-Kantian* type of analysis that would place them within the framework of objectivity, truth, and knowledge characteristic of late modernism: the *improvisations* of postmodernism in Luban's view are a form of "self-criticism" that attempt to develop "jurisprudence within jurisprudence" and thus repudiate the negation of modern jurisprudence.[46] Luban's view suggests that recent legal criticism attempts to "live up to the quality achieved by the great premodernist (classical) works."[47]

Luban's neo-Kantian characterization of the current intellectual situation in law, however, is too self-consciously rooted in the past,[48] too caught up in Kantian rational thought, to capture the irony of the current intellectual situation in law and jurisprudence.[49] Kantian rational thought cannot survive postmodernism because postmodernism seeks to undo and transform the linguistic, conceptual, and normative underpinnings of the modernist conception of reason attributable to Kant's philosophy. Kant believed that individual freedom and human rationality were ineluctably connected, and neo-Kantians remain committed to that view. Postmoderns argue that concepts about rationality and individuality are mediated and socially constructed by a language that is incapable of grasping reality.[50] "The postmodern conception of individuality casts the individual not as the subject in control of discourse, but as an artifact produced by discourse."[51] The improvisations of postmodernism thus represent the creation of new identities and new subjects for overcoming, not improving, the vestiges of modernism.

Postmodern legal movements challenge the idea that law and legal reasoning can be the basis for establishing a universal, autonomous Kantian system of legal rights. Postmodern legal movements aspire to develop a *non*-Kantian legal tradition based on neopragmatic and postmodern criticism. Postmodern legal scholars, while diverse and hardly united in perspective, share a common aspiration of exposing and highlighting the conflict and tension of a world comprised of sharp political and economic differences—a world where scarcity, privilege, sexism, racism, and disadvantage are ubiquitous.

It is true that maturity of the new scholarly movements has brought about less ambitious claims by successive generations of legal scholars. Strong claims of legal determinacy and legal indeterminacy have been recanted and downplayed. And maturity has also created ironic oscillations in theoretical perspective, as the debate between the critical legal theorists Tushnet and Peller, on the merits of narrative jurisprudence, illustrates.[52] Indeed, it would now seem that the radical indeterminacy thesis of early critical legal writing has given way to a social-construction thesis that views ideology and politics as sources of law's determinacy rather than its indeterminacy. In law and economics, the radical determinacy thesis represented by the law-and-efficiency hypothesis has in turn given way to a new acceptance of legal indeterminacy.[53] Law and economics analysts now seem to place less attention on legal rights and instead focus on behavioral consequences of cultural and legal practices.[54] Law and economics and critical legal studies movements have consequently exhibited oscillations between claims of legal determinacy and legal indeterminacy.

The scholarly debate that pitted legal determinacy against legal indeterminacy within the critical legal studies and law and economics movements no longer captures the imagination of its members. In the legal feminist movement, essentialist claims made by feminists who argued that a universal "women's" experience can be discovered for developing a truly feminist jurisprudence are now downplayed. The essentialist claims of cultural feminists, for example, have been criticized by other feminists who argue that the full complexity of women's experience belies the assertion of a universal female experience. In law and literature, a debate occurred over the issue of whether essential literary methods of interpretation can be used to discover the best interpretive framework for legal studies, or whether all that can be expected is an open-ended "ethic" of interpretation for uncovering the complexity of legal texts.[55] Feminist legal theory has moved from early claims of a universal women's perspective to a multicultural and anti-essentialist feminist position, and the law and literature movement similarly moved away from the essentialism of "law-in-literature" to an anti-essentialist "law-as-literature" perspective.

Although the critical race theory movement has just recently formed, there are indications that this movement rests upon a situated discourse of race, problematized by particularized descriptions of racial oppression and historical experience and generalized insights of a rights-based, race-conscious law. The essentialism of rights-based law, however, has been questioned as critical race scholars examine the particularity of race-conscious narratives. The disintegration of race-neutral law has set the stage for the development of postmodern critical race theory. The postmodern idea of race consciousness has been informed by investigations of the relation between *self* and *other*.[56] The new discourses of economics, politics, literature, gender, and race have thus established their own problematic and paradoxical practices.

Like traditional forms of jurisprudence, the new forms of jurisprudence have ultimately failed to ground their critical theory and practice in a monolithic explanation of law and legal decision making. Instead, local critique and microanalysis of the particularity of the contextual setting are increasingly becoming the favored theoretical approach in legal studies. This shift in theoretical perspective has occurred because the boundaries of jurisprudence have been challenged, and because the discourses and methodologies of law have diversified and proliferated. Jurisprudence is now a multicultural study. Legal scholars who once looked inside law to discover answers to law's problems now look outside to culture to find solutions that are satisfactory to local communities. A growing number of legal scholars have consequently rejected the modernist's belief in essences, foundations, and right answers that supports legal modernism.

## Paradigm Shifts

By 1990, contemporary legal theory had fragmented into different theoretical perspectives and interpretive communities. These developments in legal theory followed the pattern of paradigm shifts in science described by Thomas Kuhn and Paul Feyerabend.[57] The confidence that once characterized legal scholarship during the 1950s and 1960s had vanished in the wake of the criticism endlessly waged throughout the decade of the eighties. The political consensus that had supported the confidence in law's autonomy had been slowly dissipating since the early 1970s as new interdisciplinary approaches to law offered new perspectives and methods for legal studies.[58]

During the 1970s, Gilmore reported that the great structure of Langdellian jurisprudence had crumbled sometime during the period between the two world wars.[59] By the mid-1980s, the process of fragmentation had reached such epidemic proportions that Richard Posner was able to report that the faith in law's autonomy was dead:

The supports for the faith in law's autonomy have now been kicked away. First, the political consensus associated with the 'end of ideology' has shattered. The spectrum of political opinion in law schools, which in 1960 (except in Catholic law schools) occupied a narrow band between mild liberalism and mild conservatism, today runs from Marxism, radical feminism, and nihilism on the left to economic and political libertarianism and Christian fundamentalism on the right. Even if we lop off the extremes, a broad middle area remains, running from, say, Ronald Dworkin and William Brennan on the left to Robert Bork and Antonin Scalia on the right—two pairs of entirely respectable, 'establishment' figures but so distant from each other ideologically that there is little common ground of discourse. We now know that if we give a difficult legal question to two equally distinguished legal thinkers chosen at random, we may well get opposite answers.[60]

This did not mean that legal modernism had ceased to inspire legal scholars at the academy. To the contrary, the spirit of the Enlightenment could still be found in the interdisciplinary work of legal scholars who looked outside of law to find a methodological foundation for legal analysis. The trappings of Langdellian formalism could be found in the interdisciplinary analysis of modern legal movements such as Posner's law and economics, which exhibited considerable optimism and confidence in the ability of economic analysis to offer the missing disciplinary authority for law. Gilmore believed that a new Langdell was waiting to make "his appearance on front-and-center stage" promising a "new conceptualism" for legal studies of the future.[61] The Langdell that Gilmore had in mind was Richard Posner, who represented the "New Conceptualism" of the law and economics movement. Gilmore's prediction, however, turned out to be inaccurate. By 1990, Richard Posner largely rejected legal formalism and instead embraced the postmodern pragmatic philosophy of Richard Rorty, a leading postmodern philosopher.[62] By 1990, a paradigm shift had transformed the jurisprudential thinking of one of the best-known advocates of the modern theory of economic analysis of law.

From the vantage of the early 1970s, there was good reason for believing that a new conceptualism in legal studies was about to form. Interdisciplinary formalism could be found within legal analyses that sought to discover the missing disciplinary authority of law in economics, critical theory, feminist theory, literary criticism, and critical race theory. Interdisciplinary legal studies of the 1970s and early 1980s developed structuralist accounts of law that purported to describe the inner logic or "structure" of law. Like nineteenth-century doctrinal formalists who attempted to describe the "essential" or "true" categories of law, contemporary legal scholars seemed to advance a similar formalist agenda in their effort to locate the structure of law in a nonlegal methodology. Langdellian formalism remained a dominant feature of legal scholarship throughout the 1970s and early 1980s, although it came with a new methodology claiming greater sophistication and power.

By the mid-1980s, however, a theoretical transformation could be detected in legal scholarship. A transformatory process resulted in surprising new positions being advanced by well-known modern legal thinkers. An "epistemological break"[63] can be found by comparing the early 1980s and late 1980s scholarship of a number of prominent legal scholars. For example, Richard Posner's ECONOMIC ANALYSIS OF LAW[64] and Roberto Unger's KNOWLEDGE AND POLITICS[65] projected neo-Aristotelian perspectives or essentialist views in their 1970s analyses of American law. For Posner, economic analysis provided the essential foundation for understanding American law. For Unger, the fundamental contradictions of liberal legalism were the foundation. By the mid-1980s, both authors moved away from their earlier foundational orientations. Posner's 1990 book on jurisprudence, THE PROBLEMS OF JURISPRUDENCE,[66] embraced the postmodern pragmatic orientation of Richard Rorty, while Unger's mid-1980s work, THE CRITICAL LEGAL STUDIES MOVEMENT,[67] advanced an antifoundational or "local critique" strategy for progressive legal criticism.

Ronald Dworkin's early 1970s text, TAKING RIGHTS SERIOUSLY,[68] presented a strong foundationalist argument about rights based on claims of moral theory. In his more recent book, LAW'S EMPIRE,[69] however, Dworkin argues that justice as "integrity" requires judges to come up with the "best" legal arguments constructed from different literary interpretive practices. The shift from "right answers" to "best interpretation" represents a subtle change in the intellectual perspective of Dworkin; he seems less confident about his assertions of a universal constitutional foundation. John Rawls's recent book, POLITICAL LIBERALISM,[70] offers a political conception of justice which rejects the universalistic idea of a well-ordered society developed in his 1971 book, A THEORY OF JUSTICE.[71] The theoretical shift in perspective of these important contemporary legal thinkers is symptomatic of larger changes unfolding in the academy.

The new scholarly movements have encouraged legal thinkers to redefine the key terms for analyzing jurisprudential questions about law and adjudication in the future. The new movements in jurisprudence have challenged the once widely held view that law is an *autonomous* subject distinct from politics and moral philosophy. In bringing an interdisciplinary perspective to legal studies, the new jurisprudential movements have stimulated debate and forced new inquiry about the nature of law. While the result of this has been partly subversive, it has also led to the discovery of new insights about law.

For many legal scholars, the new discourses about law seem threatening, and even dangerous. On the other hand, it is also becoming evident that the new movements in jurisprudence are in the process of becoming institutionalized in the legal academy. The jurisprudential movements of the 1980s are becoming part of the established landscape as more and more law schools begin to offer separate courses organized around these movements and as legal academics begin to study the work of new movement scholars. Initial fears and claims of protest are now giving way to resignation, acceptance, and an overall "upbeat" mood.[72] Academic interest in the new movements is now extraordinarily high, as recent legal symposiums illustrate.[73]

The transitional state of contemporary jurisprudence reflects both the dawning significance of major trends in twentieth-century social theory, and ironically, a nostalgic interest in understanding the complicated relation between law and society. Diversity in intellectual practices and discourses about law has created a condition in jurisprudence that promises nothing less than total subversion of the modernist conception of jurisprudence. The break in the link with legal modernism can be discovered in the stunning paradigm shifts of a number of prominent legal thinkers. The possibility of a major paradigm shift in jurisprudence can also be discovered by considering how modern legal scholars have reacted to the new developments in jurisprudence.

# 11. Reaction of Modern Legal Scholars

History indicates that when a new theory or paradigm appears to challenge the view and methods of an established theory or paradigm, a crisis in confidence emerges, provoking a response from the mainstream.[1] The reason is clear. Professional reputations and careers are at stake; the old guard must hold off the challenge posed by the "Young Turks" in order to maintain their status and privilege. It is thus not surprising that new movements in legal thought have provoked heated response from a number of distinguished legal scholars. Some questioned the new critics' professional and ethical commitment to law, and the legal profession.[2] Others argued that the new critics are practicing dangerous or unethical forms of criticism.[3] Still others questioned whether the new movements will make communication and discourse within the profession impossible.[4] Criticism of new scholarly movements developed throughout the 1980s as the voice of outsiders gained momentum and the new movements matured. The ensuing criticism has been waged in terms of standard arguments about academic merit, scholarly standards, professionalism, and even the Rule of Law itself. The nature of this debate suggests that paradigm conflicts will not be resolved by theoretical proofs, but that their resolution will instead depend on the force of conviction and pleas for commitment to preserve the status quo.

## "Rule of Law" and Professionalism

Perhaps the most notorious reaction to the new movements was Paul Carrington's metaphoric essay, *Of Law and the River*,[5] which several years ago sparked a heated controversy in the pages of the JOURNAL OF LEGAL EDUCATION.[6] Carrington, the former dean of Duke University School of Law, argued that law teachers who "embrace nihilism and its lesson that who decides is everything, and principle is nothing but cosmetic [have] an ethical duty to depart the law school, perhaps to seek a place elsewhere in the academy."[7] The essay was controversial because it was generally viewed as a broadside attack on the critical legal studies movement.[8]

A number of legal scholars, including a few who are identified with the mainstream position that CLS criticizes, objected to Carrington's position. Former dean Guido Calabresi of Yale University Law School retorted that if "in all honesty what the scholar sees seems false, then the scholar must declare it to be false even if that opens him or her up to the charge of nihilism."[9] Professor Owen Fiss of Yale University Law School rejected Carrington's suggestion of a purge of the so-called nihilists and argued that "[w]e cannot shut off an avenue of inquiry, for fear that it would render the professional training [in law school] pointless. . . . [I]t is of the essence of academic freedom to allow all sides to speak."[10] Carrington subsequently stated that it was not his intent to question the professional ethics of all persons "having sympathy or connection with CLS" but "to comment instead on Legal Nihilism."[11] Additionally, Carrington made clear his "oppos[ition] to Red Hunts and loyalty oaths."[12]

More recently, Judge Harry Edwards from the Washington, D.C., Circuit Court of Appeals (formerly a law professor at the University of Michigan Law School) authored an essay that gave a new twist to Carrington's diatribe.[13] Edwards's thesis is that the new emphasis on interdisciplinary studies, theoretical scholarship, and jurisprudential theory prevents law schools from satisfying their primary mission of training effective lawyers and judges. Edwards expressed his deep concern about the growing disjunction between legal education and the legal profession, and argued that law schools and law firms are moving in opposite directions.[14] Edwards's position is that law "schools should be training ethical practitioners and producing scholarship that judges, legislators, and practitioners can use."[15] To support his thesis, Edwards relied on a survey of letters from his former law clerks who said that they were not adequately prepared by law schools for law practice. Edwards claimed that this was "proof" that law schools had become overly theoretical and of little use to practicing lawyers and judges.

Edwards's essay sparked a controversy among legal scholars, who voiced their views in a symposium on legal education in the MICHIGAN LAW REVIEW.[16] The critical reactions to Edwards's essay included lively responses from Richard Posner, who defended the "pragmatic" utility of interdisciplinary legal education and scholarship;[17] there were also representative responses from the law and economics,[18] law and literature,[19] feminist,[20] critical legal studies,[21] and postmodern perspectives.[22] Although Edwards drafted a reply to the responses of his many critics,[23] his plea for a return to an old-fashioned practical and ethical lawyering did not convince many members of the new generation of legal academics. Indeed, many legal scholars who participated in the symposium found Edwards's plea for old-fashioned doctrinal-skills training quaint.

Carrington and Edwards's essays implicitly articulated what many older legal scholars may have felt after being introduced to the new scholarly movements: they viewed the new scholarly developments as a threat to the profession and the professional status of the legal academy. It is not difficult to explain why they might feel this way. The message of the new scholarly movements was critical of the majoritarian worldviews they had internalized and refined during their initiation into the profession. The postwar paradigms that established the academic standards for their tenure initiation became the filter *they* internalized for evaluating the merits of the scholarly works of younger legal scholars. Thus, their views about the character of legal reasoning, the nature of legal education, and their definition of the profession became the normative standards used in evaluating legal scholarship for tenure and promotion.[24] Deviations from those standards were not permitted.

Modernist views about objectivity, truth, and knowledge have understandably become the framework for making normative judgments about law, legal practice, legal pedagogy, and legal scholarship. Those standards reflected a longstanding consensus of opinion. Academic standards for judging meritorious scholarship were thought to be determined by objective and neutral standards derived from indubitable foundations about the nature of law and legal practice since the 1950s. But these views reflected the normative orientation of the old doctrinal scholarship of legal moderns, the *normativity* of which was critiqued by younger scholars in the academy. And there was now reason to question whether those views were sufficient to prepare the next generation of lawyers for the challenges of a multicultural society.[25]

Moreover, while debates and controversies have always been the hallmark of the law school, law school faculties were experiencing unprecedented tensions as the younger generation attempted to develop and follow the insights of the new scholarly movements. Law faculties were, however, supposed to conduct their affairs much in the same way the typical American family depicted by the Nelson family on *Ozzie and Harriet* resolved family disputes—academic disputes should be resolved by warm-hearted, sensitive, tolerant judgment. The importance of maintaining a consensus underscored the enforcement of scholarly and civil norms. The 1950s vision of legal process embedded within the normative ideas of modern legal scholars reflected this idyllic view of the world in general.

It is not surprising then that the new scholarly movements might be perceived by mainstream legal scholars as threatening. The reason for this is not complicated. The postwar generation of legal scholars' normative vision was threatened by the critique of Young Turks. They questioned the normativity of older scholars, and their sense of civility. The historian Patricia Nelson Limerick offers a provocative reason for the older scholar's fear: "They were, their inner script and scenario told them, on their way to being the grand old men of their fields; they would be admirals of the big fleet of American history, or American literature, or American legal studies. But then something very disorienting happened to the fleet, and to its chain of command and its navigation."[26] The older scholars suddenly realized that they were "piloting ships that suddenly seemed small, and that were headed in a completely different direction from the rest of the fleet."[27] Postwar legal academics such as Carrington and Edwards saw the baby-boomer generation sailing away in a different intellectual direction. "No wonder, then, that the admirals turned to laments and grim prophesies: without their leadership, the fleet would disintegrate, and with it would go national identity and unity and common purpose."[28]

One way to get the Young Turks back in line would be to discourage forms of scholarship that departed from the majoritarian standards of academic achievement. Hence, the most frequently heard reason for discouraging new scholarly forms of legal criticism is to require that they conform to the legal modernist's professional standards of civility. Postmodern criticism is rejected because it is found to be unintelligible, impractical, and fraudulent when analyzed in terms of the modernist's legal aesthetic. Legal moderns thus fail to take seriously the critique of normativity. For postmodernists, the "law" of the legal academy justifies its pronouncement with an almost religious worship of "reason," which many find to be passé, defensive, and authoritarian.[29] "Thus, when the 'law' of the academy encounters new intellectual currents— everything from hermeneutics, to poststructuralism, to anthropology— the first contact tends to exhibit a sort of violent adjudicatory character. . . . [W]hat we typically get is the academic equivalent of a ruling from the bench on whether the foreign insight or idea is or is not useful to law's empire."[30]

One way to maintain peace has been to threaten to banish the unruly youngsters from the academic family for breaching professional standards. The critique of normative legal thought is therefore judged by some to be uncivil and therefore unprofessional. The "family" of legal scholars should never be allowed to deviate from the normativity of their "family"; professionalism requires that they agree on the basic normative values of American society. While Carrington expressly disapproved of the idea, the implication drawn from his essay is that legal educators should be required to pledge allegiance to the normative standards of their profession. Edwards seemed to imply this in arguing that legal educators should first and foremost be doctrinal and legal practice scholars. In performing their gatekeeping function, modern legal scholars seem to be demanding that new members of the profession demonstrate a scholarly commitment to the old scholar's aesthetic practice. Former students, trained under their view, are likely to be strong supporters of the prevailing dogma.

The effort to dampen dissent in the academy is a normal and expected reaction. The function of normative legal thought is to identify forms of argument that satisfy the modernist framework of objectivity, truth, and knowledge.[31] Normative legal thought thus establishes an internal mode of social control that "identifies and polices the bounds of legitimate legal thought."[32] The assertion of professional "standards" has always been a subterranean basis for mainstreamers to defend their *particular* normative conception of law and adjudication.[33] The reactions of modern legal scholars to the new scholarly movements were therefore normal and understandable given their normative orientation.

Members of the new scholarly movements thus risk ultimate exclusion in advancing scholarly projects which mainstreamers find objectionable. Some have already been suppressed from advancing alternative professional conceptions of law and practice for fear of expulsion. But many of the Young Turks successfully weathered the reactions of modern legal scholars and earned tenure. The fleet of American legal studies thus continued to sail away in a different intellectual direction. The *zeitgeist* was going against the normativity of older scholars.

## Legal Nihilism and the Death of the Law?

Perhaps the most eloquent defender of the mainstream position of modern liberal legal scholars is Owen Fiss. Professor Fiss of Yale University School of Law offers honest criticism of the new movements without embracing the more extreme positions taken by Carrington and Edwards. He is extremely forthright in explaining his strongly held liberal convictions about law and adjudication. In his Stevens Lecture at Cornell University School of Law, Fiss presented a very forceful argument and defense of the conception of law that now represents the position of many modern liberal scholars. This argument was based on the idea that law and adjudication express a public morality, and an objective process for discovering law's legitimacy.

Fiss's 1986 lecture, ominously entitled *The Death of the Law?*,[34] argued that at least two of the jurisprudential movements of the 1970s, law and economics and CLS, "were dangerous" because practitioners of those movements "distort the process of law and threaten its very existence."[35] Fiss criticized the strand of law and economics associated with the Chicago School because its arguments and methodology depended on what Fiss deems "contestable assumptions" about law and adjudication.[36] Fiss claimed that the new economic analysis of law "fails to supply the explanatory mechanism needed to give [the movement's claims] predictive validity, or even descriptive credibility."[37] He argued that the "normative" claims of the Chicago School theorists rested upon a "crude instrumentalism" that would lead to the "relativization of all values."[38] Finally, Fiss asserted that the law and economics movement failed to reflect the way the judiciary understands its own role—"judges do not see themselves as instruments of efficiency, but rather as engaged in a process of trying to understand and protect the values embodied in the law."[39]

Fiss argued that CLS practitioners critique without a vision of what might replace that which is destroyed—a form of critique Fiss found "unappealing and politically irresponsible."[40] Fiss claimed that the indeterminacy claims that Crits assert about law are suspect because the assertions have not been empirically established or defended.[41] Fiss then argued that the "law is politics" creed of CLS is threatening to both law and public morality because there is no way of confining the "law is politics" criticism.[42] His primary objection was that the CLS movement generated a dangerous form of *legal nihilism* that threatened the ability of law to sustain or generate a public morality.[43]

In defense of liberal jurisprudence, Fiss invoked the great struggles of the civil rights movement and the liberal values associated with the Warren Court era of constitutional law as examples of the public morality and concept of law he favors. He claimed that "[t]he proponents of law and economics would have us believe that the typical nuisance case, or for that matter, a case like *Brown v. Board of Education*,[44] was simply a conflict over preferences, and that it arises because the preference of all parties cannot be fully satisfied."[45] Fiss argued that the nihilism of CLS is dangerous because it undermines the law's belief in the fundamental values fostered by cases like *Brown*.[46] Like other modern liberal scholars, Fiss believes that an objective interpretive process can establish a necessary baseline for defending the conception of public morality symbolized by Chief Justice Earl Warren.[47]

Although Fiss recanted much of his criticism of the CLS movement in a published speech,[48] he remains staunchly committed to his overall jurisprudential position, a position that members of CLS and the other movements of the 1980s criticized. Many of Fiss's views about the law must be seen in terms of his firmly felt convictions about the fundamental rights revolution associated with the Warren Court.[49] Fiss's intellectual agenda is aimed at protecting the jurisprudential values he associates with the Warren Court. For Fiss, normative legal thought was constructed once and for all by the 1960s Supreme Court. All other normative conceptions of law are rejected as unacceptable because they fail to subscribe to the public morality Fiss attributes to the Warren Court.

The conviction that an objective legal process can guarantee and preserve the values of civil rights, equality, or an entire constitutional era is a highly debatable view in the legal academy during the 1980s. Critical race theorists, for example, are quite pessimistic and skeptical about the lessons to be drawn from the Warren Court.[50] Derrick Bell observed, "[J]ubilant predictions of victory in the struggle against racism based on a favorable court decision or helpful statute have always proved premature."[51] Bell demonstrates how antidiscrimination law accommodates conservative as well as liberal views of race and equality. He argues that there is no guarantee that a particular form of jurisprudence fosters a particular moral vision.[52] Critical race scholars show that there is no evidence, in theory or practice, to support the conviction that fundamental rights jurisprudence will ever *overcome* racism, sexism, and economic disadvantage. Critical race theorists instead offer alternative conceptions of law that promise to preserve the very values which Fiss and other liberal scholars try to defend.

Responding to the reactions of modern liberal scholars, critical race theorists challenge the view that public morality can be consistently and intelligently developed through an objective interpretive legal process, uninfluenced by the particular perspective of a universally defined law interpreter. They doubt that judges can discover shared values in a society where vast disparities of wealth and power exist between social and economic classes. Some argue that a conception of public morality can be defended, but only by using different, race-conscious methods. Others question the belief that a community of law interpreters can be trusted with the absolute authority to define public morality under law. Still others wonder whether the very idea of shared values, in denying the value of difference, is itself a dangerous idea for those at the margins of power. Instead of offering pleas for shared values, critical race scholars re-examine the legal perspectives that now dominate the legal imagination. Modern legal scholars such as Fiss are right to wonder if the new movements may signify the death of their particular conception of law. It is unclear whether the death of a perspective of law which dominated the legal imagination of Fiss's generation is cause for celebration or concern. It is clear, however, that the new movements in jurisprudence successfully challenged a concept of law that dominated legal analysis for nearly three decades.

Thus, one can understand why Fiss might fear that the movements of the 1980s might lead to the "death of the law." As Pierre Schlag noted, "[W]hen a discipline is then challenged (as it is here) disciplinary thinkers are very likely to experience this challenge as an attack on the self—their selves."[53] It is not surprising that modern legal theorists might fear the "death" of their work objects, which are related to their very subjective definitions of their professional identity. Schlag also notes: "This is perfectly understandable. It is also unfortunate."[54]

## Comprehensible Discourses

In reacting to the possibilities of sheer incomprehensibility of different legal discourses, some legal scholars, not all of whom are opposed to the new movements in law, have called for the creation of a new "constructive" or "comprehensible" discourse.[55] Martha Minow argued in a 1986 essay, *Law Turning Outward*, that the new interdisciplinary movements in law make it increasingly difficult for members of the profession to speak together or to speak to members of other disciplines because they require a different language and form of discourse.[56] Minow called for a new "comprehensible discourse" that would allow legal academics to engage in a public debate about their differences in methodology and outlook.

Minow wanted this discourse to "relinquish the claim of exclusive truth, and [evince] a willingness to hear competing vantage points, all of which are partial."[57] She asserted that "[r]ather than creating some new distanced categories and methods of legal analysis removed from popular understanding, legal scholars [should] look to local, specific problems that crop up in their experiences."[58] Minow recommends dialogue, listening, and efforts to make one's own claims comprehensible to others, while advocating the recognition of the inevitable partiality of one's own understanding and perspective. The idea is that "legal scholarship should look outward by looking inward to how it has insulated law from communication with nonlawyers, and cut off the sound of legal meaning in people's daily lives."[59]

Other legal academics have made similar arguments proposing the creation of a new comprehensive form of legal discourse. Bruce Ackerman once argued that the legal profession needs a "common language" that will enable its practitioners to engage in a "main line of conversation in a more constructive direction."[60] Unlike Minow, Ackerman

called for a "technocratic" discourse to provide a new source of authority and to stabilize the rhetoric of lawyers. Then lawyers could "translate
their clients' grievances into a language that powerholders will find
persuasive."[61] Ironically, the new "common language" that Ackerman
advocated was based at least in part on the language of "law and
economics."[62]

These divergent proposals for a new common discourse suggest that
the decision to use a particular "descriptive" discourse, such as feminism's discourse of difference, or the language of law and economics,
would be just as controversial and perhaps as polarizing as the current
substantive debate being waged by different discourses. It is unlikely that
legal scholars could agree on a common language, because those who
define the official language will have the power to entrench their particular conception of law and adjudication.

Even a language that seeks to valorize difference may abuse its power
and cut off alternative conversations that are necessary for presenting
new and contrary perceptions of the world. Martha Minow recognized
this danger, noting that "[i]n critiques of the 'male' point of view and in
celebrations of the 'female,' feminists run the risk of treating particular
experiences as universal and ignoring differences of racial, class, religious, ethnic, national, and other situated experiences."[63] Of course, the
same danger exists with critiques of CLS that come close to asserting
that a particular contradiction in legal thought is "fundamental" and
hence is the universal basis for critiquing American law. There seems to
be a common tendency within the new jurisprudential movements to
privilege a particular perspective as "truth" and thereby repeat the mistakes these movements identified in mainstream legal thought. Indeed,
the tendency to privilege some view as the universal view for understanding the world may be a powerful tendency affecting all perspectives.[64]

The call for new comprehensive or comprehensible forms of legal
discourse will probably never escape the very conflict it is designed to
avoid. The concept of a pure descriptive discourse for communication is
itself subject to the fact that social power is always at stake, that change
can only come through struggle and conflict, and that "there is no such
metadiscourse that is itself immune to being placed within its particular
'interpretive framework.'"[65] The fact that a person or some group has
the power to define the acceptable standards of professional discourse
too often remains submerged, unexpressed, and unappreciated. If differ-

ent languages and perspectives are allowed to coexist and compete, then perhaps other perspectives can be acknowledged and appreciated, or at least tolerated. If there is a single lesson to be gleaned from the new jurisprudential movements of the 1980s, it is that method itself is ideological and political; that there is no escape from the link between law and politics.

## Integrity and Judgment

In reacting to the "call of stories" in the narrative jurisprudence of feminist and critical race scholars, Professor Mark Tushnet, a first-generation CLS scholar, seemingly agreed with the reaction of modern legal scholars and complained that storytelling in law is flawed by "failures of integrity and judgment, some more serious than others." [66] Tushnet contended that the pedagogy of narrative jurisprudence is based on the idea that general conclusions about law can be drawn from the narrative accounts of particular events, some of which are true, others that are imagined. Tushnet believes the problem is that the listeners' "general conclusions may be held hostage to the accounts of the particular events." [67]

Tushnet is concerned that narrative jurisprudence may turn out to be "false jurisprudence." [68] For Tushnet, the problem with some forms of narrative jurisprudence is that "the determination of the general problem depends . . . on the integrity of the story or, perhaps, of the narrator." [69] This is a concern that has recently been voiced by Daniel A. Farber and Suzanna Sherry. [70]

Farber and Sherry, law professors at the University of Minnesota, suggest that legal storytelling in the feminist and critical race theory movements is a highly problematic form of jurisprudence because there are presently no objective standards for evaluating the merit and validity of storytelling in the law. While they find that "legal stories, particularly those 'from the bottom,' can play a useful role in legal scholarship," [71] they conclude that "storytellers need to take greater steps to ensure that their stories are accurate and typical, to articulate the relevance of the stories, and to include an analytical dimension to their work." [72] Like Tushnet, Farber and Sherry are concerned that legal storytelling must satisfy the expectation that scholarship in the law be based on practical "reason and analysis." For them, "A legal story without analysis is much like a judicial opinion with 'Findings of Fact' but no 'Conclusion of Law.' "[73]

Gary Peller, a second-generation CLS scholar and professor of law at Georgetown Law Center, has situated this debate within a broader debate about jurisprudence. Peller argues that Tushnet's "narrative" is itself a narrative that reflects a traditional jurisprudential understanding about law.[74] According to Peller, "Tushnet's approach to the scholarship he evaluates is itself historically and culturally constructed."[75] Peller believes that Tushnet's argument reflects a deeply conservative nineteenth-century positivistic conception of law.[76] He argues that Tushnet's criticism of race and gender storytelling "reads in many respects like a replay of Herbert Wechsler's *Neutral Principles* article."[77] As Peller explained:

Like Wechsler, Tushnet's main concern is that attention to particularity, the justice of the case at hand, not obscure the need for 'general rules' (what Wechsler calls 'neutral principles') that will apply to future cases as well. Like Wechsler, Tushnet rests legitimacy on an economy of institutional differentiation, where the requirements of judicial lawmaking are distinguished from political lawmaking because the judicial role requires the overcoming of passion, particularity, and personal identity in favor of neutrality. And like Wechsler, the limits of Tushnet's analysis are revealed in his inability to resolve the issues of particularity and the differences posed by African Americans.[78]

Peller's critique would apply to Farber and Sherry's criticism of legal storytelling by feminist and critical scholars. In suggesting that storytelling in legal scholarship must comply with the standards of practical reason and analysis of judicial opinions, Farber and Sherry attempt to preempt the rhetorical field by postulating that the rhetorical forms of modern jurisprudence establish a universal framework for judging the merits of legal scholarship. Their argument assumes automatically, *as a matter of its own form*, that it provides an uncontroversial and neutral medium for judging the "merit" or "truth" of legal scholarship.[79] This has, in fact, been one of the only "winning" moves advanced by defenders of modern jurisprudence: "If you never allow 'the other' (i.e., here, postmodernism) the possibility of changing your consciousness, your thought patterns, your cognitive or affective disposition, your text etc., then you will always be able to defeat 'the other.' "[80]

However, as Richard Delgado noted, "[M]ajoritarians tell stories too. But the ones they tell about—merit, causation, blame, responsibility, and racial justice—do not seem to them like stories at all, but the *truth.*[81] Indeed, Delgado argued, "Voice is a false issue."[82] At stake is the intellectual vitality of the aesthetics that Tushnet, Farber, and Sherry seek to defend against different sensibilities, discourses, and legal aesthetics. Outsider scholarship exposes how the "grand conversation" of modern jurisprudence is a story that has failed to capture the different values, experience, and "voice" of the "counterstories" told by racial and cultural minorities. The purpose of "counterstory" telling is aimed at challenging the stories told by the "majoritarians" of modern legal thought who assumed that their stories are the complete truth.[83] It is far from clear whether the discourse of modern jurisprudence is capable of sustaining its own normative stories in the face of the counterstories of outsider scholarship.

Tushnet, Farber, and Sherry seem to place themselves within the modernist framework of objectivity and truth. Their claim that new scholarly movements must establish the "truth" of their criticism on the basis of practical reason is characteristically a modernist argument. The counterstories told within the feminist and critical race theory movements, however, challenge the validity of modernist conceptions of objectivity and truth. Outsider narratives by feminists and critical race scholars seek to reveal how truth and objectivity are paradigm-dependent on the worldview of the storyteller. "The lesson is this: the question, 'Is this belief true'? Must be replaced with the question, 'How is this belief to be understood within a particular community or culture'? And, can it be understood differently within the story?' "[84] This question encourages legal thinkers to contemplate the politics of different narrative forms used in jurisprudence and to be wary of fundamentalism in normative arguments generally.

Farber and Sherry do not regard themselves as critics of the new scholarly movements, yet their form of criticism places them squarely within the normative framework of modern legal scholars who evaluate the merit of legal scholarship on the basis of acceptable academic standards. Their standards are the same conventional standards once used by other legal scholars to criticize the Warren Court and judicial activism. Their commitment to the modernist conception of reason identifies them with an older, more traditional and conservative generation. Peller argues that "Tushnet is drifting to the right in general, that he is beginning to embrace the kind of philosophical premises that he had throughout his career rejected."[85] The same can be said of Farber and Sherry; their recent criticism of narrative jurisprudence places them in alliance with more traditional and conservative critics. This may be an indication of the shifting stages of modern jurisprudential discourse—the categories of the political "right" and "left" are shifting as we move from modernism to postmodernism.

Legal scholars who viewed themselves as "liberal" are discovering that the critique of their normativity has placed them within a conservative intellectual legal tradition. Normative legal thought of both the political "right" and the "left" now stands "in the same place as legal formalism did just before the realists came on the scene."[86] Modern legal scholars have become the defenders of a legal tradition not unlike Langdellian formalism. The critique of normativity arising from the new scholarly movements has brought about a recognition that the old ways of understanding political issues must be revised. The critique of normativity has thus prefigured the political positions of modern legal scholars.

## The "Politics of Form"

The reaction of modern legal scholars to new forms of jurisprudence surfacing throughout the 1980s can be understood as a manifestation of the rhetoric of legal modernism. Modern legal scholars have argued that there exists a set of established norms of legal scholarship and pedagogy that defines the true and essential nature of legal writing, reasoning, and the practice of law. Writing differently becomes threatening to this way of thinking because it challenges the bureaucratic forms of power justified, legitimated, and manipulated by the rhetorical arguments and norms of legal modernism.[87] The ".politics of form"[88] thus characterizes the conceptual and normative arguments modern legal thinkers use to shield themselves from criticism that challenges the normativity of the genre and rhetoric of their writing and analysis.

The debate between modern legal scholars and their critics is a war of texts, discourse, and normative form. Legal moderns contend that rational, objective standards must be applied when evaluating the merits of legal scholarship. Reason and analysis of legal modernism is held out as the universal normative vision for acceptable legal criticism. Farber and Sherry thus argue that good legal scholarship is "much like a judicial opinion" in that it must "contain reason and analysis." Tushnet argues

that it must satisfy the requirement of "integrity of judgment." Ackerman and Minow argue that the discourse of legal scholarship must be
"comprehensible." Fiss, Edwards, and Carrington contend that it must
be faithful to the shared values and public morality of the legal system.
The text and discourse of modern jurisprudence are defended by these
scholars because they establish their identity as legal subjects.[89]

This strategy and argument have been successful, in part, because
they create an "essentialist trap"[90] for the Young Turks who critique
the normative vision of modern legal scholars. Legal moderns argue that
outsider scholarship has failed to prove the existence of its "different"
voice. To establish the merit of their narrative stories, different-voice
scholars are thus put to the task of proving the objectivity and truth of
their different voices. This places different-voice scholars in the position
of proving the essentialism of their work, a theoretical move that would
be inconsistent with their critique. Because different voice scholars believe that objectivity and truth are culturally contingent, they are committed to the nonessentialists' framework of truth. They argue that voice
is not the issue, that the real question is one that is directed at the
relationship between normative argument and power.

In arguing that truth is a pluralistic concept dependent upon culture,
different-voice scholars claim that legal scholars can still discern and
evaluate the validity of different conceptions of truth. Their claim is that
the critique of normativity will enable legal scholars to uncover the role
of power in normative judgment. Once power has been uncovered, legal
scholars would presumably be in a more intelligent position to judge
normative argument. Normative judgment would still exist after the
critique of normativity. The critique of normativity does not have to
lead to the abyss of nihilism, or moral relativity.

Legal moderns have assumed that the production of intellectual work
is the product of autonomous rational agents who participate for the
purpose of explaining, improving, and advancing the values of legal
modernism discovered in normative legal thought. The forms of legal
criticism developing throughout the 1980s question the integrity and
coherence of this endeavor. In responding to the challenge, legal moderns have attempted to preempt the rhetorical field by arguing that
normative legal thought, "as a matter of its own form," is a universal
form of discourse that defines the universe of acceptable discourse in
law. The justification in support of this is the autonomous rational

subject: it is assumed that normative legal thought "is authored by and addressed to an autonomous, coherent, integrated, rational, originary self, receptive to moral argument through a medium of language that is itself weightless and neutral."[91] Normative legal thought thus "begins repeating itself" as it defends itself against foreign criticism. "And like most routines, it remains unseen and unobserved—which is why it is so powerful."[92] Postmodern jurisprudence enters to break this routine.

# 12. Postmodern Jurisprudence

Postmodernism is an elusive idea that is not easily defined. Postmodernism is neither a theory nor a concept; it is rather a skeptical attitude or aesthetic that "distrusts all attempts to create large-scale, totalizing theories in order to explain social phenomena."[1] Postmodernists resist the idea that "there is a 'real' world or legal system 'out there,' perfected, formed, complete and coherent, waiting to be discovered by theory."[2] As developed in linguistics, literary theory, art, and architecture, postmodernism is also a style that signals the end of an era, the passing of the modern age.[3] It marks a certain "chronological progression" that comes after modernism, describing what happens when one rejects the epistemological foundations of modernity.

Modernity, as distinguished from artistic modernism, relies upon a foundational concept of reason[4] identified with the spirit of the Enlightenment. At one time, this spirit was expressed in the romantic confidence of philosophers like Kant and Hegel who thought that human emancipation could be achieved through reason. Today, modernity expresses *Weberian despair*[5] but clings to the belief in the ability of "man" to emancipate humanity through empirical knowledge, scientific innovation, and rational thought. Modernists attempted to bring order and stability to the world through the rational construction of meta-theories. A central characteristic of modernity is the belief in epistemological foundations—the idea that knowledge can be justified only if it rests on indubitable foundations.[6]

In law, modernity characterizes the view of traditional jurisprudential scholars who shared a common belief in the possibility of systematizing legal knowledge using coherent and verifiable propositions about the nature of law and adjudication. Legal modernity purported to secularize jurisprudential thought. Legal moderns thought about law in essentialist terms, viewing it as an autonomous, self-generating activity. They fostered the development of grand-scale narratives and discourses. They believed that a distinct legal method is discoverable and that such a method could unlock the door to the ultimate truths of the law. The legal scholar's responsibility was to discover, develop, and refine that method. The canons of traditional scholarship were thus thought capable of revealing the "evidence" for truth determination. As one modern legal scholar, Matthew Finkin, recently put it: "The canons of responsible scholarship require the scholar to play fair; to report all the evidence; neither to distort nor to ignore. But assuming that to have been done, the conclusion offered will rise or fall on the cogency of the reasoning, on the closeness of fit of the argument to the evidence."[7]

While the distinctive discourse of modernity is aimed at prediction and control, postmodernism brings out the diversity of multiple discourses and is skeptical of all universal knowledge claims. Postmodernism rejects the belief in stable, transcontextual foundations. Postmoderns claim that there is no logical correspondence between language and the "objective" world because "language is socially and culturally constructed, it is [thus] inherently incapable of representing or corresponding to reality; hence all propositions and all interpretations, even texts, are themselves social constructions."[8] Postmodernists do not deny that there can be knowledge of reality; what they deny is that we can rely on theory and language to objectively fix the meaning of reality.

Postmodernism is an essentially contested movement of thought that is defined by practices that resist and react against modernism. It is not a movement or school, and more than just a description of a style or aesthetic. Postmodernists disagree about objectives and methods of postmodern criticism. "What's at stake is the definition of an era—our era—and, along with it, the relevance and meaningfulness of *our* political, intellectual, and aesthetic practices."[9] Postmodernism is a contested idea associated with "a rising sentiment that we are coming to the close not only of a century and a millennium but of an era."[10] One indication of this sentiment is present in the disagreement about the meaning and existence of postmodernism. Another indication is the chaos and diversity of the "industrial process of commodification, bureaucratization, consumerization, and saturation" of social and cultural practices.[11] Postmoderns are cultural critics who attempt to bring attention to the ambivalence and confusion prevailing in the contemporary intellectual and social situation.

## The Postmodern Condition

Postmoderns say that we are now living in the *postmodern condition*, the *postmodern era*, or *postmodernity*, a time that entails new conditions and requires new critical techniques of investigation.[12] One way to understand this claim is to consider how individual identities of subjects are constructed in the dominant electronic media of our culture, television. A shift in cultural images can be seen by considering how the cultural images of the fifties generation compare to those of the contemporary generation. David Halberstam, in his recent book, THE FIFTIES, describes how the fifties generation became "wired for television," and how a new electronic medium reflected a sense of "goodness" and "expanding affluence" that characterized the feeling and mood of that era.[13]

The popular mid-fifties sitcom, *The Adventures of Ozzie and Harriet*, depicted the average American family (the Nelsons) as having "no economic crises, no class divisions or resentments, no ethnic tensions, few if any hyphenated Americans, few, if any, minority characters."[14] The Cleaver family portrayed similar images in the popular 1950s TV comedy *Leave It to Beaver*. The Cleavers, like the Nelsons, also lived in television suburbia. No one knew in which state or suburb they lived, or what Ward Cleaver and Ozzie Nelson did for a living, except that they were respectable, and they dressed in a white shirt, tie, and suit.[15] The cultural images of the families in these TV sitcoms suggested that America was a well-ordered and good society, even though the reality facing many Americans was far from perfect.[16]

By the late 1970s, television imitated the diverse, fragmented, and confusing cultural images of social life. The 1979 *Saturday Night Live* late-night television comedy made fun of the fifties sitcoms in a show featuring a special guest appearance by Ricky Nelson, who played the wholesome all-American teenager in the Ozzie and Harriet show. The *Saturday Night Live* skit turned the suburban world of Ozzie and Harriet into the Twilight Zone. Dan Aykroyd, playing Rod Serling, began as the narrator: "Meet Ricky Nelson, age sixteen. A typical American kid, in a typical American kitchen in a typical American black-and-white-TV family home. But what's about to happen to Ricky is far from typical unless you happen to live in the Twilight Zone."[17] The scene then switches to Ricky, wandering home from school, who appears in the home of the Cleavers, from *Leave It to Beaver*.

The Cleavers treat Ricky as part of their family. "June offers him a brownie but warns him against spoiling his appetite."[18] When Ricky tells June his name, she responds, "What a lovely name."[19] Ricky becomes confused; he leaves and wanders into the home of the Andersons, of *Father Knows Best*. Jim Anderson (the father) assumes that Ricky is his daughter Betty's blind date. Jim asks Ricky his name, "Nelson," he says. Jim says, "What a nice name. Presbyterian?"[20] Ricky answers: "My father is, sir. My mother is Episcopal." Jim replies: "Well, I certainly hope you'll stay for dinner." Margaret, Jim's wife, says, "You'll want to wash up and have a brownie first."[21] Ricky then continues on his journey, wandering through the family of *Make Room for Daddy* and then on to the Ricardos of *I Love Lucy*, where Ricky arrives just in time to see Lucy burn a turkey in the oven.[22] Ricky then disappears as he continues his journey, attempting to understand the meaning of the different "forms of life" he encountered in the families of other 1950s sitcoms. Serling (Aykroyd), narrating in the background, stated: "Submitted for your approval. A sixteen-year-old teenager walking through Anytown, USA, past endless Elm, Oak, and Maple Streets, unable to distinguish one house from the other."[23]

The *Saturday Night Live* skit made fun of the fifties sitcoms by using the postmodern technique of *pastiche* to bring out the experience of recognizing the endless connotations and references for defining individual identity.[24] The word "pastiche" describes the experience of multiple identities of the self defined by a contingent set of relations with other individuals and groups. Pastiche helps capture the postmodern condition by bringing out the contingency and fragility of the concept of identity. Pastiche is the experience one encounters after realizing that the universal discourses of Western culture (discourses based on the notion of a universal concept of self) are fragile, unstable, and contingent. Pastiche becomes a powerful tool for gaining critical insight about the fragility of the modernist concept of self.

In the *Saturday Night Live* skit, Ricky Nelson attempted to find his identity in relation to the new families he meets. Like the sampling technique of modern rap music, pastiche uses different styles and cultural codes to create new patterns and combinations. This experience describes the "schizophrenia" of living in a fragmented society where self-identity is constantly redefined by the intertextuality of diverse images, symbols, and cultural practices.[25] Ricky's odyssey on *Saturday Night Live* brings out the dead styles of the 1950s. Although amusing, it is also somewhat unsettling, because it helps to frame countercultures and multiple communities of *postmodern culture*.

The postmodernist Fredric Jameson uses the word "pastiche" to describe the experience of living in a society dissected and bombarded by endless symbols and messages of the electronic media that seek to give meaning to the market, bureaucratic, and social processes.[26] In such a world "we are imprisoned, bombarded, connected, inspected, and (potentially) dissected by electronic media: the TV, the VCR, the phone, the fax, and the computer."[27] The idea of society is fragmented into multiple communities of different cultural and racial perspectives: "In postmodernity, all is diversity and heterogeneity; any discourse of 'community' is suspect as a discourse of oppression. The byword is resistance, the refrain 'Watcha mean we'?"[28]

Jean-François Lyotard's account of the postmodern condition emphasizes the diversity of local narratives within scientific and academic discourse and the process by which a particular form of knowledge can claim legitimacy.[29] The grand narratives of Western knowledge are said to rest on the suppression and denunciation of local narratives that help define and support the dominant narrative. According to Lyotard, "Scientific knowledge cannot know and have made known that it is the true knowledge without resorting to the other, narrative, kind of knowledge, which is from its point of view no knowledge at all."[30] Lyotard's main conclusion is that since the Second World War, these grand narratives have lost power, giving rise to the "incredulity towards metanarratives." The loss of confidence in foundational narratives has helped bring about diversity, fragmentation, and new scholarly interest in pragmatic "local narratives." The spirit of the Enlightenment and the organizing power of science is said to have weakened.[31]

Postmoderns attempt to bring attention to the diversity of the current cultural condition by constrasting how the language and theories of modernists attempt to hide, marginalize, and homogenize the fragmentary and chaotic nature of our multicultural society. There are many different ways that postmoderns attempt this (including psychoanalytic, poststructuralist, deconstruction, and feminist approaches), but all efforts aim to expose how the postindustrial process of commodification and consumerization has disintegrated the cultural symbols of the fifties generation and recombined those values in ironic new combinations to produce a postmodern system of bureaucratic thought. Diversity and fragmentation of jurisprudential theories signal the postmodern condition.

## The Two Sides of Postmodernism

In law, postmodern criticism has come to represent two dominant perspectives. One group of postmodern social critics adopted a neopragmatic stance framed by the antifoundational philosophy of Richard Rorty. Rorty, the leading living philosopher of neopragmatism (a form of critical pragmatism derived from the pragmatist philosophy), rejects the foundational theories of analytic philosophy.[32] Following the ideas of Wittgenstein, Dewey, and Heidegger, Rorty argues that "investigations of knowledge or morality or language or society may be simply apologetic attempts to externalize a certain contemporary language-game, social practice, or self-image."[33] Rorty believes that the representational systems of meaning used in philosophical discourse derive meaning from social practices and conventions of society. "Nothing counts as justification unless by reference to what we already accept and . . . there is no way to get outside our beliefs and our language so as to find some test other than coherence."[34] Rorty's neopragmatism coupled with "his insistence on our being determinately embedded in the social and historical is quintessentially postmodern."[35]

Neopragmatism is in some ways only a "close cousin" of postmodernism. It is like postmodernism in that its practitioners accept the postmodern view that truth and knowledge are culturally and linguistically conditioned.[36] On the other hand, neopragmatist practice is unlike postmodern (or what some theorists call *poststructuralist*)[37] criticism because it is less concerned with exposing the contradictions of modern conceptual and normative thought than revealing instrumental, empirical, and epidemiological solutions for the problem at hand.[38] The neopragmatic critic attempts to use the modernist framework when it seems to work, after "correct[ing] for biases to which the culturally situated framework is prone."[39]

Neopragmatists thus attempt to explain how one can do theoretical work without rejecting all pretenses of foundational knowledge. Neopragmatists argue that the theorists must take a situated stance in their scholarship and adopt an instrumental approach to theory. Whatever works in context becomes the standard for their theoretical investigation and judgment. The goal of these postmodern critics is freedom from theory. Once we move away from the Enlightenment spirit of reason and science, Rorty argues, we can "substitute Freedom for Truth as the goal of thinking and of social progress."[40]

When applied to legal studies, neopragmatism forms the academic perspective of scholars who reject all foundational claims of legal theory but remain committed to the view that legal theory can be useful for resolving legal problems. For neopragmatics like Rorty or Stanley Fish, theory is a tool that can be used to help decision makers resolve problems pragmatically. Neopragmatists thus believe in and are committed to the Enlightenment idea of progress, even while they resist using the modernist's framework. For this reason, neopragmatists may only be "close cousins" of postmodernists. On the other hand, because neopragmatists reject foundational arguments and the idea of cultural universalism, they distinguish themselves from Enlightenment moderns as well as from traditional pragmatic philosophers.

Another group of postmodern critics, the *ironists*,[41] attempt to facilitate the crisis and fragmentation of modern theory by employing postmodern criticism to "displace, decenter, and weaken" central concepts of modern legal Western thought. They are ironists because they claim that the discourse of modern Western thought has been effective—very effective—but not for the reason modernists imagine. Ironists assert that the significance of modernism lies not in specific prescriptions or social tasks, but rather that it lies in the intellectual pursuit of theory as an end to itself. In philosophy, modernism is said to have "become more important for the pursuit of private perfection rather than for any social task."[42] In law, modernism is said to have established a form of normative legal thought which is "so concerned with producing normatively desirable worldly effects [it] has , ironically, become its own self-referential end."[43]

Ironists attempt to "intensify the irony" of modern discourse by exposing how the descriptions and prescriptions of the discourse fail to support the objective truth claims that the theorists make for advancing social progress. Ironists argue that the modernist framework for theoretical and practical discourse fails to have worldly effects. Postmoderns such as Jacques Derrida,[44] Michel Foucault,[45] and Edward Said[46] thus employ deconstructive practices and other critical techniques for displacing and decentering the modes, categories, and normative concepts of Western thought.

Derrida's deconstruction of Western philosophy and literature attempts to bring out the play of *différance* (a word created by Derrida to signify the "other") in various texts to reveal how Western reason excludes different self-identities and life-styles. Foucault and Said attempt to show how Western concepts of humanism and reason have functioned to define social identities in ways that exclude the social conventions and identities of other groups. *Postmodern ironists* attempt to expose exclusionary effects of rational thought by bringing attention to the relationship between knowledge and power. The goal is to uncover the human identities and dead styles defined by the symbolic system of meaning in modern thought and then to expose how the universal identity of the self excludes and disciplines other self-identities.

Neopragmatists and ironists have thus worked to redefine the political orientation of traditional labels such as *liberal* and *conservative*. Modernists are divided between "left," "liberal," and "right" political orientations, but no matter what political label modernists subscribe to, they believe in the Enlightenment idea of a politically correct vocabulary for thinking about political problems. They think it essential to get the "right" political vocabulary and program for government, law, and social relations. The left, liberal, and political right are regarded by postmoderns as different instances of the same universal motif of modernity. Postmoderns resist and react against the different political orientations of modernists because they view modernist conception of politics to be embodied in the fabric of a contradictory and problematized conception of reason. They attempt to decenter this conception of knowledge and politics by exposing contradiction, paradox and irony embedded within modernist discourse. Neopragmatists attempt to transcend the traditional categories of politics through an antifoundational instrumental perspective. Ironist theorists attempt to do the same by employing deconstructive interpretive strategies to show the irony of the modernists' political scenarios of "social hope." The irony is that the modernists' political scenarios have become a self-referential end rather than a means for achieving a particular social goal or task.[47]

Each side of postmodernism seeks to highlight the disintegration and fragmentation of modern culture in the representational practices of various intellectual disciplines. Culture, language, and context are the common themes of postmodern criticism. Postmoderns are cultural and literary critics who seek to reveal how intellectual discourses, language, and fields of knowledge reproduce and present questions about social relations and cultural practices. Postmoderns report on the complex motif of the postmodern condition in order to better understand the politics of our time.

## Postmodern Jurisprudence

Postmodern jurisprudence emerges from the postmodern intellectual condition. It represents the view expressed by Lyotard that the search for new legal theories and metanarratives to solve law's problems has been exhausted. It "announces or implies that a rupture has occurred, an irreparable break with the past, and that nothing can ever be the same again."[48] By 1990 there were signs that this had happened in jurisprudential studies. There was a loss of belief in a secular and autonomous jurisprudence as the "Rule of Law" for all rules. Indeed, as the century approaches its end and we enter the next millennium, it is no longer possible to identify a mainstream view of jurisprudence. Even though jurisprudence constantly develops new theories about law and adjudication, the same argumentative patterns are played out. New jurisprudential developments include new twists, new words, and new emphases on common argumentative stories told about jurisprudence.

Jurisprudence at century's end exhibits a certain postmodern aesthetic—an aesthetic that accepts the problematic nature of its own foundations. The experience of pastiche is felt as each new cycle of legal theory of jurisprudence recasts the same structure and same argumentative patterns in different combinations. The study of jurisprudence has thus become like Ricky Nelson's odyssey through the sitcom families of 1950s suburbia. The exhilarating experience of discovering a new idea or theory of jurisprudence soon dissipates as one realizes that the new idea or theory merely recycles an old one.

This experience of pastiche characterizes the *routine* of modern jurisprudence reflected within the various theoretical trends or "schools" of legal thought. Postmoderns reveal how new schools of jurisprudence, and new ideas about law and adjudication, emerge only to fade as they are revealed as flawed attempts to overcome modern problems of jurisprudence. The process of creating the new from the old (the presentation of a new theory eventually revealed to be a copy of an old theory) has weakened legal modernism. Postmoderns believe that the breakdown of the *performative* significance of modern theory has now established a crisis in representation such that the old categories and normative positions of legal modernism are no longer credible.[49]

The current intellectual mood in jurisprudence is captured by the experience of "exhilaration" that soon gives way to "ennui" as the latest "provocative new piece of legal thought" is classified as "yet another possibly clever, perhaps thoughtful, but nonetheless utterly failed contribution."[50] In jurisprudence, pastiche describes the experience of *déjà vu*—the feeling Ricky Nelson had as he realized that each new family he visited represented a slightly different variation of the same old Nelson family. For postmoderns, the current situation of American jurisprudence is a lot like Ricky Nelson's odyssey on *Saturday Night Live:* like Ricky, legal moderns have embarked on an odyssey in search of the "right" jurisprudence for American law. The contemporary problem of jurisprudence, however, is that jurisprudence is *the* problem. The diverse modes of contemporary legal thought project legal identities of many different legal subjects: critical subjects, neopragmatic subjects, feminist subjects, literary subjects, and the like. The fragmentation of subject formations in the law has become a serious problem for legal theorists. The postmodern condition of jurisprudence comes from the awareness that legal subjects have lost confidence in the distinctiveness of the "performative enterprise"[51] of their discipline that had heretofore defined their professional identity. The problem of jurisprudence is thus the problem of culture and politics.

As an intellectual and political practice, postmodernism views knowledge as mediated by the current social, cultural, linguistic, and historical condition of our time. Postmoderns understand truth and knowledge as contingent social constructions, incapable of being grasped by a fixed, determinate theory or conceptional construct. For some postmoderns, "Rational argument is expressed as . . . a privileging of a perspective, a move in a power game."[52] For others, truth can never be transparent because truth is a social construction mediated by a language inherently incapable of capturing reality. Thus, postmodern jurisprudence is not a theory of law, but a kind of *antitheory*—an antitheory that strives, however problematically, to resist the adjudicatory impulse, the regulatory obsession of modern legal thought.

Postmodern jurisprudence can be found within the legal scholarship of postmoderns who have adopted either the neopragmatist or ironist stance in their legal criticism. Richard Posner is the best-known neopragmatic postmodern legal scholar in the academy today. Pierre Schlag is the leading champion of ironist legal criticism. To understand how these postmodern scholars practice their postmodern criticism, it is helpful to examine how they position themselves in relation to ideas about the nature of theory, language, knowledge, and the identity of the subject.

## The Nature of Theory

Postmodern neopragmatism is evident in the *Pragmatic Manifesto* outline in Posner's book, THE PROBLEMS OF JURISPRUDENCE.[53] Posner renounced the *scientism* of the law and economics movement and embraced the pragmatic manifesto of neopragmatic philosophers such as Richard Rorty. According to Posner, pragmatism overcomes the essentialism of legal conceptualism and formalism without falling prey to the moral relativism of legal realism or its modern counterpart, critical legal studies. Posner believes the pragmatic approach is a "middle way" that avoids the exaggerations and pitfalls of legal formalism on the right, and the fundamental contradiction thesis on the left. Instead of relying on abstract propositions of "theory," Posner argues that judges should rely on instrumental logic; he uses theory and legal reasoning as tools to get a job done. His true test of every legal analytic is whether it "works" instrumentally in maximizing human goals and aspirations.[54] Posner justifies the application of economics to law on a practical level; economics wins because it "gets the job done" better than any other method.[55]

Richard Posner's pragmatism exhibits what Thomas Grey calls "freedom from theory-guilt,"[56] a scholarly temperament liberated from the necessity of devising a theory of law rooted in some total perspective.[57] Freedom from theory-guilt places neopragmatists in a theoretical position that is critical of modern legal theory as well as the interdisciplinary theories associated with the 1980s movements. Grey believes that the liberation of freedom from theory-guilt enables these legal critics to avoid the logical paradoxes posed by the contradictory views of "perspectivist self-reference" (there are no universal truths) and "perspectivist dogmatism" (my truth is the *real* truth), which characterize the perspectives of modern legal theory as well as critical social theories such as Marxism. Postmodern pragmatists argue that their "real interest is not in truth at all but in belief justified by social need."[58]

Posner's pragmatism helps to identify the perspective characterizing the post-Chicago law and economics movement. Although they differ in many respects, post-Chicago law and economics practitioners have unwittingly committed themselves to antifoundationalism, anti-essentialism, and the rejection of any one-dimensional interpretive guide to law and legal decision making. This is also the credo of Posner's pragmatic jurisprudence. The pragmatist argues that no universal perspective exists for resolving problems of jurisprudence. Neopragmatists thus turn their back to jurisprudence and legal theory. They instead embrace a pragmatic form of reasoning that exhibits qualities associated with postmodernism—antifoundational and skeptical attitudes about the study of law. Legal feminists and critical race scholars have also relied on neopragmatism in their work. Pragmatic feminists such as Margaret Jane Radin and Mary Becker, for example, have argued that legal feminists should stop arguing among themselves about feminist approaches and instead use whatever approach works for dealing with gender discrimination in the law. Critical race theorist Cornel West of Harvard University has been a forceful advocate of a "prophetic pragmatic" approach for understanding how structures of domination in society operate to the disadvantage of people of color.[59]

Neopragmatic legal critics also follow Rorty's skeptical attitude toward science and empiricism.[60] Rorty's brand of neopragmatism is also a form of antitheory that insists that truth and authority are social and therefore always contingent upon the meaning constructed by a particular community.[61] What is accepted as truth is merely the expression of universally shared community beliefs about the truth of something. Neopragmatists reject truth assertions based on dogma; they believe that truth is socially constructed by each community in order to achieve certain ends. In keeping with the pragmatic philosophy of James and

Dewey, neopragmatists approach theory as merely a tool or instrument for the achievement of human ends. Unlike James and Dewey, however, neopragmatists do not believe that the scientific method is "efficacious."[62]

Neopragmatists believe that theory merely establishes the rules for playing a particular language game. They view theory as a function of language, rather than reason, logic, or analytical method.[63] Neopragmatists have accepted two paradoxical ideas about law: first, that it is possible to know the truth without accepting the idea of universal essences; and second, that it is possible to reach principled decisions even though there are *no* right answers. These ideas are not really paradoxes for legal pragmatists since they reject the philosophy of foundationalism upon which universal truth and right answers rest.

Ironists, inspired by the critical practices of Derrida, Foucault, and Said, reject the essentialist claims of modern theory. Unlike neopragmatists, ironists reject the idea of a "middle ground" of a pragmatic intuition for avoiding the essentialism of foundation theories. They believe that there is no way to avoid the predicaments of modern theory because no "middle ground" exists. These nonpragmatic postmoderns have given up on the Enlightenment idea of normative or regulative theory altogether, and attempt to look beyond theory to recognize and redescribe the normative narratives and discourses of law.

One way to understand the difference between neopragmatists and ironists is to consider how they position themselves in relation to the foundational claims of modern legal theory. While neopragmatists reject the idea of an intellectual foundation, they nevertheless believe that intuition and practical reason can situate the pragmatic theorist and enable her to develop an instrumental way of knowing what to do. Ironists claim that the situatedness and instrumentalism of neopragmatists is merely another manifestation of the modernists' attempt to discover a foundation for legal analysis. Pierre Schlag, for example, concludes that "[n]eopragmatism . . . remains a protest against philosophical idealism, rationalism, and transcendentalism that ironically remains confined to the realms, the matrices already carved in the self-images of philosophical idealism, rationalism, and transcendentalism."[64] Hence, Schlag argues that neopragmatism is *prefigured* in a way quite unconscious to itself, by an aesthetic, a rhetoric, a discourse that is quite inhospitable to neopragmatism's own stated aims and projects.[65]

Neopragmatism's foundation is the intuition and common sense of the situated pragmatist. Ironists attempt to decenter the foundation of neopragmatism by revealing how pragmatic judgment reflects the view of a situated subject who tries to be very pragmatic in reacting to the postmodern condition. As Schlag has amusingly put it: "The pragmatist subject, understood in pragmatic terms, is the shopper at the universal mall making meaning with the commodified signs of our traditions and culture while the social aesthetics of techno-bureaucratic strategies are making him think he means something. Everything else is just nostalgia." [66]

Another way to see the difference between these two sides of postmodern jurisprudence is to consider how each side understands the nature of legal theory. For neopragmatists, legal theory is a tool used for getting a job done. They don't see any sense in debating the truth or objectivity of law; the only thing that matters is deciding which particular conceptions of law work best under the circumstances. While neopragmatists view legal theory as a tool, ironists understand legal theory as a type of theater. Ironists argue that the conceptualist and normative forms of modern jurisprudence are a "kind of theater" for directing the action and subjects of a particular kind of scene in a play. Postmodern ironists seek to bring out the power of this theater to control and limit the type of narratives found in the law. As Schlag stated: "The rhetorical script of normative legal thought is already written, the social scene is already set and play after play, article after article, year after year, normative legal thought" offers the same normative choices.[67]

Ironists maintain an ironic stance in claiming that the bureaucratic practices and values of modern law and society (re)inscribe and monitor the aesthetics of all forms of contemporary legal thought, including those represented by postmodernists. The goal of ironist criticism is to decenter foundational narratives in legal thought, without claiming to stand outside that system. Schlag thus does not attempt to get beyond the "text" of the law; he rejects the idea that the text stands outside of culture. He maintains that the politics of postmodernism must be understood in relation to modern legal thought; the goal of ironists' criticism is to decenter and displace modernist claims of a universalist method guided by a detached and autonomous subject unaffected by the situatedness of her context.

Ironists do not share the same intellectual position of antifoundationalist philosophers following Rorty.[68] In philosophy, antifoundationalism has become a popular theme that rejects the idea of shared intellectual foundations. Antifoundationalism is akin to postmodernism in that both reject attempts to explicate rational and objective argument.[69] Unlike foundationalists, ironists seek to (re)describe the normative subject of all foundational and antifoundational accounts of reality and knowledge claims. Through the process of (re)description, postmoderns seek to highlight the different subject formations within foundational and antifoundational accounts of law. They do this to decenter the authoritarian claims of modern theorists in order to reveal how language and reason mediate the modernists' understanding of the world, and to show how modernists lack the ability to grasp the world "as it really is."

Ironists thus refuse to take sides in the debate between foundationalists and antifoundationalists. Ironists express "incredulity" toward all meta-narratives, even those that claim to be antifoundational in nature. They point out the ironic juxtapositions of different "styles" between foundational and antifoundational arguments. They seem to be saying: "Here, look how this style embodies a particular vision . . . and how it is challenged by the style next to it, and by the style next to that."[70] Ironists remain agnostic about whether one style or another is the "correct" or "best" style for understanding social phenomena. Instead, they seek to expose how intellectual practices in the law are mediated and constructed by their own "self-referential end [which is] coextensive with the operation, performance, reproduction, and proliferation of bureaucratic practices and institutions."[71]

## The Nature of Language

Modern legal scholars uncritically assume that language is like a mirror capable of accurately reflecting the meaning of objects in reality.[72] The metaphor that captures the modernists' view of language is conduit— language is viewed as a conduit used by lawyers and judges to "get their message across."[73] In this schema, words are (re)presented as containers of meaning. Postmoderns reject this objectivist view of language. They argue that language must be understood in relation to the cognitive processes of the people who speak it. Postmodern neopragmatists argue that language must be understood as a "language game" based on socially contingent rules for determining the truth or falsity of judgments. Ironists adopt a similar stance in arguing that language in the law is a "normative language game."[74] Both strands of postmodern legal thought embrace Wittgenstein's view of language as a "form of life" or "language game."

In describing language as a "game," Wittgenstein meant that language was a practice used by communities to determine the truth and reality of judgments. "The upshot of Wittgenstein's view of language is that all of our language has meaning only within the language games and 'forms of life' in which they are embedded. One must understand the use, the context, the activity, the purpose, the game which is being played."[75] Wittgenstein's view was that human understanding occurs within language games and that there is no way to get outside of the game to ascertain the truth or reality of judgments. Legal postmoderns have adopted this view of language in their effort to bring attention to the underlying context, activity, and purpose of modern legal thought.

Postmoderns thus reject the "common sense" understanding of language which associates the meaning of words with fixed objects in the world. What is challenged is the image of legal discourse as a neutral medium capable of reflecting the true meaning of social events.[76] Postmoderns claim that the common-sense idea that meanings of words reside "in" language is "fundamentally misguided."[77] For them language constructs, rather than reflects, the meaning of things and events in the world. The revival of Wittgenstein's language-game hermeneutics in contemporary legal scholarship suggests that legal thought is slowly assimilating postmodern developments in the theory of language and culture.[78]

## The Nature of Knowledge

While postmoderns agree that "truth" is a relative concept, they disagree on the possibility of progress through "knowledge." Neopragmatists believe that practical reason is a form of knowledge that exists and can be relied on in reaching judgment. Legal neopragmatists believe that knowledge of the world can be obtained through the trial and error process of experiences. As Richard Posner states: "There is knowledge if not ultimate truth, and a fallibilist theory of knowledge emphasizes, as preconditions to the growth of scientific and other forms of knowledge, the continual testing and retesting of accepted 'truths,' the constant kicking over of sacred cows—in short, a commitment to robust and free-wheeling inquiry with no intellectual quarter asked or given."[79] Postmodern neopragmatists believe that "[t]he soundness of legal interpretations and other legal propositions is best gauged . . . therefore, by an examination of their consequences in the world of fact."[80]

Ironists have a different orientation toward knowledge. Taking Foucault's mandate that "power comes from everywhere" seriously, ironists argue that law is a form of knowledge that creates and constitutes power. Thus, Pierre Schlag forcefully argues that "the value (if any) of normative legal thought depends on a decentered economy of bureaucratic institutions and practices—such as those constituting and traversing the law school, the organized bar, the courts—that define and represent their own operations, their own character, their own performances, in the normative currency."[81] Law as a form of cultural knowledge "becomes the mode of discourse by which bureaucratic institutions and practices (re)present themselves as subject to the rational ethical-moral control of autonomous individuals (when indeed they are not), just as normative legal thought constructs us (you and me) to think and act as if we were at the center—in charge, so to speak—of our own normative legal thought *(when indeed we are not)*."[82] Ironists alter the concept of knowledge by revealing its political, social, rhetorical, institutional, and aesthetic dimensions.

Ironists thus try to decenter, displace, and weaken the knowledge-claims of conceptual and normative jurisprudence. Their goal is to uncover how bias, prejudices, and normative perspectives affect theories of evaluation and types of knowledge. The point is not merely criticism. It is to show how limits are set, how possibilities are established—in short, to show how law works. Ironists attempt to reveal the ideological bias that prefigures theories of knowledge.[83] Ironist philosophers want to expose how the boundaries of philosophy can be (re)described in ways to enlarge the canons of philosophy to permit cultural and literary criticism.[84] Legal ironists serve a similar function in enlarging the canons of legal interpretation to permit legal thinkers to better understand how the official perspective of the law is culturally and linguistically conditioned.

## Identity of the Self

Of the four key ideas relevant for understanding postmodern legal criticism, the concept of self is critical. Indeed, one way to understand legal postmodernism is to view postmodernism as a subject-formation type of criticism—postmoderns criticize and react against the liberal definition of the legal subject found within modern conceptual and normative jurisprudence. The concept of self in modern theory defines the legal subject or person "back there" in control of the analysis and reason of the law. In modern legal theory, the subject is the judge who engages in "reasoned elaboration" and applies "neutral principles." In fundamental-rights discourse, this subject is the idealized judge whom Ronald Dworkin identified as Hercules in *Law's Empire*.[85] As Schlag puts it, he "*is* the idealized self-image of the legal academic who by virtue of his intellectual prowess and his commitment to the rule of law applies his overarching legal knowledge to rewrite the case law in a way that is morally appealing."[86] Schlag calls this idealized definition of the subject the *relatively* autonomous subject of normative legal thought.[87]

While modern legal theory adopted a "centered sense of the self," postmodern critics adopted either a *situated* or *decentered* concept of self.[88] The idea of the *situated self* is based on an understanding of subjectivity that "emphasizes that self is formed only through a relationship with others."[89] The implications of situated subjectivity can be found in Posner's postmodern legal pragmatism. For Posner, "law is functional, not expressive or symbolic either in aspiration or—so far as yet appears—in effect."[90] The functional nature of law is understood by examining how law functions in context. To comprehend this, judges must develop a situated understanding of human subjectivity in the decision-making process. The individual is seen as an economic rational actor in the context of transactions with other individuals. The economic concept of self is thus defined by a theory of behaviorism of situated individuals. As Posner explained: "The law is not interested in the soul or even the mind. It has adopted a severely behaviorist concept of human activity as sufficient to its ends and traceable to its means."[91] The behaviorists' concept of human subjectivity commits postmodern legal pragmatists to a concept of situated self as a product of human relationships.

Ironists are committed to a decentered form of subjectivity. They believe there is no core component of the self, only a shifting set of unstable references of multiple identities,[92] and attempt to bring out the multiple identities of human subjects that contemporary legal scholars have uncritically ignored. As Schlag stated: "Postmodernism questions the integrity, the coherence, and the actual identity of the humanist individual self—the knowing sort of self produced by Enlightenment epistemology and featured so often as the dominant self-image of the professional academic."[93]

Ironists' legal criticism is thus based on the idea that the "subject is a problem." "The problem arises as each school (of jurisprudence) recognizes that its own intellectual architecture, its own normative ambitions rest upon the presupposition of a subject—a subject whose epistemic, ontological, and normative status is now very much in question."[94] The goal of postmodern criticism is to decenter the subject so that the human agents of law can appreciate their responsibility for the normativity of law. For ironists, "the humanist individual subject has now become one of the main disciplinary vehicles by which bureaucratic institutions stylize, construct, organize and police their clientele."[95] Ironists view the politics of postmodernism as the *politics of form*,[96] which refers to their claims about the way representational practice in modern legal thought reproduces and defines the "political and jurisprudential field" that shapes the identity of legal subjects.

Postmodernists have not limited their criticism to the subject formation of modern legal thought. They also criticize the subject formation represented in interdisciplinary legal studies. Ironists claim that the interdisciplinary work of law and economics is committed to a type of subject formation found in work of Langdellian formalists. Both law and economics and Langdellian formalism define the subject as relatively autonomous. Ironists charge that interdisciplinary approaches in law merely replaced "law" as the source of law's autonomy.

Interdisciplinary legal formalism reproduces the same autonomous subject reflected in normative legal thought. As Pierre Schlag stated in his 1991 essay, *The Problem of the Subject:* "The story is the story of formalism and the problem is the problem of the subject. The story of formalism is that it never deals with the problem of the subject. The problem of the subject is that it's never been part of the story."[97] Schlag demonstrated how Langdellian formalism presumed the existence of a conscious sovereign subject whose normative and ontological status gives the illusion of law's autonomy. Ironists argue that the history of legal modernism can be understood as a story of the missing subject.

Rejecting the possibility of finding "correct" solutions to legal problems based on conceptual formulations of some ideal Rule of Law,

postmodernists argue for new understandings derived from an awareness of the reciprocal nature of law, culture, and individual subjectivity.
Ironist criticism has inspired legal scholars to contemplate the possibility
of a new framework of analysis law, one that offers a transformed
concept of what it means to solve legal and theoretical issues generally.
What is different about postmodernists is their unabashed acceptance of
the impossibility of solving legal problems under an ideal set of conceptual solutions. One way to understand postmodernism is to consider
how postmoderns understand the relationship between law and culture.

Postmodernists reveal how Langdellian formalism and Holmesian
instrumentalism have reproduced themselves in the contemporary patterns of interdisciplinary legal studies. Postmoderns expose how repetitive sameness in the various modes of interdisciplinary legal studies fail
to maintain the modernists' faith in the powers of reason to penetrate
the truth of the legal system. They argue that the faith in one true "rule
of law" wore out; the belief in law's autonomy ceased to inspire the
imagination of the current generation of legal scholars. They recognize
this in acknowledging that "[m]any of the critiques developed over the
past twenty years or so seem to have reached, if not dead ends, then at
least a measure of exhaustion." [98]

The transition from the old to the "new" jurisprudence began with
the breakdown of the core beliefs and theories that served to define
modern jurisprudence. The breakdown is partly a manifestation of the
proliferation of new jurisprudential discourses and new movements in
legal thought. What energizes jurisprudential discourse today, however,
is a general skepticism of all structural, deterministic, and foundational
arguments in the law. What is rejected is the "bed rock assumption . . .
that we are capable of representing reality more or less precisely and
that some knowledge transcends particular perspectives and contexts." [99] Postmodern jurisprudence challenges modern conceptions of
law and jurisprudence by undermining the modernist belief in foundations, essences, objectivity, and autonomous law.

## Postmodern Politics

It would be misleading to say that everyone finds the postmodern developments in jurisprudence attractive. To the contrary, judging from the
academic hype in the general university, postmodernism is held responsi-

ble for a multitude of ills in the modern university—multicultural curricula, political correctness, affirmative action, restrictions on hate speech, and the general disinterest in the great classics of Western culture.[100] In the legal academy, the most frequently voiced objection to postmodernism is that it is a nihilistic scholarly movement that is a recipe for inaction.[101] Modern legal scholars tend to see postmodernism as threatening the progress of modern jurisprudence by destabilizing and rendering uncertain the process of interpretation. Progressives worry that postmodernism may undermine the collective optimism necessary for progressive resistance and renewal.[102]

Progressive legal criticism has presumed that the analyst is already mobilized for action, such that normative legal scholars can activate a form of political action through their normative writing. Postmoderns argue that progressive legal scholars are not mobilized and that their normative law review prescriptions are an exhaustive genre of politics. Postmoderns claim that progressive legal criticism has fallen prey to a type of false empowerment that has led legal scholars (liberals and conservatives) in the law schools to believe in nonexistent forms of abstract power. Legal progressives see postmodernism as demobilizing because they think they are already doing something to engage political action when they are not. Postmoderns start from a different place— they try what is and what is not currently practiced and considered without attempting to resolve the predicaments and paradoxes of the texts and discourses they investigate.

Postmodern legal scholars argue that there are "no necessary contradictions between a continuing loyalty to a postmodern perspective and the practical implementation of a radical political agenda."[103] For Allan C. Hutchinson "postmodernism is the only critical resource that a progressive activist can have or want."[104] Pierre Schlag believes that the attempt to locate law within some conventional understanding of politics "is bound to miss the politics of postmodernism because the politics of postmodernism [attempts] to decenter and displace [the] traditional conception of politics."[105]

For postmoderns the problem with contemporary politics is that the subject thinks he/she is in control of normative legal thought when in fact he/she is not. In short, where the subject thinks it is in control of its discourse, it turns out that the discourse controls the subject by structuring the social system of signification in which that subject participates.[106]

Postmoderns argue that "old-style lefties," liberals, and legal progressives are mistaken in their commitment to "pure" beliefs and the "right theory of human nature."[107] They contend that "[t]here is no better foundation for our values than our own actions. Without that ground, there are no foundations and no values worth speaking of."[108]

Postmodernism thus challenges legal thinkers to reconsider their most basic understanding of the nature of law and politics—their belief in an objective and autonomous law. Postmoderns argue that decision making according to rule is not possible, because rules are dependent upon language, and language is socially and culturally constructed and hence incapable of directing decision makers to make consistent and objective choices. Objectivity is possible only if agreement or consensus about different interpretive practices can be reached. Consensus about acceptable meanings of words is possible, but only if legal interpreters can agree about the "correct" method for legal interpretation. The proliferation of different interpretive methods in law means that consensus is no longer possible.

This, of course, is not to suggest that postmodernism will "rescue" modern legal theory from its current dilemmas. Essentialist impulses in postmodern thought, whether they be new claims of legal determinacy in law and economics or literary studies, identity-based politics of CLS or feminism, or the situated subjectivity of postmodern pragmatism, will surely continue to pose a curious paradox for postmodern legal scholars. There is a pull within new movement discourses toward some new metanarrative or separatist identity politics, although their adherents warn against the mistakes of essentialism. A practical strategy for fostering constructive engagement across the frontiers of race, class, gender, and language needs to be developed. New neopragmatic and ironist criticism offers no new vantage points for analyzing and confronting these problems as the monolithic forms of jurisprudence fragment and break down.

One thing seems certain. The two sides of postmodern legal criticism are working to redefine the benchmarks for evaluating the cogency of legal reasoning and the validity of the legal truth. Postmoderns are cultural critics; they are interested in tracing the various ways law represents different cultural practices, norms, and ideologies. For them "truth" and "knowledge" cannot be empirically verified by the simple process of examining the closeness of fit of the argument to the evidence. Postmoderns claim that "evidence" is a contingent social construction, and thus reject the belief in a metanarrative of jurisprudence, favoring instead an understanding of law and adjudication in terms of what Lyotard called complex multinarratives or "local discourses" of different cultural and theoretical perspectives. For postmoderns, law cannot be an autonomous, self-generating activity because there are no fixed foundations on which one can ground legal justification once and for all.

# Conclusion: Jurisprudence at Century's End

Academic trends in legal scholarship do not occur in a vacuum, nor are law schools and legal scholars autonomous. To understand what has been going on in contemporary legal theory, one must look to what has been going on at the university. American university campuses have recently witnessed a form of organized dissent not seen since the turbulent 1960s and 1970s. Commentators report that "[a]n intellectual and cultural revolution is now under way at American Universities."[1] The revolution has been stirred in part by cultural changes unfolding in American society brought about by the *diversity movement.* This movement consists of people of different races, ethnicities, genders, and cultures who share a common desire to bring more diversity to academic studies. The diversity movement calls for a more diversified curriculum of different intellectual and cultural perspectives.

Students and faculty are also protesting the validity of the canons of the Western classics which represent the core curriculum at American universities.[2] They are demanding that a new multicultural curriculum be developed to take account of the interests and perspectives of different cultures, life-styles, and people. *Multicultural studies* are said to be needed to meet the demands of a multicultural student body that wants to seriously study the history and culture of their different ethnic and racial backgrounds. A multicultural curriculum is thus demanded to meet the needs of Indians, Hispanics, African Americans, Asian Americans, and women of all ethnicities.[3]

The inclusion of multicultural perspectives in the university curriculum has made the study of history, politics, economics, psychology, and art more realistic and relevant to a wider audience of students. It has also inspired a debate about the validity of the traditional canons that made the Western classics of philosophy, literature, and art the "official" university curriculum. The exclusion of different perspectives and discourses made mainstream university scholars unable to say much that was relevant to non-white Americans, women and other non-Western people. It made it difficult for the current generation, "Generation X," to understand and evaluate the complexity and diversity of the forms of bureaucratic institutions and practices of late capitalism and the multicultural content of American culture.

This canon debate has been fueled by new academic interests in critical social theory, which revolutionized the way academic scholars think about fundamental ideas of modern theory: the nature of theory, knowledge, language, and human subjectivity. Deconstruction, neopragmatism, social construction, neo-Marxism, feminism, and other new transformative ideas associated with critical social theory have motivated academics in a variety of fields to question the most fundamental categories of their discipline. The development of these ideas has brought about a distinctive *postmodern temperament* in various academic disciplines. This emerging postmodern temperament celebrates the discovery of contradiction, contingency, and indeterminacy; it uses the techniques of metaphor, narrative, and storytelling for discovering surprising new insights; it embraces a new neopragmatic position, and it justifies the use of "situated" and "local" critiques as a means for decentering foundational theories.

The objective of postmodern criticism is not merely one of exposing contradiction or indeterminacy. Rather, the goal is to recover contradiction, paradox, and so forth, from official knowledges which police thought by disguising, denying, marginalizing, or silencing contradiction, paradox, and so forth. One of the paradoxes of Enlightenment thought, as exemplified in analytical philosophy and rule of law thinking, is that it has become a kind of thought control—making certain inquiries unthinkable. What is appealing about postmodernism is the possibility of recovering aspects of intellectual life that are generally erased by Enlightenment perspectives and knowledges. Postmoderns attempt to bring to life the forms of thought and practice unheard and unseen in the official discourses of law.

New histories, texts, and narrative practices have developed as a new generation of academics turned to critical social theory and the transformative practices of continental philosophers. Critical social theory enabled these scholars to rethink the fundamentals of Western thought. The critical interpretive strategies of Michel Foucault, Jacques Derrida, Fredric Jameson, Edward Said, and others helped precipitate a *crisis in confidence* over the validity of the canons of interpretation in both the fine arts and in academia. This crisis in confidence concerned the credibility of the traditional canons of interpretation for defining and categorizing knowledge and professional technique. It was only a matter of time until these academic trends in the university would be felt in the law schools.[4]

It is only now becoming clear that the current malaise and crisis in legal thought is shared by a wide range of intellectual thinkers, involving a variety of subjects and disciplines in the university. This common condition represents what social commentators call "a crisis of representation" or, more accurately, a series of crises of representation. The older modes of defining, appropriating, and evaluating the objects of artistic, philosophical, literary, and social sciences were no longer credible because the boundary between subjects and their objects had dissolved; this has, in turn, resulted in exciting new possibilities as the plurality of theoretical perspectives and interpretive practices have developed.[5] The *crisis of representation,* known as *postmodernism,* has reached the legal academy and it is represented by a new form of *postmodern jurisprudence.*[6]

There is a rising sentiment in the legal academy that modern legal theory has failed to sustain the modernists' hopes for social progress. Contemporary legal academics are becoming more cynical and skeptical as they realize that legal theorists have been participating in a "recycling process" in which "[e]ach [new] generation . . . offers a different meta-theory to explain or understand legal phenomena, rejecting the perspectives of the previous generation in the hope of more successfully solving [law's] paradox."[7] Cynicism comes with the realization that each succeeding generation of modern legal scholars has merely recycled the work of the previous generation, moving from new and improved conceptual theories to increasingly more complex normative theories, without ever achieving a successful conceptual or normative theory that can withstand the criticism of the next generation. In the face of this, mainstream legal scholars proclaim that chaos is "good," that the future will be secured by the development of a new "chaos theory" for law.[8]

Postmoderns assert that the current mood of the cynic is quite normal and to be expected. They assert that this cynicism is what the current postmodern condition in legal studies signifies. To better appreciate the significance of this condition, postmodern legal critics persuade students of the law (professors and law students) to adopt a new metaphor for legal studies. They favor metaphors like "law as a theater," because they believe that modern legal thought is "a kind of theater."[9] Postmodern legal critics argue that the problem with normative legal thought is that "[t]he rhetorical script . . . is already written, the social scene is already set and play after play, article after article, year after year, normative legal thought [repetitively] requires [us] to choose: 'what should we do? Where should we go?' "[10] Postmoderns argue that these are the wrong questions. What is needed is a drama and a new kind of "scene, *agon*, and actors."[11] The theater of modern jurisprudence has not permitted other stories to be told, until now.

There are now many different stories being told in the law, different theaters and rich new plots and scenes depicting new vantage points for understanding previously ignored characteristics and subjects of the law. While at one time the study of jurisprudence reflected the 1950s pluralist consensus of the legal process school, the idea of social consensus has long been discarded as legal scholars turn to new, diverse, and eclectic approaches in theory and practice. The "theater" of the 1950s generation of legal scholars reflected the values and consensus of television sitcoms such as *The Adventures of Ozzie and Harriet*. Like the Nelsons, the 1950s generation was optimistic about the future and believed that progress was possible through the legal system. They believed in the ever increasing pie (the national economy), and a color-blind society defined by the life experiences of upwardly mobile middle-class white males. By the late 1980s, however, the legal academy reflected the more cynical edge of Ricky Nelson's odyssey through the pristine sitcom families as parodied in the *Saturday Night Live* skit, except in the case of our culture there is much more diversity encountered along the journey.

Like Ricky Nelson on *Saturday Night Live*, the student of jurisprudence today embarks on a jurisprudential odyssey by studying the different disciplinary families and movements of law: legal process, fundamental rights, law and economics, critical legal studies, feminism, law and literature, critical race theory, Asian American law, gay and lesbian legal studies, Native American law, and so on. Each of these new disciplinary families of jurisprudence are studied to learn about different cultural, linguistic, and theoretical perspectives for legal studies, as they attempt to modernize the dead styles of legal modernism. Generation X is confronted with fragmented and somewhat confusing images and stories about law. These diverse images and stories require the current generation of law students to think more explicitly about the difficulties and opportunities of reaching agreement and consensus in a multicultural world. The experience of this may be unsettling and may even be described as being schizophrenic. The "schizophrenia" of modern jurisprudence, however, may be another *signification* of the breakdown in the recycling chain of modern discourse.[12]

Unlike legal moderns who have become increasingly cynical, postmodern legal critics remain optimistic. They point to the increased academic interest in new scholarly movements as a healthy and hopeful development for legal studies.[13] They argue that these movements have become part of the established landscape at the legal academy, and now allow excluded groups to participate in the discourse of jurisprudence. They note how initial fears and claims of protest are giving way to resignation and an overall upbeat mood.[14] While these movements have provoked considerable anxiety, postmoderns seek to show how they have helped to discover new insights about law and how their criticism has stimulated new intellectual activity at the law school. They encourage the current generation to rethink basic jurisprudential assumptions and premises.

The good news is that there is new energy and interest in the legal academy focusing on questions of jurisprudence. Annual meetings of the Association of American Law Schools and various leading legal symposiums now focus on postmodern interpretive strategies, as well as the American Law Institute's Restatements of the Law. Law professors argue about the pitfalls of deconstruction and narrative pedagogy, as well as common law distinctions of bailment and suretyship. These changes in academic discourse and interest are symptomatic of larger changes. The new movements in jurisprudence, unlike jurisprudence of the post-World War II generation, have helped foster a new form of jurisprudence without fixed foundations and formal boundaries.

Unlike traditional legal theorists who attempt to define autonomous law from the neutral perspective of a critical observer, postmoderns refocus the inquiry on the nature of the *subject* who interprets and creates legal reasoning. The new scholarly movements compel legal theorists to rethink and examine how law is the product of particular unstated normative conventions of law, our legal analysis and scholarship. The social construction of legal meaning in jurisprudential thought has become the new focus as contemporary legal scholars seek to understand the "politics of form." Further work is needed to reveal the way in which predilection and normative precommitment are embedded in legal form. For postmodern legal scholars, choosing the "best" answer for legal problems requires "tactical judgments and questions regarding the values of the decision maker much more than a quest for a so-called 'best' argument." [15] One consequence of this has been the realization that there exists a multiplicity of answers for law's many problems.

The bad news is that legal academics have become more skeptical and pessimistic about the possibility of resolving the big questions of jurisprudence. It is now recognized that there are no quick or easy fixes for dealing with problems of judicial decision making. In opening up the political and moral dimensions of law, new-movement legal scholars have broadened the scope of the debate and discourse about law and jurisprudence. The proliferation of different jurisprudential discourses has, however, erased the lines between description and advocacy, making it much more difficult for traditionalists to maintain that there is a distinct legal method for resolving law's many problems. There is concern that the new focus on language, meaning, and culture rather than on law and legal reasoning, will divert contemporary jurisprudence from its central mission of enlightening lawyers on the shared values of the profession. Finally, serious communication problems have resulted from too little cross-talk between the movements and minuscule scholarly exchange between advocates of the new movements and the more traditional jurisprudential thinkers.

The tension between foundational and antifoundational approaches will probably continue to structure debates among contemporary jurisprudential writers, thus preventing contemporary legal scholars from ever reaching an intellectual consensus. This tension is reflected in the continuing debate between legal moderns, who cling to foundational accounts of law, and postmodern antifoundationalists. It is also reflected in the subtle tension between postmodern neopragmatists and ironists who disagree over the possibility of developing an intellectual legal practice from the dynamic of social practices or practical reason. Neopragmatists believe that such a project is possible. Ironists reject the project as another manifestation of the false hope of modernism. ﹨

The new scholarly movements have consequently offered different theoretical discourses and practices, but the conflict between foundational and antifoundational approaches recycles the same arguments and theoretical positions that have divided legal scholars since Holmes and Langdell. The disagreement between postmodern neopragmatists and ironists is not unlike the disagreement between Langdell and Holmes, who agreed that conceptualism in law was inevitable, but disagreed on the possibility that conceptualization in legal analysis would make law like a science. Thus, Posner and Schlag agree that legal analysis is culturally and linguistically contingent, but disagree on the possibility of discovering a situated, instrumental analysis to coherently guide legal analysis to reach correct answers, pragmatically defined. Postmodern neopragmatists seek to reform modern legal analysis and instruct its practitioners on how to be more pragmatic and instrumental in their method. Postmodern ironists attempt to intensify the awareness of the repetitive nature of legal discourse, including neopragmatic discourse, in an effort to facilitate closure and transition.

Closure seems unlikely as the themes of contemporary jurisprudence repeat themselves in surprising new patterns but always reproducing the same common argumentative and normative structures. Because modern jurisprudence never seems to get beyond the structure and content of its own cognitive and normative form, legal scholars yearn for a more realistic jurisprudence—a jurisprudence that is relevant for dealing with the bureaucratic power structures and multicultural communities of postmodern American culture. Modern jurisprudence has become tired as its older scholars have worn themselves out recycling the same argumentative structures and dichotomies, even while the next generation of scholars claims to have developed new, refined methods and approaches.

The rising skepticism has been especially pronounced in other intellectual fields as a new breed of theorists questioned the objective descriptions and truth claims of modern theory. The implications of these intellectual currents have just recently been felt in the legal academy. Throughout the 1980s, the legal academy was an intellectual hothouse, spinning out new ideas, new discourses, and new solutions for dealing with problems of a changing and culturally diverse society. The proliferation of theories, discourses, and perspectives of the new scholarly movements in law set the stage for the development of a new jurisprudence and a new theoretical paradigm for law.

One indication of this is the view of contemporary legal scholars and practitioners who wonder whether traditional understandings about law and jurisprudence are exhausted. Another is the heightened disagreement between legal scholars over the most elementary issues of jurisprudence, such as the possibility of identifying objective methods and a shared intellectual foundation for legal studies. Yet another is the recognition that modern legal theory has failed to sustain the modernists' hopes about social progress. There is also the cynicism that comes from the realization that legal theorists have participated in a recycling process, coupled with a desire to move on to something else.

The sources motivating the new scholarly movements are, of course, complex and diverse, including internal pressures of tenure, the desire to write new and innovative legal theory, and a myriad of psychological and economic factors that have historically motivated legal scholars to take risks by developing controversial ideas and arguments. While legal scholars have always aspired to say something new and provocative about the law, there has never been a period in the history of American legal theory that approaches the level of intellectual diversity and fragmentation witnessed during the 1980s as intellectual eclecticism intensified and legal scholars became fragmented within different schools and movements. The new scholarly movements shared a common orientation that was defined by their shared opposition to the traditional modes of scholarship and the modern theory of jurisprudence such scholarship sought to refine.

Contemporary legal scholars consider new and different kinds of jurisprudential intellectual inquiry—inquiries about language and the kind of subjects that inhabit the world of legal thought. These new inquiries enable a different kind of jurisprudential "critique"—one that would criticize a school of legal thought, a legal theory, or a doctrine, not in terms of truth, adequacy, or normative appeal of its representations in the objective realm, but rather in terms of the kind of subject that the school, theory, concept, or doctrine presupposes or celebrates. The goal of such work is to better understand the type of subjects that have been unconsciously reproduced and constituted in legal discourse. Unlike traditional legal theorists who attempt to defend law's autonomy, legal scholars who have adopted a postmodern temperament in their work have refocused the jurisprudential inquiry toward the nature of the *subject* who interprets and creates legal meaning. These scholars have sought to provoke debate and inquiry on the social construction of legal subjects, or what has been dubbed the "problem of the subject in legal studies," [16] which refers to the many ways judges and lawyers avoid "the question of who or what thinks or produces law." [17] It is this forgetting of the "we" who do the "expounding" that a new group of legal scholars claims has been ignored in the debate about law and politics. [18]

On the other hand, postmodern trends in legal scholarship have generated considerable anxiety and discomfort. In challenging traditional notions of jurisprudence, postmodern criticism seems to challenge the very idea of law itself. If decision makers cannot render decisions according to law, then how can we expect "law" to protect us against the many injustices and invasions of the day? If the Rule of Law depends on different normative and theoretical perspectives, how will "law" protect itself against the subjective desires of legal subjects? As we approach the next millennium, it seems certain that anxiety about these questions will heighten.

Postmodernists attempt to heighten, for better or worse, the predicament of our time. Postmodernism may eventually fade into something else, but for now it is here to stay because it best describes the condition of our era. Postmodernism underscores the anxiety and uncertainty of living in a highly fragmented and diverse society at the end of the twentieth century, though it cannot be held responsible for this condition, nor can it be blamed by those who feel alienated by that condition. It is not the lack of a foundational vision or objective perspective that renders postmodernism troublesome; what is troubling is the intellectual bias against politically committed scholarship and action in legal studies. Postmodernists attempt to rectify that problem by providing intellectual legitimacy to a theoretical practice informed by social and political experience.

It may be that the temperament of contemporary jurisprudence evidences a general cultural anxiety that occurs whenever a century ends. [19] In moving from one century to the next, it is hard not to believe that an era is ending and that the old ways are exhausted. [20] Perhaps the current postmodern condition is part of a historically anxious, contingent moment. In the next millennium, new frontiers and new energy may reinvigorate the quest for answers to the dilemmas of modernism.

What may seem to be "impending annihilation"[21] may in fact be the basis for satisfaction, hope, and new intellectual inquiry in the next millennium. Constructive engagement between the different jurisprudential movements may lead to new jurisprudential insights about law.[22] Law and economics advocates may discover the social-construction thesis that gives their theory the appearance of determinacy. Critical legal studies scholars might discover that a renewed interest in understanding the process of market commodification may provide the vehicle for developing a new agenda for jurisprudence. Law and literature scholars may deepen their interest in the cultural forces of race, class, and gender that influence legal interpretation. Feminists and critical race scholars might develop a new understanding of the relation between the particular and general from their unique method of consciousness-raising.

Perhaps new canons of interpretation for the legal profession can be discovered for developing a new constructive jurisprudence for the discourse of postmodern legal movements. The two sides of postmodernism may be reconstructed and reformed so that they will be absorbed within the two sides of legal modernism created by the forms of legal thought developed from Langdell and Holmes. However, postmoderns would be quick to remind us that we can never go back to the good old days of political and intellectual consensus. They would warn us that all canons of law are man-made and thus always subject to reinterpretation. They would resist the idea of a postmodern theory of jurisprudence; they would instead emphasize diversity, contradiction, and paradox. Postmoderns would say that the future of jurisprudence remains in our hands, that it is up to us to build the legal world we wish to inhabit.

It is a critical time for jurisprudential studies in America. It is a time for self-reflection and reevaluation of methodological and theoretical legacies in the law. At stake is not only the status of modern jurisprudence, but also the validity of the Rule of Law itself. In the current era of academic diversity and disagreement, the time has come to seriously consider the transformative changes now unfolding in American legal thought. The challenge for the next century will certainly involve new ways of understanding how the legal system can preserve the authority of the Rule of Law while responding to the different perspectives and interests of multicultural communities. It is without a doubt an anxious and exciting time for jurisprudence.

Whether the jurisprudential movements discussed in this book are praised, condemned, or (as I have argued) transformed by a new form of postmodern jurisprudence will ultimately depend on how successful these movements have been in hastening the death, not of jurisprudence, but of the particular methods that modern legal scholars have employed in thinking about their subject: law and adjudication. The proliferation of new forms of competing jurisprudential discourses, the willingness of some to try new methods, and the expression of discontent and resistance signify the end of neither professional discourse nor law as we have known it—all may simply be symptomatic of change from the old to the new.[23]

What was once understood as the mainstream or modern view has broken into a diverse body of jurisprudential theories and perspectives. The current state of law and modern jurisprudence has become like a delta just before a river empties into the sea. The mighty river that was once modern jurisprudence has broken down into separate rivulets as it merges into a larger and different body of water. The modern river of jurisprudence splinters and is transformed by the sea change of a new perspective. It is time to consider the significance of these sea changes for "[n]o matter how troubling it may be, the landscape of the postmodern [now] surrounds us. It simultaneously delimits us and opens our horizons. It's our problem and our hope."[24]

# Notes

## Notes to Introduction

1. Jurisprudence is the branch of legal philosophy devoted to the study of law and adjudication. *See, e.g.,* GEORGE C. CHRISTIE, JURISPRUDENCE: TEXT AND READINGS ON THE PHILOSOPHY OF LAW (St. Paul: West Publishing Co. 1973). For the most part, jurisprudence deals with general theories of legal rights, problems of judicial decision making, and the nature of law. Until recently, jurisprudence, as taught at most American law schools, was organized around a number of central themes that attempted to explain the nature of law and judicial decision making in terms of an objective theory distinct from political and moral philosophy.

2. *See* David Kennedy, *Critical Theory, Structuralism and Contemporary Legal Scholarship,* 21 NEW ENG. L. REV. 209, 210 (1985–86).

3. Fredric Jameson stated in his study of postmodernism: *"Postmodernism* is not something we can settle once and for all and then use it with a clear conscience. The concept, if there is one, has to come at the end, and not at the beginning of our discussions of it. . . . [W]e are within the culture of postmodernism to the point where its facile repudiation is as impossible as any equally facile celebration of it is complacent and corrupt." FREDRIC JAMESON, POSTMODERNISM, OR, THE CULTURAL LOGIC OF LATE CAPITALISM, xxii, 62 (Durham: Duke University Press 1992). *See also* Stephen Feldman, *Diagnosing Power: Postmodernism in Legal Scholarship,* 88 N.W.U.L. REV. 1046 (1994).

4. *See* Gary Minda, *One Hundred Years of Modern Legal Thought: From Langdell and Holmes to Posner and Schlag,* forthcoming in INDIANA LAW REVIEW. David Luban's essay *Legal Modernism,* 84 MICH. L. REV. 1686 (1986), offers a somewhat different description of the term *legal modernism* in attempting to identify the intellectual roots of the critical legal studies movement with artistic modernism. According to Luban, "CLS is to legal theory as modern art was to traditional art." *Id.* at 1656. This book attempts to highlight a different understanding of modernism, one that

259

takes into account the significance of Enlightenment *(Weltanschauung)* as an intellectual and political condition of social and philosophical thought. *See, generally,* JÜRGEN HABERMAS, THE PHILOSOPHICAL DISCOURSE OF MODERNITY (Cambridge, Mass.: MIT Press 1987). The view of this book is that artistic modernism fails to capture the meaning of legal modernism because legal moderns conceive law as a political rather than artistic enterprise. *See, e.g.,* Ronald Dworkin, *Law as Interpretation, in* THE POLITICS OF INTERPRETATION 264 (W. J. T. Mitchell ed.) (Chicago: University of Chicago Press 1983).

5. Roy Boyne and Ali Rattansi, *The Theory and Politics of Postmodernism: By Way of an Introduction, in* POSTMODERNISM AND SOCIETY 1, 3 (R. Boyne and A. Rattansi, eds.) (New York: St. Martin's Press 1990). The liberating potential of reason and science has enabled American legal thinkers to have what Neil Duxbury has called "faith in reason." *See* Neil Duxbury, *Faith in Reason: The Process Tradition in American Jurisprudence,* 15 CARDOZO L. REV. 601 (1993). *See also* NEIL DUXBURY, PATTERNS OF AMERICAN JURISPRUDENCE (Oxford: Oxford University Press, 1995) (describing how "faith in reason" has structured the patterns of recent American jurisprudence).

6. CHARLES FRIED, ORDER AND LAW: ARGUING THE REAGAN REVOLUTION— A FIRSTHAND ACCOUNT 216 (New York: Simon & Schuster 1990).

7. *See* ROBERTO M. UNGER, LAW IN MODERN SOCIETY 134–242 (New York: Free Press 1976).

8. P. John Kozyris, *In the Cauldron of Jurisprudence: The View from within the Stew,* 41 J. LEGAL EDUC. 421 (1991).

9. The "canon debate" became public in 1987 with the late Allan Bloom's best-seller, THE CLOSING OF THE AMERICAN MIND: HOW HIGHER EDUCATION HAS FAILED DEMOCRACY AND IMPROVED THE SOULS OF TODAY'S STUDENTS (New York: Simon & Schuster 1988). Bloom argued that a new generation of university teachers trained in the techniques of literary criticism, Freudian criticism, Marxist criticism, structuralism, deconstructionism, poststructuralism, and feminism came to reject the existence of ultimate truths that were essential to a liberal education. For Bloom and others like him it was time for the university to return to the classic discovery of the "canons" of Western liberal thought. *See, e.g.,* ROGER KIMBALL, TENURED RADICALS: HOW POLITICS HAS CORRUPTED OUR HIGHER EDUCATION (New York: Harper Collins 1990); DAVID LEHMAN, SIGNS OF THE TIMES: DECONSTRUCTION AND THE FALL OF PAUL DeMAN (New York: Poseidon Press 1992); DINESH D'SOUZA, ILLIBERAL EDUCATION: THE POLITICS OF RACE AND SEX ON CAMPUS (New York: Random House 1992); GERALD GRAFF, BEYOND THE CULTURE WARS: HOW TEACHING THE CONFLICTS CAN REVITALIZE AMERICAN EDUCATION (New York: Norton 1993).

10. Posner, a federal judge and a former law professor at the University of Chicago, is best known for his work in law and economics. More recently, however, Posner's interest has turned to jurisprudence and neopragmatic

philosophy, which can be identified as a form of postmodern jurisprudence. His recent articles and books on jurisprudence, and especially his embrace of the neopragmatic philosophy of Richard Rorty, justify treating Posner as a postmodern writer. *See* RICHARD A. POSNER, THE PROBLEMS OF JURIS-PRUDENCE (Cambridge, Mass.: Harvard University Press 1990); OVERCOM-ING LAW (Cambridge, Mass.: Harvard University Press 1995). Pierre Schlag, currently a law professor at the University of Colorado, is largely responsi-ble for developing the postmodern critique of normative legal thought. *See, e.g.,* Pierre Schlag, *Normativity and the Politics of Form,* 139 U. PA. L. REV. 801 (1991); *Normative and Nowhere to Go,* 43 STAN. L. REV. 167 (1990). Schlag is one of the best-known postmodern legal critics in the academy today.

11. *See* JEAN-FRANÇOIS LYOTARD, THE POSTMODERN CONDITION: A REPORT ON KNOWLEDGE (Geoff Bannington and Brian Massumi, TRANS.) (Minneap-olis: University of Minnesota Press 1984). The postmodern attitude was expressed by Lyotard's declaration: "I define *postmodernism* as incredulity towards meta-narratives." *Id.* at xxiv.

12. DAVID LEHMAN, SIGNS OF THE TIMES: DECONSTRUCTION AND THE FALL OF PAUL DEMAN, *supra* at 41. Lehman argues that postmodernism with its deconstructive strategies "is a catastrophe theory inasmuch as it proceeds from the perception of an extreme linguistic instability that undermines the coherence of any statement—a breakdown in our collective confidence in the power of words to communicate ideas and represent experience." *Id.* The view of this book is that postmodernism cannot be held responsible for the breakdown in intellectual representational practices. Postmodernists merely point out that a crisis and fragmentation exist. Postmodernism is a reflective temperament that invites us to see the fluidity of law; it is not a theory, but a practice which defines itself in relation to modernist aspira-tions and practices.

## Notes to Chapter 1

1. C. C. LANGDELL, A SELECTION OF CASES ON THE LAW OF CONTRACTS i–v (Boston: Little, Brown & Co. 1871). *See also Address by C. C. Langdell to the Harvard Law School Association, 1886, in* A. SUTHERLAND, THE LAW AT HARVARD 175 (Cambridge, Mass.: Belknap Press of Harvard University Press 1967). Langdell was dean of Harvard University Law School from 1870 until 1895.

2. Langdell's idea of "law as science" developed at the time that scientific naturalism, associated with Darwin's theory of evolution, became a highly influential theory in American intellectual thought. Darwin's evolutionary thesis placed mankind within the animal kingdom and "made it plausible to treat human mental capacities as evolved functions of natural organisms, arising from simpler forms of animal behavior as a result of their survival-promoting tendencies." Thomas C. Grey, *Holmes and Legal Pragmatism,*

41 STAN. L. REV. 787, 796 (1989). This evolutionary form of thinking encouraged philosophers and social thinkers to reject the positivist autonomy that separated mind from matter. It enabled intellectuals to contemplate the possibility that nonbiological processes of social relations developed in an evolutionary manner. Scholars in various academic fields used evolutionary thinking in their analyses of nonbiological processes, such as social and political events. See EDWARD A. PURCELL, THE CRISIS OF DEMOCRATIC THEORY, SCIENTIFIC NATURALISM & THE PROBLEM OF VALUE 5 (Lexington: University Press of Kentucky 1973). Scientific naturalism nurtured the modernists' obsession with the existence of autonomous spheres of pure reason for discovering the objective order of the universe. As scientific naturalism spread, American lawyers developed new approaches to legal studies that reflected a new legal conceptualism.

3. Grant Gilmore (1910–82), was a highly respected legal scholar known for his writings on the Uniform Commercial Code, Contracts, Admiralty, and Jurisprudence. Gilmore taught his students at Yale Law School to be skeptical about interdisciplinary legal studies and to be wary of the danger of "false certainties." See Guido Calabresi, Grant Gilmore and the Golden Age, 92 YALE L.J. 1, 2 (1982). Gilmore's skeptical philosophy is helpful for understanding the dynamics of legal modernism and the conditions leading to postmodern jurisprudence. See GRANT GILMORE, THE DEATH OF CONTRACT (Columbus: Ohio State University Press 1974); GRANT GILMORE, THE AGES OF AMERICAN LAW (New Haven: Yale University Press 1977).

4. GILMORE, THE AGES OF AMERICAN LAW, supra at 43.

5. See Thomas C. Grey, Langdell's Orthodoxy, 45 U. PITT L. REV. 1 (1983). Grey is a professor of law at Stanford University.

6. Id. at 7–8.

7. Id. at 8.

8. Id.

9. See K. LLEWELLYN, THE COMMON LAW TRADITION—DECIDING APPEALS 35–45 (Boston: Little, Brown & Co. 1960). Grey states that conceptualism "describes legal theories that place a high value on the creation (or discovery) of a few fundamental principles and concepts at the heart of a system, whether reasoning from them is formal or informal." Grey, Langdell's Orthodoxy, supra at 9–10.

10. "The result [was] platonism: the idea that concepts exist 'out there,' like trees on rocks, rather than are created." Richard A. Posner, Legal Formalism, Legal Realism, and the Interpretation of Statutes and the Constitution, 37 CASE W. L. REV. 179, 182 (1986).

11. Grey, Holmes and Legal Pragmatism, supra at 822.

12. See Pierre Schlag, The Problem of the Subject, 69 TEX. L. REV. 1627, 1632–62 (1991).

13. Christopher Columbus Langdell, A Brief Survey of Equity Jurisdiction, 1 HARV. L. REV. 55, 68 (1987), quoted in Pierre Schlag, The Problem of the Subject, supra at 1632.

14. As Schlag put it, "Langdell's work reads like law's immaculate conception." Schlag, *The Problem of the Subject, supra* at 1632.

15. *See* Pierre Schlag, *Normativity and the Politics of Form,* 139 U. PA. L. REV. 801, 814–28 (1991); Thomas Grey, *Langdell's Orthodoxy, supra* at 9. Nonformalist conceptualists want clear autonomous rules, but they place little importance on abstract doctrinal formulations. They believe, as Holmes believed, that "general principles do not decide concrete cases." Lochner v. New York, 198 U.S. 45, 76 (1905). *See also* Grey, *Langdell's Orthodoxy, supra* at 9, nn. 29, 44.

16. "Transcendental" means that which makes experience possible. *Transcendental object* refers to the order of the legal categories and definitions of the law (the object). *Transcendental subject* refers to the "gaze of the observer, the Langdellian legal scientist" that renders the experience of law possible. Schlag, *The Problem of the Subject, supra* at 1645, n. 66. The Langdellian vision of "law" can thus be understood as both the experience of a transcendental object and as transcendental subject. Sometimes Langdell viewed law as an object and sometimes as a subject.

17. *See* GILMORE, THE DEATH OF CONTRACT, *supra* at 43–44.

18. *See* Schlag, *The Problem of the Subject, supra* at 1632–56. *See also* David S. Caudill, *Pierre Schlag's "The Problem of the Subject": Law's Need for an Analyst,* 15 CARDOZO L. REV. 707, 709–12 (1993).

19. *See* Ernest J. Weinrib, *The Jurisprudence of Legal Formalism,* 16 HARV. J. L. & PUB. POL'Y 583, 594 (1993).

20. *See* Pierre Schlag, *Fish v. Zapp: The Case of the Relatively Autonomous Self,* 76 GEO. L.J. 37, 42–50 (1987); Pierre Schlag, *"Le Hors de Texte, C'est Moi": The Politics of Form and the Domestication of Deconstruction,* 11 CARDOZO L. REV. 1631, 1667–73 (1990). *Autonomy* is a word used in legal analysis to mean different things to different people. For example, autonomy may refer to qualities of people, processes, theories, and even the law itself. The idea of *relatively autonomous self* is used by legal writers such as Pierre Schlag to denote how modern legal subjects have become defined by causal forces, involving the fluidity and interconnectivity of human institutions and social practices. In Schlag's view, the legal understanding of "autonomy" is relative to social, economic, and political context.

21. *See* Drucilla Cornell, *Toward a Modern/Postmodern Reconstruction of Ethics,* 133 U. PA. L. REV. 291, 308 (1985).

22. *See, e.g.,* Owen M. Fiss, *Objectivity and Interpretation,* 34 STAN. L. REV. 739, 744.

23. Steven L. Winter, *Indeterminacy and Incommensurability in Constitutional Law,* 78 CAL. L. REV. 1441, 1445 (1990).

24. *Id.* at 57. *See also* Robert Stevens, *Two Cheers for 1870: The American Law School, in* LAW IN AMERICAN HISTORY (D. Flemming and B. Baily, eds.) (Boston: Little, Brown & Co. 1971).

25. GILMORE, THE AGES OF AMERICAN LAW, *supra* at 42. Gilmore also said,

"Langdell seems to have been an essentially stupid man who, early in his life, had one great idea to which, thereafter, he clung with all the tenacity of genius." *Id.*

26. *See, generally,* Roy Boyne and Ali Rattansi, *The Theory and Politics of Postmodernism: By Way of an Introduction, in* POSTMODERNISM AND SO-CIETY 3 (R. Boyne and A. Rattansi, eds.) (New York: St. Martin's Press 1990).

27. Holmes, America's most famous jurist, was a student at Harvard Law School from 1865 to 1866. He briefly served as a professor at the law school until he became a judge on the Massachusetts Supreme Judicial Court. He eventually took a seat on the United States Supreme Court and remained active on that bench into his nineties. *See, e.g.,* BERNARD SCHWARTZ, MAIN CURRENTS IN AMERICAN LEGAL THOUGHT 376–96 (Dur-ham, N.C.: Carolina Academic Press 1993). Holmes was a deeply skeptical but practical man. Gilmore said that Holmes "was savage, harsh, and cruel, a bitter and lifelong pessimist who saw in the course of human life nothing but a continuing struggle in which the rich and powerful impose their will on the poor and weak." GILMORE, THE AGES OF AMERICAN LAW, *supra* at 49. The "real Holmes" may never be known, since he was an intensely private and enigmatic person. One fact is certain, however: Holmes's com-plex thought established a second path for the development of modern jurisprudence. *See* G. EDWARD WHITE, JUSTICE OLIVER WENDELL HOLMES: LAW AND THE INNER SELF (New York: Oxford University Press 1993); Morton J. Horwitz, *The Place of Justice Holmes in American Legal Thought, in* THE LEGACY OF OLIVER WENDELL HOLMES, JR. (R. W. Gor-don, ed.) (Stanford, Calif.: Stanford University Press 1992).

28. GILMORE, THE AGES OF AMERICAN LAW, *supra* at 48.

29. *See* OLIVER WENDELL HOLMES, THE COMMON LAW (Boston: Little, Brown & Co. 1881). The success of these lectures earned Holmes an appointment at Harvard Law School as a professor of law. Holmes's position at Harvard Law School lasted only three months after being appointed to the Supreme Court of Massachusetts, where he served until his appointment to the United States Supreme Court in 1902. *See* ROBERT STEVENS, LAW SCHOOLS: LEGAL EDUCATION IN AMERICA from the 1850s to the 1980s 138 (Chapel Hill: Univ. of North Carolina Press, 1983).

30. *See* Grey, *Holmes and Legal Pragmatism, supra* at 795. It is generally recognized that Holmes was influenced by the American pragmatist philoso-phy of Charles Sanders Peirce and John Dewey. *Id.* at 788. Holmes's views were pragmatic in spirit, but his philosophy was not the same as that of Pierce's or Dewey's. *See* Gary Minda, *One Hundred Years of Modern Legal Thought: From Langdell and Holmes to Posner and Schlag,* forthcoming in INDIANA LAW REVIEW.

31. HOLMES, THE COMMON LAW, *supra* at 5.

32. The sources and analysis of this point are developed more fully in Grey, *Holmes and Legal Pragmatism, supra* at 793–801.

33. *Id.* at 805.
34. *Id.* at 809.
35. *Id.* at 847.
36. Holmes was a member of the Metaphysical Club, a discussion group that met regularly in Boston and Cambridge from 1870 to 1872. Members of this club included, in addition to Holmes, a number of leading American pragmatic philosophers such as William James and Charles Peirce. *See* GILMORE, THE AGES OF AMERICAN LAW, *supra* at 50. It is a fair assumption that Holmes was influenced by the pragmatic theories of these philosophers. *See, e.g.,* Thomas C. Grey, *Pragmatism and Democracy,* 71 OR. L. REV. 521 (1992); Grey, *Holmes and Legal Pragmatism, supra* at 788; Catharine W. Hantzis, *Legal Innovation within the Wider Intellectual Tradition: The Pragmatism of Oliver Wendell Holmes, Jr.,* 82 Nw. U. L. REV. 541, 579– 891 (1988).
37. *See, e.g.,* Grey, *Holmes and Legal Pragmatism, supra* at 788. *See also* CHARLES S. PEIRCE, *The Fixation of Belief, in* WRITINGS OF CHARLES SANDERS PEIRCE 242, 248–49 (Christian J. W. Kloesel, ed.) (1986). *See also* Leslie Pickering Francis, *Law and Philosophy: From Skepticism to Value Theory,* 27 LOY. L.A. L. REV. 65, 72 (1993).
38. "The felt necessities of the time," Holmes wrote, "the prevalent moral and political theories, intuitions of public policy, avowed or unconscious, even the prejudices which judges share with their fellow men, have had a good deal more to do than the syllogism in determining the rules by which men should be governed." HOLMES, THE COMMON LAW, *supra* at 1.
39. R. RANDALL KELSO and CHARLES D. KELSO, STUDYING LAW: AN INTRO- DUCTION 115 (St. Paul, Minn.: West Publishing Co. 1984).
40. Holmes's critique of Langdellian formalism was based on the "philosophi- cal" reconceptualization of the old doctrinal classification system of the common law, based on Blackstone and the Writ system. Holmes's doctrinal formulations of the common law were based on the external standard of the "reasonable man." *See* Grey, *Holmes and Legal Pragmatism, supra* at 816. The conceptual approach of Holmes, however, was subordinated to the judges' "views of public policy" and "considerations of social advantage." *Id.* at 819, *citing* HOLMES, THE COMMON LAW, *supra* at 32; *The Path of the Law, supra* at 184. Hence, while Holmes was critical of Langdellian formalism, he was not an "unequivocal" antiformalist; he advocated a conceptual form of pragmatic jurisprudence based on actual facts and expe- rience that was very much part of the tradition of Langdell. *See* NEIL DUXBURY, PATTERNS OF AMERICAN JURISPRUDENCE, 46 (Oxford: Oxford University Press, forthcoming 1995): "[W]hile Holmes was certainly an important forerunner of American legal realism, it would be wrong straight- forwardly to categorize him as an unequivocal anti-formalist." *See also* GRANT GILMORE, THE AGES OF AMERICAN LAW, supra at 48–56. Holmes's pragmatic jurisprudence was anti-formalistic to the extent that Holmes rejected Langdell's thesis that law was a closed, formal system. *See, e.g.,*

*Southern Pacific Co. v. Jensen*, 244 U.S. 205, 221 (1917): "Ours is not a closed system of existing precedent. The law is not such a formal system at all" (Holmes, J., dissenting). On the other hand, Holmes also attempted to make the study of law intellectually respectable by offering a deeper understanding of law's logic. *See, e.g.*, OLIVER WENDELL HOLMES, JR., THE COMMON LAW 219 (Boston: Little, Brown & Co. 1881): "The business of the jurist is to make known the content of the law; that is, to work upon it from within, or logically, arranging and distributing it, in order, from its *sumorum genus* of its *infima species*, so far as practicable."

41. *See, e.g.*, Oliver W. Holmes, *Review of* LANGDELL, A SELECTION OF CASES ON THE LAW OF CONTRACTS, 14 AM. L. REV. 233 (1880).

42. Grey, *Holmes and Legal Pragmatism, supra* at 816.

43. *Id.*

44. *See* Schlag, *Normativity and the Politics of Form, supra* at 803.

45. *Id.* at 929.

46. *Id.* at 803.

47. *Id.* at 804.

48. *See generally* PURCELL, THE CRISIS OF DEMOCRATIC THEORY, *supra* at 75–76; Robert Summers, *Pragmatic Instrumentalism in Twentieth-Century American Legal Thought—A Synthesis and Critique of Our Dominant General Theory about Law and Its Uses*, 61 CORNELL L. REV. 861 (1981). David Lyons, *Foundation and Instrumentalism: A Pathological Study*, 61 CORNELL L. REV. 949 (1981).

49. This mediation was characteristic of American pragmatic philosophy. *See* Grey, *Holmes and Legal Pragmatism, supra* at 789.

50. *See* Robert M. Cover, *Forward: Nomos and Narrative*, 97 HARV. L. REV. 1, 11 (1983). *See also* ROBERT POST, *The Relative Autonomous Discourse of Law*, *in* LAW AND THE ORDER OF CULTURE vii (Berkeley: University of California Press 1991).

51. GILMORE, THE AGES OF AMERICAN LAW, *supra* at 50.

52. As Thomas Grey noted, "The application of this idea to law has been one of the central themes of the Critical Legal Studies movement." Grey, *Holmes and Legal Pragmatism, supra* at 814, *citing* Robert W. Gordon, *New Developments in Legal Theory*, *in* THE POLITICS OF LAW: A PROGRESSIVE CRITIQUE 281, 286 (D. Kairys, ed.) (New York: Pantheon Books 1982).

53. OLIVER W. HOLMES, *The Path of the Law* (1897), *in* COLLECTED LEGAL PAPERS 200 (New York: Pantheon Books 1982).

54. *Id.* at 167, 171. *See also* Grey, *Holmes and Legal Pragmatism, supra* at 832.

55. *Id.* at 833.

56. *Id.* at 831. Holmes's intellectual influence has since "placed a tilt on American jurisprudence from which it has not altogether recovered, that is, the limitation of legal theory to a theory of judicial decision making." JAMES E. HERGET, AMERICAN JURISPRUDENCE, 1870–1970: A HISTORY 46 (Houston: Rice University Press 1990).

57. *See* POSNER, THE PROBLEMS OF JURISPRUDENCE, *supra* at 19.

58. BENJAMIN N. CARDOZO, THE NATURE OF THE JUDICIAL PROCESS 167 (New Haven: Yale University Press 1923). Cardozo seemed to imply a revolutionary message: judges make law. *See also* GILMORE, THE AGES OF AMERICAN LAW, *supra* at 77 ("Cardozo was, we might say, a revolutionary *malgré lui* who was affectionately attached to the structure which, imperceptibly, almost surreptitiously, he proceeded to subvert and destroy"). Holmes, on the other hand, believed that the law should give effect to the dominant majority desires of the community. As Gilmore described Holmes's view: "[I]f the dominant majority desires to persecute blacks or Jews or communists or atheists, the law, if it is to be 'sound', must arrange for the prosecution to be carried out with, as we might say, due process." *Id.*

59. Schlag, *Normativity and the Politics of Form, supra* at 818.

60. POST, *The Relatively Autonomous Discourse of Law, supra* at vii.

61. *Id.* at viii.

62. GILMORE, THE AGES OF AMERICAN LAW, *supra* at 56.

63. *See, e.g.,* NEIL DUXBURY, PATTERNS OF AMERICAN JURISPRUDENCE (Oxford: Oxford University Press forthcoming 1995). Another explanation for this can be found in Duncan Kennedy's explanation of the "fundamental contradiction" of classical legal thought. *See* Duncan Kennedy, *The Structure of Blackstone's Commentaries,* 28 BUFF. L. REV. 209, 211–13 (1979).

64. Pierre Bourdieu, *The Force of Law: Toward a Sociology of the Juridical Field,* 38 HASTINGS L.J. 805, 814 (1987).

65. *See* POST, *The Relatively Autonomous Discourse of Law, supra* at viii.

66. Schlag, *Normativity and the Politics of Form, supra* at 816, *quoting* Walker Kennedy, *Functional Nonsense and the Transcendental Approach,* 5 FORDHAM L. REV. 272, 292 (1936).

67. Duncan Kennedy has identified this *mind-set* as the *legal consciousness* of classical legal thought (1885–1935). *See* Duncan Kennedy, *Towards an Historical Understanding of Legal Consciousness: The Case of Classical Legal Thought in America, 1850–1940,* 3 RES. L. & SOC'Y 3 (1980). "Legal consciousness" refers to commonly understood ideas about interpretation, law, knowledge, and truth, which lawyers, judges, and legal scholars took for granted. These underlying premises were shaped by ideas of legal formalism, Langdellian conceptualism, and Holmesian jurisprudence. *See* MORTON HORWITZ, THE TRANSFORMATION OF AMERICAN LAW 1870–1960, 9–32 (New York: Oxford University Press 1992). *See also* Elizabeth Mensch, *The History of Mainstream Legal Thought, in* THE POLITICS OF LAW: A PROGRESSIVE CRITIQUE 13, 18–24 (D. Kairys, ed.) (New York: Pantheon Books, rev. ed. 1990).

68. *See* Schlag, *Politics of Form, supra* at 1668.

69. The image of a depersonalized judiciary policing the boundaries of legal actors enabled judges to think of themselves as disinterested subjects who discovered the objective order of law. "The justification of this judicial role," according to Duncan Kennedy, "was the existence of a peculiar

legal technique rendering the task of policing the boundaries of spheres an objective, quasi-scientific one." Kennedy, *Towards an Historical Understanding, supra* at 7. Thus, Samuel Williston, a post-Langdell professor at Harvard Law School, published a treatise on the law of contract in 1920 to explain how an objective definition of free contract structured the entire corpus of contract law. Williston assumed that judges could derive these foundational principles of contract law from this objective theory of contract. *See* SAMUEL WILLISTON, THE LAW OF CONTRACTS (New York: Baker, Voorhis & Co. 1920).
70. *See* Schlag, *The Problem of the Subject, supra* at 1634.

## Notes to Chapter 2

1. GRANT GILMORE, THE AGES OF AMERICAN LAW 15 (New Haven: Yale University Press 1977).
2. *See* Steven L. Winter, *Indeterminacy and Incommensurability,* 78 CAL. L. REV. 1441, 1461 (1990). The substantive due process era thus defined a style of judicial reasoning popular at the end of the nineteenth century which permitted the Supreme Court to read common law principles of contract and property into the Due Process clause of the Fourteenth Amendment. For example, in the notorious decision of *Coppage v. Kansas,* 236 U.S. 1 (1915), the Supreme Court held that the concept of liberty found within the Due Process clause of the Fourteenth Amendment forbid a state from prohibiting so-called yellow dog employment contracts (an employment contract requiring that the employee not engage in union activities). The Due Process clause thus became a *substantive* limitation on the power of state and federal governments to enact social welfare legislation. The Supreme Court "equat[ed] the liberty secured by the Due Process clause . . . with the 'free will' from which they believed they could deduce the common law rules." *Id.* at 1754. The power of the "one true rule of law" had consequently entrenched a formalistic approach to constitutional interpretation during the 1920s.
   Legal realists exposed the underlying politics of the substantive due process decisions by revealing how those decisions reinforced the existing status quo of property entitlements. New Deal liberals and the legal realists wanted the Supreme Court to embrace a constitutional jurisprudence more tolerant of the activist welfare state erected by the New Deal.
3. *See, e.g.,* Gitlow v. New York, 268 U.S. 652, 672 (1925) (Holmes J., dissenting); Abrams v. United States, 250 U.S. 616, 624 (1919) (Holmes J., dissenting). *See also* Winter, *Indeterminacy and Incommensurability, supra* at 1461, n. 93 (recounting how Herbert Wechsler, as a student at Columbia in the late 1920s, was told by his teachers that the latest Holmes and Brandeis dissents were "virtually sacred texts to be read and studied." *Id.*)
4. Legal realism began as a critique of legal conceptualism but, as it turned

out, legal realism served to lay the groundwork for a new form of social science conceptualism that grounded objectivity in empirical observation.

5. James Boyle, *The Politics of Reason: Critical Legal Theory and Local Social Thought,* 133 U. PA. L. REV. 685, 711 (1985).

6. Roscoe Pound, *The Call for a Realist Jurisprudence,* 44 HARV. L. REV. 697 (1931).

7. Karl Llewellyn, *Some Realism about Realism—Responding to Dean Pound,* 44 HARV. L. REV. 1222 (1931). Grant Gilmore notes that Llewellyn and Frank jointly prepared the essay, but that it was published under Llewellyn's name only. GILMORE, AGES OF AMERICAN LAW, *supra* at 78, n. 25. Llewellyn's reply to Pound represented "a model for disciplined polemics" that shaped the future course of the legal realist movement. *See* WILLIAM TWINING, KARL LLEWELLYN AND THE REALIST MOVEMENT, 77–83 (Norman: University of Oklahoma Press 1973).

8. Llewellyn, *Some Realism about Realism, supra* at 1233. Twining asserts that this was an unfortunate strategy on the part of Llewellyn (and Frank): "Failure to identify who were 'the realists' has been the most fruitful source of error." *See* TWINING, KARL LLEWELLYN AND THE REALIST MOVEMENT, *supra* at 81. On the other hand, by 1931 (the year Llewellyn and Frank published their reply to Pound) the realist movement, and the key figures writing in the realist tradition (Corbin, Hohfeld, Cook, Moore, Oliphant, Llewellyn, and Frank), consciously made it difficult for even the realists to classify anyone under a single theory or legal label. As Twining acknowledged: "The [only] unifying element was the attempt to work out an alternative to the 'orthodox' approach to legal education and legal research that was symbolized by the popular images of Harvard and Langdell" (*id.* at 82). The same could be said today of contemporary legal movements such as critical legal studies, law and economics, feminism, law and literature, and critical race theory—all attempt to work out alternatives to the 'orthodox' approach to legal education and law symbolized by the popular images of Harvard and the new Langdellians: the legal process theorists who came after Langdell.

9. *Id.*

10. *See, generally,* Pierre Schlag, *Normativity and the Politics of Form,* 139 U. PA. L. REV. 801 (1991).

11. *See* TWINING, KARL LLEWELLYN AND THE REALIST MOVEMENT, *supra* at 82. *See also* Golding, *Jurisprudence and Legal Philosophy in Twentieth-Century America—Major Themes and Developments,* 36 J. LEGAL EDUC. 441, 452 (1986).

12. *See, e.g.,* Roscoe Pound, *The Scope and Purpose of Sociological Jurisprudence* (pts. 1–3), 24 HARV. L. REV. 591 (1911), 25 Harv. L. Rev. 140, 489 (1912); BENJAMIN N. CARDOZO, THE NATURE OF THE JUDICIAL PROCESS (New Haven: Yale University Press 1921). Legal realism emerged from such early nineteenth century traditions as pragmatism, instrumentalism, and

progressivism. *See* M. WHITE, SOCIAL THOUGHT IN AMERICA: THE REVOLT
AGAINST FORMALISM (Boston: Beacon Press 1967); Joseph Singer, *Legal
Realism Now*, 76 CAL. L. REV. 465 (1988). The work of the legal realists
that has served as the bedrock of American realist thought includes Felix
Cohen, *The Ethical Basis of Legal Criticism*, 41 YALE L.J. 201 (1931); Felix
Cohen, *Transcendental Nonsense and the Functional Approach*, 35 COLUM.
L. REV. 809 (1935) [hereinafter *Transcendental*]; Morris Cohen, *The Basis
of Contract*, 46 HARV. L. REV. 553 (1933); Morris Cohen, *Property and
Sovereignty*, 13 CORNELL L.Q. 8 (1927); Walter Wheeler Cook, *Privileges
of Labor Unions in the Struggle for Life*, 27 YALE L.J. 779 (1918); Robert
Hale, *Bargaining, Duress, and Economic Liberty*, 43 COLUM. L. REV. 603
(1943).

13. It is thus ironic that Roscoe Pound came to be viewed as an "arch-reaction-
ary" by many legal realists.

14. Lochner v. New York, 198 U.S. at 76 (Holmes, J., dissenting).

15. *Id.* at 75.

16. 198 U.S. 45 (1905).

17. This argument was made by Professor Cass Sunstein in his article, *Lochner's
Legacy*, 87 COLUM. L. REV. 873 (1987). Sunstein's analysis of the *Lochner*
decision represents a modern-day application of legal realism. *See id.* at n.
51, *citing* Cohen, *Property and Sovereignty*, 13 CORNELL L.Q. 8 (1927);
Robert L. Hale, *Coercion and Distribution in a Supposedly Noncoercive
State*, 38 POL. SCI. Q. 470 (1923).

18. Sunstein, *Lochner's Legacy*, *supra* at 883. In *Lochner*, the Court assumed
that common law notions of freedom of contract were embedded in the
concept of liberty secured by the Due Process clause. Such a concept established a "neutral," "objective," and "prepolitical" baseline for evaluating
the constitutionality of state welfare legislation. *Id.* at 882–83. Sunstein
argued that, as a result of this "*Lochner*-like premise," the Supreme Court
assumed that disparities of wealth and privilege were natural and legitimate.
*See* Coppage v. Kansas, 236 U.S. 1, 17–18 (1915).

19. *See* Lon L. Fuller, *American Legal Realism*, 82 U. PA. L. REV. 429, 443
(1934).

20. *Id.* at 452.

21. The realists claimed that the Supreme Court's liberty of contract cases were
decided by formalistic methods of legal analysis that concealed or deflected
attention away from the social consequences of judicial decision making.
The realists argued that decisions like *Lochner* should be condemned as
"formalistic" because the Court attempted to mask a political choice by
decision making according to rule. Modern legal scholars now accept this
criticism as one of the "vices" of legal formalism. *See, e.g.,* Frederick
Schauer, *Formalism*, YALE L.J. 509, 513–14 (1988).

22. *See* Felix Cohen, *Transcendental Nonsense and the Factional Approach*, 35
COLUM. L. REV. 809 (1935).

23. *See* Walter Wheeler Cook, *Privileges of Labor Unions in the Struggle for Life*, 27 YALE L.J. 779 (1918).
24. *See, e.g.,* Robert L. Hale, *Bargaining, Duress and Economic Liberty*, 43 COLUM. L. REV. 253 (1943); John Davison, *Economic Duress—An Essay in Perspective*, 45 MICH. L. REV. 253 (1947).
25. *See* Gary Peller, *The Metaphysics of American Law*, 73 CAL. L. REV. 1151, 1227 (1985). Peller reveals how the "political" strand of radical realism can be found in the work of legal realists such as Felix Cohen and Robert Hale. *Id.* at 1222–24. Peller's scholarship established how the realist scholarship of Cohen, Hale, Cook, and others was marked by a distinctly political bent aimed at debunking formalism and thereby exposing the power dimension of all legal institutions. *See also* Robert E. Scott, *Chaos Theory and the Justice Paradox*, 35 WM. & MARY L. REV. 329, 339 (1993).
26. Cohen, *Transcendental, supra* at 810.
27. *Id.* at 812.
28. *See, e.g.,* Karl Llewellyn, *The Constitution as an Institution*, 34 COLUM. L. REV. 1 (1934).
29. JEROME FRANK, LAW AND THE MODERN MIND (Garden City, N.Y.: Doubleday 1963, 1949) (orig. ed. 1930).
30. *See, e.g.,* Felix Cohen, *Transcendental Nonsense and the Functional Approach*, 35 COLUM. L. REV. 809 (1935).
31. *See, e.g.,* Cooke, *Privileges of Labor Unions in the Struggle for Life, supra* at 799.
32. *See, e.g.,* Robert Hale, *Bargaining, Duress and Economic Liberty*, 43 COLUM. L. REV. 603 (1943); Robert Hale, *Coercion and Distribution in a Supposedly Non-Coercive State*, 33 POL. SCI. Q. 470 (1923).
33. *See, e.g.,* Robert L. Hale, *Force and the State: A Comparison of "Political" and "Economic" Compulsion*, 35 COLUM. L. REV. 149 (1935); Hale, *Coercion and Distribution in a Supposedly Non-Coercive State, supra* at 38. For a highly useful account of Hale's theory of compulsion, *see* Neil Duxbury, *Robert Hale and the Economy of Legal Force*, 53 MOD. L. REV. 421 (1990).
34. Joseph William Singer, *Legal Realism Now*, 76 CAL. L. REV. 467, 474 (1988).
35. Gary Peller, *The Metaphysics of American Law*, 73 CAL. L. REV. 1151, 1222 (1985).
36. *See* EDWARD A. PURCELL, JR., THE CRISIS OF DEMOCRATIC THEORY 91 (Lexington: University Press of Kentucky 1973).
37. *See* GILMORE, THE AGES OF AMERICAN LAW, *supra* at 78, 81–85, 87–88. *See also* TWINING, KARL LLEWELLYN AND THE REALIST MOVEMENT, *supra* at 375–87 (evaluating the work of progressive realists that many claim to have "concertize[d] sociological jurisprudence," *id.* at 383).
38. *Id.* at 85. Gilmore was a member of the drafting staff of the Code in 1946 and served until the staff was disbanded in 1954. He also served as a

consultant to committees charged with considering revisions of the Code. Karl Llewellyn was the first "Chief Reporter" of the Code.

39. See Pierre Schlag, The Problem of the Subject, 69 TEX. L. REV. 1627, 1731–38 (1991). This point has been more recently developed by Neil Duxbury in his book PATTERNS OF AMERICAN JURISPRUDENCE (Oxford: Oxford University Press 1995).

40. The idea of "Realistic Jurisprudence" comes from Llewellyn's famous article, A Realistic Jurisprudence—The Next Step, 30 COLUM. L. REV. 431 (1930) [hereinafter Realistic]. Llewellyn argued that "Realistic Jurisprudence" would require judges to look beyond abstract legal verbalism and instead focus on behavioral factors—"the area of contact, of interaction, between official regulatory behavior and the behavior of those affecting or affected by official regulatory behavior." Id. at 464. The idea of "Realistic Jurisprudence" made the social sciences, including economics, relevant for legal study.

41. Id. at 431.

42. Another example of such an effort can be found in Lasswell and McDougal, Legal Education and Public Policy: Professional Training in the Public Interest, 52 YALE L.J. 203 (1943).

43. See GILMORE, THE AGES OF AMERICAN LAW, supra at 85.

44. See Llewellyn, Some Realism about Realism, supra at 1222.

45. See GILMORE, THE AGES OF AMERICAN LAW, supra at 87, citing CARL BECKER, THE HEAVENLY CITY OF THE EIGHTEENTH-CENTURY PHILOSOPHERS (New Haven: Yale University Press 1932).

46. See Winter, Indeterminacy and Incommensurability, supra at 1464, citing THOMAS KUHN, THE STRUCTURE OF SCIENTIFIC REVOLUTIONS 35–38 (Chicago: University of Chicago Press, 2d ed. 1970).

47. Progressive legal realists could thus claim that "Holmes, Roscoe Pound, and [their] exponents [were] relatively primitive and confused precursors of the more rigorous and sophisticated form of scientific instrumentalist jurisprudence represented by contemporary law and economics, cost-benefit analysis and public choice theory." Grey, Holmes and Legal Pragmatism, supra at 789.

48. See RICHARD POSNER, THE PROBLEMS OF JURISPRUDENCE 19 (Cambridge, Mass.: Harvard University Press 1990). Some contemporary legal theorists, however, regard legal realism as a movement that "failed" to sustain itself in the wake of the legal process tradition of the 1950s and 1960s. See Neil Duxbury, Faith in Reason: The Process Tradition in American Jurisprudence, 15 CARDOZO L. REV. 601, 704 (1993): "[L]egal realism failed. Whereas realism was weak in opposition to tyranny, process jurisprudence was premised on the rationality of democracy. Inevitably, the latter prospered as the former fell from grace." Citing Thurmond Arnold, Judge Jerome Frank, 24 U. CHI. L. REV. 633, 635 (1957) ("realism, despite its liberating virtues, is not a sustaining food for a stable civilization"). My view of this is that realism, as an intellectual aesthetic, has re-emerged in the

post-process tradition known as "post-realist jurisprudence." The post-process tradition is represented by new forms of legal criticism emerging in the 1980s that rejected the values of legal rationality and the consensus theories of process jurisprudence. *See also* note 96 *infra.*

49. *See* GILMORE, THE AGES OF AMERICAN LAW, *supra* at 74–98. The reason for this was that legal academics have never given up on Langdell's image of law as a discipline worthy of the university. *See* Schlag, *The Problem of the Subject, supra* at 1732.

50. "All Ages of Faith may be of brief duration. . . . The specifics of the breakdown, like the specifics of the original construction, are determined by the accidents of time." *See* GILMORE, THE AGES OF AMERICAN LAW, *supra* at 68.

51. *Id.* at 72. William Draper Lewis, dean of the University of Pennsylvania Law School, was the founder and "guiding spirit" of the Institute and Reinstatement projects. *See* Herbert Goodrich, *The Story of the American Institute,* 1951 WASH. U. L.Q. 283. The first Reinstatements, which were intended to be a "once only" project, lasted less than a generation. The Reinstatements are now in their "Second Series."

52. *See* BRUCE ACKERMAN, WE THE PEOPLE: FOUNDATIONS 50–56 (Cambridge, Mass.: Harvard University Press 1984).

53. *See* M. McDOUGAL, H. LASSWELL, AND I. VLASIC, LAW AND PUBLIC ORDER IN SPACE 1–127 (New Haven: Yale University Press 1963); Howard Lasswell and Myres McDougal, *Legal Education and Public Policy: Professional Training in the Public Interest,* 52 YALE L.J. 203 (1943). *See, generally,* BRUCE ACKERMAN, RECONSTRUCTING AMERICAN LAW 41–42 (Cambridge, Mass.: Harvard University Press 1984).

54. The progressive strand of legal realism was thus disrupted by a new "prudential" rather than empirical or positivist understanding of the judicial process. *See* Gary Peller, *Neutral Principles in the 1950s,* 21 U. MICH. J.L. REF. 4 (1988).

55. *See* Henry M. Hart, Jr., and Albert M. Sacks, *The Legal Process: Basic Problems in the Making and Application of Law* (tent. ed. 1958) (Foundation Press 1994) (Eskridge W. & Frickey P. eds.). Hart and Sacks's law school teaching materials on the legal process were widely read and highly regarded even though they were never published during their life. Hart and Sacks regarded their materials as "unfinished research." *Id.* And yet these famous photocopied materials have come to define post–World War II process jurisprudence. *See* William N. Eskridge, Jr., *Metaprocedure,* 98 YALE L.J. 945, 962 (1989). The materials were published posthumously in 1994.

56. *See* ROBERT DAHL, A PREFACE TO DEMOCRATIC THEORY (Chicago: University of Chicago Press 1956).

57. *See* Hart and Sacks, *The Legal Process, supra* at 1–123.

58. *See* Peller, *Neutral Principles in the 1950s, supra* at 586–91.

59. *Id.* at 593.

60. *See* Hart and Sacks, *The Legal Process, supra* at 3.
61. *I.e.,* they believed that judges should avoid grounds of decision that would require them to involve themselves with the messy world of politics.
62. *See* Peller, *Neutral Principles in the 1950s, supra* at 594.
63. Henry M. Hart, Jr., *The Supreme Court 1958 Term—Forward: The Time Chart of the Justices,* 78 HARV. L. REV. 84, 99, 125 (1959). As Richard Posner noted, the "shift in terms" from "experience" to "reason" was "portentous" for the development of modern jurisprudence. *See* Richard Posner, *The Material Basis of Jurisprudence,* 69 IND. L.J. 1, 2, n. 1 (1993). *See also* Neil Duxbury, *Faith in Reason: The Process Tradition in American Jurisprudence,* 15 CARDOZO L. REV. 601 (1993).
64. The "Neutral Principles School" was a leading movement of the legal process tradition, popular during the 1960s. The neutral principles school purported to develop a theory of adjudication missing in Hart and Sacks's theory of legal process. In doing so, the neutral principles school shaped the jurisprudence of the 1960s. Richard Posner stated that the "1960s can be identified as the highwater mark of the American legal profession's cartel, and hence of jurisprudence conceived of as the ideology of the legal profession's guild or cartel, rather than merely as a stuffy, old-fashioned term for legal theory." Richard Posner, *The Material Basis of Jurisprudence,* 69 IND. L.J. 1, 23 (1993).
65. 347 U.S. 483 (1954).
66. 163 U.S. 537 (1896).
67. *See* ACKERMAN, WE THE PEOPLE: FOUNDATIONS, *supra* at 132–42.
68. The debate over the separate but equal doctrine of *Plessy* and the meaning of slavery has had a profound impact on the development of modern forms of American jurisprudence. *See* GILMORE, THE AGES OF AMERICAN LAW, *supra* at 36–39; Paul Finkelman, *The Centrality of the Peculiar Institution in American Legal Development,* 68 CHI.-KENT L. REV. 1009 (1993).
69. Wechsler, *Towards Neutral Principles of Constitutional Law,* 73 HARV. L. REV. 1 (1959).
70. *See, e.g.,* Smith v. Allwright, 321 U.S. 649 (1944).
71. *See, e.g.,* Shelley v. Kraemer, 334 U.S. 1 (1948); Barrows v. Jackson, 346 U.S. 249 (1953).
72. Wechsler, *Neutral Principles, supra* at 12.
73. *Id.* at 15.
74. *Id.* at 34.
75. ALEXANDER M. BICKEL, THE LEAST DANGEROUS BRANCH: THE SUPREME COURT AT THE BAR OF POLITICS (Indianapolis: Bobbs-Merrill Co. 1962).
76. *Id.* at 16–17.
77. *Id.* at 25.
78. *See, e.g.,* EUGENE ROSTOW, THE SOVEREIGN PREROGATIVE (New Haven: Yale University Press 1962).
79. This point is accepted by both conservative and progressive legal scholars

today. *See, e.g.*, Posner, *The Material Basis of Jurisprudence, supra* at 32–33; Peller, *The Neutral Principles in the 1950s, supra* at 611–13.

80. Jan G. Deutsch, *Neutrality, Legitimacy, and the Supreme Court: Some Intersections between Law and Political Science*, 20 STAN. L. REV. 169, 195 (1968).

81. Addison Mueller and Murray L. Schwartz, *The Principle of Neutral Principles*, 7 U.C.L.A. L. REV. 571, 586 (1960).

82. Louis Pollack, *Racial Discrimination and Judicial Integrity: A Reply to Professor Wechsler*, 108 U. PA. L. REV. (1959).

83. *Id.* at 28. *See also* Louis Henkin, *Some Reflections on Current Constitutional Controversy*, 109 U. PA. L. REV. 637, 653 (1961) ("I, like Professor Pollack, believe that the particular cases which bother Professor Wechsler, can be justified in 'neutral principles' although the Court perhaps did not do so effectively." *Id.*).

84. *See* Alexander Bickel, *The Supreme Court, 1960 Term—Forward: The Passive Virtues*, 75 HARV. L. REV. 40 (1961). *See also* BICKEL, THE LEAST DANGEROUS BRANCH, *supra*.

85. Bork's article became famous as the focus of the Senate Judiciary Committee's hearings that resulted in the rejection of his nomination to the Supreme Court. He is currently a research scholar at the American Enterprise Institute.

86. Robert H. Bork, *Neutral Principles and Some First Amendment Problems*, 47 IND. L.J. 1,7 (1971).

87. *Id.*

88. *Id.*

89. *Id.* at 14–15.

90. 381 U.S. 479 (1965).

91. *Id.* at 484.

92. Bork, *Neutral Principles and Some First Amendment Problems, supra* at 10.

93. *See* Mueller and Schwartz, *The Principle of Neutral Principles, supra* at 586.

94. Schlag, *Politics of Form, supra* at 1668.

95. *See* ROSTOW, THE SOVEREIGN PREROGATIVE, *supra* at 28.

96. For an explanation of the continuing hold of Langdellian formalism in modern conceptual jurisprudence, *see* Neil Duxbury, *Faith in Reason: The Process Tradition in American Jurisprudence, supra* at 704. Duxbury, however, concludes that "legal realism failed." He finds that its failure was largely due to the success of process theorists in developing and emphasizing the "rationalistic premises of process thinking." *Id.*

My view is that legal realism never really failed; its radical opposition to judicial tyranny was merely suppressed for a time by what Duxbury calls the "faith in reason." Legal realism has also been around in American jurisprudence since the time of Holmes, and its legacy can be discovered in the work of law and economics and critical legal scholars.

## Notes to Chapter 3

1. While it is true that legal process scholars wanted to avoid making subjective value choices in their analysis of legal principles, especially constitutional principles, they nonetheless believed that their conceptualization of reasoned elaboration and neutral principles would lead to a normatively correct judicial decisions. Legal process scholars thus attempted to be normative without discussing normativity. By the late 1960s, legal scholars sought to be more explicitly normative by discussing the normativity of judicial decisions, especially those involving constitutional principle. The form of this normativity was highly rationalistic in character and therefore could be understood as a normative version of conceptualist jurisprudence, or what Pierre Schlag has called "normative legal thought." *See* Pierre Schlag, *Normativity and the Politics of Form,* 139 U. PA. L. REV. 801 (1991); Pierre Schlag, *Normative and Nowhere to Go,* 43 STAN. L. REV. 167 (1990).
2. *See* Schlag, *Normative and Nowhere to Go, supra* at 179.
3. *See* Schlag, *Normativity and the Politics of Form, supra* at 804.
4. The significance of Bickel's lecture was not missed by the popular press. As Anthony Lewis of the NEW YORK TIMES reported, Bickel's lecture was "[o]ne of those intellectual events whose reverberations gradually disturb a widening circle. . . . It was an event in the law." NEW YORK TIMES, October 10, 1969, at 46, col. 5, quoted in J. Skelly Wright, *Professor Bickel, the Scholarly Tradition, and the Supreme Court,* 84 HAR. L. REV. 769 (1971).
5. The lecture was subsequently published as a book; *see* ALEXANDER M. BICKEL, THE SUPREME COURT AND THE IDEA OF PROGRESS (New York: Harper & Row 1970).
6. *Id.* at 175.
7. *Id.* Bickel explained: "The judicial process is principle-prone and principle-bound—it has to be, there is no other justification or explanation for the role it plays." *Id.* at 177.
8. *See* ALEXANDER M. BICKEL, THE MORALITY OF CONSENT 11–25 (New Haven: Yale University Press 1975) (discussing the views of Edmund Burke).
9. J. Skelly Wright, *Professor Bickel, the Scholarly Tradition, and the Supreme Court,* 84 HARV. L. REV 769 (1971) [hereinafter *Scholarly Tradition*].
10. *Id.* at 783.
11. *Id.* at n. 68, 789, *citing* ROBERT DAHL, WHO GOVERNS? (New Haven: Yale University Press 1961).
12. *Id.* at n. 68, 789, *citing* P. BACHRACH, THE THEORY OF DEMOCRATIC ELITISM 83–92 (Lanham, Md.: University Press of America 1967); R. WOLFF, THE POVERTY OF LIBERALISM 122–61 (Boston: Beacon Press 1968).
13. Wright, *Scholarly Tradition, supra* at 781.
14. *Id.* at 797.
15. *Id.* at 780, 799.

16. *Id.* at 803.
17. *Id.* at 804.
18. *Id.*
19. *Id.*
20. *Id.* at 805.
21. The Senate's rejection of President Reagan's nomination of Robert Bork to the Supreme Court was an official rejection of the jurisprudential philosophy of the Wechslerian generation. In protracted televised proceedings, the public saw senators embarrass Bork by pointing out the inconsistencies in his theory of neutral principles as applied to constitutional interpretation. *See, generally,* RONALD DWORKIN, LIFE'S DOMINION: AN ARGUMENT ABOUT ABORTION, EUTHANASIA, AND INDIVIDUAL FREEDOM 132–43 (New York: Alfred A. Knopf 1993).
22. *See* BRUCE ACKERMAN, WE THE PEOPLE: FOUNDATIONS 144 (Cambridge, Mass.: Belknap Press of Harvard University Press 1991.)
23. *Id.* at 149.
24. JOHN AUSTIN, THE PROVINCE OF JURISPRUDENCE DETERMINED (New York: Humanities Press 1965); LECTINE VI (New York: Humanities Press 1965) (1954 ed.).
25. *See* H. L. A. HART, THE CONCEPT OF LAW 16 (Oxford: Clarendon Press 1961).
26. Austin assumed that the rules of the legal system provide binding or "positive" answers to legal questions, whether or not they conform to moral principles. Austin and the English positivists made a distinction between what law is at a given moment and whether that law can survive moral criticism. Legal positivists following Austin believed that law was devised to govern public order and that sovereign authority was the source of all law. While legal positivists once believed that most legal questions had a right answer specified by sovereign authority, they now acknowledge that gaps and uncertainties in the law make the search for sovereign authority a difficult matter. Ultimately, the simplicity of Austin's model led to a more sophisticated concept of law. *See* RONALD DWORKIN, TAKING RIGHTS SERIOUSLY 16–22 (Cambridge, Mass.: Harvard University Press 1977).
27. *See, generally,* HART, THE CONCEPT OF LAW, *supra.*
28. *See* DWORKIN, TAKING RIGHTS SERIOUSLY, *supra* at 21.
29. *Id.*
30. H. L. A. Hart, *Positivism and the Separation of Law and Morals,* 71 HARV. L. REV. 593 (1958).
31. *Id.* at 607.
32. *Id.*
33. GRANT GILMORE, THE AGES OF AMERICAN LAW 22 (New Haven: Yale University Press 1977).
34. *See* DWORKIN, TAKING RIGHTS SERIOUSLY, *supra* at 3.
35. A good example of this is Fuller's response to Hart's "bicycle-in-the-park" hypothetical. Lon Fuller, *Positivism and Fidelity to Law—A Reply to Pro-*

*fessor Hart,* 71 HARV. L. REV. 630 (1958). Fuller gave an example of a truck erected as a war memorial by a group of patriotic citizens. Fuller argued that his example illustrated how even a simple rule, like Hart's rule prohibiting vehicles in the park, might lack a settled core of meaning. According to Fuller, a judge could not determine, simply by looking up the word "vehicle" in a dictionary, whether the truck falls within the rule's core meaning. For Fuller, decision making according to rules necessarily requires judges to consider the *purpose* of the rule they seek to enforce. *Id.* at 633. Judicial inquiry of purpose, however, necessarily entails much more than simply deciding according to rules. Fuller thus argued in favor of a functional or *purposive* approach to legal decision making. *Id.*

36. Law students continue to read Lon Fuller's *The Case of the Speluncean Explorers,* 62 HARV. L. REV. 616 (1949), as well as Fuller's debate with Hart over *Positivism and Fidelity to Law,* 71 HARV. L. REV. 630, 631, 635 (1958), as a classic jurisprudential account of judicial decision making.

37. The phrase is used by James Boyle to describe Fuller's jurisprudence of process in LON L. FULLER, THE MORALITY OF LAW (New Haven: Yale University Press 1965) (2d ed. 1969). *See* James Boyle, *Legal Realism and the Social Contract: Fuller's Public Jurisprudence of Form, Private Jurisprudence of Substance,* 78 CORNELL L. REV. 371, 377 (1993).

38. For the view that Hart's idea of "core meaning" could yield "rule-consistent-with-its-justification" results. *See* FREDERICK SCHAUER, PLAYING BY THE RULES—A PHILOSOPHICAL EXAMINATION OF RULE-BASED DECISION-MAKING IN LAW AND IN LIFE 212–15 (Oxford: Clarendon Press 1991).

39. *See, generally,* FULLER, THE MORALITY OF LAW, *supra.*

40. *See* Hart, *The Separation of Law and Morals, supra.* Hart demonstrated in this article how English postivists relied upon the distinction between legality and morality to effectively evaluate law against an external moral standard.

41. Lon Fuller also thought that American legal realism and forms of sociological jurisprudence were indistinguishable from legal positivism. In Fuller's mind, legal realists represented an American variant of English positivism since both attempted to anchor law's objectivity in some datum of nature. LON FULLER, THE LAW IN QUEST OF ITSELF 47 (Chicago: Foundation Press 1940). This led Georgetown Law Center professor Francis Lucey to claim that legal realism breeds totalitarian legal regimes. Francis Lucey, *Natural Law and American Legal Realism: Their Respective Contributions to a Theory of Law in a Democratic Society,* 30 GEO. L.J. 494 (1942) ("Realism is being tried today in Germany and Russia. . . . There is not a single tenet of Realism that these dictatorships do not cherish, adhere to, and try to apply." *Id.* at 513, n. 14). It is now recognized, however, that legal positivism and legal realism are contradictory approaches to law.

It is more correct to say that H. L. A. Hart's brand of legal positivism coheres with American legal formalism: "positivism but under another name," and that legal realism as practiced in the 1930s and 1940s was antagonistic to both formalism and positivism. *See* ANTHONY JAMES SEBOK, LEGAL POSITIVISM AND THE GROWTH OF TWENTIETH-CENTURY AMERICAN JURISPRUDENCE (1993) (unpublished dissertation, Princeton University). One point is clear and undisputable: legal realism had a profound impact on American jurisprudential studies.

42. *See* Mark Tushnet, *Truth, Justice and the American Way: An Interpretation of Public Law Scholarship in the Seventies*, 57 TEX. L. REV 1307, 1316 (1979).

43. *See* MARK TUSHNET, RED, WHITE AND BLUE: A CRITICAL ANALYSIS OF CONSTITUTIONAL LAW 139 (Cambridge, Mass.: Harvard University Press 1988).

44. The literature is reviewed in Paul Brest, *The Fundamental Rights Controversy: The Essential Contradictions of Normative Constitutional Scholarship*, 90 YALE L.J. 1063 (1981).

45. *See* Stephen M. Feldman, *Republican Revival/Interpretive Turn*, 1992 WIS. L. REV. 679, 701–14 (discussing how fundamental rights theory developed from two fundamentally different approaches to the problem of judicial review—*interpretivism* and *noninterpretivism*. *Id.* at 702).

46. *See, e.g.,* LAWRENCE TRIBE, AMERICAN CONSTITUTIONAL LAW (Westbury, N.Y.: Foundation Press 1978); Kenneth Karst, *The Freedom of Intimate Association*, 89 YALE L.J. 624 (1980); J. Harvey Wilkinson and G. Edward White, *Constitutional Protection for Personal Lifestyles*, 62 CORNELL L. REV. 563 (1977); David A. J. Richards, *Sexual Autonomy and the Constitutional Right to Privacy: A Case Study in Human Rights and the Unwritten Constitution*, 30 HASTINGS L.J. 957 (1979). *See, e.g.,* Michael Perry, *Abortion, the Public Morals, and the Police Power: The Ethical Function of Substantive Due Process*, 23 U.C.L.A. L. REV. 689 (1976); Harry Wellington, *Common Law Rules and Constitutional Double Standards: Some Notes on Adjudication*, 83 YALE L.J. 221 (1973).

47. Stephen M. Feldman, *Republican Revival/Interpretive Turn*, *supra* at 703.

48. RICHARD EPSTEIN, TAKINGS: PRIVATE PROPERTY AND THE POWER OF EMINENT DOMAIN (Cambridge, Mass.: Harvard University Press 1988).

49. *See* DWORKIN, TAKING RIGHTS SERIOUSLY, *supra* chap. 5. Ronald Dworkin has since become a leading spokesperson for the interpretivist strand of fundamental rights. *See* Ronald Dworkin, LAW'S EMPIRE, chaps. 10–11 (Cambridge, Mass.: Belknap Press of Harvard University Press 1986).

50. *See* ACKERMAN, WE THE PEOPLE: FOUNDATIONS, *supra* at 12.

51. *See* Schlag, *Normative and Nowhere to Go, supra* at 175.

52. *See* Schlag, *Normativity and the Politics of Form, supra* at 818–28 (discussing the nature of *moralist* jurisprudence).

53. *Id.* at 850.

54. *Id.*

55. *See* FULLER, THE MORALITY OF LAW, *supra*.

56. *See* JOHN RAWLS, A THEORY OF JUSTICE (Cambridge, Mass.: Belknap Press of Harvard University Press 1971).

57. *Id.* at 120.
58. *Id.*
59. This was the "interpretive turn" in constitutional law scholarship. For discussion of the "interpretive turn" in legal scholarship of the early 1980s; see *Symposium,* 60 TEX. L. REV. 373–586 (1982); David Kennedy, *The Turn to Interpretation,* 58 S. CAL. L. REV. 251 (1985).
60. Owen M. Fiss, *Objectivity and Interpretation,* 34 STAN. L. REV. 739, 744 (1982).
61. *Id.* Fiss is a law professor at Yale University and a leading constitutional law scholar.
62. As Professor Stephen Feldman of the University of Tulsa College of Law explained: "Fiss argues that the courts must give meaning to our public values—especially constitutional values—by engaging in 'a special dialogue.' Fiss insists, however, the dialogue is so closely restrained that judges are, in fact, objective; judges cannot memely express 'personal beliefs.' " Stephen M. Feldman, *Republican Revival/Interpretive Turn, supra* at 699–700.
63. *Id.*
64. *Id.* at 1–73. *See also* Feldman, *Republican Revival/Interpretive Turn, supra* at 703.
65. *See* DWORKIN, LAW'S EMPIRE, *supra.*
66. *See* Fiss, *Objectivity in Interpretation, supra* at 739.
67. *See* RONALD DWORKIN, *How Law Is Like Literature, in* A MATTER OF PRINCIPLE 146 (Cambridge, Mass.: Harvard University Press 1982).
68. The field is now divided, however. While some scholars believe that interpretation can be grounded in objectivity and shared values, others working in the law-as-interpretation school argue that legal interpreters are "for all intents and purposes, free" to construct their own interpretations of legal texts and discover their own values. *See, e.g.,* Stanley Fish, *Working on the Chain Gang: Interpretation in Law and Literature,* 60 TEX. L. REV. 551 (1982). *See also* STANLEY FISH, IS THERE A TEXT IN THIS CLASS? (Cambridge, Mass.: Harvard University Press 1980).
69. *See* DWORKIN, TAKING RIGHTS SERIOUSLY, *supra* at 160–61.
70. *See* ELY, DEMOCRACY AND DISTRUST, *supra* at 1–73. *See also* Feldman, *Republican Revival/Interpretive Turn, supra* at 703.
71. *Id.* at 73–183. *See* MARK TUSHNET, RED, WHITE AND BLUE: A CRITICAL ANALYSIS OF CONSTITUTIONAL LAW, *supra* at 94–95.
72. *See* DWORKIN, A MATTER OF PRINCIPLE, *supra* at 59.
73. *See* ELY, DEMOCRACY AND DISTRUST, *supra* at 73–183. *See also* JESSE H. CHOPER, JUDICIAL REVIEW AND THE NATIONAL POLITICAL PROCESS (Chicago: University of Chicago Press 1983). *But see* Michael J. Perry, *Interpretivism, Freedom of Expression, and Equal Protection,* 42 OHIO ST. L.J. 261, 264 (1981).
74. *See* Schlag, *Normativity and the Politics of Form, supra* at 850–51.
75. *See* DWORKIN, TAKING RIGHTS SERIOUSLY, *supra* at 81, 149.

76. *See* DWORKIN, LAW'S EMPIRE, *supra* at 245–49.
77. *See* DWORKIN, TAKING RIGHTS SERIOUSLY, *supra* at chap. 5; *see also* DWORKIN, LAW'S EMPIRE, *supra* at chaps. 10–11.
78. *See* ACKERMAN, WE THE PEOPLE: FOUNDATIONS, *supra* at 11.
79. *See* Gerald Gunther, *Foreword: In Search of Evolving Doctrine on a Changing Court: A Model for a Newer Equal Protection*, 86 HARV. L. REV. 1, 12–18 (1972).
80. *Id.*
81. *Id.* at 16–32. *See also* Gerald Gunther, *The Subtle Vices of the "Passive Virtues"—A Comment on Principle and Expediency in Judicial Review*, 64 COLUM. L. REV. 1 (1964).
82. *See, generally,* DWORKIN, TAKING RIGHTS SERIOUSLY, *supra.*
83. *See, generally,* ACKERMAN, WE THE PEOPLE: FOUNDATIONS, *supra.*
84. *See* DWORKIN, TAKING RIGHTS SERIOUSLY, *supra.*
85. *See* ACKERMAN, WE THE PEOPLE: FOUNDATIONS, *supra* at 5.
86. *See* Schlag, *Normativity and the Politics of Form, supra* at 850.
87. *Id.*
88. *See* KENT GREENAWALT, LAW AND OBJECTIVITY 197 (New York: Oxford University Press 1992).
89. *Id.* at 6–7. Kent Greenawalt provides a good summary of how the postwar generation of traditional legal academics understood law and adjudication:

> For many circumstances the application of relevant legal standards is clear; for others the law is uncertain. The percentage of doubtful cases depends on the general area of law—the law of wills is more certain than constitutional law—and also on the subdivision within the general area. There is often rough agreement on the force of legal arguments. Some arguments have substantial force; others seem to have little or no genuine force but serve to obscure the true bases of decision. Law generally, and desirably, treats people in an objective or impersonal manner, but with some frequency particular, or subjective, characteristics count. Certain broader sources often underlie the law and are a basis for decision in hard cases, but neither law nor legal interpretation can be reduced to a subcategory of a single outside source or to a combination of them.

*Id.* at 6.
90. *Id.* at 208.
91. *Id.*
92. For example, it is not uncommon to hear traditional legal scholars reject the legal realist project as "a naive attempt to do empirical social science" and yet at the same time hear them proclaim that "we are all realists now." *See* Schlegel, *American Legal Realism and Empirical Social Science: From the Yale Experience*, 28 BUFF. L. REV. 459–60 (1979).
93. *See* GREENAWALT, LAW AND OBJECTIVITY, *supra* at 212. That is "when more immediate criteria, like the language of an authoritative statute, leave matters in doubt, one choice will cohere better with all the legal materials than any other." *Id.*

94. *See, e.g.*, Cass Sunstein, *Beyond the Republican Revival*, 97 YALE L.J. 539, 1566–71 (1988) (arguing for a new liberal republican philosophy of law).
95. *See* GREENAWALT, LAW AND OBJECTIVITY, *supra* at 213.
96. *Id.* at 234. This has allowed legal theorists to "generally assume . . . that judicial decisions that are required by law, and thus the things that are done to people in the name of law, normally enjoy some measure of moral justification." David Lyons, *Critical Analysis and Constructive Interpretation* in MORAL ASPECTS OF LEGAL THEORY 217 (Cambridge: Cambridge University Press 1993).
97. *Id.*
98. *Id.*
99. *Id.* at 213.
100. Frederick Schauer, *Formalism*, 97 YALE L.J. 509, 510 (1988).
101. *See* Schlag, *Normativity and the Politics of Form, supra* at 847.
102. This seems to be the position of David Luban in rejecting the implications of postmodernist criticism associated with the critical legal studies movement. *See* David Luban, *Legal Modernism*, 84 MICH. L. REV. 1656, 1682 (1986).
103. For example, one usually does not think of Richard A. Posner as a postmodernist legal thinker. And he would much dislike being associated with postmodernism. Yet, undeniably, his recent work in jurisprudence has an unwittingly postmodern character to it: his articles and books on jurisprudence are a pastiche of grand philosophical luminaries cited in the most traditional legal-authority form, combined with a nostalgic, almost romantic, yearning for common-sense neopragmatic philosophy, advertised by an appeal to a long-lost "Holmesian tradition," and an almost religious worship of human intuition. The postmodern moments in Posner's recent jurisprudential writing can be found by his recent effort to expose and "overcome" the silences, the aporias, the schisms of modern legal thought. *See* RICHARD POSNER, OVERCOMING LAW (Cambridge, Mass.: Harvard University Press forthcoming 1995).

## Notes to Chapter 4

1. Robert W. Gordon, a law professor at Stanford University and a member of the critical legal studies movement, provides an especially vivid description of what legal studies were like at the major law schools in the 1960s:

   Basically, the teachers taught us to do two things: doctrinal analysis and policy analysis. Doctrinal analysis was (as I now recognize) a kind of toned-down legal realism: we learned how to take apart the *formal* arguments from the outcome of a case and to find the underlying layer of justifications that *really* explain the case, a layer of 'principles' and 'purposes' behind the rules. Policy analysis was a kind of quickie utilitarian method for use in close cases—it was supposed to enable us to argue for outcomes that could efficiently serve social policies somehow inhering in the legal system. The polices were derived either by appeal to an assumed general consensus of values (personal security, economic growth), or to an assumed (and assumed to be good) trend of historical development (such as from protecting producers to protecting consumers). Sometimes there would be competing policies, representing conflicting 'interests'; here the function of policy analysis was to provide an on-the-spot rapid-fire 'balancing' of interests.

A really "smart" lawyer who was adept at all these techniques would be able to discover—by the use of legal reasoning alone—socially optimal solutions for virtually all legal problems. The image of the ideal lawyer was that of the technocrat with mildly reformist-liberal sympathies—half hotshot, half benevolent country squire. Smart corporate lawyer-technicians on one side would be counterbalanced by smart government lawyer-technicians on the other. Moreover, the corporate types, trained to see deeper purposes, policies, and historical trends underlying the rules, would advise their corporate clients to play by the deep-level rules in their own long-term interests, and would engage in law-reform efforts in their spare time to keep the rules consistent with principles and up-to-date with changing conditions.

R. W. Gordon, *New Developments in Legal Theory, in* THE POLITICS OF LAW: A PROGRESSIVE CRITIQUE 414–15 (D. Kairys, ed.) (New York: Pantheon Books 1982).

2. Grant Gilmore argued that the Age of Anxiety commenced with Benjamin Cardozo's Storrs Lectures at Yale Law School in 1920, subsequently published as THE NATURE OF THE JUDICIAL PROCESS (New Haven: Yale University Press 1921). *See* Grant Gilmore, *The Storrs Lectures: The Age of Anxiety,* 84 YALE L.J. 1022 (1975). In this lecture, Cardozo argued that legal decison making was a creative process in which judges made law by adopting the methods of philosophy, history, tradition, and sociology. Gilmore believed that Cardozo's lecture set the stage for the legal realist movement and the Age of Anxiety. After World War II, however, postwar legal scholars developed new consensus theories based on legal process theory and fundamental rights theory. *See* chapter 2, *supra.* In this chapter, I will discuss the forces that were responsible for finally bringing about the Age of Anxiety that had been dormant since the 1930s.

3. *See, e.g.,* Roy Boyne and Ali Rattansi, *The Theory and Politics of Postmodernism: By Way of an Introduction, in* POSTMODERNISM AND SOCIETY 12 (R. Boynes and A. Rattansi, eds.) (New York: St. Martin's Press 1990).

4. A *performative enterprise* has operative significance in bringing about specific kinds of actions. *See* JEAN-FRANÇQIS LYOTARD, THE POSTMODERN CONDITION 46 (Minneapolis: University of Minnesota Press 1984). Pierre Schlag, *Normative and Nowhere to Go,* 43 STAN. L. REV. 167, 183–84, n. 47 (1990).

5. The intellectual enterprise thus becomes identified as a language game in which the participants search for new opportunities to increase the performative significance of their work. *See* STEVEN CANNON, POSTMODERN CULTURE: AN INTRODUCTION TO THEORIES OF THE CONTEMPORARY 32 (New York: Blackwell 1989).

6. *See* Schlag, *Normative and Nowhere to Go, supra* at 183–84.

7. *See* Gordon, *New Developments in Legal Theory, supra* at 283.

8. Gary Peller, *Neutral Principles in the 1950s,* 21 U. MICH. J.L. REF. 561, 613 (1988). Peller is a law professor at Georgetown Law Center and a member of the critical legal studies movement.

9. *Id.* at 5.

10. BRUCE A. ACKERMAN, RECONSTRUCTING AMERICAN LAW 39–40 (Cambridge, Mass.: Harvard University Press 1984).

11. *See* Peller, *Neutral Principles in the 1950s, supra* at 594.

12. *Id.*

13. Bruce Ackerman, a professor of law at Yale University and a leading liberal constitutional law theorist, is largely responsible for popularizing this view. *See* BRUCE ACKERMAN, WE THE PEOPLE: FOUNDATIONS 149 (Cambridge, Mass.: Belknap Press of Harvard University Press 1991).

14. *Id.*

15. *See* Gordon, *New Developments in Legal Theory, supra* at 283.

16. *See* Peller, *Neutral Principles in the 1950s, supra* at 562.

17. Gordon, *New Developments in Legal Theory, supra* at 283.

18. Peller, *Neutral Principles in the 1950s, supra.*

19. ACKERMAN, WE THE PEOPLE: FOUNDATIONS, *supra* at 11.

20. RICHARD A. POSNER, THE PROBLEMS OF JURISPRUDENCE 23 (Cambridge, Mass.: Harvard University Press 1990).

21. Peter Gabel, *Rectification in Legal Reasoning,* 3 RES. IN L. & SOC. 25, 28 (1979); James Boyle, *Introduction, in* CRITICAL LEGAL STUDIES XVII (J. Boyle, ed.) (New York: New York University Press 1992).

22. *See, e.g.,* Mark Tushnet, *Darkness on the Edge of Town: The Contributions of John Hart Ely to Constitutional Theory,* 89 YALE L.J. 1037, 1045 (1980).

23. Stephen M. Feldman, *Republican Revival/Interpretive Turn,* WIS. L. REV. 679, 704 (1992).

24. DAVID HALBERSTAM, THE FIFTIES, 497 (New York: Random House 1993).

25. The angst of Generation-X was captured in an amusing novel. *See* DOUGLAS COUPLAND, GENERATION X: TALES FOR AN ACCELERATED CULTURE (New York: St. Martin's Press 1991).

26. Charles Reich, *The New Property,* 73 YALE L.J. 733 (1964).

27. Ronald Coase, *The Problem of Social Cost,* 3 J. L. & ECON. 1 (1960).

28. Pierre Schlag was the first to identify these as "transitional articles." Schlag explained: "[T]hey are transitional in the sense that they exemplify a renewed interest of American legal thought in rights and rights-discourse; they are transitional in the sense that they mark a change in the mode in which American legal thinkers have thought about law and rights; and they are transitional in the sense that they exhibit both the continuation of the realist project as well as the routes of its denial." Pierre Schlag, *Rights in the Postmodern Condition,* 21–22 (unpublished manuscript, 1992).

29. Ronald Coase's article challenged the conventional wisdom of basic microeconomic theory in its failure to appreciate the centrality of transaction costs in the operation of markets. *See* Ronald H. Coase, *Coase on Posner on Coase,* 149 J. OF INST'L & THEORETICAL ECONOMICS 96 (1993). *See*

*also* Richard Posner, *Ronald Coase and Methodology, in* OVERCOMING LAW (1994 forthcoming).

30. Charles Reich, *The New Property,* 73 YALE L.J. 733 (1964).
31. *Id.* at 733.
32. *Id.*
33. *Id.*
34. Charles Reich, *Beyond the New Property: An Ecological View of Due Process,* 56 BROOK. L. REV. 731, 735 (1990).
35. Felix Cohen, *Dialogue on Private Property,* 9 RUTGERS L. REV. 357, 375 (1954).
36. *See* Reich, *The New Property, supra* at 771.
37. *Id.*
38. *Id.*
39. *Id.* at 785.
40. Goldberg v. Kelly, 397 U.S. 254 (1970).
41. The New Property of *Goldberg v. Kelly,* however, was shortlived. In Jefferson v. Hackney, 406 U.S. 535 (1972), and Dandridge v. Williams, 397 U.S. 471 (1970), the Court held that state governments could control the level of welfare benefits generally. In Matthews v. Eldridge, 424 U.S. 319 (1976), the Court restricted the due process requirement of *Goldberg* to AFDC entitlements. *See, generally,* J. HANDLER, THE CONDITIONS OF DISCRETION: AUTONOMY, COMMUNITY, BUREAUCRACY CHAP. 2 (New York: Russell Sage Foundation 1986).
42. Coase, *The Problem of Social Cost, supra.*
43. An externality is a cost or benefit visited by one party upon another without compensation. *See* Scitovsky, *Two Concepts of External Economies,* 62 J. POL. ECON. 143 (1954).
44. For a description of the structure of the Coasian arguments, *see* Pierre Schlag, *The Problem of Transaction Costs,* 62 S. CAL. L. REV. 1661 (1989).
45. Coase did recognize the possibility that Pigouvian analysis of externalities might be rehabilitated by a system of taxes that imposed all effects of the externality on the factors of production. Yet Coase rejected this possibility on the basis that too much information would be needed to determine the preferences, interrelations among the damages caused, and the calculation of the resulting loss. *Id.*
46. Coase articulated his argument at a seminar at the University of Chicago at the time his article was published. *See* Robert Cooter, *The Cost of Coase,* 11 J. LEG. STUD. 1, 14, n. 10 (1982). George Stigler later labeled the argument as a "theorem." *See* RONALD COASE, THE FIRM, THE MARKET AND THE LAW 14, 157 (Chicago: University of Chicago Press 1990).
47. The other work was Guido Calabresi's *Some Thoughts on Risk Distribution and the Law of Torts,* 70 YALE L.J. 499 (1961).
48. *See* Coase, *The Problem of Social Cost, supra* at 19.
49. *See* RONALD COASE, THE FIRM, THE MARKET AND THE LAW, *supra* at 820–21.

50. In a world of zero transaction costs, legal rights would not affect efficient transactions unless enforcement leads to positive transaction costs, and then the costs of legal enforcement may still block efficient transactions. In a world of positive transaction costs, however, the assignment of legal rights will affect efficient outcomes. In such a world, legal rights should be defined to make the market work and, failing that, they should attempt to bring about outcomes likely to occur in the market (*i.e.,* rights should mimic the market).
51. *See* Reich, *The New Property, supra* at 733.
52. *See* Coase, *The Problems of Social Costs, supra* at 32–41.
53. *See* Schlag, *The Problem of Transaction Costs, supra* at 1667.
54. *See* Coase, *The Problem of Social Cost, supra* at 2.
55. The insight for this was not fully appreciated until 1991. If the legal subject is defined by the values and rhetoric of law, then the subject cannot be relatively autonomous. *See* Pierre Schlag, *Normativity and the Politics of Form,* 139 U. PA. L. REV. 801 (1991); Pierre Schlag, *The Problem of the Subject,* 69 TEX. L. REV. 1627 (1991).
56. *See* ACKERMAN, WE THE PEOPLE: FOUNDATIONS, *supra* at 144.
57. *Id.* at 147.
58. Brown v. Board of Education, 347 U.S. 483, 493 (1954).
59. Plessy v. Ferguson, 163 U.S. 537 (1896).
60. BRUCE ACKERMAN, WE THE PEOPLE: FOUNDATIONS, *supra* at 150.
61. *Id.* at 147.
62. *See* KENT GREENAWALT, LAW AND OBJECTIVITY, 214 (New York: Oxford University Press 1992).
63. *See* Richard A. Posner, *The Decline of Law as Autonomous Discipline: 1962–1987,* 100 HARV. L. REV. 761, 766 (1987).
64. Abram Chayes, *The Role of the Judge in Public Law Litigation,* 89 HARV. L. REV. 1281 (1976).
65. Duncan Kennedy, *Form and Substance in Private Law Adjudication,* 89 HARV. L. REV. (1976).
66. RICHARD A. POSNER, ECONOMIC ANALYSIS OF LAW (Boston: Little, Brown & Co. 1977).
67. ROBERT M. COVER, JUSTICE ACCUSED (New Haven: Yale University Press 1950).
68. *See, e.g.,* J. Allen Smith, *The Coming Renaissance in Law and Literature,* 30 J. LEGAL EDUC. 13 (1979).
69. Arthur Allen Leff, *Economic Analysis of Law: Some Realism about Nominalism,* 60 VA. L. REV. 451, 454 (1974).
70. *Id.* at 454.
71. *See* David M. Trubek and John Esser, *"Critical Empiricism" in American Legal Studies: Paradox, Program, or Pandora's Box?,* 14 J. L. & SOC. INQUIRY 3 (1989).
72. *See* Pierre Schlag, *"Le Hors De Texte, C'est Moi": The Politics of Form and the Domestication of Deconstruction,* 11 CARDOZO L. REV. 1631, 1653–

57 (1990) (making a similar point about Richard Posner's law and economics jurisprudence).

73. *Id.* at 1655.
74. *Id.* at 1656.
75. *See* ACKERMAN, WE THE PEOPLE: FOUNDATIONS, *supra* at 12.
76. *Id.*
77. Stephen M. Feldman, *Republican Revival/Interpretive Turn, supra* at 705.
78. *See* Rosemary J. Coombe, *"Same As It Ever Was": Rethinking the Politics of Legal Interpretation,* 34 McGILL L.J. 603 (1989).
79. THOMAS KUHN, THE STRUCTURE OF SCIENTIFIC REVOLUTIONS (Chicago: University of Chicago Press 1970).
80. PAUL FEYERABEND, AGAINST METHOD: OUTLINE OF AN ANARCHISTIC THEORY OF KNOWLEDGE (London: Verso 1978).
81. *See* Coombe, *"Same As It Ever Was," supra* at 606.
82. *See, generally,* STANLEY FISH, IS THERE A TEXT IN THIS CLASS? THE AUTHORITY OF INTERPRETIVE COMMUNITIES (Cambridge, Mass.: Harvard University Press 1980).
83. *Id.*
84. *See* HANS-GEORG GADAMER, TRUTH AND METHOD (Joel Weinsheimer and Donald Marshall, trans.) (New York: Continuum Publishing, 2d rev. ed. 1989).
85. JACQUES DERRIDA, OF GRAMMATOLOGY (Gayatri Spivak, trans.) (Baltimore: Johns Hopkins University Press 1977).
86. *See* Feldman, *Republican Revival/Interpretive Turn, supra* at 706.

## Notes to Chapter 5

1. *See* RICHARD POSNER, THE ECONOMIC ANALYSIS OF LAW 21 (Boston: Little, Brown & Co., 4th ed. 1992).
2. *See* Ronald Coase, *The Problem of Social Cost,* 3 J. L. & ECON. 1 (1960).
3. *See* Guido Calabresi, *Some Thoughts on Risk Distribution and the Law of Torts,* 70 YALE L.J. 499 (1961).
4. GUIDO CALABRESI, THE COST OF ACCIDENTS: A LEGAL AND ECONOMIC ANALYSIS (New Haven: Yale University Press 1970).
5. RICHARD POSNER, ECONOMIC ANALYSIS OF LAW (Boston: Little, Brown & Co., 1st ed. 1973).
6. Neil Duxbury argues that responsibility for this "ambivalence" lies at the feet of critical legal scholars, like myself, who have argued that law and economics and critical legal studies movements share a common historical legacy with the legal realist movement. *See* Neil Duxbury, PATTERNS OF AMERICAN JURISPRUDENCE 434 (Oxford University Press forthcoming 1995). *See also* Gary Minda, *"The Law and Economics and Critical Legal Studies Movements in American Law"* in Nicholas Mercuro ed., LAW AND ECONOMICS (Dordrecht: Kluwer 1989). Duxbury claims that arguments emphasizing intimacy between law and economics and critical legal studies

have brought about ambivalence about the true jurisprudential pedigree of the law and economics movement.

My view is that the jurisprudential connection between law and economics and critical legal studies was justified by first-generation law and economics scholars who, like critical legal studies scholars, challenged the jurisprudential claims of traditional legal scholars for lacking a "realistic" understanding of the world. *See, e.g.,* Frank H. Easterbrook, *Method, Result, and Authority: A Reply,* 98 HARV. L. REV. 622 (1985). Some of these early law and economics scholars also claimed legal realism as the jurisprudential source of their movement. *See, e.g.,* Edmund W. Kitch, *The Intellectual Foundations of* LAW AND ECONOMICS 533 J. OF LEGAL ED. 184 (1983). Ambiguity in the jurisprudence of law and economics has been brought about by shifts in the jurisprudential direction of second-generation scholarship. The first generation was wedded to legal realism; the second generation has embraced an eclectic jurisprudence defined in part by postmodern trends in the academy.

7. RICHARD POSNER, ECONOMIC ANALYSIS OF LAW 189 (Boston: Little, Brown & Co., 2d ed. 1977). Posner's subsequent writing, however, especially his work in jurisprudence, indicate that he has rejected Langdellian formalism. Posner now associates himself with a brand of pragmatic philosophy that views economics instrumentally as a mere tool for predicting human behavior. Posner thus attempts to define a "middle ground" between formalism and realism in modern jurisprudence. *See* Neil Duxbury, *Pragmatism without Politics,* 55 MOD. L. REV. 594 (1992). The pragmatic approach has enabled Posner to duck the criticism of those, like myself, who have dubbed law-and-economics as the "new Langdell." *See* Gary Minda, *The Lawyer-Economist at Chicago: Richard A. Posner and the Economic Analysis of Law,* 39 OHIO ST. L.J. 439 (1978).

8. Jack M. Balkin, *The Domestication of Law and Literature,* 14 LAW & SOC. Inquiry 787, 798 (1989).

9. MARK KELMAN, A GUIDE TO CRITICAL LEGAL STUDIES 114 (Cambridge, Mass.: Harvard University Press 1987).

10. Richard A. Posner, *The Present Situation in Legal Scholarship,* 90 YALE L.J. 1113, 1120 (1981).

11. *Id.*

12. *See* RICHARD A. POSNER, THE PROBLEMS OF JURISPRUDENCE 239–44, 441–42 (Cambridge, Mass.: Harvard University Press 1990).

13. *Id.* at 441.

14. *Id.* at 440. Posner does not say that Holmes was a full-blown Nietzschian. He seems to say that Holmes was like Nietzsche in embracing the idea that questions of morality are relative, and that knowledge is a product of social circumstances. *Id.* at 239–40.

15. Richard Posner, *What Has Pragmatism to Offer Law?* 63 S. CAL. L. REV. 1653, 1661 (1990).

16. *Id.* at 1660–61. Posner now follows the neopragmatism of Richard Rorty.

See RICHARD A. POSNER, OVERCOMING LAW (forthcoming 1995). *See also* Richard Rorty, *The Banality of Pragmatism and the Poetry of Justice,* 63 S. CAL. L. REV. 1811, 1813 (1990).

17. *See* POSNER, THE PROBLEMS OF JURISPRUDENCE, *supra* at 441.

18. *Id.* at 442.

19. This point is more fully explored in chapter 12, *infra* at 234–36. Neopragmatism is associated with postmodern philosopher Richard Rorty, who denies the possibility of universal laws or foundational constraints to "govern" modern analysis and interpretation. *See* RICHARD RORTY, PHILOSOPHY AND THE MIRROR OF NATURE (Princeton, N.J.: Princeton University Press 1979). *See also* chap. 12 *infra.*

20. *See* Richard Posner, *Pragmatism, Economics, Liberalism, in* OVERCOMING LAW (forthcoming 1994).

21. *See* Posner, *The New Institutional Economics Meets Law and Economics, in* OVERCOMING LAW, *supra.*

22. *Id.* at 453.

23. *See, e.g.,* Gary S. Becker, *Nobel Lecture: The Economic Way of Looking at Behavior,* 101 J. OF POL. ECONOMY 385 (1993).

24. Robert C. Ellickson, *Bringing Culture and Human Frailty to Rational Actors: A Critique of Classical Law and Economics,* 65 CHI.-KENT L. REV. 23, 23 (1989).

25. *See* GARY BECKER, THE ECONOMIC APPROACH TO HUMAN BEHAVIOR (Chicago: University Chicago Press 1976).

26. *See* POSNER, ECONOMIC ANALYSIS OF LAW, *supra* at 3.

27. *Id.* at 4.

28. *Id.*

29. *See id.* at 4–12.

30. *Id.*

31. *Id.* at 5.

32. POSNER, ECONOMIC ANALYSIS OF LAW (2d ed.), *supra* at 7.

33. *Id.* at 9.

34. *Id.* at 10.

35. *Id.* (emphasis in original).

36. *Id.* at 37–39.

37. *Id.* at 37.

38. *See* Coase, *The Problem of Social Cost, supra.*

39. *See* Richard Posner, *Ronald Coase and Methodology, in* OVERCOMING LAW (forthcoming 1995).

40. *See* Duncan Kennedy, *Cost-Benefit Analysis of Entitlement Problems: A Critique,* 33 STAN. L. REV. 387 (1981).

41. *See, generally,* Minda, *The Lawyer-Economist At Chicago: Richard A. Posner and the Economic Analysis of Law, supra* at 461–66.

42. *See* A. PIGOU, THE ECONOMICS OF WELFARE (New York: AMS Press, 4th ed. 1932).

43. This point is more fully developed in chap. 4, *supra.*

44. *See* Pierre Schlag, *The Problem of Transaction Costs,* 62 S. CAL. L. REV. 1661, 1667 (1989).
45. *See, e.g.,* Arthur Leff, *Economic Analysis of Law: Some Realism about Nominalism,* 60 VA. L. REV. 451 (1974); GRANT GILMORE, THE AGES OF AMERICAN LAW 107–8 (New Haven: Yale University Press 1977).
46. *See, e.g.,* Edwin Baker, *The Ideology of the Economic Analysis of Law,* 5 PHIL. & PUB. AFF. 3 (1975); Arthur A. Leff, *Economic Analysis of Law: Some Realism about Normalism,* 60 VA. L. REV. 451 (1974).
47. *See* A. Mitchell Polinsky, *Economic Analysis as a Potentially Defective Product: A Buyer's Guide to Posner's Economic Analysis of Law,* 87 HARV. L. REV. 655 (1974).
48. POSNER, ECONOMIC ANALYSIS OF LAW (2d ed., 1977), *supra* at 13. Paul Samuelson characterized a similar defense made by Milton Friedman as the "F-twist—the idea that [a] theory is vindicable if (some of) its consequences are empirically valid to a useful degree of approximation." Paul Samuelson, *Discussion,* 75 AM. ECON. ASS'N 227, 231 (Papers and Proceedings) 211 (1952). According to Samuelson, it is "fundamentally wrong to" assume that "factual inaccuracy even to a tolerable degree of approximation is anything but a demerit for a theory of hypothesis." *Id.* at 233. *See also* Minda, *The Lawyer-Economist at Chicago, supra* at 469.
49. *See* Richard Posner, *Utilitarianism, Economics, and Legal Theory,* 8 J. LEGAL STUD. 103 (1979).
50. *Id.* at 136, *quoting* Devine, *Adam Smith and the Problem of Justice in Capitalist Society,* 6 J. LEGAL STUD. 399 (1977).
51. *See* Posner, *Utilitarianism, Economics, and Legal Theory, supra* at 119.
52. *See* Ulen, *Law and Economics: Settled Issues and Open Questions, in* LAW AND ECONOMICS 210 (N. Mercuro, ed.) (Boston: Kluwer Academic 1989).
53. *See* Susan Rose-Ackerman, *Progressive Law and Economics—And the New Administrative Law,* 98 YALE L.J. 341 (1988).
54. *See* Owen Fiss, *The Death of the Law?,* 72 CORNELL L. REV. 1, 7 (1986).
55. *See* Roberta Romano, *Metapolitics and Corporate Law Reform,* 36 STAN. L. REV. 923 (1984).
56. *See* C. Goetz and R. Scott, *Principles of Relational Contracts,* 67 VA. L. REV. 1089 (1981). Scott's recent embrace of "Chaos theory" places him firmly into the second generation. *See* Robert E. Scott, *Chaos Theory and the Justice Paradox,* 35 WM. & MARY L. REV. 329 (1993) (chaos theory concerns the phenomenon of "orderly disorder created by simple processes." *Id.* at 331).
57. *See* Rowley, *The Common Law in Public Choice Perspective,* 12 HAMLINE L. REV. 355–83 (1989) [hereinafter *Public Choice*].
58. *See* KENNETH ARROW, SOCIAL CHOICE AND INDIVIDUAL VALUES (New Haven: Yale University Press, 2d ed. 1970).
59. *See* W. ESKRIDGE AND P. FRICKEY, CASES AND MATERIALS: CONSTITUTIONAL LAW THEMES FOR THE CONSTITUTION'S THIRD CENTURY 28–36 (St. Paul, Minn.: West Publishing Company 1993).

60. *See* Frank Easterbrook, *Ways of Criticizing the Court,* 95 HARV. L. REV. 802 (1982).

61. *See, e.g.,* ROBERT DAHL, A PREFACE TO DEMOCRATIC THEORY (Chicago: University of Chicago Press 1956); Jane J. Mansbridge, *The Rise and Fall of Self-Interest in the Explanation of Political Life, in* BEYOND SELF-INTEREST 8–9 (Jane J. Mansbridge, ed.) (Chicago: University of Chicago Press 1990); Gary Minda, *Interest Groups, Political Freedom, and Antitrust,* 41 HASTINGS L.J. 905, 937–42 (1990). The intellectual history of American pluralism is discussed in Purcell, *The Crisis in Democratic Theory, supra* at 235–66.

62. *See* chap. 2, *infra.*

63. *See* Peller, NEUTRAL PRINCIPLES IN THE 1950S, *supra* at 571.

64. MANCUR OLSON, THE LOGIC OF COLLECTIVE ACTION (Cambridge, Mass.: Harvard University Press 1965).

65. *See* Rowley, *Public Choice, supra.* OLSEN, THE LOGIC OF COLLECTIVE ACTION, *supra.*

66. *See, e.g.,* SOCIO-ECONOMICS: TOWARD A NEW SYNTHESIS (A. Etzioni and P. R. Lawrence, eds.) (Armonk, N.Y.: M. E. Sharpe 1991) (advancing the idea of a socioeconomic school of thought).

67. *See, e.g.,* MANSBRIDGE, ED., BEYOND SELF-INTEREST, *supra;* Marleen A. O'Connor, *The Human Capital Era: Reconceptualizing Corporate Law to Facilitate Labor-Management Cooperation,* 78 CORNELL L. REV. 899 (1993).

68. *See* DENNIS MUELLER, THE PUBLIC CHOICE APPROACH TO POLITICS (Brookfield, Vt.: Ashfield Publishing 1993).

69. Lewis A. Kornhauser, *The Great Image of Authority,* 36 STAN. L. REV. 349, 353 (1984).

70. *See, e.g.,* Susan Rose-Ackerman, *Progressive Law and Economics—and the New Administrative Law,* 98 YALE L.J. 341 (1988). There is some disagreement about what to call this new school of law and economics. Susan Rose-Ackerman does not like the label "New Haven School" because she believes that this school is "not pervasive enough at Yale Law School to warrant using [her] hometown as a label." *Id.* at 253, n. 1. (Rose-Ackerman is a professor of law at Yale Law School.) However, at least one member of Yale Law School, Owen Fiss, has used the New Haven label to describe this school of law and economics. *See also* Owen Fiss, *The Death of the Law?,* 72 CORNELL L. REV. 1, 7 (1986). Moreover, a leading advocate of this school is Guido Calabresi, former dean of the Yale Law School, and currently a federal count of appeals judge. *See, e.g.,* Guido Calabresi and Douglas Melamed, *Property Rules, Liability Rules, and Inalienability: One View of the Cathedral,* 85 HARV. L. REV. 1089 (1972).

71. *Id.* at 354–55.

72. *Id.* at 355.

73. Ulen, *Law and Economics: Settled Issues and Open Questions, supra* at 210.

74. R. COOTER AND T. ULEN, LAW AND ECONOMICS 11 (New York: HarperCollins College 1987).

75. See Posner, What Has Pragmatism to Offer Law?, supra at 1668.

76. Id.

77. See, e.g., Robin Paul Malloy, Toward a New Discourse of Law and Economics, 42 SYRACUSE L.REV. 27 (1991); Kenneth G. Dau-Schmidt, Relaxing Traditional Economic Assumptions and Values: Toward a New Multidisciplinary Discourse of Law, 42 SYRACUSE L. REV. 181 (1991).

78. See Randy E. Barnett, Symposium on Post-Chicago Law and Economics: Foreword: Chicago Law and Economics, 65 CHI.-KENT L. REV. 3, 4 (1989) [hereinafter Forward]; Robert C. Ellickson, Bringing Culture and Human Frailty to Rational Actors: A Critique of Classical Law and Economics, 65 CHI.-KENT L. REV. 23 (1989).

79. See Lewis A. Kornhauser, An Economic Perspective on Stare Decisis, 65 CHI.-KENT L. REV. 63 (1989). See also Arthur Leff, Economic Analysis of Law: Some Realism about Normalism, 60 VA. L. REV. 451 (1974).

80. See Randal C. Picker, Law and Economics: Intellectual Arbitrage, 27 LOY. L.A. L. REV. 127 (1993).

81. See Jonathan R. Macey, The Internal and External Costs and Benefits of Stare Decisis, 65 CHI.-KENT L. REV. 93 (1989).

82. See Kornhauser, An Economic Perspective on Stare Decisis, supra at 3.

83. Compare POSNER, ECONOMIC ANALYSIS OF LAW, supra note 1.

84. POSNER, THE PROBLEMS OF JURISPRUDENCE, supra at 459–60.

85. Id.

86. Id.

87. Posner now concludes that the "methods of practical reason are [sometimes] inarticulate" because such reason relies upon "a non-rational process alien to conversation." Id.

88. Id.

89. Id.

90. Id.

91. Id.

92. Id.

93. Id. at 387. See also Posner, What Has Pragmatism to Offer Law?, supra at 1670.

94. Id. Some legal scholars argue that Posner's pragmatism resembles classical legal formalism. Like a classic legal formalist, Posner believes that instrumental rationality and common sense can specify formal criteria for legal decision making. The problem with Posner's pragmatism is that the moral predilections of the pragmatic analyst are merely deferred by the privileged inquiry of the instrumental analysis of economics. Given that the test for Posner's pragmatism is whether the method works, we must still ask, "works for what purpose, and for whom?" See Pierre Schlag, "Le Hors De Texte, C'est Moi": The Politics of Form and the Domestication of Deconstruction, 11 CARDOZO L. REV. 1631, 1655 (1990). See also Mark

M. Hager, *The Emperor's Clothes Are Not Efficient: Posner's Jurisprudence of Class,* 41 AM. U. L. REV. 7 (1991).

95. *See, e.g.,* Duncan Kennedy, *Cost-Benefit Analysis of Entitlement Problems: A Critique, supra. See also* Charles Fried, *The Artificial Reason of the Law or: What Lawyers Know,* 60 TEX. L. REV. 35 (1981). *See also* Pierre Schlag, *An Appreciative Comment on Coase's: The Problem of Social Cost: A View from the Left,* 1986 WIS. L. REV. 919; Schlag, *The Problem of Transaction Costs, supra.*

96. Meta-narratives are what postmoderns call the "grand discourses of Western society, which is to say all of the legitimating narratives that purport to provide valid and definitive principles, in any sphere, applicable across all societies." JEAN-FRANCQIS LYOTARD, THE POSTMODERN CONDITION XXII (Manchester: Manchester University Press 1984). In law, meta-narrative refers to the rhetorical modes of conceptual and normative legal thought that presume the existence of a correct answer for every legal problem.

97. One indication of this shift can be seen in recent symposium topics such as *Symposium: The Future of Law and Economics,* 20 HOFSTRA L. REV. 757–1137 (1992); or *Symposium: Post-Chicago Law and Economics,* 65 CHI.-KENT L. REV. 3–191 (1989). Another indication is the work of Posner and other law and economics scholars who have adopted a more pragmatic approach to economic analysis of law. *See* Randy E. Barnett, *Introduction: A New Era of Law and Economics,* 65 CHI.-KENT L. REV. 3 (1989) (summarizing the more pragmatic directions of law and economic practitioners). Further indication can be gleaned from commentators who suggest that a new era of law and economics is evolving, an era in which the rational-actor theory of the Chicago School of Economics no longer dominates. A "post-Chicago" law and economics movement is emerging in its place. *Id.*

98. *See* Jules L. Coleman, *Afterword: The Rational Choice Approach to Legal Rules,* 65 CHI.-KENT L. REV. 177, 179 (1989).

99. *Id.*

100. Barnett, *Forward, supra* at 19.

101. *See* Coleman, *Afterward: The Rational Choice Approach to Legal Rules, supra.*

102. *Id.* at 177.

103. *Id.*

104. *Id.*

105. *Id.* at 188.

106. *Id.* at 189. The complexity of the new transaction analysis is highlighted by Colman as follows: "First, identify the standard or typical *context* within which the problem is embedded. Second, identify the factors in the environment that contribute to uncertainty and those factors which constitute the pool of resources upon which parties in those circumstances might typically draw. Third, see whether the central problem which the

legal rules addresses (given the context) is one of *coordination, division* or *defection* uncertainty." *Id.*

## Notes to Chapter 6

1. The history of the origins of CLS can be found in Mark Tushnet, *Critical Legal Studies: A Political History,* 100 YALE L.J. 1515 (1991); John Henry Schlegel, *Notes toward an Intimate, Opinionated, and Affectionate History of the Conference on Critical Legal Studies,* 36 STAN. L. REV. 391 (1984). For a bibliography of CLS literature, *see* Duncan Kennedy and Karl Klare, *Bibliography of Critical Legal Studies,* 94 YALE L.J. 461 (1984).

2. For an excellent introduction to the intellectual projects of the movement, *see* James Boyle, *Introduction, in* CRITICAL LEGAL STUDIES SELECTED READINGS (J. Boyle, ed.) (New York: New York University Press 1992). *See also* MARK KELMAN, A GUIDE TO CRITICAL LEGAL STUDIES (Cambridge, Mass.: Harvard University Press 1987); A. ALTMAN, CRITICAL LEGAL STUDIES: A LIBERAL CRITIQUE (Princeton, N.J.: Princeton University Press 1989); THE POLITICS OF LAW: A PROGRESSIVE CRITIQUE (D. Kairys, ed.) (New York: Pantheon Books 1982); CRITICAL LEGAL STUDIES (A. Hutchinson, ed.) (Totowa, N.J.: Rowman & Littlefield 1982); ESSAYS ON CRITICAL LEGAL STUDIES SELECTED FROM PAGES OF THE HARVARD LAW REVIEW (Cambridge, Mass.: Harvard University Press 1986). For an examination of the *New Left* origins of CLS thought, *see* NEIL DUXBURY, PATTERNS OF AMERICAN JURISPRUDENCE (Oxford University Press forthcoming 1995).

3. *Statement of Critical Legal Studies Conference, in* CRITICAL LEGAL STUDIES (P. Fitzpatrick and A. Hunt, eds.) (New York: Basil Blackwell 1987).

4. *See* Boyle, *Introduction, in* CRITICAL LEGAL STUDIES, *supra* at xliv.

5. *Id.*

6. Lewis Kornhauser, *The Great Image of Authority,* 36 STAN. L. REV. 349, 352 (1984).

7. *Id.* at 364.

8. Paul Carrington, *'Of Law and the River,'* 34 J. LEGAL EDUC. 222 (1984).

9. Mark Tushnet, *Critical Legal Studies: A Political History,* 100 YALE L.J. 1515 (1991). By "political location," Tushnet meant "a place where people with a wide but not unlimited range of political views come together for political education, sustenance, and activity." *Id.* at 1515, n.2.

10. *Id.* at 1516.

11. *Id.* at 1516–17 (footnotes omitted).

12. *Id.* at 1517. Tushnet goes on to explain: "For, if law is politics, presumably one might also believe that legal intellectual positions are politics too." *Id.* at 1517.

13. *Id.* at 1517–18.

14. Martha Minow, *Law Turning Outward,* 73 TELOS 79, 83 (1986).

15. *Id.* at 84.

16. *Id.* at 84–85.
17. *Id.* at 85.
18. *Id.* at 84–85.
19. See Kennedy, *Form and Substance in Private Law Adjudication,* 89 HARV. L. REV. 1685 (1976); Kennedy, *The Structure of Blackstone's Commentaries,* 28 BUFF. L. REV. 209 (1979).
20. ROBERTO UNGER, KNOWLEDGE AND POLITICS (New York: Free Press 1975).
21. See Gabel and Feinman, *Contract Law as Ideology, in* POLITICS OF LAW, *supra* at 172.
22. Legal scholars who reject the political theory of interest-group pluralism have recently revived a competing tradition in early American political history called *civic republicanism. See, e.g.,* Frank I. Michelman, *Law's Republic,* 97 YALE L.J. 1493 (1988); Cass R. Sunstein, *Beyond the Republican Revival,* 97 YALE L.J. 1539 (1988). Civic republican thought offers a political conception of interest-group representation that differs radically from the concept offered by political pluralists. Republican theorists argue that the prerequisites of sound government should be based on the development of a deliberative process that subordinates private interest to the public good. Republicans question the premise that the political process can be understood as merely a strategic interaction aimed at reaching bargains between competing groups. Republicans argue that the deliberative process of government must be insulated from undue interest-group influence so as to allow policy decision makers to make choices in light of collective discussion and debate, bringing together all perspectives and interests in society.
23. *See, e.g.,* MORTON HORWITZ, THE TRANSFORMATION OF AMERICAN LAW: 1780–1860 (New York: Oxford University Press 1992); MORTON HORWITZ, THE TRANSFORMATION OF AMERICAN LAW: 1780–1860 (Cambridge, Mass.: Harvard University Press 1977).
24. See Mark G. Kelman, *Trashing,* 36 STAN. L. REV. 293 (1984).
25. See Duncan Kennedy, *The Structure of Blackstone's Commentaries,* 28 BUFF. L. REV. 209 (1978).
26. See James Boyle, *Introduction, in* CRITICAL LEGAL STUDIES, *supra* at xiv–xv.
27. See Peter Gabel, *Reification in Legal Reasoning,* 3 RES. IN L. & SOC. 25 (1980). *See also* Gary Peller, *The Metaphysics of American Law,* 73 CAL. L. REV. 1151 (1985).
28. *See, e.g.,* David Kennedy, *The Turn to Interpretation,* 58 SO. CALIF. L. REV. 251 (1985); Gary Minda, *Phenomenology, Tina Turner and the Law,* 16 NEW MEXICO L. REV. 479 (1986). Traditional legal thinkers attempted to defend the possibility of legal objectivity in terms of a concept of objectivity based on shared community values. *See, e.g.,* Owen M. Fiss, *The Death of the Law?,* 72 CORNELL L. REV. 1 (1986); Owen M. Fiss, *Objectivity and Interpretation,* 34 STAN. L. REV. 739 (1982).

29. *See* Duncan Kennedy, *Psycho-Social CLS: A Comment on the Cardozo Symposium*, 6 CARDOZO L. REV. 1013 (1985).
30. DUNCAN KENNEDY, LEGAL EDUCATION AND THE REPRODUCTION OF HIER-ARCHY: A POLEMIC AGAINST THE SYSTEM (Cambridge, Mass.: A Far Press 1983).
31. *See Association in Favor of Labor,* BOSTON DAILY JOURNAL, Jan. 7, 1993; *Law Profs. Call for Hotel Boycott,* BOSTON DAILY JOURNAL, Jan. 8, 1993.
32. At the 1984 AALS convention, CLS members distributed an "alternative" newspaper called the *Lizard,* a pop-style, cartoon-like leaflet of CLS criticism of the convention events of the day. CLS members reported on convention events, distributed the leaflet, and organized an alternative CLS meeting.
33. Peter Gabel and Paul Harris, *Building Power and Breaking Images: Critical Legal Theory and the Practice of Law,* 11 N.Y.U. REV. L. & SOC. CHANGE 396 (1982–83).
34. *Id.*
35. *Id.* at 373.
36. *Id.*
37. *Id.* at 369, 374.
38. William H. Simon, *The Ideology of Advocacy: Procedural Justice and Professional Ethics,* 1978 WIS. L. REV. 29 (1978).
39. KENNEDY, *Freedom and Constraint in Adjudication: A Critical Phenomenology,* 36 J. LEGAL EDUC. 518 (1986).
40. *Id.* at 526 (emphasis in original).
41. *Id.*
42. *See* Duncan Kennedy, *A Semiotics of Legal Argument,* 42 SYRACUSE L. REV. 75 (1991); Jeremy Paul, *The Politics of Legal Semiotics,* 69 TEX. L. REV. 1779 (1991); Jack M. Balkin, *The Promise of Legal Semiotics,* 69 TEX. L. REV. 1831 (1991).
43. *See* Kennedy, *The Structure of Blackstone's Commentaries, supra.*
44. *See* RAYMOND GEUSS, THE IDEA OF A CRITICAL THEORY: HABERMAS AND THE FRANKFURT SCHOOL (Cambridge, U.K.: Cambridge University Press 1981).
45. *See* Boyle, *Introduction, in* CRITICAL LEGAL STUDIES, *supra* at xvii.
46. *Id.*
47. The *critique of false essences* refers to the problem of seeing something as representing more than it is because of the false belief that the existence of certain natural or essential qualities need no justification. The belief in false essences is a self-deception. The philosopher Richard Rorty argues that we need to abandon the notion of "essence" altogether in critical analysis. *See* RICHARD RORTY, PHILOSOPHY AND THE MIRROR OF NATURE 361–62 (Princeton, N.J.: Princeton University Press 1979).
48. *Id.*
49. *See, e.g.,* Clare Dalton, *An Essay in the Deconstruction of Contract Doctrine,* 94 YALE L.J. 997 (1985); Drucilla Cornell, *Toward a Modern/Post-*

*modern Reconstruction of Ethics,* 133 U. Pa. L. Rev. 291 (1985); Gerald
E. Frug, *The Ideology of Bureaucracy in American Law,* 97 Harv. L. Rev.
1276 (1984). *See also* Jack M. Balkin, *The Crystalline Structure of Legal
Thought,* 39 Rutgers L. Rev. 1 (1986).

50. *See* Kennedy, *The Structure of Blackstone's Commentaries, supra* at 209,
213.

51. *See* Balkin, *Deconstructive Practice and Legal Theory, supra* at 764.

52. *See* Pierre Schlag, *"Le Hors de texte, C'est Moi": The Politics of Form and
the Domestication of Deconstruction,* 11 Cardozo L. Rev. 1631 (1990).

53. Jacques Derrida, Of Grammatology 97–316 (Gayatri Chatravorty Spi-
rak, trans.) (Baltimore: Johns Hopkins University Press 1977).

54. *See* Jack M. Balkin, *Deconstructive Practice and Legal Theory, supra* at
758.

55. *See* Derrida, Of Grammatology, *supra* at 3. *See also* Balkin, *Deconstructive Practice and Legal Theory, supra* at 755.

56. Balkin, *Deconstructive Practice and Legal Theory* 141–64. *See also* Peter
C. Schanck, *Understanding Postmodern Thought and Its Implications for
Statutory Interpretation,* 65 S. Cal. L. Rev. 2505, 2527 (1992); Jack M.
Balkin, *Deconstruction Practice and Legal Theory,* 96 Yale L.J. 743, 774–
75 (1987).

57. Derrida, Of Grammatology, *supra* at 3, 11–12. This does not mean
that Derrida is silent on the question of justice of the text. On the contrary,
Derrida's position is that deconstruction is about justice and little else. See
Jacques Derrida, *Force of Law: The "Mystical Foundation of Authority,"*
11 Cardozo L. Rev. 919 (1990).

58. See Balkin, *Deconstructive Practice and Legal Theory, supra* at 760.

59. *See* Derrida, Of Grammatology, *supra* at 158.

60. Gerald F. Frug, *The Ideology of Bureaucracy in American Law,* 97 Harv.
L. Rev. 1277 (1984).

61. *Id.* at 1277–78.

62. *Id.* at 1287.

63. *Id.* at 1286.

64. *Id.*

65. *Id.* at 1287.

66. *Id.* at 1289.

67. *Id.*

68. *Id.* at 1291.

69. *Id.*

70. *Id.*

71. *See* Balkin, *Deconstructive Practice and Legal Theory,* 96 Yale L.J. 743,
763 (1987). *See also* Jack M. Balkin, *Transcendental Deconstruction, Transcendent Justice,* 92 Mich. L. Rev. 1131 (1994).

72. *See* Frug, *The Ideology of Bureaucracy, supra* at 1386.

73. Gary Peller, *The Metaphysics of American Law,* 73 Cal. L. Rev. 1151
(1985).

74. *Id.* at 1207–10.
75. *Id.* at 1208–9.
76. *See* chap. 2, *supra.*
77. Peller, *Metaphysics of American Law, supra* at 1194–98.
78. *Id.* at 1197.
79. *Id.*
80. *Id.* at 1197–98.
81. *See* Peter Gabel and Duncan Kennedy, *Roll Over Beethoven,* 36 STAN. L. REV. 1 (1984).
82. *See* David Luban, *Legal Modernism,* 84 MICH. L. REV. 1656 (1986).
83. *Id.* at 1672.
84. *Id.*
85. *Id.* at 1675.
86. *See* Fiss, *The Death of the Law?, supra.*
87. *Id.* at 15.
88. *See* Carrington, *Of Law and the River, supra.*
89. Calvin R. Massey, *The Faith Healers,* 17 J. L. & SOC'Y INQUIRY 821, 822 (1992).
90. *See* John Stick, *Can Nihilism Be Pragmatic?,* 100 HARV. L. REV. 332 (1986).
91. *See* Joel F. Handler, *Postmodernism, Protest, and the New Social Movements,* 26 LAW & SOC'Y REV. 697 (1992).
92. *See* Joseph W. Singer, *The Player and the Cards: Nihilism and Legal Theory,* 94 YALE L.J. 1 (1984). Critics have nonetheless forcefully argued that Crits have to prove that they are anything but nihilistic. *See, e.g.,* John Stick, *Can Nihilism Be Pragmatic?,* 100 HARV. L. REV. 332 (1986). Charges of legal nihilism were, however, difficult to defend since the term "legal nihilism" was never defined nor was it ever established as characteristic of scholarship authored by any CLS writer. *Id.* The fear remained that CLS promotes an unprincipled relativistic jurisprudence that encourages and sustains nihilism.
93. Within the CLS movement, the charge of legal nihilism helped fuel a debate between so-called rationalists who argued a reformist mission for CLS, and the so-called irrationalists, who argued in favor of "trashing." *See* Clare Dalton, *Book Review,* 6 HARV. WOMEN'S L.J. 229 (1983). The internal debate between the rationalists and irrationalists focused chiefly on the question of whether progressive legal strategies would be best served by legal advocacy of legal rights. Some argued that the legal concept of "rights" undermined authentic understandings of the self; *see* Peter Gabel, *The Phenomenology of Rights-Consciousness and the Pact of the Withdrawn Selves,* 62 TEX. L. REV. 1563 (1984). Others argued that "rights" were central to all progressive struggles. *See* Elizabeth M. Schneider, *The Dialectic of Rights and Politics Form the Women's Movement,* 61 N.Y.U. L. REV. 589 (1986).
94. *See* Richard Bernstein, BEYOND OBJECTIVISM AND RELATIVISM, SCIENCE, HERMENEUTICS & PRAXIS 18 (Philadelphia: University of Pennsylvania

Press 1983) ("*Either* there is some support for our being, a fixed foundation for our knowledge, *or* we cannot escape the forces of darkness that envelop us with madness, with intellectual and moral chaos." *Id.*).

95. Pierre Schlag, *Normativity and the Politics of Form*, 139 U. PA. L. REV. 801, 831 (1991).

96. *See* Richard Michael Fischl, *Privileged Positions*, 17 J. L. & SOC'Y INQUIRY 831, 834 (1992); Duncan Kennedy, *A Semiotics of Legal Argument*, 42 SYRACUSE L. REV. 75, 115 (1991); *see, generally*, Richard Michael Fischl, *The Question That Killed Critical Legal Studies*, 17 J. L. & SOC'Y INQUIRY 779 (1992); Jack M. Balkin, *Nested Oppositions*, 99 YALE L.J. 1669 (1990).

97. Even Duncan Kennedy has given up on the idea. *See* Gabel and Kennedy, *Roll Over Beethoven, supra* at 15.

98. *Id.* at 15–16 (comments by Peter Gabel and Duncan Kennedy).

99. Another reason for the demise of the radical version of the fundamental contradiction thesis is that it failed to explain why so much of American law has a distinctive political tilt. If every rule can be deconstructed in terms of rule and counterrule and if everything is truly up for grabs, then how do we explain why so much of legal doctrine has a pattern of development? This is what Professor Richard Michael Fischl of the University of Miami Law School has called "The Question That Killed Critical Legal Studies." *See* Fischl, *The Question That Killed Critical Legal Studies, supra.*

100. The feminist presence within the Conference on Critical Legal Studies surfaced in 1985 when a group of Fem-Crits organized the first national CLS feminist conference in Boston. *See* Carrie Menkel-Meadow, *Feminist Legal Theory, Critical Legal Studies, and Legal Education or "The Fem-Crits Go to Law School,"* 38 J. LEGAL EDUC. 61 (1988). A race-conscious critique developed somewhat later as minority men and women within CLS began to criticize liberals and radicals for assuming that all minorities have the same perspective. *See, e.g.,* Kimberle Crenshaw, *Demarginalizing the Intersection of Race and Sex: A Black Feminist Critique of Antidiscrimination Doctrine, Feminist Theory and Antiracist Politics*, 1989 CHI. LEGAL F. 139, 140, 152–60; Richard Delgado, *Storytelling for Oppositionists and Others: A Plea for Narrative*, 87 MICH. L. REV. 2411 (1989); Mari Matsuda, *Looking to the Bottom: Critical Legal Studies and Reparations*, 22 HARV. C.R.-C.L. L. REV. 323 (1987).

101. *See* Kennedy, *Psycho-Social CLS: A Comment on the Cardozo Symposium*, 6 CARDOZO L. REV. 1013, 1021 (1985) (discussing the internal challenge of Fem-Crits). The term "groupism" was coined by Roberto Unger in a speech given at a CLS conference, "Policy Making in the Nineties," held at Harvard Law School and Northeastern School of Law in January 1992.

102. At the 1992 CLS conference held at Harvard University, for example, critical legal theory networks (CLTNs) were organized to stimulate collec-

tive self-reflection and common group concerns. CLTNs aimed to advance distinctive programmatic approaches for engaging in transformative legal practice by emphasizing the intersectionality of critical approaches to law (*e.g.*, new feminist theories of African American women). The hope was that CLTNs would enable various groups to work out a global coalition for a new progressive social and political movement. The idea never went anywhere after the conclusion of the conference.

103. See Gary Peller and William Eskridge, Jr., *The New Public Law Movement: Moderation as a Postmodern Cultural Form,* 89 MICH. L. REV. 707, 776–87 (1991).

104. See Pierre Schlag, *Normativity and the Politics of Form,* 139 U. PA. L. REV. 801, 804–5 (1991). *See also* Pierre Schlag, *The Problem of the Subject,* 69 TEX. L. REV. 1627 (1991).

105. See Mark Tushnet, *The Degradation of Constitutional Discourse,* 81 GEO. L.J. 251 (1992); Gary Peller, *The Discourse of Constitutional Degradation,* 81 GEO. L.J. 313 (1992); Mark Tushnet, *Reply,* 81 GEO. L.J. 343 (1992). Tushnet and Peller disagree over what should constitute politically correct political strategies, arguments, and methods for progressive legal politics. Mark Tushnet, a first-generation CLS scholar, finds the technique of storytelling and narrative in critical race and feminist scholarship a dangerous degradation of constitutional discourse. Tushnet, *The Degradation of Constitutional Discourse, supra* at 258–77. Gary Peller, on the other hand, a second-generation CLS scholar, sees Tushnet's argument as advancing a deeply conservative functional analysis of authority, identity, and power that is itself part of a discourse of "constitutional degradation." Peller, *Discourse, supra* at 315. Generational conflicts within CLS, like all generational conflicts, may have an Oedipal element, in which, according to Tushnet, "successive generations *first attack* and then come to grips with their predecessors." Tushnet, *Reply, supra* at 349. On the other hand, it may be that the particular form of generational conflict within CLS is itself part of what Peller sees as a larger cultural conflict in the profession— "a conflict with its own economies of authority, identity and power." Peller, *Discourse, supra* at 315.

106. Joel F. Handler, for example, suggested that postmodern approaches in legal criticism present serious difficulties for anyone seeking to advance the political goals of a new social movement. Joel F. Handler, *Postmodernism, Protest, and the New Social Movements,* 26 LAW & SOC'Y REV. 697, 719–22 (1992).

107. *Id.* at 722 (arguing that "even local power cannot be confronted without a comprehensive political and economic plan." *Id.*).

108. See James Boyle, *Introduction, in* CRITICAL LEGAL STUDIES, *supra* at XL.

109. See, *e.g.,* Duncan Kennedy and Karl E. Klare, *A Bibliography of Critical Legal Studies,* 94 YALE L.J. 461 (1985) (listing over 500 books and articles on the subject of CLS or influenced by CLS published by 1984). See also

*Critical Legal Studies Symposium,* 36 STAN. L. REV. 1 (1984); *Symposium on Critical Legal Studies,* 6 CARDOZO L. REV. 691 (1985); *Professing Law: A Colloquy on Critical Legal Studies,* 31 ST. LOUIS U. L.J. 1 (1986); *Symposium, Roberto Unger's Politics: A Work in Constructive Social Theory,* 81 NW. U. L. REV. 589 (1987); *Constitutional Law from a Critical Legal Perspective: A Symposium,* 36 BUFF. L. REV. 211 (1987).

## Notes to Chapter 7

1. Leslie Bender, *A Lawyer's Primer on Feminist Theory and Tort,* 38 J. LEGAL EDUC. 3 (1988). *See also* Linda J. Lacey, *Introducing Feminist Jurisprudence: An Analysis of Oklahoma's Seduction Statute,* 25 TULSA L.J. 775, 776–77 (1990).
2. *See* Linda J. Lacey, *Introducing Feminist Jurisprudence, supra* at 777.
3. *See* Deborah L. Rhode, *The "No-Problem" Problem: Feminist Challenges and Cultural Change,* 100 YALE L.J. 1731, 1738 (1991) [hereinafter *Feminist Challenges*].
4. *See* Nadine Taub and Elizabeth M. Schneider, *Women's Subordination and the Role of Law, in* THE POLITICS OF LAW: A PROGRESSIVE CRITIQUE 151 (D. Kairys, ed.) (New York: Pantheon Books 1990).
5. *Id.*
6. *See* Rhode, *Feminist Challenges, supra* at 1745.
7. *Id.* at 1744.
8. *See* DAVID HALBERSTAM, THE FIFTIES 280 (New York: Random House 1993).
9. BETTY FRIEDAN, THE FEMININE MYSTIQUE 15 (New York: Norton 1963), *quoted in* Rhode, *Feminist Challenges, supra* at 1745.
10. *Id.* at 1745.
11. Ann Scales, *Towards a Feminist Jurisprudence,* 56 IND. L.J. 375 (1981).
12. *See* Lacey, *Introducing Feminist Jurisprudence, supra* at 779.
13. *See* Robin West, *Jurisprudence and Gender,* 55 U. CHI. L. REV. 1, 4 (1988).
14. Feminist legal thought is perhaps the most powerful of the contemporary movements in legal theory—first, because the feminist movement is sufficiently diverse to include and mobilize all women (and men); second, because feminism demands a fundamental reexamination and restructuring of existing legal and social arrangements.
15. Susan Moller Okin, *Sexual Difference, Feminism, and the Law,* 16 LAW & SOCIAL INQUIRY 553, 554 (1991); [Reviewing WENDY KAMINH, A FEARFUL FREEDOM: WOMEN'S FLIGHT FROM EQUALITY (Reading, Mass.: Addison-Wesley 1990); DEBORAH L. RHODE, JUSTICE AND GENDER (Cambridge, Mass.: Harvard University Press 1989)].
16. The phrase was coined by Luce Itigaray. *See* DRUCILLA CORNELL, BEYOND ACCOMMODATION: ETHICAL FEMINISM, DECONSTRUCTION AND THE LAW 95 (New York: Routledge 1991).

17. *See* Gary Minda, *Title VII at the Crossroads of Employment Discrimination Law and Postmodern Feminist Theory*, 11 St. Louis U. Pub. L. Rev. 89 (1992).

18. Catharine A. MacKinnon, *Feminism, Marxism, Method, and the State: Toward Feminist Jurisprudence*, 8 Signs 635 (1983) [hereinafter *Toward Feminist Jurisprudence*]; West, *Jurisprudence and Gender, supra* at 1, 3–4.

19. West, *Jurisprudence and Gender, supra* at 4.

20. Martha Minow, *Law Turning Outward*, 73 Telos 79, 62–64 (1986).

21. West, *Jurisprudence and Gender, supra* at 56.

22. Scales, *Towards a Feminist Jurisprudence, supra* at 1401.

23. *See* Robin L. West, *The Difference in Women's Hedonic Lives: A Phenomenological Critique of Feminist Legal Theory*, 3 Wis. Women's L.J. 81 (1987).

24. *See* Kathryn Abrams, *Hearing the Call of Stories*, 79 Cal. L. Rev. 971 (1991) (examining the emergence of feminist narrative scholarship as a distinctive form of critical legal discourse).

25. Deborah Rhode, *The "Woman's Point of View,"* 38 J. Legal Educ. 39 (1988).

26. *See* Michel Foucault, Discipline and Punish: The Birth of the Prison (New York: Random House 1979). *See also* Robin West, *Feminism, Critical Social Theory and Law*, 1989 U. Chi. Legal F. 59.

27. *See* Abrams, *Hearing the Call of Stories, supra* at 976.

28. *Id.*

29. *Id.* at 982.

30. *See* Francis Olsen, *The Sex of Law in* The Politics of Law: A Progressive Critique (D. Kairysed. 2nd ed.) (New York: Pantheon Books 1991).

31. *See* Abrams, *Henry the Call of Stories, supra* at 982–1012 (surveying the work of Susan Estrich, Martha Mahoney, Patricia Williams, and Marie Ashe).

32. Dennis Patterson, *Postmodernism/Feminism/Law*, 77 Cornell L. Rev. 254, 261 (1992).

33. *See* Sabina Lovibond, *Feminism and Postmodernism, in* Postmodernism and Society 161 (Roy Boyne and Ali Rattansi, eds.) (Houndmills, U.K.: Macmillan 1990).

34. *See* Boyne and Rattansi, *The Theory and Politics of Postmodernisn: By Way of an Introduction, in* Postmodernism and Society, *supra* at 5.

35. *See* Sabina Lovibond, *Feminism and Postmodernism, supra* at 162.

36. West, *Jurisprudence and Gender, supra* at 65.

37. *See* Joan C. Williams, *Deconstructing Gender*, 87 Mich. L. Rev. 797, 828 (1989).

38. West, *Feminism, Critical Social Theory and Law, supra* at 70–71.

39. *Id.*

40. Feminist legal criticism offered the possibility of a feminist jurisprudence, but a modernist framework for analyzing questions of method, the nature

of feminist knowledge, and the nature of feminist critique, have remained within feminist theory. Patterson argued that even contemporary feminist theory continues to exhibit modernist beliefs in universal truths, essential categories, and the privacy of the individual. *See* Patterson, *Postmodernism/ Feminism/Law, supra.*

41. *See, generally,* JOHN MCGOWAN, POSTMODERNISM AND ITS CRITICS 3–12 (Ithaca, N.Y.: Cornell University Press 1991).

42. *See* Lacey, *Introducing Feminist Jurisprudence, supra* at 780. As Lacey notes, there has been some confusion created by attempts of others to identify different types of feminist legal thought. Professor Cass Sunstein, for example, concluded that there are three principled strands of feminist legal theory: "difference," "different voice," and "dominance." *See* Cass Sunstein, *Feminism and Legal Theory* (Book Review), 101 HARV. L. REV. 826 (1988). Following Sunstein, I presented a similar classification in Gary Minda, *Jurisprudential Movements of the 1980s,* 1989 OHIO ST. L.J. 599, 626. I now believe that Lacey's three categories are more descriptive. Lacey's liberal feminist category corresponds to Sunstein's "difference" strand.

43. *See* Ann Freedman, *Sex Equality, Sex Differences and the Supreme Court,* 92 YALE L.J. 913 (1983).

44. Minow, *Law Turning Outward, supra* at 62. *See also* Bartlett, *Book Review,* 75 CAL. L. REV. 1559 (1987).

45. Wendy Williams, *Equality's Riddle: Pregnancy and the Equal Treatment/ Special Treatment Debate,* 13 N.Y.U. REV. L. & SOC. CHANGE 325 (1985).

46. West, *The Difference in Women's Hedonic Lives, supra* at 83.

47. *See* Joan Williams, *Dissolving the Sameness/Difference Debate: A Postmodern Path beyond Essentialism in Feminist and Critical Race Theory,* 1991 DUKE L.J. 296 (1991).

48. *See* Lucinda Finley, *Choice and Freedom: Elusive Issues in the Search for Gender Justice,* 96 YALE L.J. 914 (1987).

49. Martha Minow, *Foreword: Justice Engendered,* 101 HARV. L. REV. 10 (1987).

50. *Id.* at 69–70.

51. CAROL GILLIGAN, IN A DIFFERENT VOICE (Cambridge, Mass.: Harvard University Press 1982).

52. Sunstein, *Feminism and Legal Theory, supra* at 826–27.

53. Lisa Bender, *A Lawyer's Primer on Feminist Theory and Tort,* 38 J. LEGAL EDUC. 3, 18–19 (1988).

54. Joan C. Williams, *Gender Wars: Selfless Women in the Republic of Choice,* 66 N.Y.U. L. REV. 1559, 1564–65 (1991).

55. *Id.* at 1564.

56. *Id.* at 1566.

57. *See* West, *Jurisprudence and Gender, supra* at 13, 14.

58. *Id.* at 17.

59. GILLIGAN, IN A DIFFERENT VOICE, *supra* at 25.

60. *Id.* at 26.

61. *Id.*
62. *Id.*
63. *Id.* at 32–33.
64. *Id.* at 28.
65. *Id.*
66. *Id.*
67. *Id.*
68. *Id.*
69. *Id.* at 29.
70. *Id.* at 29, 62–63.
71. *Id.* at 31–32.
72. *Id.*
73. *See* Deborah L. Rhode, *The "No-Problem" Problem: Feminist Challenges and Cultural Change,* 100 YALE L.J. 1731, 1784–89 (1991).
74. *See* Carol Gilligan, Annie Rogers, and Lyn Mikel Brown, *Epilogue: Sounding into Development, in* MAKING CONNECTIONS 314, 317–18 (Carol Gilligan, Nora P. Lyons, and Trudy J. Hammer, eds.) (Cambridge, Mass.: Harvard University Press 1990).
75. *See* Jeanne L. Schroeder, *Abduction from the Seraglio: Feminist Methodologies and the Logic of Imagination,* 70 TEX. L. REV. 109, 145–46 & nn. 89–90 (1991).
76. West, *Jurisprudence and Gender, supra* at 21.
77. *See* MacKinnon, *Toward Feminist Jurisprudence, supra* at 137.
78. *Id.* at 50.
79. *Id.* at 7.
80. *Id.* at 34.
81. *Id.* at 40.
82. *Id.*
83. Robin West, *Jurisprudence and Gender, supra* at 13.
84. *See* Marion Smiley, *Gender Justice without Foundations,* 89 MICH. L. REV. 1574, 1578 (1991).
85. *See* West, *Women's Hedonic Lives, supra* at 116–39.
86. Minow, *Law Turning Outward, supra* at 48.
87. *See* MacKinnon, *Toward Feminist Jurisprudence, supra.*
88. *See* Patterson, *Postmodernism/Feminism/Law, supra* at 220–95 (examining the feminist scholarship of Robin West and Joan Williams).
89. West, *Jurisprudence and Gender, supra* at 41.
90. *See* Carrie Menkel-Meadow, *Feminist Legal Theory, Critical Legal Studies, and Legal Education, or The Fem-Crits Go to Law School,* 38 J. LEGAL EDUC. 61 (1988).
91. *See* West, *Jurisprudence and Gender, supra* at 38–39.
92. *Id.* at 61.
93. Leslie Bender, *An Overview of Feminist Tort Scholarship,* 78 CORNELL L. REV. 575, 575 (1993). *See also* FEMINIST LEGAL LITERATURE: A SELECTED ANNOTATED BIBLIOGRAPHY (F.C. De Coste et al., eds.) (New York: Garland

Publishers 1991); Paul M. George and Susan McGlamery, *Women and Legal Scholarship: A Bibliography*, 77 Iowa L. Rev. 87 (1991).

94. *See* Mary Joe Frug, *A Postmodern Feminist Legal Manifesto* (an unfinished draft), 105 Harv. L. Rev. 1045 (1992).

95. Mary Joe Frug was a professor of law at New England College of Law and a highly regarded feminist legal theorist. She was an effective organizer within both the CLS and feminist movements. Frug was murdered in 1991, and her murder has remained unsolved to this day. Her death was a great loss to the legal community. Mary Joe was a friend and a mentor.

96. *Id.* at 1046.

97. Smiley, *Gender Justice without Foundations*, supra at 1578.

98. Williams, *Gender Wars*, supra at 1567, citing and relying on Jacques Derrida, Of Grammatology 141–64 (Gayatri Chakravorty Spivak, trans.) (Baltimore: Johns Hopkins University Press 1977); Jonathan Culler, On Deconstruction: Theory and Criticism after Structuralism 85–225 (Ithaca, N.Y.: Cornell University Press 1982).

99. Williams, *Gender Wars*, supra at 1567.

100. *Id.*

101. *Id.* at 1567–68.

102. *Id.* at 1567.

103. Abrams, *Hearing the Call of Stories*, supra at 1013.

104. *Id.* at 1013–14.

105. Patterson, *Postmodern/Feminism/Law*, supra at 276–77.

106. *Id.* at 278, *quoting* Simone de Beauvoir, The Second Sex 267 (H. M. Parshley, trans.) (New York: Alfred A. Knopf 1953).

107. Patterson, *Postmodernism/Feminism/Law*, supra at 278, *citing* Judith Busler, Gender Trouble: Feminism and the Subversion of Identity 98 (New York: Routledge 1990).

108. Zillah R. Eisenstein, The Female Body and the Law 5 (Berkeley: University of California Press 1988).

109. Williams, *Dissolving the Sameness/Difference Debate*, supra.

110. *See* West, *Jurisprudence and Gender*, supra at 55.

111. Nancy Fraser and Linda Nicholson, *Social Criticism without Philosophy: An Encounter between Feminism and Postmodernism*, in Universal Abandon? The Politics of Postmodernism (Andrew Ross, ed.) (Minneapolis: University of Minnesota Press 1988).

112. Id. at 90–91.

113. Lovibond, *Feminism and Postmodernism*, supra at 161.

114. *Id.* at 179.

115. *See* West, *Jurisprudence and Gender*, supra note 13.

116. Patterson, *Postmodern/Feminism/Law*, supra at 258.

117. Drucilla Cornell, *Sexual Difference, the Feminine, and Equivalency: A Critique of MacKinnon's "Toward a Feminist Theory of the State,"* 100 Yale L.J. 2247, 2250 (1991).

118. Williams, *Sameness/Difference Debate*, supra at 299.

119. Margaret Jane Radin, *The Pragmatist and the Feminist,* 63 S. CAL. L. REV. 1699 (1990).
120. *Id.* at 1718–19.
121. Mary Becker, *Strength in Diversity: Feminist Theories Approach Child Custody and Same-Sex Relationship,* 23 STETSON L. REV. (forthcoming 1994).
122. *See* Patterson, *Postmodernism/Feminism/Law, supra.* "Feminists seem to have two choices: Stick with modernism or give up feminism." *Id.* Postmoderns argue that the "choice between feminism and postmodernism is a false one." *Id.* at 256. Postmoderns assert that their critical practice "poses no threat to feminism" because "all that postmodernism threatens is a conception of reason (the modernist conception) which may have reached the end of its useful life." *Id.* at 258.
123. *See* Patterson, *Postmodernism/Feminism/Law, supra* at 279–95 (discussing how the modernist framework can be found in the feminist legal scholarship of Robin West and Joan Williams).
124. On the other hand, the essentialism in recent postmodern feminist scholarship detected by Dennis Patterson may well be a reflection of the paradoxes of the texts postmodern feminists interpret. For postmodernists, predicament and paradox are unavoidable conditions of the current intellectual state posed by the texts, discourses, vocabulary, and grammar of a socially and culturally situated profession. One does not criticize postmodernists merely because they exhibit predicaments and paradoxes in their announcements. Predicament and paradox are what postmodernists are about. They reject the idea that there exists a fixed, coherent foundational principle from which postmodern truth and knowledge can be derived.
125. *See* Kimberle Crenshaw, *Demarginalizing the Intersections of Race and Gender in Antidiscrimination Law, Feminist Theory, and Antiracist Politics,* 1989 U. CHI. LEGAL F. 139; KIMBERLE CRENSHAW, WHOSE STORY IS IT, ANYWAY? FEMINIST AND ANTIRACIST APPROPRIATIONS OF ANITA HILL IN RACE-ING JUSTICE, EN-GENDERING POWER: ESSAYS ON ANITA HILL, CLARENCE THOMAS, AND THE CONSTRUCTION OF SOCIAL REALITY 402 (Toni Morrison, ed.) (New York: Pantheon Books 1992).
126. *See* Crenshaw, *Demarginalizing the Intersection of Race and Sex, supra.*
127. CRENSHAW, WHOSE STORY IS IT, ANYWAY?, *supra* at 402, 406.
128. *Id.*
129. Crenshaw, *Demarginalizing the Intersection of Race and Sex, supra* at 166.
130. *See* MARY JOE FRUG, POSTMODERN LEGAL FEMINISM (New York: Routledge 1992).
131. *See* Jerry Frug, *Decentering Decentralization,* 60 U. CHI. L. REV. 253, 304–12 (1993).

## Notes to Chapter 8

1. JAMES B. WHITE, THE LEGAL IMAGINATION: STUDIES IN THE NATURE OF LEGAL THOUGHT AND EXPRESSION (Boston: Little, Brown & Co. 1973).

2. Law and literature studies were later structured by a "law-in-literature"/ "literature-in-law" dichotomy. *See* David Ray Papke, *Problems with an Uninvited Guest: Richard A. Posner and the Law and Literature Movement,* 69 B.U. L. Rev. 1067, 1070, n. 18 (1989) & note 9 *infra.*

3. John H. Wigmore (1863–1943), a noted authority on evidence and dean of the Law School at Northwestern University, was a prolific legal scholar who was the first to combine literature with legal studies. *See, generally,* Wigmore, *A List of Legal Novels,* 2 U. ILL. L. Rev. 547 (1908); *See also* BENJAMIN N. CARDOZO, LAW AND LITERATURE AND OTHER ESSAYS AND ADDRESSES (New York: Harcourt, Brace & Co. 1931).

4. *See* RICHARD H. WEISBERG, POETHICS AND OTHER STRATEGIES OF LAW AND LITERATURE 4 (New York: Columbia University Press 1992). *See also* the essays by Brook Thomas, *Reflections on the Law and Literature Revival,* 17 CRITICAL INQUIRY 510 (1991); Ian Ward, *Law and Literature,* 4 LAW & CRITIQUE 43 (1992).

5. The word "hermeneutics" signifies interpretation; it often implies an interpretation that treats the object of the study "reverently," *i.e.,* by assuming words "dictate meaning." *See, e.g.,* David Couzens Hoy, *Interpreting the Law: Hermeneutical and Poststructuralist Perspectives,* 58 S. CAL. L. REV. 135 (1985). Other scholars use the word to refute the idea that words can dictate meaning or universally valid interpretations. *See, e.g.,* David Kennedy, *The Turn to Interpretation,* 58 S. CAL. L. REV. 251 (1985). In law, hermeneutics generally refers to different theoretical positions on the nature of legal interpretation or the role of perspective in creating interpretation. *See, e.g.,* Paul Brest, *Who Decides?,* 58 S. CAL. L. REV. 661, 662 (1985).

6. *See, e.g.,* Owen M. Fiss, *Objectivity and Interpretation,* 34 STAN. L. REV. 739 (1982); RONALD DWORKIN, LAW AND INTERPRETATION IN THE POLITICS OF INTERPRETATION (W. J. T. Mitchell, ed.) (Chicago: University of Chicago Press 1983).

7. JAMES BOYD WHITE, JUSTICE AS TRANSLATION: AN ESSAY IN CULTURAL LEGAL CRITICISM 17 (New York: Harcourt, Brace & Co. 1990).

8. John Fischer, *Reading Literature/Reading Law: Is There a Literary Jurisprudence?,* 72 TEX. L. REV. 135, 136–37 (1993).

9. *See* Robert Weisberg, *The Law-Literature Enterprise,* 1 YALE J. L. & HUMAN. 1 (1988).

10. *See* RICHARD H. WEISBERG, THE FAILURE OF THE WORD: THE LAWYER AS PROTAGONIST IN MODERN FICTION (New Haven: Yale University Press 1984).

11. *See* WEISBERG, THE FAILURE OF THE WORD, *supra.*

12. *See* Sanford Levinson, *Law as Literature,* 60 TEX. L. REV. 373 (1982).

13. *See* ROBERT COVER, JUSTICE ACCUSED 1–7 (New Haven: Yale University Press 1975).

14. *See* Daniel A. Farber and Suzanna Sherry, *Telling Stories Out of School: An Essay on Legal Narratives,* 45 STAN L. REV. 807 (1993).

15. *See id., Pedagogy of Narrative Symposium,* 40 J. LEGAL EDUC. 1–250

(1990); James R. Elkins, *A Bibliography of Narrative*, 40 J. LEGAL EDUC. 203 (1990).

16. Fischer, *Reading Literature/Reading Law: Is There a Literary Jurisprudence?*, supra at 139.

17. *See* GREGORY LEYH, ED., LEGAL HERMENEUTICS: HISTORY, THEORY, AND PRACTICE (Berkeley: University of California Press 1992).

18. *See* STANLEY FISH, DOING WHAT COMES NATURALLY: CHANGE, RHETORIC, AND THE PRACTICE OF THEORY IN LITERARY AND LEGAL STUDIES (Durham, N.C.: Duke University Press 1989).

19. *See* Fiss, *Objectivity and Interpretation, supra.*

20. *See* Levinson, *Law As Literature, supra.*

21. Richard H. Weisberg, *Family Feud: A Response to Robert H. Weisberg on Law and Literature*, 1 YALE J. L. & HUMAN. 76 (1988).

22. *Id.* at 77.

23. JAMES BOYD WHITE, HERACLES' BOW XII (Madison: University of Wisconsin Press 1985).

24. J. B. White, *Law and Literature: 'No Manifesto,'* 39 MERCER. L. REV. 739, 741 (1988).

25. *See* RICHARD WEISBERG, THE FAILURE OF THE WORD, *supra;* Richard H. Weisberg, *Text into Theory: A Literary Approach to the Constitution,* 20 GA. L. REV. 939 (1986).

26. *See* R. DWORKIN, *How Law Is Like Literature, in* A MATTER OF PRINCIPLE (Cambridge, Mass.: Harvard University Press 1985). STANLEY FISH, IS THERE A TEXT IN THIS CLASS? THE AUTHORITY OF INTERPRETATIVE COMMUNITIES (Cambridge, Mass.: Harvard University Press 1980). See also *Symposium on Law and Literature*, 60 TEX. L. REV. (1982); *Interpretative Symposium*, 58 S. CAL. L. REV. (1985).

27. *See* Ward, *Law and Literature, supra.*

28. RICHARD POSNER, LAW AND LITERATURE: A MISUNDERSTOOD RELATION 271–81 (Cambridge, Mass.: Harvard University Press 1988). Posner has recently revisited the law-and-literature movement in RICHARD A. POSNER, OVERCOMING LAW (Cambridge, Mass.: Harvard University Press 1995) and appears to be more tentative in his criticism of the specific intersections of law · *and* literature. Nonetheless, Posner continues to believe that literary approaches to legal studies are inferior when compared to the empirical approach of economics.

29. *See* RICOEUR, THE RULE OF METAPHOR (London: Routledge 1978); P. RICOEUR, HERMENEUTICS AND THE HUMAN SCIENCES (Cambridge, U.K.: Cambridge University Press 1981).

30. *See, e.g.,* D. BELL, AND WE ARE NOT SAVED: THE ELUSIVE QUEST FOR RACIAL JUSTICE (New York: Basic Books 1987) (employing narrative to debate civil rights issues); R. Delgado, *Storytelling for Oppositionists and Others: A Plea for Narrative*, 87 MICH. L. REV. 2411 (1989) (using narrative to examine problems of racial reform); Mari S. Matsuda, *Looking to*

*the Bottom: Critical Legal Studies and Reparations,* 22 HARV. C.R.-C.L. L. REV. 323 (1987) (using narrative to reveal how the experiences of people of color are excluded in legal discussions); K. Abrams, *Hearing the Call of Stories,* 79 CAL. L. REV. 971 (1991) (using narrative to advance feminist legal theory).

31. T. SHAFFER AND J. ELKINS, SOLVING PROBLEMS AND TELLING STORIES IN LEGAL INTERVIEWING AND COUNSELING 22–45 (St. Paul, Minn.: West Publishers 1987). *See also* J. Elkins, *The Quest for Meaning: Narrative Accounts of Legal Education,* 38 J. LEGAL EDUC. 577 (1988); J. Elkins, *On the Emergence of Narrative Jurisprudence: The Humanistic Perspective Finds a New Path,* 9 LEGAL STUD. F. 123 (1985).

32. Stanley Fish, *Fish v. Fiss,* 36 STAN. L. REV. 1325, 1345 (1984); quoted in Ward, *Law and Literature, supra* at 49.

33. *See* Richard H. Weisberg, *How Judges Speak: Some Lessons on Adjudication in Billy Budd, Sailor with Application to Justice Rehnquist,* 57 N.Y.U. L. REV. 1 (1982). *See also* WEISBERG, POETHICS AND OTHER STRATEGIES OF LAW & LITERATURE, *supra.*

34. Richard H. Weisberg, *Entering with a Vengeance: Posner on Law and Literature,* 41 STAN. L. REV. 1597, 1614 (reviewing R. POSNER, LAW AND LITERATURE: A MISUNDERSTOOD RELATION, *supra*).

35. *Id.* at 1616.

36. *See* Weisberg, *How Judges Speak, supra. See also* Elizabeth Fajans and Mary Falk, *Against the Tyranny of Paraphrase: Talking Back to Texts,* 78 CORNELL L. REV. 163 (1993).

37. Weisberg, *How Judges Speak, supra.*

38. HERMAN MELVILLE, BILLY BUDD, SAILOR 44 (H. Hayford and M. Sealts, eds.) (Chicago: University of Chicago Press 1962).

39. *Id.* at 61. *See also* Weisberg, *How Judges Speak, supra* at 8.

40. *See* MELVILLE, BILLY BUDD, SAILOR, *supra* at 72–73.

41. *Id.* at 98.

42. *Id.*

43. *See* Weisberg, *How Judges Speak, supra* at 34–42. Weisberg defines the concept of "considerate communication" in relation to three elements: "(1) that the communicator's perception of the audience's well-being stand uppermost in his mind, whatever the ancillary motivations for the speech; (2) that whatever factual distortions occur involve predominantly *omissions,* or, at the worst, trivial misstatements of fact; and (3) that the communicator faithfully convey the essence of the underlying reality he is discussing (either through overt language, or tonal or structural elements), despite the omissions or mild misrepresentation of detail." *Id.* at 35.

44. *Id.* at 34–42.

45. *Id.* at 35.

46. *Id.*

47. *Id.* at 34–58. Billy Budd was convicted of murdering an officer when he

violently struck him after refusing to answer in response to a direct order. Billy's silence and his violent response were caused by his inability to speak at the moment.

48. *See* Richard H. Weisberg, *Three Lessons from Law and Literature*, 27 LOY. L.A. L. REV. 285, 289 (1993).

49. *See* Weisberg, *How Judges Speak, supra* at 43. Weisberg examines how Justice Rehnquest's opinion in Paul v. Davis, 424 U.S. 693 (1976), is a "brilliant contemporary example of narrative prose in the service of the adjudicator's unspoken desires." Weisberg, *How Judges Speak, supra* at 43. The case involved the distribution of a police bulletin of "Active Shoplifters" to local merchants, warning them of possible shoplifters. The plaintiff Edward Charles Davis was named in the bulletin even though the charges of shoplifting against him were dropped six days after the bulletin was distributed. Davis then commenced a civil rights action against Paul, the chief of police. In finding that Davis's lawsuit failed to establish a viable claim under the civil rights law, Weisberg shows how Justice Rehnquist used a form of narrative in his opinion not unlike the narrative used to justify Billy Budd's fate in the mutiny trial in BILLY BUDD, SAILOR. As Weisberg explained: "Justice Rhenquist continue[d] to depict Davis as opposing, in turn, the basic premises of the federal system, the police who [were] trying 'to calm the fears of an aroused populace,' the natural limits of legal liability, and the studious reflectiveness of the Court itself." *Id.* at 53. Justice Rehnquist is not considerate of his readers because, as Weisberg claims, he distorts the record and the reliance of legal precedent to achieve his own subjective desires. *Id.* at 45–58.

50. *Id.* at 43–52.

51. *See also* Elizabeth Fajans and Mary Falk, *Against the Tyranny of Paraphrase, supra* at 196–201 (discussing the significance of considerate communication in reader-response theories of legal interpretation).

52. *See* Richard H. Weisberg, *Legal Rhetoric under Stress: The Example of Vichy*, 12 CARDOZO L. REV. 1371 (1991).

53. *See* WEISBERG, POETHICS, *supra* at 16–17.

54. Richard Delgado, *Storytelling for Oppositionists and Others: A Plea for Narrative, supra* at 2414; *see also* Farber and Sherry, *Telling Stories Out of School: An Essay on Legal Narrative, supra* at 825.

55. *See* Mark Tushnet, *The Degradation of Constitutional Discourse*, 81 GEO. L.J. 251 (1992).

56. *Id.*

57. *See* BELL, AND WE ARE NOT SAVED: THE ELUSIVE QUEST FOR RACIAL JUSTICE, *supra.*

58. In this sense, the book is characteristic of other narratives found within African-American literature. *See* TONI MORRISON, BELOVED (New York: NAL/Dutton 1987).

59. Linda R. Hirshman, *Bronte, Bloom, and Bork: An Essay on the Moral Education of Judges*, 137 U. PA. L. REV. 177, 179 (1988).

60. *But see* Tushnet, *The Degradation of Constitutional Discourse, supra* at n. 55.
61. STEPHEN L. CARTER, REFLECTIONS OF AN AFFIRMATIVE ACTION BABY (New York: Basic Books 1991).
62. *Id.* at 48–49.
63. PATRICIA J. WILLIAMS, THE ALCHEMY OF RACE AND RIGHTS (Cambridge, Mass.: Harvard University Press 1991).
64. *Id.* at 128.
65. *Id.* at 126–28.
66. *See, e.g.,* FISH, IS THERE A TEXT IN THIS CLASS?, *supra.*
67. *See* Levinson, *Law as Interpretation, supra.*
68. *Id.* at 686.
69. *See* Fiss, *Objectivity and Interpretation, supra.* Fiss's reaction to Levinson's essay raised the "specter of nihilism"—the fear that "all law is masked power." *Id.* at 740–42.
70. *See* ROBERT BORK, THE TEMPTING OF AMERICA (New York: Free Press 1990); Robert H. Bork, *Neutral Principles and Some First Amendment Problems,* 47 IND. L.J. 1 (1971).
71. *See, e.g.,* Owen M. Fiss, *Objectivity and Interpretation, supra*; Stanley Fish, *Fish v. Fiss, supra.*
72. David Papke, *Problems with an Uninvited Guest, supra* at 1084–85.
73. J. B. White, *Law and Literature: 'No Manifesto,' supra* at 740.
74. Weisberg, *Coming of Age Some More: 'Law and Literature' beyond the Cradle,* 13 NOVA L. REV. 107 (1988); Weisberg, *The Law-Literature Enterprise, supra* at 1.
75. Robin West, *Economic Man and Literary Woman: One Contrast,* 39 MERCER L. REV. 867 (1988); Robin West, *Jurisprudence as Narrative: An Aesthetic Analysis of Modern Legal Theory,* 60 N.Y.U. L. REV. 145 (1985). *See also* Robin West, *Authority, Autonomy, and Choice: The Role of Consent in the Moral and Political Visions of Franz Kafka and Richard Posner,* 99 HARV. L. REV. 384 (1985).
76. POSNER, LAW AND LITERATURE, *supra.*
77. *See, e.g.,* R. Dworkin, *Law As Interpretation,* 60 TEX. L. REV. 527; R. DWORKIN, LAW'S EMPIRE 379–80 (Cambridge, Mass.: Belknap Press of Harvard University Press 1986).
78. *See* Fiss, *Objectivity and Interpretation, supra.*
79. *See* White, *Law as Language: Reading Law and Reading Literature,* 60 TEX. L. REV. 415, 417 (1982). (All that we can expect is that law be interpreted by an "ideal reader.") *Id.*
80. *Id.*
81. *See* Weisberg, *Family Feud: A Response to Robert Weisberg on Law and Literature, supra* at 70.
82. *See* Rosemary J. Coombe, *Same As It Ever Was: Rethinking the Politics of Legal Interpretation,* 34 McGILL L.J. 603, 630–52 (1989).
83. *Id.* at 632.

84. *Id.*
85. *Id.*
86. Fischer, *Reading Literature/Reading Law: Is There a Literary Jurisprudence?, supra* at 156.
87. In other respects, West is distinctly a legal modernist. In her article, *Jurisprudence and Gender*, 55 U. CHI. L. REV. 1 (1988), West argues that women possess an essential human subjectivity that is different from the masculine subjectivity reflected in jurisprudence. *Id.* at 42. As Dennis Patterson has argued, Professor West's theory of women's human subjectivity is "distinctly modernist." Dennis Patterson, *Postmodern/Feminism/Law*, 77 CORNELL L. REV. 254, 284 (1992). The text emphasizes the way West uses literary works to bring out the complex and multiple consciousness of the individual self in her critique of Posner's modernist analysis of law and economics. On this point, West is distinctly postmodern.
88. Patricia J. Williams, *Alchemical Notes: Reconstructory Ideals from Deconstructed Rights*, 22 HARV. C.R.-C.L. L. REV. 401 (1987).
89. *See, e.g.,* Delgado, *Storytelling for Oppositionalists and Others: A Plea for Narrative, supra*; Matsuda, *Looking to the Bottom: Critical Legal Studies and Reparations, supra*; Abrams, *Hearing the Call of Stories, supra.*
90. See *Symposium, Legal Storytelling*, 87 MICH. L. REV. 2073 (1989).
91. *See* Farber and Sherry, *Telling Stories Out of School: An Essay on Legal Narratives, supra.*
92. *See* Stephanie B. Goldberg, *The Law, a New Theory Holds, Has a White Voice*, NEW YORK TIMES, July 17, 1992, at A23.
93. *See* Kimberle W. Crenshaw, *Foreword: Toward a Race-Conscious Pedagogy in Legal Education*, 11 NAT'L BLACK L.J. 1 (1989).
94. *See* Stanley Fish, *Working on the Chain Gang: Interpretation in the Law and in Literary Criticism*, CRITICAL INQUIRY, vol. 9 (1982); Stanley Fish, *Fish v. Fiss, supra*; Stanley Fish, *Dennis Martinez and the Uses of Theory*, 96 YALE L.J. 1773 (1987).
95. *See* Thomas Morawetz, *Understanding Disagreement, the Root Issue of Jurisprudence: Applying Wittgenstein to Positivism, Critical Theory and Judging*, 141 U. PA. L. REV. 371 (1992).
96. *See* RICHARD RORTY, PHILOSOPHY AND THE MIRROR OF NATURE 6, 11 (Princeton, N.J.: Princeton University Press 1979).
97. *See* RICHARD RORTY, CONTINGENCY, IRONY AND SOLIDARITY (Cambridge, U.K.: Cambridge University Press 1989).
98. *Id.* at 141–88.
99. *Id.* at 81–84.
100. *Id.* at 97.
101. RICHARD RORTY, CONSEQUENCES OF PRAGMATISM (Minneapolis: University of Minnesota Press 1982).

102. *Id.* at 221. *See also* Scott Brewer, *Introduction: Choosing Sides in the Racial Critiques Debate,* 103 HARV. L. REV. 1844, 1849, n. 20 (1990).

103. *Id.*

104. *Id.* at 220.

105. *Id.*

106. *See* Milner S. Ball, *The Legal Academy and Minority Scholars,* 103 HARV. L. REV. 1855, 1859, n. 30 (1990) ("Stories create worlds, characters, and experiences and invite us to recreate them in good readings"). *Id.*

107. RORTY, CONSEQUENCES OF PRAGMATISM, *supra* at 160.

108. *See* Thomas C. Grey, *Holmes and Legal Pragmatism,* 41 STAN. L. REV. 787, 789 at n. 12 (1989).

109. *Id.* at 97.

110. RORTY, CONTINGENCY, IRONY AND SOLIDARITY, *supra* at 81.

111. Joseph W. Singer, *The Player and the Cards: Nihilism and Legal Theory,* 94 YALE L.J. 1, 35 (1984).

112. Martha Minow and Elizabeth V. Spelman, *In Context,* 63 S. CAL. L. REV. 1597, 1611 (1990).

113. *See* RORTY, PHILOSOPHY AND THE MIRROR OF NATURE, *supra;* RICHARD A. POSNER, OVERCOMING LAW (Cambridge, Mass.: Harvard University Press 1995); Morawetz, *Understanding Disagreement, the Root Issue of Jurisprudence, supra.*

114. *See* Thomas Grey, *Hear the Other Side: Wallace Stevens and Pragmatist Legal Theory,* 63 S. CAL. L. REV. 1569, 1591 (1990).

115. *See* FISH, IS THERE A TEXT IN THIS CLASS?, *supra* at 14.

116. *See, e.g.,* Morawetz, *Understanding Disagreement, supra.*

117. *See* WEISBERG, POETHICS AND OTHER STRATEGIES OF LAW AND LITERATURE, *supra* at 117–23.

118. *See* Gary Peller, *The Discourse of Constitutional Degradation,* 81 GEO. L. REV. 313, 337–41 (1992).

119. *See* POSNER, LAW AND LITERATURE: A MISUNDERSTOOD RELATION, *supra* at 1.

120. White, *Law and Literature: 'No Manifesto,' supra* at 840.

121. Papke, *Problems with an Uninvited Guest, supra* at 1083.

122. *Id.* at 1086. *See, generally,* T. Chase, *Lawyers and Popular Culture: A Review of Mass Media Portrayals of American Attorneys,* 1986 AM. B. FOUND. RES. J. 281; T. Chase, *Toward a Theory of Popular Culture,* 1986 WIS. L. REV. 527; J. Jaff, *Law and Lawyers in Pop Music: A Reason for Self-Reflection,* 40 U. MIAMI L. REV. 659 (1986); Leonard, *From Perry Mason to Kurt Waldheim: The Pursuit of Justice in Contemporary Film and Television,* 12 LEGAL STUD. 377 (1988); G. Minda, *Phenomenology, Tina Turner and the Law,* 16 N. MEX. L. REV. 479 (1986); R. Post, *On the Popular Image of the Lawyer: Reflections on a Dark Glass,* 75 CAL. L. REV. 379 (1987).

123. See Coombe, *"Same As It Ever Was"*: *Rethinking the Politics of Legal Interpretation, supra* at 632.
124. See Fischer, *Reading Literature/Reading Law: Is There a Literary Jurisprudence?, supra* at 153, citing WEISBERG, POETHICS AND OTHER STRATEGIES OF LAW AND LITERATURE, *supra* at 117.
125. Fischer, *Reading Literature/Reading Law, supra* at 153.
126. Weisberg, *Three Lessons from Law and Literature, supra*.
127. *Id.* at 302.
128. See WEISBERG, POETHICS AND OTHER STRATEGIES OF LAW AND LITERATURE, *supra* at 119.

## Notes to Chapter 9

1. Mari J. Matsuda, *Looking to the Bottom: Critical Legal Studies and Reparations*, 22 HARV. C.R.-C. L. REV. 323, 325 (1987). For a bibliography of the relevant literature, *see* Richard Delgado and Jean Stefancic, *Critical Race Theory: An Annotated Bibliography*, 79 VA. L. REV. 461 (1993).
2. Jerome M. Culp, Jr., *Toward a Black Legal Scholarship: Race and Original Understanding*, 1991 DUKE L.J. 39, 40 (1991).
3. *Id.* See also Richard Delgado, *The Imperial Scholar: Reflections on a Review of Civil Rights Literature*, 132 U. PA. L. REV. 561 (1984) [hereinafter *The Imperial Scholar*]; Richard Delgado, *The Imperial Scholar Revisited: How to Marginalize Outsider Writing, Ten Years Later*, 140 U. PA. L. REV. 1349 (1992).
4. *See* Robin D. Barnes, *Race Consciousness: The Thematic Content of Racial Distinctiveness in Critical Race Scholarship*, 103 HARV. L. REV. 1864, 1864 (1990).
5. *See* Kimberle Williams Crenshaw, *Race, Reform, and Retrenchment: Transformation and Legitimation in Antidiscrimination Law*, 101 HARV. L. REV. 1331 (1988). A central tenet of this movement is premised on the view that the law of civil rights is culturally and ideologically biased against people of color. The bias in American law is said to be the consequence of rational meritocratic judgments that purport to evaluate legal questions of race under "color-blind," *i.e.*, racially neutral, legal standards.
6. *See* Peggy C. Davis, *Law as Microaggression*, 98 YALE L.J. 1559 (1989) (highlighting the racists attitudes in the criminal justice system).
7. *See* Harlon L. Dalton, *The Clouded Prism*, 22 HARV. C.R.-C.L. L. REV. 435 (1987).
8. *See* Richard Delgado, *When a Story Is Just a Story: Does Voice Really Matter?*, 76 VA. L. REV. 95 (1990).
9. *See* Patricia J. Williams, *Alchemical Notes: Reconstructing Ideals from Deconstructed Rights*, 22 HARV. C.R.-C.L. L. REV. 401 (1987).
10. Derrick Bell's imaginative narrative in *The Unspoken Limit on Affirmative*

*Action: The Chronicle of the DeVine Gift, in* AND WE ARE NOT SAVED 140–61 (New York: Basic Books 1987), is an early example of this genre of critical race literature.

11. *See supra* note 3 at 561. Delgado is a professor of law at the University of Colorado.

12. *Id.* at 566.

13. *See* Richard Delgado, *The Ethereal Scholar: Does Critical Legal Studies Have What Minorities Want?*, 22 HARV. C.R.-C.L. REV. 301, 307 (1987). Critical race theory thus emerged in part from the "critique of the critique" of progressive white scholars within the CLS movement.

14. *See* Crenshaw, *Race, Reform, and Retrenchment, supra* note 5.

15. The intellectual history of critical race theory is as old as the question of race in American history. Critical race theorists attempt to resurrect that history by uncovering the stereotypes and racial biases in the early history of America. S. DRAKE, BLACK FOLK: HERE AND THERE (Los Angeles: UCLA Center for Afro-American Studies 1987); Neil Gotanda, *Origins of Racial Categorization in Colonial Virginia, 1619–1705* (1980) (LL.M. thesis, Harvard Law School).

16. *See* DERRICK BELL, AND WE ARE NOT SAVED: THE ELUSIVE QUEST FOR RACIAL JUSTICE (New York: Basic Books 1987). Derrick Bell resigned from Harvard Law School in protest of the law faculty's failure to hire more minority teachers. He is now a visiting professor of law at New York University School of Law. *See* D. Bell, CONFRONTING AUTHORITY: REFLECTIONS OF AN ARDENT PROTESTER (Boston: Beacon Press 1994).

17. *See, e.g.,* THOMAS SOWELL, BLACK EDUCATION: MYTHS AND TRAGEDIES (New York: McKay 1972).

18. This discussion draws from Crenshaw's article, *Race, Reform and Retrenchment, supra.*

19. THOMAS SOWELL, CIVIL RIGHTS, RHETORIC OR REALITY? 109 (New York: Morrow 1985).

20. *Id.* at 37–48.

21. *See* chap. 2, *infra.*

22. SOWELL, CIVIL RIGHTS, *supra* at 119.

23. *See, e.g.,* Derrick Bell, *Foreword,* 61 OR. L. REV. 151 (1982).

24. Derrick Bell, *Foreword: The Civil Rights Chronicles,* 99 HARV. L. REV. 4, 10 (1985).

25. 347 U.S. 483 (1954).

26. Bell has advanced an *interest-convergence thesis* to explain *Brown:* the decision in favor of the interests of African Americans was made because it converged with the interests of the white majority. *See* Derrick A. Bell Jr., *Brown v. Board of Education and the Interest-Convergence Dilemma,* 93 HARV. L. REV. 518 (1980) (arguing that the *Brown* decision converged with the interests of the majority of whites who: [1] wanted to enhance the "immediate credibility of America's struggle with Communist countries to

win the hearts and minds of the emerging third world peoples"; [2] wanted to appease African-Americans, especially World War II veterans, who faced continuing discrimination; and [3] "realized that the South could make the transition from a rural, plantation society to the sunbelt with all its potential and profit only when it ended the struggle to remain divided by state-sponsored segregation." *Id.* at 524–25).

27. *See id.*
28. Gary Peller, *Notes Toward a Postmodern Nationalism,* 1992 U. ILL. L. REV. 1095 (1992).
29. Crenshaw, *Race, Reform and Retrenchment, supra* at 93.
30. *See, e.g.,* Regina D. Austin, *Sapphire Bound,* 1989 WIS. L. REV. 539 (1989); Robin Barnes, *Race Consciousness: The Thematic Content of Racial Distinctiveness in Critical Race Scholarship,* 103 HARV. L. REV. 1864 (1989); Kimberle Crenshaw, *Foreword: Toward a Race-Conscious Pedagogy in Legal Education,* 11 NAT'L BLACK L.J. 1 (1989); Anthony E. Cook, *Beyond Critical Legal Studies: The Reconstructive Theology of Dr. Martin Luther King, Jr.,* 103 HARV. L. REV. 985 (1990); Richard Delgado, *When a Story Is Just a Story: Does Voice Really Matter?,* 76 VA. L. REV. 95 (1990); Gerald Torres, *Critical Race Theory: The Decline of the Universalist Ideal and the Hope of Plural Justice—Some Observations and Questions of an Emerging Phenomenon,* 75 MINN. L. REV. 993 (1991); John O. Calmore, *Critical Race Theory, Archie Shepp, and Fire Music: Securing an Authentic Intellectual Life in a Multi-Cultural World,* 65 SO. CAL. L. REV. 2129 (1992).
31. Delgado, *The Imperial Scholar, supra.*
32. *Id.* at 563.
33. Mari Matsuda, *Affirmative Action and Legal Knowledge: Planting Seeds in Plowed-Up Ground,* 11 HARV. WOMEN'S L.J. 1, 2–4 & n. 12 (1988). Matsuda is a professor of law at Georgetown Law Center. She has been an active participant in the feminist, critical legal studies, and critical race theory movements.
34. Matsuda, *Looking to the Bottom: Critical Legal Studies and Reparations, supra* at 326.
35. *Id.* at 346.
36. *See* Randall L. Kennedy, *Racial Critiques of Legal Academia,* 102 HARV. L. REV. 1745, 1745–46 (1989).
37. *Id.* at 1746. According to Professor Randall L. Kennedy, the racial distinctiveness thesis posits: (1) "that minority scholars, like all people of color in the United States, have experienced racial oppression;" (2) "that this experience causes minority scholars to view the world with a different perspective than their white colleagues;" and (3) "that this different perspective displays itself in valuable ways in the work of minority scholars." *Id.*
38. Delgado, *The Imperial Scholar, supra* at 566–73.
39. *See* Matsuda, *Affirmative Action and Legal Knowledge: Planting Seeds in Plowed-Up Ground, supra.*

40. Matsuda, *Looking to the Bottom: Critical Legal Studies and Reparations,* *supra* at 324.
41. *See, e.g.,* Richard Delgado, *Rodrigo's Eighth Chronicle; Black Crime, White Fears—On the Social Construction of Threat,* 80 VA. L. REV. 503 (1994).
42. *See, generally,* Sharon Elizabeth Rush, *Understanding Diversity,* 42 FLA. L. REV. 1, 22 (1990). *See also* Jerome M. Culp, Jr., *Toward a Black Legal Scholarship: Race and Original Understandings,* 1991 DUKE L.J. 39, 103 (1991).
43. *See* Mari J. Matsuda, *Public Response to Racist Speech: Considering the Victim's Story,* 87 MICH. L. REV. 2320, 2324 (1989).
44. *See, e.g.,* Crenshaw, *Race, Reform and Retrenchment, supra* at nn. 96–136.
45. *Id.*
46. *Id.* at 1356.
47. *Id.*
48. *Id.* at 1357.
49. *Id.*
50. Alan D. Freeman, *Legitimizing Racial Discrimination through Antidiscrimination Law: A Critical Review of Supreme Court Doctrine,* 62 MINN. L. REV. 1049 (1978).
51. *Id.* at 1052.
52. Crenshaw, *Race, Reform and Retrenchment, supra* at 1360.
53. *Id.* at 1361–64.
54. *Id.* at 1364. As a result of the minority critique, CLS scholars developed their own critical race theories on the question of race and affirmative action. Duncan Kennedy's essay, *A Cultural Pluralist Case for Affirmative Action in Legal Academia,* 1990 DUKE L.J. 705 (1990), and Gary Peller's essay, *Race Consciousness,* 1990 DUKE L.J. 758 (1990), are good examples of the new race-conscious perspective in CLS criticism.
55. Randall L. Kennedy, *Racial Critiques of Legal Academia,* 102 HARV. L. REV. 1745 (1989) [hereinafter *Racial Critiques*]. Kennedy is a professor of law at Harvard Law School.
56. *Id.* at 1796.
57. *Id.*
58. *Id.*
59. *Id.* at 1794–95.
60. *Id.* at 1793.
61. *Id.*
62. *Id.* at 1794–95. Kennedy stated that "the use of *race* as a proxy is specially disfavored because, even when relatively accurate as a signifier of the trait sought to be identified, racial proxies are especially prone to misuse. " *Id.* at 1794. He further noted that "[b]y requesting that white scholars leave the field or restrict their contributions to it, Delgado seems to want to transform the study of race-relations law into a zone of limited intellectual competition." *Id.* at 1795.

63. *See* Richard Delgado, *Mindset and Metaphor*, 103 HARV. L. REV. 1872, 1874 & n. 20 (1990).
64. *See* Derrick Bell, *Letter to the Editor*, NEW YORK TIMES, Jan. 26, 1990, at A30, col. 6. *See also* Scott Brewer, *Introduction: Choosing Sides in the Racial Critiques Debate*, 103 HARV. L. REV. 1844, 1846 (1990).
65. See *Colloquy*, 103 HARV. L. REV. 1844–86 (1990) (comments by Professors Scott Brewer, Milner S. Ball, Robin D. Barnes, Richard Delgado, and Leslie G. Espinoza).
66. Brewer, *Introduction: Choosing Sides in the Racial Critiques Debate, supra* at 1844, 1851. Brewer went on to state: "Surely it is similarly possible for Kennedy and his critics to share that broad goal [the goal of equal respect and concern] while disagreeing vigorously over the method of reaching it. And if they are struggling for a shared goal, might they not both be better off acknowledging that?" *Id.*
67. *See* Milner S. Ball, *The Legal Academy and Minority Scholars*, 103 HARV. L. REV. 1855, 1857 (1990), *citing* C. Geertz, LOCAL KNOWLEDGE 155 (New York: Basic Books 1983).
68. Robin D. Barnes, *Race Consciousness: The Thematic Content of Racial Distinctiveness in Critical Race Scholarship*, 103 HARV. L. REV. 1864, 1869–70 (1990).
69. Kennedy, *A Cultural Pluralist Case for Affirmative Action in Legal Academia, supra* at 705. *See also* Gary Peller, *Race Consciousness*, 1990 DUKE L.J. 758.
70. Kennedy, *A Cultural Pluralist Case for Affirmative Action in Legal Academia, supra* at 726–27.
71. *Id.* at 705.
72. Duncan Kennedy's thesis is that rational meritocratic judgments cannot be culturally and ideologically neutral and, therefore, race consciousness of the author is inevitable. *See* Kennedy, *A Cultural Pluralist Case for Affirmative Action, supra* at 705.
73. *See* Alex M. Johnson, Jr., *The New Voice of Color*, 100 YALE L.J. 2007, 2020 (1991) (suggesting that voice of color scholarship is "undergoing evolution analogous to the theoretical diversification within Critical Feminist Theory." *Id.*).
74. *See* Robin West, *Jurisprudence and Gender*, 55 U. CHI. L. REV. 1 (1988); Richard A. Wasserstrom, *Racism, Sexism, and Preferential Treatment: An Approach to the Topics*, 24 U.C.L.A. L. Rev. 581 (1977). *See also* Robert E. Scott, *Chaos Theory and the Justice Paradox*, 35 WM. & MARY L. REV. 329, 345, n. 85 (1993).
75. Johnson, *The New Voice of Color, supra* at 2022.
76. *Id.* at 2024.
77. Crenshaw, *Race, Reform and Retrenchment, supra* at 1332, n. 2.
78. Patricia J. Williams, *Alchemic Notes: Reconstructing Ideals from Deconstructed Rights*, 22 HARV. C.R.-C.L. L. REV. 401, 404 n. 4 (1987).
79. Catharine MacKinnon, *Feminism, Marxism, Method, and the State: An*

*Agenda for Theory,* 7 Signs: J. Women in Culture & Soc'y 515, 516 (1982).

80. Matsuda, *Looking to the Bottom: Critical Legal Studies and Reparations, supra.*

81. See Delgado, *Storytelling for Oppositionists and Others: A Plea for Narrative,* 87 Mich. L. Rev. 2411 (1989); Delgado, *When a Story Is Just a Story: Does Voice Really Mater?, supra;* Delgado, *The Imperial Scholar: Reflections on a Review of Civil Rights Literature, supra.*

82. See J. Derrida, Of Grammatology 49 (Baltimore: Johns Hopkins University Press 1977). See also J. Balkin, *Deconstructive Practice and Legal Theory,* 96 Yale L.J. 743, 747 (1987).

83. *Id.* at n. 155.

84. *Id.* at nn. 156–57.

85. *Id.* at 748.

86. Crenshaw, *Race, Reform and Retrenchment, supra* at 1372.

87. *Id.* at n. 200.

88. *Id.* at 1387.

89. *Id.* at 1386.

90. A. Gramsci, Selections from the Prison Notebooks (Q. Hoare and G. Smith, trans.) (London: Lawrence & Wishart 1971).

91. See R. Gordon, *New Developments in Legal Theory, in* The Politics of Law: A Progressive Critique 284–86 (D. Kairys, ed.) (New York: Pantheon Books 1982); Crenshaw, *Race, Reform and Retrenchment, supra* at n. 90.

92. Crenshaw, *Race, Reform and Retrenchment, supra* at 1356 (discussing the work of Gordon, Tushnet, and Gable).

93. *Id.* at 1358. Crenshaw explained: "Black people are boxed in largely because there is a consensus among many whites that the oppression of Blacks is legitimate. This is where consensus and coercion can be understood together; ideology convinces one group that the coercive domination of another is legitimate. It matters little whether the coerced group rejects the dominant ideology and can offer a competing conception of the world; if they have been labeled 'other' by the dominant ideology, they are not heard." *Id.* at 1358–59.

94. As Crenshaw explained: "The challenge for Blacks may be to pursue strategies that confront the beliefs held *about* them by whites. For Blacks, such strategies may take the form of reinforcing some aspects of the dominant ideology in attempts to become participants in the dominant discourse rather than outsiders defined, objectified, and reified by that discourse. In this sense, the civil rights movement might be considered as an attempt to deconstruct the image of 'the Negro' in the white mind. By forcing the political system to respond to Black demands, Blacks rejected images of complacency and docility that had been invoked by some whites to dismiss Black demands." *Id.* at n. 103.

95. *Id.* at 1371.

96. *Id.* at nn. 157–90.
97. *Id.* at 1381.
98. *See* Gary Peller, *Race Consciousness,* 1990 Duke L.J. 758 (1990).
99. *See* Peller, *Postmodern Nationalism, supra* at 1095.
100. *Id.* at 1097.
101. *Id.* at 1096.
102. *Id.* at 1100. *See also* Peller, *Race Consciousness, supra;* Kennedy, *A Cultural Pluralist Case for Affirmative Action, supra* at 705.
103. *Id.* at 1100.
104. *See* Robert S. Chang, *Toward an Asian American Legal Scholarship: Critical Race Theory, Post-Structuralism, and Narrative Space,* 81 Cal. L. Rev. 1243, 1245 (1993). The emergence of an Asian American voice in legal scholarship thus disproves the recent observation of Professor Alex M. Johnson, Jr., that "although critical race theorists come in many colors with many different ethnic backgrounds, by and large its theorists have thus far been unable to expand their voice beyond the prototypical Black experience that is socioeconomically class-based and rooted in oppression." Johnson, *The New Voice of Color, supra* at 2039.
105. *Id.,* quoting Culp, *Toward a Black Legal Scholarship, supra* at 40.
106. *Id.* at 1247.
107. *Id.* at 1258.
108. *See* Reginald Leamon Robinson, *"The Other against Itself": Deconstructing the Violent Discourse between Korean and African Americans,* 67 So. Cal. L. Rev. 15 (1993); Jerome M. Culp Jr., *Notes from California: Rodney King and the Race Question,* 70 Denv. U. L. Rev. 199, 202 nn. 8–9 (1993). *See, generally, Colloquy: Racism in the Wake of the Los Angles Riots,* 70 Denv. U. L. Rev. 187 (1993).
109. Chang, *Toward an Asian American Legal Scholarship, supra* at 1267.
110. Neil Gotanda, *A Critique of "Our Constitution Is Color-Blind,"* 44 Stan. L. Rev. 1, 68 (1991).
111. *Id.* at 66–68.
112. Johnson, *The New Voice of Color, supra* at 2055.
113. *Id.*
114. *See, e.g.,* Paulette M. Caldwell, *A Hair Piece: Perspectives on the Intersection of Race and Gender,* 1991 Duke L.J. 365 (1991); Angela P. Harris, *Race and Essentialism in Feminist Legal Theory,* 42 Stan. L. Rev. 581 (1990); Pamela J. Smith, *We Are Not Sisters: African-American Women and the Freedom to Associate and Disassociate,* 66 Tul. L. Rev. 1467 (1992).
115. Kimberle Crenshaw, *Whose Story Is It? Feminist and Antitrust Appropriations of Anita Hill, in* Race-ing Justice, En-gendering power 402 (T. Morrison, ed.) (New York: Pantheon Books 1992).
116. *Id.* at 406.

*Notes to Chapter 10*

1. Peter Schanck, *Understanding Postmodern Thought*, 65 S. CAL. L. REV. 2505 (1992). *See also* BAILEY KUKLIN AND JEFFREY W. STEMPEL, FOUNDATIONS OF THE LAW: AN INTERDISCIPLINARY AND JURISPRUDENTIAL PRIMER 183–84 (St. Paul, Minn.: West Publishing 1994).

2. *See also* Stephen M. Feldman, *Diagnosing Power: Postmodernism in Legal Scholarship and Judicial Practice (with an Emphasis on the Teague Rule against New Rules in Habeas Corpus Cases)*, 88 Nw. U. L. REV. 1046 (1994).

3. Frank H. Easterbrook, *Method, Result, and Authority: A Reply*, 98 HARV. L. REV. 622, 629 (1985) (arguing that the Supreme Court's constitutional decisions have become increasingly coherent as the Court has adopted the L/E perspective). Judge Easterbrook's view of statutory interpretation reflects a public choice theory that views legislation as the product of political bargains. *See* Eleanor M. Fox, *The Politics of Law and Economics in Judicial Decision Making: Antitrust as a Window*, 61 N.Y.U. L. REV. 554, 560 (1986). Moreover, unlike liberal constitutional scholars who advance noneconomic goals such as fairness and justice, Easterbrook can only see efficiency for statutory interpretation. *See id.*

4. *See, e.g.*, Easterbrook, *Method, Result and Authority, supra* (arguing that "scarcity," "choice," and "self-interested conduct" are "the facts of life" which judges must sometimes respond to in legal decision making); *see also* Gary Peller, *The Politics of Reconstruction*, 98 HARV. L. REV. 863, 864 (1985) (describing how "liberal reformist legal thinkers" are challenged by "law-and-economics" adherents' claim to scientific rigor and hardheaded realism about "the way things are").

5. *See, e.g.*, MARK KELMAN, A GUIDE TO CRITICAL LEGAL STUDIES 4–5 (Cambridge, Mass.: Harvard University Press 1987).

6. JAMES B. WHITE, JUSTICE AS TRANSLATION: AN ESSAY IN CULTURAL AND LEGAL CRITICISM xi (Chicago: University of Chicago Press 1990).

7. R. WEISBERG, POETHICS AND OTHER STRATEGIES OF LAW AND LITERATURE 5 (New York: Columbia University Press 1992).

8. *Id.*

9. *See* PATRICIA J. WILLIAMS, THE ALCHEMY OF RACE AND RIGHTS (Cambridge, Mass.: Harvard University Press 1991).

10. *See, e.g.*, Roy Brooks, *Racial Subordination through Formal Equal Opportunity*, 25 SAN DIEGO L. REV. 881 (1988); Kimberle Crenshaw, *Race, Reform and Retrenchment: Transformation and Legitimation in Antidiscrimination Law*, 101 HARV. L. REV. 1331 (1988); Richard Delgado, *Recasting the American Race Problem*, 79 CAL. L. REV. 1389 (1991).

11. Gary Peller, *The Discourse of Constitutional Degradation*, 81 GEO. L.J. 313, 335 (1993).

12. Richard A. Posner, *The Decline of Law as an Autonomous Discipline: 1962–1987*, 100 HARV. L. REV. 761, 762 (1987). Reacting to Judge

Posner's essay, Erwin N. Griswold wrote: "[Judge Richard A. Posner's] essay is thoughtful and penetrating, but it does take me by surprise. It has never occurred to me that the law is an 'autonomous discipline,' and I do not think that was the lore of the Harvard Law School when Judge Posner was a student or at any other time in the twentieth century. It always seemed to me—and I was taught—that the law sought light from any source, and that contributions from other fields were welcome and relevant." Erwin N. Griswold, *Essays Commemorating the One Hundredth Anniversary of the Harvard Law Review: Introduction*, 100 HARV. L. REV. 728, 729–30 (1987).

While it may be true, as former dean Griswold argues, that modern legal scholars look to sources "outside the law" for insight about their subject, modern legal scholars nevertheless rely upon implicit philosophical assumptions about foundationalism; they believe that objectivity, truth, and knowledge can be grounded in some intellectual foundation.

13. Richard A. Posner, *The Decline of Law as an Autonomous Discipline, supra* at 773.

14. *Id.*

15. DUNCAN KENNEDY, SEXY DRESSING, ETC. 68 (Cambridge, Mass.: Harvard University Press 1993).

16. A feminist critique of law and economics would seek to show how the principle of wealth maximization serves to entrench sexism and patriarchal structures by solidifying the position of the status quo. If wealth is maximized in a society structured by the values of patriarchy, then disadvantages resulting from gender differences would probably be worsened. The hand of the dominant class would be strengthened at the expense of the weaker class. Hence, while Chicago School law and economics scholars argue that efficiency or wealth maximization should be the general welfare standard, feminist legal scholars would argue that a broader definition of substantive equality should be the standard.

17. John Henry Schlegel, *Searching for Archimedes—Legal Education, Legal Scholarship, and Liberal Ideology*, 34 J. LEGAL EDUC. 103, 103 (1984).

18. David Ray Papke, *Problems with an Uninvited Guest: Richard A. Posner and the Law and Literature Movement*, 69 B.U. L. REV. 1067 (1989).

19. Anthony E. Cook, *The Spiritual Movement towards Justice*, 1992 U. ILL. L. REV. 1007, 1008.

20. *Id.* at 1009.

21. *See, generally*, Amy Gutmann, *The Challenge of Multiculturalism in Political Ethics*, 22 PHIL. & PUB. AFFAIRS 171 (1993).

22. An early example of gaylaw jurisprudence was Rhonda R. Rivera, *Our Straight-Laced Judges: The Legal Position of Homosexual Persons in the United States*, 30 HASTINGS L.J. 799 (1979).

23. *See* William N. Eskridge, Jr., *A Social Constructionist Critique of Posner's Sex and Reason: Steps toward a Gaylegal Agenda*, 102 YALE L.J. 333, 335 (1992). Eskridge is a law professor at Georgetown Law Center.

24. *Id.*
25. *Id.* at 366.
26. The reference is to the generation of gays and lesbians who came of age during the Stonewall riots in New York City on the nights of June 27 and 28, 1969, following a police raid on a gay bar.
27. *Id.*
28. *Id.*
29. *See* ROBERT A. WILLIAMS, JR., THE AMERICAN INDIAN IN WESTERN LEGAL THOUGHT (New York: Oxford University Press 1990). *See also Symposium: Native American Law,* 28 GEO. L. REV. 299–553 (1994).
30. *See* Kevin J. Worthen, *Sword or Shield: The Past and Future Impact of Western Legal Thought on American Indian Sovereignty,* 104 HARV. L. REV. 1372 (1991). *See also* Joseph W. Singler, *Well Settled? The Increasing Weight of History in American Indian Land Claims,* 28 GEO. L. REV. 481, 485–86 (1994) (illustrating how "the courts have adopted an approach to Indian property rights that has the intended or unintended consequence of treating American Indians as second-class citizens, and even as not fully human").
31. Robert S. Chang, *Toward an Asian American Legal Scholarship: Critical Race Theory, Post-Structuralism, and Narrative Space,* 81 CAL. L. REV. 1241 (1993). *See also* chap. 9, *supra.*
32. *See also* Angela P. Harris, *Race and Essentialism in Feminist Legal Theory,* 42 STAN. L. REV. 581 (1990). *See also* chap. 9, *supra.*
33. *See* KENNEDY, SEXY DRESSING, ETC., *supra* at vii.
34. *Id.*
35. *See* Kimberle Crenshaw, *Demarginalizing the Intersection of Race and Gender in Antidiscrimination Law, Feminist Theory, and Antiracist Politics,* 1989 U. CHI. LEGAL F. 139 (1989).
36. Jules L. Coleman and Judy Kraus, *Rethinking the Theory of Legal Rights,* 95 YALE L.J. 1335 (1986).
37. Some CLS practitioners claim that abstract concepts of rights cannot be rendered determinant by either theory or social context. As Mark Tushnet has claimed: "Specifying a particular right is thus either an act of political rhetoric or a commitment to social transformation." Tushnet, *An Essay on Rights,* 62 TEX. L. REV. 1363, 1380 (1984).
38. *See* Gabel, *The Phenomenology of Rights—Consciousness and the Pact of the Withdrawn Selves,* 62 TEX. L. REV. 1563 (1984); Olsen, *Statutory Rape: A Feminist Critique of Rights Analysis,* 63 TEX. L. REV. 207 (1984). *But see* Williams, *Alchemical Notes: Reconstructed Ideals from Deconstructed Rights,* 22 HARV. C.R.-C.L. L. REV. 401 (1987) (arguing that rights can empower the disadvantaged).
39. Robin West, *Jurisprudence of Gender,* 55 U. CHI. L. REV. 1, 52 (1988).
40. "As a consequence, [the Rule of Law] can be used and occasionally is used to ameliorate the sorrow we feel as a consequence of our alienation, as well as to protect the autonomy we value against the very real threat of annihilation." *Id.*

41. *See* Peter Teachout, W*orlds beyond Theory: Toward the Expression of an Integrative Ethic for Self and Culture,* 83 MICH. L. REV. 849 (1985).
42. *See, e.g.,* RICHARD H. WEISBERG, THE FAILURE OF THE WORD: THE PRO-TAGONIST AS LAWYER IN MODERN FICTION (New Haven: Yale University Press 1984).
43. *See, e.g.,* RONALD DWORKIN, LAW'S EMPIRE (Cambridge, Mass.: Belknap Press of Harvard University Press 1986).
44. *See* Crenshaw, *Demarginalizing the Intersection, supra* at n. 1000.
45. *Id.* at n. 137.
46. David Luban, *Legal Modernism,* 84 MICH. L. REV. 1656, 1663 (1986). "Modernist art is the *determinate* negation of premodernism." *Id.*
47. *Id.*
48. As Luban acknowledges: "I am no fan of the avant-gardist interpretations of modernism. . . . I revere too much of the past—too much art, too much history, too many ideas and institutions—to have any real sympathy with the avant-gardist sensibility." *Id.* at 1681–82.
49. Postmodernists are "ironist philosophers" because they seek to bring out the irony of modern philosophy within an "ironist culture." RICHARD RORTY, CONTINGENCY, IRONY, AND SOLIDARITY 73–94 (New York: Cambridge University Press 1989). Rorty defines an "ironist" as someone who "has radical and continuing doubts about the final vocabulary she currently uses . . . [and] realizes that argument phrased in her vocabulary can neither underwrite nor dissolve these doubts . . . [and] does not think that her vocabulary is closer to reality than others, that it is in touch with a power not herself." *Id.* at 73. Rorty claims that the ironist realizes that modern philosophy "has become more important for the pursuit of private perfection rather than any social task." *Id.* at 94. Rorty's idea of the "ironist theorist" describes the critical stance of those legal critics who have sought to critique the normativity of modern legal thought. See *Symposium: The Critique of Normativity,* 139 U. PA. L. REV. 801–1002 (1991) (papers by Pierre Schlag, Richard Delgado, and Steven Winter). *See also* chap. 12, *infra.*
50. *See* Schanck, *Understanding Postmodern Thought, supra* at 2514 (discussing the strand of postmodernism associated with the poststructuralism of French theorists such as Roland Barthes, Jean Baudrillard, Jacques Derrida, Jacques Lacan, and Jean-François Lyotard). Schanck also identifies a second strand of postmodern thought which he associates with neopragmatism. Schanck explained: "The second strain, neopragmatism, agrees with poststructuralism that language mediates our understanding of the world and that we lack the ability to grasp reality 'as it really is,' but neopragmatism emphasizes the social construction of knowledge and language." *Id.,* citing RICHARD RORTY, CONSEQUENCES OF PRAGMATISM xix–xx (Minneapolis: University of Minnesota Press 1982). For a discussion of the two sides of postmodern thought, *see* chap. 12, *infra.*
51. Dennis Patterson, *Postmodernism/Feminism/Law,* 77 CORNELL L. REV. 254, 276–77 (1992).

52. *See* chap. 6, *supra*.
53. Second-generation law and economics scholars admit that "[m]ost law and economics questions are still open and likely [will] remain so for a long time." Ulen, *Law and Economics: Settled Issues and Open Questions, in* LAW AND ECONOMICS 224–25 (N. Mercuro, ed.) (Boston: Kluwer Academic 1989).
54. *See* Kornhauser, *Legal Rules as Incentives, in* LAW AND ECONOMICS, *supra* at 27.
55. *See Symposium: Law As Literature*, 60 TEX. L. REV. 373–586 (1982).
56. *See, generally*, Anthony E. Cook, *Foreword: Towards a Postmodern Ethic of Service*, 81 GEO. L.J. 2457, 2458 (1993).
57. *See* PAUL FEYERABEND, AGAINST METHOD: OUTLINE OF AN ANARCHISTIC THEORY OF KNOWLEDGE (London: Verso 1978); THOMAS KUHN, THE STRUCTURE OF SCIENTIFIC REVOLUTIONS (Chicago: University of Chicago Press, 2d ed. 1970).
58. During the 1970s, Gilmore reported that it was "clear enough that the great structure of Langdellian jurisprudence crumbled during the period between the two world wars." GRANT GILMORE, THE AGES OF AMERICAN LAW 68 (New Haven: Yale University Press 1977). During this new "Age of Anxiety," the rule skepticism of the legal realist set in motion "[t]he process of disintegration of unitary theory and [the] return toward a pre-Langdellian pluralism." *Id.* at 81. Gilmore found this new form of pre-Langdellian pluralism to be represented in the scholarship of legal realists such as Karl Llewellyn who rejected the Langdellian attempt to reduce law to a finite set of universal principles and instead developed descriptions of "atomized" law based on an understanding of the dynamic of law in context. Jurisprudential studies had thus become fragmented and diversified after the 1970s.
59. *See* GILMORE, THE AGES OF AMERICAN LAW, *supra* at 68.
60. RICHARD A. POSNER, THE PROBLEMS OF JURISPRUDENCE 428 (Cambridge, Mass.: Harvard University Press 1990). *See also* Richard A. Posner, *The Decline of Law as an Autonomous Discipline: 1962–1987*, 100 HARV. L. REV. 761, 762 (1987).
61. *Id.* at 107–8.
62. *See* chap. 12, *infra*. Contemporary critics find that Posner is still willing to "embrace the formalism of the economic analysis of law." Neil Duxbury, *Pragmatism without Politics*, 55 MOD. L. REV. 594, 605 (1992).
63. The term "epistemological break" is used by Cornel West to describe how Unger's critical legal scholarship has moved from a "a self-styled neo-Aristotelian perspective (or a teleological and essentialist view) to a full-blown antifoundational orientation." WEST, KEEPING FAITH: PHILOSOPHY AND RACE IN AMERICA 208 (Reading, Mass.: Routledge 1993).
64. RICHARD A. POSNER, ECONOMIC ANALYSIS OF LAW (Boston: Little, Brown, & Co., 2d ed. 1977).
65. ROBERTO M. UNGER, KNOWLEDGE AND POLITICS (New York: Free Press 1975).

66. POSNER, THE PROBLEMS OF JURISPRUDENCE, *supra*.
67. ROBERTO M. UNGER, CRITICAL LEGAL STUDIES MOVEMENT (Cambridge, Mass.: Harvard University Press 1986).
68. RONALD DWORKIN, TAKING RIGHTS SERIOUSLY (Cambridge, Mass.: Harvard University Press 1977).
69. *See* DWORKIN, LAW'S EMPIRE *supra*.
70. JOHN RAWLS, POLITICAL LIBERALISM (New York: Columbia University Press 1993).
71. *Id.* at xvi. *See also* JOHN RAWLS, A THEORY OF JUSTICE (Cambridge, Mass.: Harvard University Press 1971).
72. For example, in 1989, at a meeting of the Jurisprudence section of the American Association of Law Schools, Owen Fiss publicly retracted much of his early criticism of CLS and L/E in his essay *The Death of the Law?* 72 CORNELL L. REV. 1 (1986), and affirmed what he saw as the positive contributions of the new jurisprudential movements. *See* Jurisprudence Meeting, AALS Conference, San Antonio, Texas, January 1989 (unpublished speech) (recorded transcript on file with author). In 1989, I was the chair of the Jurisprudence section of the AALS where Fiss reported what he saw in the academy in 1990, stating "oddly enough I think my mood is more upbeat." *Id.*
73. *See, e.g., Symposium—Beyond Critique: Law, Culture, and the Politics of Form,* 69 TEX. L. REV. 1595–2041 (1991); *Symposium: The Critique of Normativity,* 139 U. PA. L. REV. 801–1075; *Symposium: Frontiers in Legal Thought,* 1990 DUKE L.J. 375 (1990).

## Notes to Chapter 11

1. *See* THOMAS S. KUHN, THE STRUCTURE OF SCIENTIFIC REVOLUTIONS 77–91 (Chicago: University of Chicago Press, 2d ed. 1970).
2. *See, e.g.,* Paul D. Carrington, *Of Law and the River,* 34 J. LEGAL EDUC. 222 (1984).
3. *See, e.g.,* Owen M. Fiss, *The Death of Law?,* 72 CORNELL L. REV. 1 (1986).
4. *See, e.g.,* BRUCE ACKERMAN, RECONSTRUCTING AMERICAN LAW (Cambridge, Mass. Harvard University Press 1984).
5. Carrington, *Of Law and the River, supra.*
6. *See* Peter W. Martin, *"Of Law and the River" and of Nihilism and Academic Freedom,* 35 J. LEGAL EDUC. 1 (1985).
7. Carrington, *Of Law and the River, supra* at 227.
8. *See, e.g., Robert W. Gordon to Paul D. Carrington,* 35 J. LEGAL EDUC. 1 (1985); *Paul Brest to Phillip E. Johnson,* 35 J. LEGAL EDUC. 16 (1985).
9. *Guido Calabresi to Paul D. Carrington,* 35 J. LEGAL EDUC. 23 (1985).
10. *Owen M. Fiss to Paul D. Carrington,* 35 J. LEGAL EDUC. 24 (1985). "Every law school should confront the question of whether law exists, and it is of the essence of academic freedom to allow all sides to speak, even those who

would answer that question in the negative and thus recommend that our doors be closed and resources be used for other purposes." *Id.*

11. *Paul D. Carrington to Robert W. Gordon,* 35 J. LEGAL EDUC. 9, 10 (1985).

12. *Id.*

13. *See* Harry T. Edwards, *The Growing Disjunction between Legal Education and the Legal Profession,* 91 MICH. L. REV. 34 (1992).

14. *Id.* at 34. *See also* Harry T. Edwards, *The Growing Disjunction between Legal Education and the Legal Profession: A Postscript,* 91 MICH. L. REV. 2191 (1993) [hereinafter *Postscript*].

15. *Id.*

16. See *Symposium: Legal Education,* 91 MICH. L. REV. 1921–2219 (1993).

17. *See* Richard Posner, *The Deprofessionalization of Legal Teaching and Scholarship,* 91 MICH. L. REV. 1921 (1993).

18. *See* George L. Priest, *The Growth of Interdisciplinary Research and the Industrial Structure of the Production of Legal Ideas: A Reply to Judge Edwards,* 91 MICH. L. REV. 1929 (1993).

19. James Boyd White, *Law Teachers' Writing,* 91 MICH. L. REV. 1970 (1993).

20. *See* Barbara Bennett Woodhouse, *Mad Midwifery: Bringing Theory, Doctrine, and Practice to Life,* 91 MICH. L. REV. 1977 (1993).

21. *See* Paul Brest, *Plus Ça Change,* 91 MICH. L. REV. 1945 (1993); Robert W. Gordon, *Lawyers, Scholars, and the "Middle Ground"* 91 MICH. L. REV. 2075 (1993).

22. *See* Pierre Schlag, *Clerks in the Maze,* 91 MICH. L. REV. 2053 (1993).

23. *See* Edwards, *Postscript, supra.*

24. *See* Richard Delgado, *Norms and Normal Science: Toward a Critique of Normativity in Legal Thought,* 139 U. PA. L. REV. 933 (1991).

25. See *Symposium: The Critique of Normativity,* 139 U. PA. L. REV. 801–1002 (1991) (papers by Pierre Schlag, Richard Delgado, and Steven L. Winter).

26. Patricia Nelson Limerick, *The Canon Debate from a Historian's Perspective,* 43 J. of LEGAL EDUC. 4, 9 (1993).

27. *Id.*

28. *Id.* at 10.

29. *See* Pierre Schlag, *Clerks in the Maze,* 91 MICH. L. REV. 2053 (1993) (arguing that normative legal thought reflects the persona of a judge who announces authoritarian judgments from the bench).

30. *Id.* at 2062.

31. Richard Delgado, for example, has noted how even "well-meaning senior professors often counsel young scholars of color to postpone writing about race until they have first demonstrated their skills at mainstream doctrinal analysis." Richard Delgado, *On Telling Stories in School: A Reply to Farber and Sherry,* 46 VAND. L. REV. 665, 676 n. 84 (1993). *See also* Richard Delgado, *The Imperial Scholar: Reflections on a Review of Civil Rights Literature,* 132 U. PA. L. REV. 561–62 (1984).

32. Pierre Schlag, *The Critique of Normativity*, 139 U. PA. L. REV. 801, 932 (1991).
33. The plea to obey "the law" may represent a "strategy utilized to shift the debate within the profession about the conduct of law and legal education over to a debate about the necessity of protecting law and its institutions from non-believers." Minda, *Of Law, the River and Legal Education*, 10 NOVA L.J. 705, 721 (1986). What may be at stake in the debate provoked by Dean Carrington's essay is the question of whether a particular conception of professionalism should be allowed to displace other conceptions for no reason other than some felt necessity about the faith in the need to protect the Rule of Law from nonbelievers. *See also* Minda, *The Politics of Professing Law*, 31 ST. LOUIS U. L.J. 61 (1986).
34. *See* Fiss, *The Death of Law?, supra.*
35. *Id.* at 1.
36. *Id.* at 4.
37. *Id.* at 5
38. *Id.*
39. *Id.* at 8. Fiss acknowledges, however, that "some practitioners of Law and Economics (originally based in New Haven)" offer a more acceptable view of law and adjudication—a view that shifts its focus from private law subjects to "the great public law cases of our day." *Id.* at 7. He defends the liberal school of law-and-economics because he finds that the scholars of this school better understand the "larger role for law . . . in qualitatively different terms." *Id.* According to Fiss, "The role of the law is neither to perfect nor to replicate the market, but rather to make those judgments that the adherents of law and economics claim are only 'arbitrary,' i.e., a mere matter of distribution." *Id.*
40. *See* Fiss, *The Death of Law?, supra* at 10.
41. *Id.* at 12.
42. *Id.* at 13.
43. *Id.* at 15.
44. 347 U.S. 483 (1954), *supplemented by* 349 U.S. 294 (1955).
45. Fiss, *The Death of Law?, supra* at 8.
46. *Id.* at 11.
47. *See, e.g.,* RONALD DWORKIN, LAW'S EMPIRE 29–30 (Cambridge, Mass.: Belknap Press of Harvard University Press 1986) (using Justice Warren's decision in *Brown* as an example of the public morality that can be defended under his interpretation of the Constitution). While Fiss acknowledges that feminism is a "new cause" which he sees as having "achieved (at least in New Haven) the momentum that once belonged to the civil rights movement," he warns feminists that they may fall prey to the dangers that have befallen the CLS and the law and economics movements. Fiss argued that the "bearers of the (feminist) cause" must "cease to view gender issues as a matter of individual or group interests, and recognize the claim to sexual equality as an expression of the ideals and values we hold in common." Fiss

thus admonishes feminist legal thinkers to commit their movement to a view of law that embraces the fundamental ideals of liberalism. *Id.*

48. *See* Owen M. Fiss, *The Law Regained,* 74 CORNELL L. REV. 245 (1989).

49. For nearly a decade Fiss has been warning of the dangers of new jurisprudential trends that depart from the style of jurisprudence characterized by the Warren Court era in constitutional law. Fiss asserts that during the Warren Court era of the 1960s, judges sought to provide "structural reform" by giving "meaning to our public values." Fiss, *The Supreme Court, 1978 — Foreword: The Forms of Justice,* 93 HARV. L. REV. 1 (1979) [hereinafter *Foreword*]. According to Fiss, Earl Warren symbolizes the "great judge" — "someone whom the specter of authority both disciplines and liberates, someone who can transcend the conflict." *Id* at 17. "The task of a judge, then, should be seen as giving meaning to our public values and adjudication as the process through which that meaning is revealed or elaborated." *Id.* at 14. Fiss admits that he is "a romantic and an innocent." *Owen M. Fiss to Paul D. Carrington,* 35 J. LEGAL EDUC. 24 (1985). It is becoming increasingly difficult, however, to sustain the conviction and romanticism of the Warren Court when the Burger and Rehnquist Courts have established examples of what a Supreme Court can be. *See* Froomkin, *Climbing the Most Dangerous Branch: Legisprudence and the New Legal Process,* 66 TEX. L. REV. 1071, 1093 (1988).

50. *See, e.g.,* DERRICK BELL, AND WE ARE NOT SAVED: THE ELUSIVE QUEST FOR RACIAL JUSTICE (New York: Basic Books 1987). *See also* Kimberle Crenshaw, *Race, Reform and Retrenchment: Transformation and Legitimation in Antidiscrimination Law,* 101 HARV. L. REV. 1331 (1988). Alan Freeman, *Racism, Rights and the Quest for Equality of Opportunity: A Critical Legal Essay,* 23 HARV. C.R.- C.L. L. REV. 295 (1988).

51. Bell, *Foreword,* 61 OR. L. REV. 151 (1982). According to Bell, "The modern civil rights movement and its ringing imperative, 'We Shall Overcome,' must be seen as part of the American racial fantasy." Bell, *Foreword: The Civil Rights Chronicles,* 99 HARV. L. REV. 4, 10 (1985).

52. *See* Crenshaw, *Race, Reform and Retrenchment: Transformation and Legitimation in Antidiscrimination Law, supra* (demonstrating how antidiscrimination law represents "an ongoing ideological struggle in which occasional winners harness the moral, coercive, consensual power of law." *Id.* at 1335).

53. Pierre Schlag, *Normative and Nowhere to Go,* 43 STAN. L. REV. 167 (1990).

54. *Id.*

55. *See, e.g.,* Louis B. Schwartz, *With Gun and Camera through Darkest CLS Land,* 36 STAN. L. REV. 413, 416 n. 6 (1984) (commenting on "CLS theories and vocabulary"). *See also* Ulen, *Law and Economics: Settled Issues and Open Questions, in* LAW AND ECONOMICS 210 (N. Mercuro, ed.) (Boston: Kluwer Academic 1989) (arguing that "practitioners of CLS have seemed to be talking only to each other speaking in tongues, as it were, intelligible only to the true believers" [footnote omitted]). The problem of communica-

tion has also been raised in reaction to the new form of power-talk associated with the law and economics movement. *See* B. ACKERMAN, RECONSTRUCTING AMERICAN LAW, *supra* at 44–45.

56. Martha Minow, *Law Turning Outward*, 73 TELOS 79, 95 (1986).

57. *Id.*

58. *Id.* at 99.

59. *Id.*

60. ACKERMAN, RECONSTRUCTING AMERICAN LAW, *supra* at 44–45.

61. *Id.* at 3.

62. *Id.* at 42. Ackerman argues that there are two structures to his new discourse: one for establishing "facts," the other for establishing "values." *Id.* at 45. The language of law and economics would be used to determine facts, and common discourse of the "people" would be used to determine "values." *Id.* at 29, 79–80. *See also* Gary Peller, *The Politics of Reconstruction*, 98 HARV. L. REV. 863, 867–69 (1985).

63. Martha Minow, *Feminist Reason: Getting It and Losing It*, 38 J. LEGAL EDUC. 47, 48 (1988). Indeed, Minow acknowledges that the problem of mediating between different discourses and perspectives renders the idea of a universal discourse difficult, if not impossible. *See* Minow, *supra* n. at 92–93. *See also* Kathryn Abrams, *Law's Republicanism*, 97 YALE L.J. 1591, 1600–1601 (1988).

64. Minow suggests that this tendency is the product of "our attraction to simplifying categories; our own contests over power include contests over what version of reality prevails." Minow, *Feminist Reason, supra* at 51.

65. Peller, *The Politics of Reconstruction*, 98 HARV. L. REV. 863, 880–81 (1985).

66. Mark Tushnet, *The Degradation of Constitutional Discourse*, 81 GEO. L.J. 251, 251 (1992).

67. *Id.* at n. 198 (commenting on the narratives of Anita Hill and the Clarence Thomas judicial appointment hearings).

68. *Id.*

69. Tushnet believes that the main problem in judicial decision making is reconciling particular events with general rules. Tushnet, *The Degradation of Constitutional Discourse, supra* at 252–53. He argues that the process of adjudication is plagued by the problem of the general and the particular. Generality of abstract rules leads to "avid abstractions," *id.* at 253; but overemphasis on particular factual events can lead to "emotional flooding" and "bad" legal decisions, *id.* at 254. He views the task of judging as a process of mediating the general and the particular without falling prey to the "pathologies" of each, *id.* at 253–54. Ultimately, Tushnet concludes that judges must rely upon the exercise of virtue—integrity and judgment—to successfully mediate the general and the particular in legal decision making. Tushnet argues for "a shift in focus from 'law,' which is validated by correctness, to 'judging,' which is validated by the exercise of the judicial virtues." *Id.* at 256.

70. Daniel A. Farber and Suzanna Sherry, *Telling Stories Out of School: An Essay on Legal Narratives*, 45 STAN. L. REV. 807 (1993).
71. *Id.* at 854.
72. *Id.* at 809.
73. *Id.* at 854. *See also* Daniel A. Farber and Suzanna Sherry, *The 200,000 Cards of Dimitri Yurasov: Further Reflections on Scholarship and Truth*, 46 STAN. L. REV. 647, 648 (1994).
74. *See* Gary Peller, *The Discourse of Constitutional Degradation*, 81 GEO. L.J. 313 (1992).
75. *Id.* at nn. 7–8.
76. *Id.* at 102.
77. *Id.* at 108.
78. *Id.*
79. *See, generally*, Schlag, *Normative and Nowhere to Go, supra* at 175.
80. *Id.* at 176.
81. Richard Delgado, *On Telling Stories in School: A Reply to Farber and Sherry*, 46 VANDERBILT L. REV. 665, 666 (1993) [emphasis added].
82. *Id.* at 669.
83. *Id.* at 670–71. Farber and Sherry's critique of narrative jurisprudence has been criticized, for example, for failing to mention the important contribution of gaylegal narratives. *See* William Eskridge, Jr., *Gaylegal Narratives*, 46 STAN. L. REV. 607 (1994).
84. Dennis Patterson, *Postmodernism/Feminism/Law*, 77 CORNELL L. REV. 254, 307–9 (1992).
85. Peller, *Constitutional Degradation, supra* at 336. *See also* Mark V. Tushnet, *Introduction: Perspectives on Critical Legal Studies*, 52 GEO. WASH. L. REV. 239 (1984).
86. Delgado, *Norms and Normal Science, supra* at 935.
87. *See, generally*, MICHEL FOUCAULT, LANGUAGE, COUNTER-MEMORY, PRACTICE: SELECTED ESSAYS AND INTERVIEWS (D. F. Bourchard, ed.) (Ithaca, N.Y.: Cornell University Press 1980).
88. *See* Pierre Schlag, *Normativity and the Politics of Form*, 139 U. PA. L. REV. 801 (1991).
89. "This much should be clear, for a politics located in the academy readily should recognize that the text is the normative territory of legal life, and that the discourse of law is the constitution of the sociality, the civility, of legal subjects, 'the children of the text.' " Peter Goodrich, *Sleeping with the Enemy: An Essay on the Politics of Critical Legal Studies in America*, 68 N.Y.U. L. REV. 389, 403 (1993).
90. *See* Robert S. Chang, *Toward an Asian American Legal Scholarship: Critical Race Theory, Post-Structuralism, and Narrative Space*, 81 CAL. L. REV. 1243, 1270 (1993) (discussing how Farber and Sherry have created the "equivalent of an essentialist trap" for different-voice scholars).
91. Schlag, *Normative and Nowhere to Go, supra* at 175.
92. *Id.* at 180.

*Notes to Chapter 12*

1. COSTAS DOUZINAS, POSTMODERN JURISPRUDENCE: THE LAW OF TEXTS IN THE TEXTS OF LAW (New York: Routledge 1991).
2. *Id.*
3. *Id.* at 14. *See also* JOHN LUKACS, THE END OF THE TWENTIETH CENTURY AND THE MODERN AGE 281 (New York: Ticknor & Fields 1993).
4. *See* Dennis Patterson, *Postmodernism/Feminism/Law,* 77 CORNELL L. REV. 254, 258 (1992). As Patterson defined the modernist conception of reason: "I identify modernism with the spirit of Enlightenment. 'In the most general sense of progressive thought, Enlightenment has always aimed at liberating men from fear and establishing their sovereignty.' " *Id.* at 258, n. 11, *quoting* MAX HORHEIMER AND THEODORE W. ADORNO, DIALECTIC OF ENLIGHTENMENT 3 (John Comming, trans.) (New York: Continuum Publishing Company 1975).
5. *See* Stephen M. Feldman, *An Interpretation of Max Weber's Theory of Law: Metaphysics, Economics, and the Iron Cage of Constitutional Law,* 16 LAW & SOC. INQ. 205 (1991) (Max Weber's sociology is riddled with the irreconcilable contradictions of modern thought—what Feldman calls the *Weberian despair*).
6. *See* Nancy Murphy and James W. McClendon Jr., *Distinguishing Modern and Postmodern Theologies,* 5 MOD. THEOLOGY 199 (1989). *See also* Neil Duxbury, *Faith in Reason: The Process Tradition in American Jurisprudence,* 15 CARDOZO L. REV. 601 (1993) (describing how the propensity for foundationalism and faith in reason has influenced American jurisprudence).
7. Matthew W. Finkin, *Reflections on Labor Law Scholarship and Its Discontents: The Reveries of Monsieur Verog,* 46 U. MIAMI L. REV. 1101, 1106 (1992).
8. Peter C. Schanck, *Understanding Postmodern Thought,* 65 S. CAL. L. REV. 2505 (1992).
9. Steven L. Winter, *For What It's Worth,* 26 LAW & SOC'Y REV. 789, 792 (1992).
10. ALBERT BORGMANN, CROSSING THE POSTMODERN DIVIDE 2 (Chicago: University of Chicago Press 1992).
11. Steven L. Winter, *For What It's Worth, supra* at 793.
12. *See* JEAN-FRANCQIS LYOTARD, THE POSTMODERN CONDITION: A REPORT ON KNOWLEDGE (Geoff Bannington and Brian Massumi, trans.) (Minneapolis: University of Minnesota Press 1984). There has been some confusion about what postmoderns mean by "postmodern condition." Peter Schanck, for example, claims that the label "is used to convey the idea that the present world is fundamentally different from previous periods, that life today—compared with the modern era—is seriously uncertain, fragmented, disjointed, incoherent, uncentered, pluralistic, that the master narratives that once structured our lives are absent." Schanck, *Understanding Postmodern Thought, supra* at 2518. From this, Schanck concludes that by

announcing the existence of the postmodern condition, postmoderns declare that "postmodern philosophy" has successfully led us to "a postmodern way of life." *Id.* at 2560.

Postmodernists, however, would be the first to concede that the vocabulary, grammar, and worldview of modernity remains pervasive and continues to shape the thinking of people generally. *See, e.g.,* Jacques Derrida, *Sign and Play in the Discourse of the Human Sciences, in* WRITING AND DIFFERENCE 280 (Chicago: University of Chicago Press 1980). Legal postmoderns assert that the vocabulary and grammar of modernism are the only vocabulary and grammar available. *See* Pierre Schlag, *Normative and Nowhere to Go,* 43 STAN. L. REV. 167, 174, n. 18 (1990) ("[T]he problem for postmodernists [not to mention everybody else] is that while the normative vocabulary and grammar are no longer an acceptable currency for intellectuals to use in advancing claims for human beings, there is no other vocabulary, no other grammar, as of yet." *Id.*). Postmoderns are "never quite able to take themselves seriously because [they are] always aware that the terms in which they describe themselves are subject to change, always aware of the contingency and fragility of their final vocabularies, and thus of their selves." RICHARD RORTY, CONTINGENCY, IRONY, AND SOLIDARITY, 73–74 (London: Cambridge University Press 1989). The postmodern condition describes the fragile condition of the modernist's concept of self.

13. *See* DAVID HALBERSTAM, THE FIFTIES, 508–14 (New York: Villard Books 1993).
14. *Id.* at 508.
15. *Id.* at 511–12.
16. As Halberstam put it: "The low-key Ozzie Nelson of the sitcoms had little in common with the real-life Ozzie, who was a workaholic." *Id.* at 515. For "millions of other Americans, coming from flawed homes, it often seemed hopelessly unfair to look on families like this." *Id.* at 512.
17. *Id.*
18. *Id.*
19. *Id.*
20. *Id.*
21. *Id.*
22. *Id.*
23. *Id.*
24. Jerry Frug, *Decentering Decentralization,* 60 U. CHI. L. REV. 253, 309 (1993). The word "pastiche" is attributed to the postmodernist Fredric Jameson, who used the word to describe the "dead styles" expressed in cultural discourse. *See* FREDRIC JAMESON, POSTMODERNISM, OR, THE CULTURAL LOGIC OF LATE CULTURALISM 16–25 (Durham, N.C.: Duke University Press 1991).
25. As Jerry Frug explained: "Everyone knows that his or her actions are understandable only because they can be compared to actions already taken by others; the postmodern subject bases her/his presentation of self on this

recognition of inter-textuality and quotation. In the postmodern world there are no originals, only copies." Frug, *Decentering Decentralization, supra* at 309.

26. *See* JAMESON, POSTMODERNISM, OR, THE CULTURAL LOGIC OF LATE CAPITALISM, *supra* at 16–25. *See also* Frug, *Decentering Decentralization, supra* at 309.

27. Winter, *For What It's Worth, supra* at 789, 794. The confusion is evident in the cultural symbols used today in the electronic media and product advertising, which have appropriated and transformed political and social symbols of the past. As Winter explained:

> At the level of social practices, postmodernism signals postindustrial processes of commodification, bureaucratization, consumerization, and saturation. Nowhere is this more apparent than with respect to signs that, notwithstanding their political or artistic origins, have been appropriated and redeployed for corporate commercial ends. John Lennon's "Revolution" and Jerry Rubin's "Do It!" have both been appropriated by Nike to sell its running shoes. Signs, moreover, have become the primary products of bureaucracies which design, market, and disseminate images and other symbolic forms through media that are literally everywhere. As Russell Baker writes: "Nowadays Whitman would not hear America singing . . . He would write, 'I see America listening to a nearly perfect Japanese technological reproduction of singing.' "

*Id.* at 794, *quoting* Russell Baker, *Hear America Listening*, NEW YORK TIMES at 23, col. 6 (Nov. 2, 1991).

28. *Id.*

29. LYOTARD, THE POSTMODERN CONDITION: A REPORT ON KNOWLEDGE, *supra.*

30. *Id.* at 29.

31. *See* STEVEN CONNOR, POSTMODERNIST CULTURE: AN INTRODUCTION TO THEORIES OF THE CONTEMPORARY 32 (New York: Blackwell 1989).

32. *See* RICHARD RORTY, PHILOSOPHY AND THE MIRROR OF NATURE (Princeton, N.J.: Princeton University Press 1979). Rorty defines pragmatism as "an attempt to replace the notion of true beliefs as representations of 'the nature of things' and instead to think of them as successful rules of action." Richard Rorty, *Pragmatism without Method, in* OBJECTIVITY, RELATIVISM, AND TRUTH: PHILOSOPHICAL PAPERS 63, 65 (Cambridge, U.K.: Cambridge University Press 1991).

33. RORTY, PHILOSOPHY AND THE MIRROR OF NATURE, *supra* at 9–10.

34. *Id.* at 178.

35. JOHN MCGOWAN, POSTMODERNISM AND ITS CRITICS, 192 (Ithaca, N.Y: Cornell University Press 1991).

36. *See* Schanck, *Understanding Postmodern Thought, supra* at 2515.

37. *Structuralism* is essentially a modern, rather than postmodern, technique of analysis which seeks to demonstrate how law (or knowledge) is organized by an underlying structure of organization that is fundamentally true or real. Structuralists maintain an objective critical stance, independent of their

subject, for the purpose of examining and uncovering the true nature of things. *Poststructuralism* is said to be a postmodern perspective (although some postmoderns would disagree) which rejects the belief in stable structures, origins, or foundational essences for grasping the true nature of things. Poststructuralists maintain a skeptical stance in relation to the subjects of their analysis; they believe that the underlying structures of knowledge are merely the result of interpretative practices which are themselves socially and culturally situated. *See* Schanck, *Understanding Postmodern Thought, supra* at 2514–34.

38. *See* Margret J. Radin and Frank Michelman, *Pragmatism and Poststructuralist Critical Legal Practice,* 139 U. PA. L. REV. 1019, 1031–32 (1991).

39. *Id.*

40. RORTY, CONTINGENCY, IRONY, AND SOLIDARITY, *supra* at xiii. *See also* McGOWAN, POSTMODERNISM AND ITS CRITICS, *supra* at 21.

41. My use of the label *ironist* is drawn from Richard Rorty's notion of *ironist theorist* in CONTINGENCY, IRONY, AND SOLIDARITY, *supra* at 73. According to Rorty, an ironist is someone who fulfills three conditions: "(1) She has radical and continuing doubts about the final vocabulary she currently uses, because she has been impressed by other vocabularies, vocabularies taken as final by people or books she had encountered; (2) she realizes that argument phrased in her present vocabulary can neither underwrite nor dissolve these doubts; (3) insofar as she philosophizes about her situation, she does not think that her vocabulary is closer to reality than others, that it is in touch with a power not herself." *Id.* An ironist "who [is] inclined to philosophize see[s] the choice between vocabularies as made neither within a neutral and universal metavocabulary nor by an attempt to fight one's way past appearances to the real, but simply by playing the new off against the old." *Id.* Rorty calls himself an ironist theorist, but the irony is that his brand of neopragmatic philosophy has been used by pragmatic critics to sustain the usefulness of the modernist framework and vocabulary. *See* Margret Jane Radin and Frank Michelman, *Pragmatist and Poststructuralist Critical Legal Practices,* 55 U. PA. L. REV. 619 (1992).

Other commentators use the term *poststructualism* to distinguish this separate strand of postmodern thought from neopragmatism. *See* Schanck, *Understanding Postmodern Thought, supra* at 2514; Radin and Michelman, *supra* at 1031–32. Postmoderns, however, disagree about whether the poststructualism is a modernist or postmodernist concept. *See* ANDREAS HUYSSEN, AFTER THE GREAT DIVIDE: MODERNISM, MASS CULTURE, POST-MODERNISM 207–16 (Bloomington: Indiana University Press 1987) (claiming that poststructuralism is a modernist concept). *See also* Frug, *Decentering Decentralization, supra* at 304, n. 221.

42. *Id.* at 94.

43. *See* Pierre Schlag, *Normative and Nowhere to Go,* 43 STAN. L. REV. 167 (1990). For examples of other postmodern ironist criticism, *see* Jack Balkin, *Understanding Legal Understanding: The Legal Subject and the Problem of*

*Legal Coherence*, 103 YALE L.J. 105 (1993); Rosemary Coombe, *"Same As It Ever Was": Rethinking the Politics of Legal Interpretation*, 34 McGILL L.J. 603 (1989); Drucilla L. Cornell, *Institutionalization of Meaning, Recollective Imagination and the Potential for Transformative Legal Interpretation*, 136 U. PA. L. REV. 1135 (1988); Steven L. Winter, *Indeterminacy and Incommensurability in Constitutional Law*, 78 CAL. L. REV. 1441 (1990); Frug, *Decentering Decentralization, supra* at 253; MARY JOE FRUG, POST-MODERN LEGAL FEMINISM (New York: Routledge 1992).

44. *See, e.g.*, JACQUES DERRIDA, OF GRAMMATOLOGY (Baltimore: Johns Hopkins University Press 1976).

45. *See, e.g.*, MICHEL FOUCAULT, POWER/KNOWLEDGE (New York: Pantheon Books 1980).

46. *See, e.g.*, EDWARD W. SAID, CULTURE AND IMPERIALISM (New York: Knopf 1993).

47. *See* RICHARD RORTY, CONTINGENCY, IRONY, AND SOLIDARITY, *supra* at 86, 94.

48. DAVID LEHMAN, SIGNS OF THE TIMES: DECONSTRUCTION AND THE FALL OF PAUL DeMAN 41 (New York: Poseidon Press 1991). Lehman argues that postmodernism with its deconstructive strategies "is a catastrophe theory inasmuch as it proceeds from the perception of an extreme linguistic instability that undermines the coherence of any statement—a breakdown in our collective confidence in the power of words to communicate ideas and represent experience." *Id.* at 41. My view is that postmodernism cannot be held responsible for a breakdown in intellectual activity. Postmodernism merely highlights the different metanarratives about law now prevailing in the academy. Postmodernists point out the ironic juxtapositions of different "styles" of jurisprudential analysis. They seem to be saying: "Here, look how this style embodies a particular vision . . . and how it is challenged by the style next to it, and by the style next to that." James Boyle, *Is Subjectivity Possible? The Post-Modern Subject in Legal Theory*, 62 U. COLO. L. REV. 489, 503 (1991). In other words, postmodernism is a reflective temperament that invites us to see the fluidity of law.

49. *See, e.g.*, Schlag, *Normative and Nowhere to Go, supra* at 183–84 (developing Lyotard's postmodern criticism of modern and premodern science).

50. Schlag, *Normative and Nowhere to Go, supra* at 184.

51. That is, "one that uses normative words and normative grammars instrumentally to induce specific kinds of social action." Schlag, *Normative and Nowhere to Go, supra* at 183–84.

52. Schanck, *Understanding Postmodern Thought, supra* at 2509.

53. RICHARD A. POSNER, THE PROBLEMS OF JURISPRUDENCE 454–69 (Cambridge, Mass.: Harvard University Press 1990).

54. *Id.* at 460.

55. *Id.*

56. Thomas C. Grey, *Hear the Other Side: Wallace Stevens and Pragmatist Legal Theory*, 63 S. CAL. L. REV. 1569, 1569 (1990).

57. *Id.* at 1576–77.
58. POSNER, THE PROBLEMS OF JURISPRUDENCE, *supra* at 464, Posner's pragmatic approach is further developed in RICHARD A. POSNER, OVERCOMING LAW (Cambridge, Mass.: Harvard University Press 1995).
59. CORNEL WEST, KEEPING FAITH: PHILOSOPHY AND RACE IN AMERICA 89–105 (New York: Routledge 1993).
60. *See* Schanck, *Understanding Postmodern Thought, supra* at 2540.
61. *See* RORTY, PHILOSOPHY AND THE MIRROR OF NATURE, *supra.*
62. Schanck, *Understanding Postmodern Thought, supra* at 2540.
63. *See* Dennis M. Patterson, *Law's Pragmatism: Law As Practice and Narrative,* 76 VA. L. REV. 937 (1990).
64. Pierre Schlag, *The Problem of the Subject,* 69 TEX. L. REV. 1627, 1721 (1991).
65. *See* Pierre Schlag, *Pre-Figuration and Evaluation,* 80 CAL. L. REV. 965 (1992). Prefiguration is the unthought bias embedded within all theoretical perspectives.
66. Schlag, *The Problem of the Subject, supra* at 1721.
67. Schlag, *Normativity and the Politics of Form, supra* at 807.
68. *See* Thomas Morawetz, *Understanding Disagreement, the Root Issue of Jurisprudence: Applying Wittgenstein to Positivism, Critical Theory and Judging,* 140 U. PA. L. REV. 371 (1992).
69. *Id.*
70. Boyle, *Is Subjectivity Possible?, supra* at 503.
71. Pierre Schlag, *Normative and Nowhere to Go, supra* at 186.
72. *See* RICHARD RORTY, PHILOSOPHY AND THE MIRROR OF NATURE, *supra.*
73. *See* Steven L. Winter, *Transcendental Nonsense, Metaphoric Reasoning, and the Cognitive Stakes for Law,* 137 U. PA. L. REV. 1105, 1107–8 (1989); Michael J. Reddy, *The Conduit Metapahor—A Case of Frame Conflict in Our Language about Language, in* METAPHOR AND THOUGHT 284 (A. Ortony, ed.) (Cambridge, U.K.: Cambridge University Press 1979).
74. Schlag, *Normative and Nowhere to Go, supra* at 183.
75. Brian Langille, *Revolution without Foundations: The Grammar Skepticism and Law,* 33 McGILL L.J. 451, 495–96 (1988). *See also* Schlag, *Normative and Nowhere to Go, supra* at 183, n. 45.
76. *See* Gary Peller, *The Metaphysics of American Law,* 73 CAL. L. REV. 1151, 1159 (1985).
77. Coombes, *"Same As It Ever Was," supra* at 611.
78. *Id.* at 613.
79. Posner, *Problems of Jurisprudence, supra* at 466.
80. *Id.* at 467.
81. *See* Schlag, *Normative and Nowhere to Go, supra* at 175.
82. *Id.*
83. *See* RORTY, CONTINGENCY, IRONY, AND SOLIDARITY, *supra* at 81.
84. *See* Schlag, *Normative and Nowhere to Go, supra* at 174, n. 18.
85. *See* Schlag, *Politics of Form, supra* at 1665–66.

86. *Id.* at 1665.
87. *Id.* at 1668. According to Schlag, "This self is relatively autonomous in several senses of the term relative. First, this self is only *relatively* autonomous as opposed to say *fully* autonomous or *non*-autonomous. At the same time, however, this self is also *relatively* autonomous in the sense that it takes a 'relative' stance concerning its own autonomy. The relatively autonomous self is *relatively* so in yet a third sense of relative . . . *[p]aradoxically*, this self is a creature whose structure is in part constituted by the legal texts, but who is in part constituted to act and understand itself to be autonomous." *Id.* at 1668. *See also* Schlag, *The Problem of the Subject, supra.*
88. *See, generally,* Frug, *Decentering Decentralization, supra* at 253–312.
89. *Id.* at 273. As Frug notes, the form of subjectivity has inspired a "wide variety of communitarians, civic republicans, and feminists, among others." *Id.*
90. Posner, *Problems of Jurisprudence, supra* at 462.
91. *Id.*
92. *See* Frug, *Decentering Decentralization, supra* at 304–12.
93. Schlag, *Normative and Nowhere to Go, supra* at 173.
94. Schlag, *The Problem of the Subject, supra* at 1738.
95. Schlag, *Normative and Nowhere to Go, supra* at 173.
96. *See* Schlag, *"Le'Hors de texte, C'est Moi": The Politics of Form and the Domestication of Deconstruction,* 11 CARDOZO L. REV. 1631 (1990).
97. Schlag, *The Problem of the Subject, supra* at 1628.
98. Sanford Levinson, *Strolling Down the Path of the Law (and toward Critical Legal Studies?): The Jurisprudence of Richard Posner,* 91 COLUM. L. REV. 1221, 1252 (1991).
99. Schanck, *Understanding Postmodern Thought, supra* at 2510.
100. *See, e.g.,* ALLAN BLOOM, THE CLOSING OF THE AMERICAN MIND: HOW HIGHER EDUCATION HAS FAILED DEMOCRACY AND IMPOVERISHED THE SOULS OF TODAY'S STUDENTS (New York: Simon & Schuster 1987); ROGER KIMBALL, TENURED RADICALS: HOW POLITICS HAS CORRUPTED OUR HIGHER EDUCATION (New York: Harper & Row 1990); LEHMAN, SIGNS OF THE TIMES: DECONSTRUCTION AND THE FALL OF PAUL DEMAN, *supra;* DINESH D'SOUZA, ILLIBERAL EDUCATION: THE POLITICS OF RACE AND SEX ON CAMPUS (New York: Random House 1992).
101. Handler, *New Social Movements, supra.*
102. *Id.*
103. Allan C. Hutchinson, *Doing the Right Thing? Toward a Postmodern Politics,* 26 LAW & SOC'Y REV. 773, 774 (1992).
104. *Id.*
105. Schlag, *Normative and Nowhere to Go, supra* at 169.
106. *Id.* at 797.
107. *Id.* at 806.
108. *Id.* at 807.

## Notes to Conclusion

1. *See, e.g.*, DINESH D'SOUZA, ILLIBERAL EDUCATION: THE POLITICS OF RACE AND SEX ON CAMPUS 13 (New York: Free Press 1991). D'Souza's text is representative of the modernist viewpoint that sees the diversity movement as a dangerous threat to the liberal tradition of Western classics, which some believe is now undermining liberal education. *See also* ALLAN BLOOM, THE CLOSING OF THE AMERICAN MIND: HOW HIGHER EDUCATION HAS FAILED DEMOCRACY AND IMPOVERISHED THE SOULS OF TODAY'S STUDENTS. (New York: Simon & Schuster 1987); EDWARD D. HIRSCH, JR., CULTURAL LITERACY: WHAT EVERY AMERICAN NEEDS TO KNOW (Boston: Houghton Mifflin 1987); ROGER KIMBALL, TENURED RADICALS: HOW POLITICS HAS CORRUPTED OUR HIGHER EDUCATION (New York: Harper & Row 1990).

2. This sentiment is best expressed by the 1990s student protest chant: "Hey, hey, ho, ho, Western culture's got to go." D'SOUZA, ILLIBERAL EDUCATION, *supra* at 59. The chant received national media coverage when it was used by Jesse Jackson and some five hundred students marching at Stanford University. KIMBALL, TENURED RADICALS, *supra* at xii.

3. *See, e.g.*, Patricia Nelson Limerick, *The Canon Debate from a Historian's Perspective*, 43 J. LEGAL EDUC. 4 (1993).

4. The interdisciplinary approaches of the "law and" movements encouraged legal academics throughout the 1970s and the 1980s to look to the general university for academic insight in developing new forms of legal analysis. One can now imagine what happened. When law professors came to the university, they discovered critical social theory and were welcomed with a slogan: "Welcome to the Revolution." This revolution concerned the world of ideas. It questioned fundamental beliefs about the nature of truth, language, and theoretical method used by legal academics in their intellectual work. This revolution was stirred by a loss of confidence in the viability of universal canons of interpretation. An "epistemological break" seemed inevitable because the old methods of defining and categorizing the world no longer seemed to work. Legal academics studied the crisis and applied the new learning to their discipline.

5. Roy Boyne and Ali Rattansi, *The Theory and Politics of Postmodernism: By Way of an Introduction, in* POSTMODERNISM AND SOCIETY 12 (New York: Macmillan 1990).

6. *See* Peter C. Schanck, *Understanding Postmodern Thought and Its Implications for Statutory Interpretation*, 65 S. CAL. L. REV. 2505 (1992); *Postmodernism and Law: A Symposium*, 62 U. COLO. L. REV. 439 (1991); *Symposium—Beyond Critique: Law, Culture, and the Politics of Form*, 69 TEX. L. REV. 1595 (1991) [hereinafter Texas Symposium II]. The postmodern attitude was expressed by Lyotard's declaration: "I define *postmodernism* as incredulity towards metanarratives." LYOTARD, THE POSTMODERN CONDITION: A REPORT ON KNOWLEDGE (Geoff. Bannington and Brian

Massumi, trans.) (Minneapolis: University of Minnesota Press 1984). For accounts of postmodern jurisprudence, *see* COSTAS DOUZINAS et al., POST-MODERN JURISPRUDENCE: THE LAW OF TEXTS IN THE TEXTS OF LAW (New York: Routledge 1991); PETER FITZPATRICK, ED., DANGEROUS SUPPLE-MENTS: RESISTANCE AND RENEWAL IN JURISPRUDENCE (Durham, N.C.: Duke University Press 1991). I have traced the postmodern temperament in legal scholarship dealing with regulatory takings and Title VII employment discrimination law. *See* Gary Minda, *Title VII at the Crossroads of Employment Discrimination Law and Postmodern Feminist Theory: United Auto Workers v. Johnson Controls, Inc. and Its Implications for Women's Rights Movement,* 11 ST. LOUIS U. PUB. L. REV. 89 (1992); Gary Minda, *The Dilemmas of Property and Sovereignty in the Postmodern Era: The Regulatory Takings Problem,* 62 U. COLO. L. REV. 599 (1991) [hereinafter, Minda, *Dilemmas*].

7. *See* Robert E. Scott, *Chaos Theory and the Justice Paradox,* 35 WM. & MARY L. REV. 329, 330 (1993).

8. *Id. at* 331. According to Scott: "Chaos Theory concerns the phenomenon of 'orderly disorder created by simple processes.' It is the notion that the law of the physical world cannot predict what is going to happen in the future. This is not because the laws are invalid, but because even when we understand interactions very well, and even when the applicable laws are quite accurate and clear, results in specific cases still can be impossible to predict—even though recurring patterns are discernable and remarkably durable. In sum, there is chaos in order, and there is order in chaos." *Id.* at 331.

9. *See* Pierre Schlag, *Normativity and the Politics of Form,* 139 U. PA. L. REV. 801, 807 (1991).

10. *Id.*

11. *Id.*

12. *See* FREDRIC JAMESON, POSTMODERNISM, OR, THE CULTURAL LOGIC OF LATE CAPITALISM 25–31 (Durham, N.C.: Duke University Press 1991) (schizophrenia as the breakdown in the signifying chain). For a primer on the recycling chain of modern jurisprudence, *see* BAILEY KUKLIN and JEFFREY W. STEMPEL, FOUNDATIONS OF THE LAW: AN INTERDISCIPLINARY AND JURISPRUDENTIAL PRIMER (St. Paul, Minn.: West Publishing 1994).

13. See *Symposium—Beyond Critique: Law, Culture, and the Politics of Form,* supra at 1595–2041; *Symposium: New Frontiers in Legal Theory,* 1990 DUKE L.J. 375.

14. For example, in 1989, at a meeting of the Jurisprudence section of the American Association of Law Schools, Professor Owen Fiss publicly retracted much of his early criticism of CLS and law and economics in his essay *The Death of the Law,* 72 CORNELL L. REV. 1 (1986), and affirmed what he saw as the positive contributions of the new jurisprudential movements. *See* Jurisprudence Meeting, AALS Conference, San Antonio, Texas, January 1989 (unpublished speech) (recorded transcript).

15. *Id.* at 1829.
16. *See* Pierre Schlag, *The Problem of the Subject,* 69 TEX. L. REV. 1 (1991).
17. *Id.*
18. *Id.*; Rosemary Coombe, *Objects of Property and Subjects of Politics: Intellectual Property Laws and Democratic Dialogue,* 69 TEX. L. REV. 1853 (1991).
19. Consider, for example, how Lawrence M. Friedman described the mood prevailing at the end of the last century: "a narrowing sky, a dead frontier, life as a struggle for position, competition as a zero-sum game, the economy as a pie to be divided, not a ladder stretching out beyond the horizon." A HISTORY OF AMERICAN LAW 296 (New York: Simon & Schuster Trade, 2d ed. 1986).
20. There is a rising sentiment that as the century and millennium come to a close, so too does an era. *See* Alan Borgman, CROSSING THE POSTMODERN DIVIDE 2 (Chicago: University of Chicago Press 1992).
21. DAVID LEHMAN, SIGNS OF THE TIMES: DECONSTRUCTION AND THE FALL OF PAUL DEMAN 41 (New York: Poseidon Press 1991).
22. For a recent example of this, *see* James Boyle, *A Theory of Law and Information: Copyright, Spleens, Blackmail, and Insider Trading,* 80 CAL. L. REV. 1413 (1992).
23. *See* THOMAS S. KUHN, THE STRUCTURE OF SCIENTIFIC REVOLUTIONS 91 (Chicago: University of Chicago Press, 2d ed. 1977) (describing revolutionary paradigm shifts in scientific thought). Kuhn's theory of paradigm shifts is controversial among philosophers of science; *see, e.g.,* FREDERICK SUPPE, THE STRUCTURE OF SCIENTIFIC THEORIES (Champaign, Ill.: University of Illinois Press, 2nd ed. 1977); but Kuhn's fundamental insights about the nature of paradigms make sense and are helpful for understanding paradigmatic shifts in the law.
24. Andreas Huyssen, *Mapping the Postmodern,* 33 New German Critique 5, 52 (1984).

# Index